W9-BZY-940

The Rise of Modern Prose Style

The Rise of Modern Prose Style

Robert Adolph

The M.I.T. Press
Massachusetts Institute of Technology
Cambridge, Massachusetts, and London, England

ABIGAIL E. WEEKS MEMORIAL LIBRARY
UNION COLLEGE
BARBOURVILLE, KENTUCKY

823.09
A239

Copyright © 1968 by
The Massachusetts Institute of Technology

Set in Linotype Janson
and printed and bound
in the United States of America
by The Colonial Press Inc.

All rights reserved. No part of this book may be
reproduced or utilized in any form or by any means,
electronic or mechanical, including photocopying,
recording, or by any information storage and retrieval
system, without permission in writing from the publisher.

Library of Congress catalog card number: 68-14459

For
Rheba, Jack, *and* Ben

Acknowledgments

I would like to thank, in alphabetical order, Anne Ferry, Norman Holland, Louis Kampf, Roy Lamson, Harry Levin, and Travis Merritt for reading and criticizing various drafts of this book. Needless to say, that these scholars have read it does not necessarily mean that they approve of everything in it. The anonymous but lynx-eyed readers to whom my publisher sent the manuscript steered me away from some horrendous *gaffes*. I have also benefited from the comments on specific points of Donald Morse, William Watson, and Henry West. Twenty-five M.I.T. students in an experimental course in seventeenth-century literature and philosophy helped me more than they will ever realize. If my wife had not been at my side, the language of this book would have been quite impenetrable. Finally, my task would have been much more difficult without funds from the Department of Humanities at M.I.T. for summer research in 1964 and a leave of absence in the spring term of 1965.

Andrews Wanning has kindly allowed me to quote from his unpublished Cambridge dissertation, "Some Changes in the Prose Style of the Seventeenth Century" (1936).

Robert Adolph

Cambridge, Mass.
September 1967

Contents

CONTENTS

The Rise of Modern Prose Style

Introduction

Scholars, critics, and more common readers agree that to-day's standard literary prose style arose around the time of the Restoration. Even in recent editions, with spelling and orthography modernized, the sermons and meditations of a Donne or a Browne or an Andrewes are difficult or strange for us, while South's and Tillotson's only a few decades later are at least superficially easy to read and seem modern. Of course there was much plain prose, especially among the Puritans, before 1660. Most readers feel, though, that even the bourgeois fiction of a chiefly "plain" Elizabethan writer like Deloney is somehow not "plain" in the more modern way Bunyan's is.

For the study of English style then the period is especially significant. Yet thus far there has been little success in describing the change adequately, perhaps because we have no suitable discipline. Linguistics must rest content with describing those aspects of language, such as phonemes and syntactic structures, which can be described and compared with some exactness. Once the description is complete, the historian of style can analyze the reappearance of these elements — or their failure to reappear — later on. For the historian of style, however, linguistics alone is inadequate. It can describe language, but not our responses to it. The re-

I

appearance of similar forms does not necessarily produce similar responses. Readers react differently to the antitheses of Lyly and Dryden.

Perhaps then literary criticism, not linguistics, must articulate our responses to style and changes of style. Because literary criticism does not claim to be a science, it can evaluate style and make statements about our responses to it better than linguistics can. But criticism of style must be, at least in part, subjective. Different readers experience the same style in different ways. Even when critics use the same word to describe style, they may mean different things by it. For example, "precision," as applied to that imprecise abstraction, Restoration prose, has meant among other things: ease of comprehension for the reader, duplication of the intended meaning of the writer, elimination of ornament, fluency, brevity, and neatness of structure. The relative "precision" of Restoration prose is often linked by the critics to its shorter sentences. But these same critics rarely cope with the problems, long familiar to linguists, of defining the sentence; nor do they deal with seventeenth-century practices of punctuation, which may make it impossible to say just where a "sentence," as we would use the term, begins and ends; and so on.[1]

What is required, then, for the study of style and its history is a method which will somehow combine the objectivity and generality of application of linguistics with the subjective and imaginative insights of literary criticism. (The objective-subjective dichotomy is not completely accurate, for the sciences of language also use imagination and insight, while literary criticism is bound by certain "scientific" rules of procedure.) There is now a considerable school working toward just such an alliance.[2] If the effort succeeds, I think it will be a most significant advance indeed. Thus far, though, it has produced little that is relevant to critical stylistic studies. Almost no one has gone beyond the many manifestos to provide us with an actual study, along new lines, of changes in prose style.

The main problem is that all such studies need an objective "control" which will be a check against — yet allow best use of — the critic's own feelings about style. An example of such a control, which I have used a few times in my last chapter, is the simple device of compiling successive seventeenth-century translations of identical passages. Successive variations can then be isolated and related to stylistic effects, and reasonable generalizations inferred about historical changes. I can then draw upon linguistics, as well as my own impressions, to describe these changes. For example, if translator A in 1675 uses a different sort of simile from that of translator B in 1615 in translating the identical passage, linguistics can supply names for and descriptions of the two different kinds of simile. I can then generalize with more assurance and (if I may use the word) precision about the objective causes of my feelings about the style of the passage. Because, as I will try to show, seventeenth-century translators sought to render their sources and previous translations into the most up-to-date idiom, I can then go on to discuss with some objectivity the history of seventeenth-century prose style, using the translations as more reliable specimens of general trends than isolated masterpieces would be. I can check practice against theory, for the seventeenth century was very self-conscious about its stylistic reforms. In an interminable series of arguments, observations, manifestos, and programs it wrestled with the problems of style and the uses of language in general. Many of these problems still vex us today.

Most of the time, however, translations were lacking, and I have resorted to the next best things. These include admittedly less objective comparisons, such as the versions of various authors (for example, Montaigne, Bacon, and Taylor) of an identical passage in another author (Seneca) or to a comparison of the handling of identical themes (Tacitus and Bacon on the accession of a king). These devices, I confess, are somewhat primitive; I await assistance from the linguist-critics for better "controls."

My work is a history of style, not of stylists. For the most part I am not attempting a commentary on masterpieces but the isolation and description of the normal literary style of the day against which these masterpieces can be compared, and thereby more fully appreciated. At first I planned to begin with a chapter on vocabulary in general, and then go on to topics like metaphor, structure, and the role of definition. Later, however, it seemed to make more sense to discuss sections of prose, in which many stylistic devices can be seen working all at once, and even individual authors, rather than isolated aspects of style taken out of their contexts.

To my knowledge there is only one work like mine. This is an unpublished thesis (Cambridge University, 1936) by Andrews Wanning, "Some Changes in the Prose Style of the Seventeenth Century." From Wanning has come the idea of comparing the translations as well as a great deal of general stimulation and inspiration.

Even more interesting than any description of the great stylistic shift is the question of why the change occurred. In practice of course these two concerns are inseparable, a state of affairs which I suspect most linguists regard as unfortunate. Linguists, I would imagine, deny that it is ever possible usefully to relate data about language to generalizations about sensibility, world view, and the like. Readers however have always felt that styles are "baroque" or "heroic" or "scientific" or "Elizabethan" or "neoclassic" or what have you. Such terms are notoriously imprecise. Yet their currency shows that perhaps the main interest in styles for most people is in how they reflect extralinguistic concerns. At least at the present state of the art the relationships between linguistic data and such concerns (even if they could be defined clearly) cannot be scientifically shown. Yet it is wrong to regard as impressionism the intuitive leaps of sensitive readers like Croll or Auerbach. And it seems downright perverse to avoid making such connections on the ground that we have not yet perfected our methods.

There has been pretty general agreement among those willing to relate *Weltanschauung* to language that the rise of modern prose style in the seventeenth century had something to do with the new science. There is a crucial disagreement however about the dates and causes of this chapter of literary history.

Ever since the articles of Morris Croll, which appeared between 1914 and 1931, many scholars have held that our standard modern English prose style dates from about 1600, appearing first in such figures as Bacon and Burton as the so-called "Anti-Ciceronian" movement. Its chief models are the alleged Anti-Ciceronians of antiquity, especially Seneca and Tacitus. According to Croll and his followers, "Anti-Ciceronianism" becomes the dominant prose style of the century. It is "the rhetorical and literary expression of science." [3]

Croll's view was vigorously challenged by R. F. Jones.[4] For Jones, the major stylistic shift so crucial for modern prose occurs suddenly about 1660. It is a result of the direct, specific influence of the new science, or at least of its Baconian aspects, on language. The new style looked not to classical models but to the spirit of the "New Philosophy" as embodied in such documents as Sprat's *History of the Royal-Society*, with its famous manifesto for a "close, naked, natural" style. For Croll, the stylistic platform of the scientists is an *adaptation* of "Anti-Ciceronian" norms; for Jones, the scientists are reacting *against* "Anti-Ciceronianism," and decisively influencing English prose style in general.

Almost all historians of the prose style of the seventeenth century are, unwittingly or not, Jonesians or Crollians. But to my knowledge, the controversy has never been seriously explored, despite acknowledgments in many a learned footnote that the issue is still unsettled. It seems to me that until the question is resolved, our understanding of the history of style in the period, so important for the development of modern prose, will remain incomplete and blurred. As I see it, Croll's "Anti-Ciceronianism" may be more a scholarly fiction than a fact of literary history. There is no doubt that Jones and his followers have exaggerated the influence of "science" on prose. Although my position is clearly closer to Jones than to Croll, the evidence suggests strongly that the ultimate influence on the new prose is neither "science" nor "Anti-Ciceronianism" but the new utilitarianism around which the values of the age are integrated.

I have concentrated on stylistic analysis, the style manifestos, and a few crucial figures like Bacon, Browne, Glanvill, Sprat, and Wilkins claimed by the school of Croll as scientific-minded "Anti-Ciceronians" and by the Jonesians as scientists reacting *against* "Anti-Ciceronianism." Since the style of all prose of the Restoration period is commonly said to reflect "scientific" norms, and since almost all prose of the entire century has been claimed for "Anti-Ciceronianism," a comprehensive treatment of the relations between "Anti-Ciceronianism" and "science" would necessitate a general history of seventeenth-century prose. I have not undertaken such a stupendous labor. Instead I have chosen the more modest course of allowing the Croll-Jones controversy to determine which authors I talk about. Those few men claimed by both sides as crucial instances either resolve the controversy or point to something else as the decisive influence on the beginnings of modern English prose style.

In addition to science and Anti-Ciceronianism, I see the other influences mentioned by critics — the new journalism, the rise of rationalism, the civil wars, neoclassicism, the various facets of the Protestant Ethic — as aspects of the general

6

requirement that prose be a vehicle of useful communication rather than a medium which calls attention to itself either as conscious art or self-expression. Perhaps Marshall McLuhan (whose own style is an extraordinary revival of "Anti-Ciceronianism") is on the right track in emphasizing how the spread of typography itself assisted utilitarians like Sprat by "purifying Latin out of existence" and abetting the "regulation and fixation of languages" by reducing all expression to "linear" sequences.[5]

I should say at the outset that I do not wish to imply that the later "linear" prose of the "print culture" is necessarily inferior or less artful. "Utilitarian" in this book is a neutral not a pejorative word. The virtues of the new prose are substantial. My intention here however is descriptive, not evaluative, and "utilitarian" seems to describe best what is distinctive about the new prose. For example, critics have argued at length whether the later Glanvill's plain style was Anglican or scientific or rationalist. Whatever the truth of the matter is, there is no doubt that Glanvill's later style differs from his earlier style in that it is a vehicle of utilitarian communication. Furthermore, the later Glanvill described himself — and defended his new prose style — as utilitarian.

By no means are all the "moderns" as self-consciously utilitarian as Glanvill. But normal prose after the age of Glanvill remains a means of useful communication rather than self-expression or overt artifice. Once the norm becomes established, infinite possibilities for artistic expression through variations from it become possible. But these variations are not my main concern. I am seeking to isolate the norm itself.

In discussing seventeenth-century ideas I have deliberately avoided strict definitions of such massive abstractions as "utility" and "science," chiefly because the age never used these terms in a clear-cut way. Seventeenth-century utilitarianism, for example, is never more than a vague, undefined instrumentalism. Except for its generally pragmatic, empirical, "English" quality, it never had much in common with the more systematic doctrines of Bentham or Mill. But though vague, it was extremely powerful. "Utility" was one of those words, like our "Freedom" or "Democracy," whose very vagueness wins it the loyalty of people who have little else in common.

"Science" is a much more potent word for us than for the seventeenth century, in which it referred, in a formal way, to any body of systematic thought or skills. Medieval philosophy and rhetoric were "sciences." The nearest equivalents to our word "Science" were tentative circumlocutions like "the New Philosophy" or "the experimental way." Even if we enlarge our word "Science" to refer not only to the specific activities of the "experimental way" but to some sort of skeptical world outlook or all-overpowering methodology or attitude inspired by its successes, we cannot attribute to it the principal motivation for the reform of prose style in the seventeenth century. Finally, never in the seventeenth century is the "New Philosophy" equated (as "Science" sometimes popularly is today) with "utility" or useful activity in general. Even in the earliest, most utilitarian days of the Royal Society, much of the research was "pure." In fact, the virtuosi were often pilloried by the Restoration wits for the uselessness of their endeavors.

Perhaps the most elusive abstraction of all, for us as for the seventeenth century, is "style" itself. Nils Enkvist, in "On Defining Style," [6] takes up the various ways people have defined style. In one kind of definition, it is some mysterious and objectively unverifiable essence, a "higher, active principle of composition by which the writer penetrates and reveals the inner form of his subject" (pp. 10–11). I think most people at times "feel" style this way. But it is hard to talk about so ineffable a notion. Less subjective, and therefore more accessible to analysis, are six other approaches: "style as a shell surrounding a pre-existing core of thought or expression; as the choice between alternative expressions; as a set of individual characteristics; as deviations from a norm; as a set of collective characteristics; and as those relations among linguistic entities that are statable in terms of wider spans of text than the sentence" (p. 12). I think that all six definitions have some validity though all raise serious problems. They help us articulate the vague feelings we all have about any work of literature when we refer to its style. In this book I have used all six, for I do not regard them as mutually exclusive. Our total conception of style is probably an amalgam of them all.

Science and Anti-Ciceronianism

All discussion of the shift in prose style in the middle of the seventeenth century must come to grips with "Anti-Ciceronianism," and any consideration of this movement begins with the classic essays of Morris W. Croll, now collected in *Style, Rhetoric, and Rhythm*.[1] His understanding of the "modern" prose written in the later seventeenth century as "Anti-Ciceronian" raises the main problems of this study. According to Croll, all this seventeenth-century Anti-Ciceronianism is a version of the *genus humile*, or plain style, of classical antiquity. Therefore it is legitimate to ask, first, whether the "moderns" were influenced by ancient and contemporary Anti-Ciceronians; and second, whether Croll's identification of seventeenth-century Anti-Ciceronianism with the ancient *genus humile* is correct. Indeed, was there ever such a thing as "Anti-Ciceronianism" at all, either in antiquity or the seventeenth century?

Croll's use of the term "Anti-Ciceronian" needs clarification. Because for the most part the Anti-Ciceronian movement was directed not against Cicero, but his imitators, Croll prefers "Attic," despite its vagueness as a critical term. (The so-called "Attic" writers were models for Cicero's Roman opponents.) Sometimes Croll and his disciples use "Anti-Ciceronian" and "Attic" interchangeably to describe both ancient and seventeenth-century prose, and I shall do so here. "Baroque," another important term for Croll, is a synonym for Attic prose of the seventeenth century, from the well-known analogy between a knotty, turbulent style and baroque painting. The chief model for seventeenth-century baroque prose is Seneca. Although "Senecan," strictly speaking, refers to only one of the various Anti-Ciceronian styles, in the usage of Croll and his followers, especially Williamson, the term becomes virtually synonymous with "Attic," "Anti-Ciceronian," and "baroque." Finally, Anti-Ciceronianism, Senecanism, and the rest make up for Croll what the seventeenth century called the "plain style" and antiquity, the *genus humile.*

In the seventeenth century, according to Croll, as well as in antiquity, the *genus humile* is the style of philosophy and the essay, as opposed to oratory. The seventeenth century "regarded the history of ancient prose style chiefly as a story of relations and conflicts between two modes or styles which — for the sake of utmost simplification — we may characterize at once (in modern terms) as the oratorical style and the essay style" (*Style*, p. 54). The invention of the oratorical style, which came first, is attributed in all classical rhetorics to Gorgias. It appears in Isocrates and in the Sophists, attacked by Socrates and Plato. Croll is "almost certain" that Gorgias' style originated in the Greeks' "love of sensuous forms" in "certain liturgical or legal customs of the primitive Greek community." It is characterized by "schemes," "chiefly similarities or repetitions of sound used as purely sensuous devices to give pleasure or aid the attention" (p. 83). With the spread of Sophistic teachings, Gorgian-Isocratic style persisted into Roman times in the oratory of Cicero, and beyond in the church fathers and medieval schools.

The origins of the essay style Croll finds in the "philosophic curiosity" of the Greeks, "quite as strong an incentive to literary art as the love of sensuous forms" (p. 56). The essay style is first described in Plato's *Gorgias* and *Phaedrus* as the appropriate method for Socrates' dialectic — the means of discovering the truth — and its inappropriateness for rhetoric, the method of persuasion. Here begins the opposition between philosophy and oratory, an opposition, as Cicero observed, fatal to the latter. The new philosophical or essay style, conforming to the laws of thought, is first codified by Aristotle in Books One and Two of the *Rhetoric*,[2] which become the principal authority, with Seneca, for the seventeenth-century plain style and "Anti-Ciceronianism." According to Croll Aristotle does not completely distinguish between the philosophical and oratorical styles. The formal distinction between the Socratic *genus humile* and the Isocratic *genus grande* comes later, with the creation of the "characters" of style.[3] Of the *genus humile*, Croll says:

Its function is to express the individual variances of experience in contrast with the general and communal ideas which the open design of the oratorical style is so well adapted to contain. Its idiom is that of conversation or adapted from it, in order that it may flow into and fill up all the nooks and crannies of reality and reproduce its exact image to attentive observation. (p. 61)

Croll maintains that "the history of Greek and Roman style is chiefly the story of the relations of the *genus grande* and the *genus humile*." Though not necessarily hostile to one another, "they almost always proved to be rivals" (p. 61).

For the principal models for the prose actually written by the seventeenth-century classicists Croll sends us not to Greek theory but to Roman practice. The history of Latin prose style repeats the rivalry between the *genera dicendi* of Greece. The pragmatic, largely unphilosophical Roman mind, however, associated the *genus humile* not with lofty Platonic speculations but with the "virility and sturdy practical purpose" (p. 83) of the old Republic. As such it was thought to be distinctively Roman. It formed the rhetorical platform of the one philosophy congenial to the Roman spirit, Stoicism. But perhaps because of the overwhelming influence of Cicero's example, perhaps because of Stoic aloofness, the style did not dominate until after Augustus. Stoic theorists of the Empire praise the styles of such Republican heroes as Brutus, Caesar, and Cato. For guidance they turn to Aristotle's two essential principles of style: clearness and appropriateness. The Stoics added a third, brevity. To clearness the Stoics paid only lip service; Stoicism was inherently obscure. Tacitus is the most obscure of all. His imitators included Donne and Bacon. Seneca, like the other Stoics, emphasized clearness "not for its own merits but as a wise corrective to . . . brevity and appropriateness, which they loved better" (p. 86).

Croll tells us that Stoics ancient and modern did practice the brevity they found emphasized in Aristotle's theory.

It is a quality that is almost necessarily involved in the attempt to portray exactly the immediate motions of the mind. In the history of all the epochs and schools of writing it is found that those which have aimed at the expression of individual experience have tended to break up the long musical periods of public discourse into short, incisive members, connected with each other by only the slightest of ligatures, each one carrying a stronger emphasis, conveying a sharper meaning than it would have if it were more strictly subordinated to the general effect of the whole. (p. 87)

In Stoics from Chrysippus on, brevity takes the form of aphorisms, maxims, *sententiae* and the like, which also appear later in a "scientific" writer like Bacon.

Appropriateness is for Croll an ill defined but important principle in Stoic theory. Writing is appropriate to *things,* that is, whatever is under discussion. Croll identifies this appropiateness with the efforts of seventeenth-century Baconians and Cartesians to make words equal things. In

Stoic theory writing must also be appropriate to *persons*, those addressed and, more important, those speaking or writing. "A style appropriate to the mind of the speaker, therefore, is one that portrays the process of acquiring the truth rather than the secure possession of it, and expresses ideas not only with clearness and brevity, but also with the ardor with which they were conceived" (p. 89). Its figures, therefore, "are not the 'schemes,' or figures of sound, which characterize oratory, but the figures of wit, the rhetorical means, that is, of conveying thought persuasively" (p. 89). Antithesis, point, and metaphor are the chief figures of wit.

Croll maintains that the seventeenth-century Stoics, like their first-century prototypes, thought they saw their ideal in the "explicit and inartificial candor" (p. 94) of the Roman Republic. They could not imitate it. As in the first century, the lonely Stoics of the seventeenth century found themselves forced into external allegiance to decadent political authority while their real loyalty was to their own internal standards.

In such an age the true literary modes are those that serve the purposes of criticism, protest, individual intelligence. The *ideal* form of style to which it refers is of course the "natural" style which expresses naïvely the candor of the soul. But in fact the style it demands for its self-expression is one that has been wrought upon with subtle art to reveal the secret experiences of arduous and solitary minds, to express, even in the intricacies and subtleties of its form, the difficulties of a soul exploring unfamiliar truth by the unaided exercise of its own faculties. (p. 95)

For intricacies and subtleties the seventeenth-century Stoics, children of the Renaissance, turned to antiquity. According to Croll, they turned not to Virgil, Cicero, Livy, Catullus, Horace, and St. Augustine but to Seneca, Tacitus, Lucan, Martial, Juvenal, Persius, Tertullian, Plutarch, and Epictetus.

Literary history in the Renaissance is a duplication of

the struggle between the *genera* of antiquity. The initial dominance in antiquity of the Gorgian-Isocratic-Ciceronian rhetoric Croll sees repeated in the Renaissance in the schematic prose of Lyly and Sidney. Its parallel in poetry is the copiousness of Spenser and his followers. It is related to the humanism of such figures as Ascham, Car, Hooker, Sturm, and Melanchthon. Opposed to this tradition is the scientific, skeptical spirit of Politian, Erasmus (whose *Ciceronianus* initiates Renaissance Anti-Ciceronianism, for all practical purposes), Machiavelli, Guicciardini, Lipsius, Montaigne, and Bacon. The struggle between the Attic and Ciceronian styles is the literary expression of the conflict between these two tendencies.

The first was the tendency to give free, or freer, play in the knowledges that were then most critically placed, to the spirit of sceptical enquiry which had been the characteristic and novel part of Petrarch's message to the modern world. . . . It was in short the growth of scientific and positive rationalism . . . what we call the "modern" world.

The other . . . was the tendency to study the *forms* of knowledge, as the Middle Ages had done, rather than the facts of nature and history. But if it was conservative and often reactionary, it was also eminently literary and classical, and was the friend of the beauties and symmetries of Renaissance art. Ciceronian imitation was, as we shall see, the representative of all that was best and worst in it. (p. 110–111)

In the career of Muret Croll sees the triumph of the scientific radicals over the humanistic conservatives. Muret began as a Ciceronian and ended an avid disciple and editor of Seneca and Tacitus, the chief models of the Anti-Ciceronian movement. For Croll it is Muret's pupil Lipsius and Montaigne who are the chief sources of the Senecan literary mode on the continent and in England. Each created a distinctive "Attic" style from Silver Latin models.

Beginning with Muret Croll sees the "Anti-Ciceronians" drawing on Aristotle's justification of oratory as necessitated by the boorishness of the public. Aristotle thus degrades oratory. The same justification was "eagerly seized on" by many other antioratorical theorists, including Bacon, Pascal, and Arnauld. Tacitus' description of the decline of Roman oratory in the *Dialogus* is another *locus classicus*, especially for Muret and Montaigne. After Bacon none of the English writers close to the New Philosophy refer to these texts. Nevertheless Croll asserts that Attic prose is the vehicle for Baconian and Cartesian ideas and methods, as well as for religious and moral controversy. "The temporary success of Puritanism and Quietism, the rapid progress of scientific method, and the diffusion of Cartesian ideas, all in their different ways helped to create a taste for a bare and level prose style adapted merely to the exact portrayal of things as they are" (p. 67).

In "The Baroque Style" Croll systematically described the varieties of Attic prose the seventeenth century derived from its Silver Latin models. This style is the equivalent in prose of the baroque in art. The outstanding difference between baroque and Ciceronian prose is the way in which the members of the period are connected. In the extreme or "curt" form of baroque prose there is no connection between members; this asyndeton is in direct contrast to Ciceronian imitation. There is another kind of baroque prose in which the members are bound together, but in a "loose and casual manner" (p. 210) unlike Ciceronian rounded formality.

The characteristics of the "concise, serried, abrupt" (p. 229) curt style are as follows:

1. There is no syntactic connection between the main members.

2. "Each member is as short as the most alert intelligence would have it" (p. 212).

3. There is a characteristic movement. The first member states the entire idea of the period, and each succeeding

member is "a new apprehension of the truth expressed in the first. We may describe the progress of a curt period, therefore, as a series of imaginative moments occurring in a logical pause or suspension. Or . . . successive flashes of a jewel or prism as it is turned about on its axis and takes the light in different ways" (p. 212).

4. The members are deliberately asymmetrical. Asymmetry is achieved in many ways: by varying the length of the members, changing from literal statement to metaphor, and making conspicuous syntactical shifts.

This is the "curt" style, based on Seneca more than anyone else, and derived by him from the Stoic schools. Often its rules are modified.

1. "And," "or," and "nor" appear between members, but with no logical force.

2. Symmetry is established in two or three members, only to be broken. In this way the asymmetry is even stronger.

3. Long periods may be introduced to clash very strongly with short.

The "informal, meditative and 'natural'" (p. 229) loose style is more difficult to describe.

1. There are coordinating conjunctions, but only those needed to "allow the mind to move straight on from the point it has reached." These are "and," "but," "for," "whereas," "nor" (meaning "and not"), "though . . . yet," and "as . . . no."

2. There are absolute participial constructions and other noncommittal, detachable syntactic units.

3. There are parenthetical expressions.

4. More rigid and binding syntactical forms, such as relative pronouns, are used in such a way as to lose their usual restrictive force in a mass of parenthetical expressions, appositives, and so on.

5. Members often relate, not to the general idea or most important word of the preceding member, but to its last word in a "linked" or trailing effect.

6. Suspensions occur, as in Ciceronian prose, but they are handled differently, ending in an imaginative soaring rather than a rounded conclusion.

These, then, are the two baroque styles. "They represent two sides of the seventeenth-century mind: its sententiousness, its penetrating wit, its Stoic intensity, on the one hand, and its dislike of formalism, its roving and self-exploratory curiosity . . . on the other" (p. 230). The seventeenth century found the curt and loose styles mingled in three Silver Latin styles. One is associated with Seneca and Stoicism, and is revived by the neo-Stoic Lipsius. A second, the "libertine," is also basically Senecan, but freer. It is adopted by Rabelais and Montaigne. The third, chiefly from Tacitus, is the model for Bacon and many others. These three styles comprise Anti-Ciceronian prose.

Having summarized Croll's analysis of Attic prose and its relation to antiquity, we are in a position to consider his understanding of the movement in relation to science, of which it is "the rhetorical and literary expression" (p. 195). Bacon was the first to sketch a rhetoric for scientific communication. His method had already been employed by the moralists Lipsius and Montaigne. Bacon codified their "habit of exact observation, sharp definition, and clear classification" (p. 198). He introduced this method into his own writings, with their aphorisms, antitheta, and topics. Descartes, Wotton, Browne, Pascal, Temple, Halifax and many others were to adopt the same habits. At first the new science, with its "courageous scepticism" and accompanying "rhetorical audacity" gave "greater imaginative range and freedom to the new Attic prose" (p. 199), as in Burton, Browne, and Pascal. The advent of Cartesianism and related influences ended this kind of Attic prose, and another took its place. The stylistic reforms of Lipsius, Montaigne, and Bacon had driven prose toward anarchy.

The syntactic connections of a sentence become loose and casual; great strains are imposed upon tenuous, frail links; parentheses are abused; digression becomes licentious; anacoluthon is frequent and passes unnoticed; even the limits of sentences are not clearly marked, and it is sometimes difficult to say where one begins and another ends. (p. 232)

Cartesianism spawned the corrective, which Croll sees as the triumph of grammar over rhetoric. The sentence replaces the period as the logical unit. Punctuation, grammar, forms of speech, and definitions are made "correct" and standardized. But Attic or baroque prose, now modified from its earlier excesses, remains the style associated with science.[4]

In the early 1930's, R. F. Jones attacked Croll's account of the relation between Anti-Ciceronianism and later seventeenth-century prose style. Jones places the style advocated by the scientists in *opposition* to the styles of such people as Burton, Browne, and even Bacon. For Jones the important conflict is not between Attic and Ciceronian, but between scientific style and the dominant manner of writing in the Puritan regime of the middle of the century,

revealed in the great figures of Jeremy Taylor, Sir Thomas Browne, and John Milton, and lesser writers like Nathanael Culverwell. As is well known, this style is characterized by various rhetorical devices, such as figures, tropes, metaphors, and similes, or similitudes, to use a term of the period. The sentences are long, often obscurely involved, and rhythmical, developing in writers like Browne a stately cadence, which, in the studied effect of inversions, is the prose counterpart of Milton's blank verse. The penchant for interlarding a work with Latin and Greek quotations is also apparent. The diction reveals a host of exotic words, many Latinisms, and frequently poetic phraseology of rare beauty. Against this style there arose a movement which later became an organized revolt. . . . the revolt had its origin in the scientific movement that determined the intellectual complexion of the seventeenth century.[5]

Jones supports his conclusions with examples of pleas for a "plain" style from men associated with science, such as Wilkins, Petty, Hobbes, Webster, Boyle, Glanvill, and Dryden. In the evolution of the styles of Glanvill and Cowley from ornate to plain, Jones sees concrete examples of the direct effect of science itself on prose rather than adjustment within the frame of Anti-Ciceronianism. The running attack on pulpit eloquence in the period 1650–1675 Jones interprets as the stylistic counterpart of the attempt to reconcile science and religion. Arguing specifically against Croll, Jones finds no connection between Attic prose and Baconian science at any time after Bacon himself. The Baconians' stylistic platform was "distinctly different" (*Seventeenth Century*, p. 105). The new philosophy rejected Aristotle in rhetorical theory as in everything else. It yearned for a style devoid of literary qualities altogether, including the aphorisms, antitheses, paradoxes, neologisms, and metaphors of Anti-Ciceronianism. This antiliterary tendency reaches its logical conclusion in the attacks on philological study in general and in the various schemes for a Baconian "Real Character" which would substitute a system of marks for words. Never, according to Jones, do the scientific reformers look to the Anti-Ciceronian movement. Although both stylistic attitudes emphasize reality and "things" over "words," the scientists meant a material reality, the Anti-Ciceronians "rationalistic explanations of human experience" (p. 106). Both objected to musical phrases and obscurities, but only the Baconians practiced what they preached. Both favored brevity, but to the Baconians this meant absence of all rhetorical devices, to the Anti-Ciceronians aphorism and "point." [6]

In his reply to Jones, Croll simply reiterated his previous

conclusion that the new science, especially in its later, Cartesian manifestations,

did not create a new, a rival style to the Anti-Ciceronian. . . . It was an attempt, a successful attempt, to take the heat and fever out of the imaginative naturalism of Montaigne, Bacon, and Browne. . . . But it did not change the form and structure of the prose of its time. . . . Glanvill's later style is a *revision* of Browne's; and Sprat's easy periods have almost exactly the form of Bacon's harder and knottier ones. Seventeenth-century prose is and remains predominantly Senecan.[7]

In a note appended to Croll's reply, R. S. Crane limits the intended application of the stylistic platform of the Royal Society to "philosophical" (that is, scientific) exposition. The scientists and their allies — such as Bacon, Cowley, Glanvill, and Boyle — derived this idea of separate styles for different subjects and audiences from classical rhetorical theory, especially Aristotle, the source of the theory of the Anti-Ciceronian "philosophical" style. At least in their rhetorical theory, the scientists are Anti-Ciceronian.

Returning Croll's fire, Jones held that "any theory which places Sir Thomas Browne and John Dryden, Jeremy Taylor and John Tillotson in the same [Senecan] stylistic category is puzzling" (*Seventeenth Century*, p. 158). Against Crane's assertion that the Baconians restricted the new plain style to scientific exposition Jones cites his own evidence of the effect of science on pulpit oratory and Sprat's advocacy of a plain style for "most other Arts and Professions." Jones also argues that Crane's examples of the scientists' approval of Aristotle's rhetorical theory are out of context.

In fairness to Jones, his case for the scientific influence on prose should not be overstated. In "Science and English Prose Style" Jones mentions the effects of rationalism and "the steady growth of the classical spirit." Referring to Spingarn's introduction to *Critical Essays of the Seventeenth Century*, Jones reminds us of "the substitution of general for technical terms, the preference for skeptical as opposed to dogmatic modes of thought and speech, the horror of pedantry, the trend toward precision of word and idea, and the attempt to make literature approximate conversation." [8] In "The Moral Sense of Simplicity" Jones contends that the scientists' insistence on plainness was adumbrated long before the Royal Society. Jones is speaking of the anti-rhetorical, predominantly Puritan pleas for English as a more moral way of writing than Latin. This thesis Jones massively documents later in *The Triumph of the English Language*.[9] Unlike Croll, Jones sees this movement as separate from Anti-Ciceronianism: "For the most part the upholders of plainness are far removed from classical models or classical authorities, and they do not develop any suggestion of the particular stylistic ideal demanded by the Anti-Ciceronians. Furthermore their ascetic and utilitarian spirit possessed little in common with the literary spirit animating Anti-Ciceronianism" ("Moral Sense," p. 2).

I intend this book to be more than the solution of a dryas-dust scholarly dispute. But the Croll-Jones controversy is crucial for our problem, and a logical starting point. I shall be referring to it continually in the ensuing chapters. Before pointing out the nub of the controversy, I would note here that in any discussion of style we can describe the linguistic features of the style itself or analyze their causes in contemporary culture. Jones at no point challenges Croll's *description* of Attic or Anti-Ciceronian prose, though he does deny Croll's assertion that it applies to most important seventeenth-century prose. Nor does Jones object to Croll's description of Anti-Ciceronianism as a self-conscious movement. Jones' fundamental disagreement has to do with Croll's interpretation of its *causes*, that is, its relation to cultural history. For Croll as much as for Jones the most significant cultural influence in the history of prose style in the seventeenth century is the new philosophy of Bacon and Descartes (for Jones, mostly the former). Croll feels that in certain like-minded classical models, principally Seneca, the scientific reformers found ready made, and adopted, a way of writing ideally suitable for what they were trying to say. This is how Croll explains seventeenth-century prose, which for him is more or less an "Attic" unity. For Croll the great watershed in prose style, in which we find the transition to true scientific modernity, occurs around 1600, the age of Muret, Lipsius, Montaigne, and Bacon. Jones does not find such a unity in seventeenth-century prose. The contrast for Jones is not between the unscientific, Ciceronian, six-teenth and the proscientific, Anti-Ciceronian seventeenth centuries. Rather, Jones distinguishes the baroque prose of the period 1600–1660 — his use of "baroque" is unlike Croll's, embracing the Ciceronian Milton as well as the Anti-Ciceronian Bacon and Browne — from the plain style of Hobbes, Dryden, Tillotson, and the later Glanvill. According to Jones, modern prose begins sixty years later than for Croll. It is largely a result, not of an adaptation of a pre-viously existing Attic style to the demands of the new science, but of the direct, specific effects of the new science itself. It has no relation to Anti-Ciceronianism but is a deliberately different and opposed style, appearing with remarkable and overwhelming suddenness in the third quarter of the century.

We have now come to the heart of the controversy, which turns on the stubborn fact that, though looking backward to classical and Christian antiquity, the Anti-Ciceronians adhere to the same skepticism, empiricism, and emphasis on induction that Jones attributes to the Restoration scientists and by which he apparently defines "science" in general. Yet it is clearly the Anti-Ciceronian style that the Restoration scientists reject, even as they call for its virtues of brevity, clarity, and appropriateness. The ultimate questions are, first, Is modern, "scientific" prose style continuous, as

Croll says, with the large Western traditions of Christian humanism? and second, What terms other than the clearly inadequate epithet "scientific" accurately describe the new style?

I should say here at the outset that my interest is not in bludgeoning Croll, to whom every student of the history of prose style owes a huge debt, or Jones, whose position is not very far from mine anyway. My disagreement with Croll (and also my debt to him) will become apparent as we go along. As for Jones, especially in his *Ancients and Moderns*, no other scholar has seen so clearly the influence of Baconian utilitarianism on the second half of the seventeenth century. My quarrel with Jones comes down to his failure to relate this utilitarianism to the Restoration shift in prose style. Rather, he preferred, in his articles on language, to attribute the shift to "science." In these articles Jones never defined "science." In a later article on a different topic he does attempt such a definition, discarding "the usual view" and considering the history of science "as a movement of ideas" rather than "a series of descriptions and evaluations of past discoveries in a more or less chronological order" (*Seventeenth Century*, p. 41). The "main principles" of science in seventeenth-century England were, "First . . . the demand for a sceptical mind. . . . Second, observation and experimentation. . . . And third, the inductive method of reasoning [which] was to be employed on these data" (p. 42). In his articles on language, Jones seemed to understand "science" more narrowly, limiting it to the "Experimental Way" of the Royal Society itself. Even if we assume that the definition quoted above was what Jones meant all along by "science," we are still left with the problem we have already discussed: as Croll points out, the style of the Anti-Ciceronians was determined by these very same principles. Now, as Jones himself has shown, it was the Anti-Ciceronian style that the scientists rebelled against.

But the scientists themselves could hardly have rejected a scientific style. There must be some other explanation for the Restoration shift in prose style.

The crucial figure in all these questions is Bacon. Jones holds that Restoration prose style, though directly traceable to Baconian science, is not the style of Bacon. Paradoxically, according to Jones, Bacon is nowhere held up by the post-1660 Baconians as a model of style. Jones, in other words, has handed Bacon over to the prescientific Anti-Ciceronians. From Jones' line of reasoning, it follows that Bacon's style, despite his Aristotelian desire for appropriateness, was felt by his followers to be unsuitable for Baconian purposes. On the other hand, if Croll is correct, there is little difference between Bacon's style and that of the later Baconians.

Since it is on the subject of Bacon's style and its relation to the stylistic practice of his followers that Croll and Jones disagree most significantly, Bacon becomes our first object of study. We must decide, first, whether his style is as Attic as Croll and, evidently, Jones think it is; second, whether it is influenced directly by the spirit of the new science itself or is an adaptation of Attic prose; and third, whether Bacon's style is as remote from the stylistic practice of his disciples later in the century as Jones says it is.[10]

ABIGAIL E. WEEKS MEMORIAL LIBRARY
UNION COLLEGE
BARBOURVILLE KENTUCKY

Bacon

Bacon and Tacitus

We have seen that Croll classifies the major seventeenth-century Anti-Ciceronians according to each one's Silver Latin model. Until Croll, Bacon was regarded as a Senecan. Croll held that Bacon "naturalized" Tacitus, "domesticating the style of Tacitus in English prose." [1] Evidently Croll understands Bacon to be engaged in a deliberate stylistic reform. The "profound moral experience" of Bacon's time required "ceremonious dignity, an ideal of deliberate and grave demeanor" embodied in a prose style "at once ingenious and lofty, intense yet also profound, acute, realistic, revealing, but at the same time somewhat grave and mysterious" (*Style*, p. 194). Not in Seneca, but in Tacitus was such a style to be found. To my knowledge, however, no one has ever attempted to prove Bacon's alleged debt to Tacitus. But for Croll it is this influence which puts the scientist Bacon in the Anti-Ciceronian camp. For our purposes then we must test the theory which, since Croll's articles, has become orthodoxy.

While it may be thought unreasonable to compare things so unlike as a history and an essay, it is Bacon's essays, as well as his *History*, which are always singled out by the

Crollian critics for their Tacitean qualities. And of all the essays, "Of Death" is perhaps closest to Croll's "ingenious and lofty . . . grave and mysterious" Tacitus. It is this essay that suggested to Shelley, in the *Defense of Poetry*, that Bacon was a poet in prose.

Men fear Death, as children fear to go in the dark; and as that natural fear in children is increased with tales, so is the other. Certainly, the contemplation of death, as the wages of sin and passage to another world, is holy and religious; but the fear of it, as a tribute due unto nature, is weak. Yet in religious meditations there is sometimes mixture of vanity and of superstition. You shall read in some of the friars' books of mortification, that a man should think with himself what the pain is if he have but his finger's end pressed or tortured, and thereby imagine what the pains of death are, when the whole body is corrupted or dissolved; when many times death passeth with less pain than the torture of a limb: for the most vital parts are not the quickest of sense. And by him that spake only as a philosopher and natural man, it was well said, *Pompa mortis magis terret, quam mors ipsa:* [it is the accompaniments of death that are frightful rather than death itself.] Groans and convulsions, and a discoloured face, and friends weeping, and blacks, and obsequies, and the like, shew death terrible. It is worthy the observing, that there is no passion in the mind of man so weak, but it mates and masters the fear of death; and therefore death is no such terrible enemy when a man hath so many attendants about him that can win the combat of him. Revenge triumphs over death; Love slights it; Honour aspireth to it; Grief flieth to it; Fear preoccupateth it; nay we read, after Otho the emperor had slain himself, Pity (which is the tenderest of affections) provoked many to die, out of mere compassion to their sovereign, and as the truest sort of followers. Nay Seneca adds niceness and satiety: *Cogita quamdiu eadem feceris; mori velle, non tantum fortis, aut miser, sed etiam fastidiosus potest.* A man would die, though he were neither valiant nor miserable, only upon a weariness to do the same thing so oft over and over. It is no less worthy to observe, how little alteration in good spirits the approaches of death make; for they appear to be the same men till the last instant. Augustus Caesar died in a compliment; *Livia, conjugii nostri memor, vive et vale:* [farewell, Livia;

and forget not the days of our marriage.] Tiberius in dissimulation; as Tacitus saith of him, *Jam Tiberium vires et corpus, non dissimulatio, deserebant:* [his powers of body were gone, but his power of dissimulation still remained.] Vespasian in a jest; sitting upon the stool, *Ut puto Deus fio:* [I think I am becoming a god.] Galba with a sentence; *Feri, si ex re populi Romani:* [strike, if it be for the good of Rome;] holding forth his neck. Septimius Severus in despatch; *Adeste si quid mihi restat agendum:* [make haste, if there is anything more for me to do.] And the like. Certainly the Stoics bestowed too much cost upon death, and by their great preparations made it appear more fearful. Better saith he, *qui finem vitae extremum inter munera ponat naturae:* [who accounts the close of life as one of the benefits of nature.] It is as natural to die as to be born; and to a little infant, perhaps, the one is as painful as the other. He that dies in an earnest pursuit, is like one that is wounded in hot blood; who, for the time, scarce feels the hurt; and therefore a mind fixed and bent upon somewhat that is good doth avert the dolours of death. But above all, believe it, the sweetest canticle is, *Nunc dimittis;* when a man hath obtained worthy ends and expectations. Death hath this also; that it openeth the gate to good fame, and extinguisheth envy. *Extinctus amabitur idem:* [the same man that was envied while he lived, shall be loved when he is gone].[2]

The English equivalents of certain features of Tacitus' language are to be found in Bacon. They are also common to the *genus humile*, at least according to Croll's description. This is especially true with regard to the form of the period. There is little or no syntactic connection between members. What links there are ("for," and "and") serve little logical purpose (like *nam* and *et* in the passage from Tacitus analyzed in the Appendix). The members are short, and move in the characteristic Anti-Ciceronian progression, embellishing a simple declarative statement in the first member, to end in a speculation or pointed "sentence" like "It is as natural to die as to be born . . . perhaps, the one is as painful as the other." Asymmetry is achieved by introducing quotations (equivalent to Tacitus' shifts into indirect discourse), varying the lengths of members and periods, parenthetical expressions, and grammatical disjunctions such as clauses dissimilar in structure connected by "and" — "nay, we read after Otho the emperor had slain himself, Pity (which is the tenderest of affections) provoked many to die, out of mere compassion to their sovereign, and as the truest sort of followers." There are many participial or absolute phrases, with their natural syntactic isolation, often asymmetrically jostling unlike grammatical forms, especially mixed singulars and plurals: "Groans and convulsions, and a discoloured face, and friends weeping, and blacks and obsequies." There is the "trailing effect": "provoked many to die out of mere compassion to their sovereign, and as the truest sort of followers. Nay, Seneca adds satiety. . . ." Symmetry is established by devices akin to Tacitus' anaphora, zeugma, antithesis, and the like, and by the device, frequent in Tacitus, of doublets ("holy and religious," "pressed and tortured," "mates and masters"). But symmetry is broken: "Revenge triumphs over death; love slights it; . . . nay, we read, after Otho the emperor. . . ." Personification (poetical and frequent in Tacitus) occurs in a quiet way ("Death is no such terrible enemy . . . Revenge triumphs . . ."), as does effective rather than merely showy assonance ("so oft over and over") and alliteration ("dolours of death") as in Tacitus. There are also Gorgian figures of sound on the jingling Euphuistic model now and then in Bacon which we also find now and then in Tacitus: "Revenge *tri*umphs over death; love *sli*ghts it; honor as*pir*eth to it; grief *fli*eth to it. . . ."

What we have said thus far about Bacon's syntax, in addition to his numerous quotations from Silver Latin writers, supports Croll's hypothesis. Yet Bacon's style cannot be described as domesticated or "naturalized" Tacitean. Despite these apparent resemblances, I am not convinced that Tacitus influenced Bacon's style at all. The Baconian period, though structurally similar, produces an entirely different *effect*.

Specific linguistic habits must be described in their contexts. For example, both Tacitus and Bacon seek brevity. But in Tacitus, as can be seen in the passage analyzed in the Appendix, the brevity is insinuating, forceful, and even melodramatic at times; this is not the case with Bacon. In the first phrase of that passage, "*Primum facinus novi principatus*," we have, instead of an introduction, the emphatic "*primum*" — emphatic because it is first in the sentence as murder is first in Tiberius' reign. The brevity insinuates that there is much more *facinus* to come in this *principatus*, as indeed there is. The dark, oppressive atmosphere characteristic of Tacitus is immediately established. Tacitus' understated, annalistic brevity sardonically emphasizes the routine quality of Tiberian crimes — and thereby their moral horror. In Bacon's "Men fear death as children fear to go in the dark" there is also brevity in rhetorical balance. The sentence is striking, like so many of Bacon's openings. But it is essentially straightforward, a statement of fact, a "natural fear." Lacking Tactitus' suggestiveness, it sets up no dark atmosphere, even though the word "dark" appears and it also has to do with death. Tacitus maintains the oppressiveness. For example, in the passage analyzed in the Appendix, the constricted, muffling effect of "*quem ignarum inermumque quamvis*" may well suggest the muffling of Postumus Agrippa. As so often in Tacitus, there is a suggestive ambiguity, and therefore innuendo: to what does "*quamvis*" refer? Is Tacitus saying that, "Although Agrippa was unarmed, the brave centurion killed him," thereby emphasizing the horror of the crime? Or does he mean, "Although the centurion was determined (*quamvis firmatus animo*) he only with difficulty (*aegre*) overcame Agrippa?" Perhaps Tacitus wishes to suggest both meanings. At any rate, he has pushed brevity to the point where his prose approaches poetry, with its greater ambiguity, compression, and suggestiveness. Tacitus even borrows from the great poets themselves, driving his prose even further toward poetry.

Bacon drives his prose in precisely the opposite direction. I do not wish to imply that Bacon's prose, especially here in the later essays, is flat or "prosaic" in the pejorative sense. On the contrary. But generally — the opening sentences of some essays are partial exceptions — for his finest effects Bacon the essayist depends not on heightened language, ambiguity, overtones, sensuousness, and the like, but on balanced strings of firm, unambiguous distinctions and a certain even-tempered boldness. It is a sense of this boldness that informs Hazlitt's excellent comments on Bacon,[3] as well as Macaulay's over-maligned essay; and it is one of the things that makes Cowley's image of Bacon as the Moses of the Royal Society so apt. Bacon achieves boldness by, first, the omission of articles and qualifiers. Unlike Tacitus, Bacon is stingy with adjectives and adverbs. He has no use at all for the weakening "rather," "somewhat," and "often." Firmness and certainty also emerge in Bacon's preference for the straightforward "is" and "are." Like Hamlet, Bacon knows not "seems." In all of these things, of course, Bacon is at the opposite pole from Tacitus. Even where he seems to be like Tacitus — as in his use of the present tense to express habitual action or eternal truth — it is with the sense of reporting a fact rather than hinting at a crime. Finally, Bacon and Tacitus are both metaphorical. But where Tacitus' metaphors open outward suggestively and dramatically, for Bacon they generally clarify, illustrate, and restrict. The Baconian metaphor is not "Anti-Ciceronian," but closer to the kind of metaphor admitted by the Baconians of the Royal Society, and by the Restoration in general (pp. 210–241, 251–256). Where Tacitus' "verbal disharmonies reflect the complexities of history and all that is ambiguous in the behavior of men,"[4] Bacon's bold, distilled certainties and progression of distinctions reflect his faith in the instructed intellect. Where brevity in Tacitus' history is for dramatic effect, in the essay it is cerebral, a means of putting Bacon's distinctions into bolder relief.

But Tacitus is a historian, Bacon here an essayist. Although Croll himself never specified in which genre Bacon was most like Tacitus, a comparison perhaps fairer to Croll's position would be between Tacitus and Bacon the historian. If Bacon were a disciple of Tacitus, then we would expect him to follow the Master in his one major historical effort, the *History of the Reign of King Henry VII* (1622). Here, by way of comparison to the *coup* of Tiberius analyzed in the Appendix, is the even more shadowy coming to power of Henry:

He on the other side with great wisdom (not ignorant of the affections and fears of the people), to disperse the conceit and terror of a conquest, had given order that there should be nothing in his journey like unto a warlike march or manner; but rather like unto the progress of a King in full peace and assurance.

He entered the City upon a Saturday, as he had also obtained the victory upon a Saturday; which day of the week, first upon observation, and after upon memory and fancy, he accounted and chose as a day prosperous unto him.

The mayor and companies of the City received him at Shoreditch; whence with great and honourable attendance, and troops of noblemen and persons of quality, he entered the City; himself not being on horseback, or in any open chair or throne, but in a close chariot; as one that having been sometimes an enemy to the whole state, and a proscribed person, chose rather to keep state and strike a reverence unto the people than to fawn upon them.

He went first into St. Paul's Church, where, not meaning that the people should forget too soon that he came in by battle, he made offertory of his standards, and had orizons and *Te Deum* again sung; and went to his lodging prepared in the Bishop of London's palace, where he stayed for a time.

During his abode there, he assembled his counsel and other

principal persons, in presence of whom he did renew again his promise to marry with the Lady Elizabeth. This he did the rather, because having at his coming out of Brittaine given artificially for serving of his own turn some hopes, in case he obtained the kingdom, to marry Anne, inheritress to the duchy of Brittaine, whom Charles the Eighth of France soon after married, it bred some doubt and suspicion amongst divers that he was not sincere, or at least not fixed, in going on with the match of England so much desired; which conceit also, though it were but talk and discourse, did much afflict the poor Lady Elizabeth herself. But howsoever he both truly intended it, and desired also it should be so believed (the better to extinguish envy and contradiction to his other purposes), yet was he resolved in himself not to proceed to the consummation thereof, til his coronation and a Parliament were past. The one, lest a joint coronation of himself and his Queen might give any countenance of participation of title; the other, lest in the entailing of the crown to himself, which he hoped to obtain by Parliament, the votes of the Parliament might any ways reflect upon her. (*Works,* XI, pp. 52–54)

These periods are clearly in the "Anti-Ciceronian" vein. They are more "loose" than in the largely "curt" essays; Civil Knowledge, as Bacon admitted, being so "immersed in matter" (*Advancement of Learning, Works,* VI, p. 347), does not reduce itself to terse aphorisms very easily, and History is close to Civil Knowledge. Asymmetry here is carried almost to the point of anarchy. For example, between the subject and verb of the first sentence Bacon has two prepositional phrases, a parenthetical expression, and an infinitive phrase. These constructions have little syntactic relation to one another or to the rest of the sentence, and are of widely varying length. Participial constructions are numerous: "himself not being on horseback," "not meaning that the people should forget," "having at his coming out of Brittaine." Symmetry is set up ("like unto . . . march or manner . . . like unto . . . peace and assurance") only to be dispelled in a mass of absolute constructions ("The one, lest a joint coronation of himself and his Queen might give any countenance of participation of title; the other, lest in the entailing of the crown to himself, which he hoped to obtain by Parliament, the votes of the Parliament might any ways reflect upon her"). The "trailing effect," in which members relate to the last element rather than the main idea of the preceding member, is present: "in case he obtained the kingdom to marry Anne, inheritress to the duchy of Brittaine, whom Charles the Eighth of France soon after married." As is the case in this sentence, the conclusion is often an idea and a construction remote from the beginning of the sentence: ". . . though it were but talk and discourse, did much affright the poor Lady Elizabeth herself." For all these devices, as we have seen, parallels are to be found in Tacitus.

But again the feeling of the passage is un-Tacitean, and again stylistic analysis confirms our general impression. In Tacitus the asymmetry in his context is dramatic. In Bacon it has the opposite effect. It is cerebral and digressive, endless subordinate constructions explaining motives and causes. Although Tacitus' syntax is loose, he never loses the dramatic unity of the paragraph as a whole. In Bacon, the unity of the paragraph is sacrificed to the individual sentence — lapidary in the essays, loosely sprawling in the *History*. Furthermore, Bacon's vocabulary is quite plain. There are none of Tacitus' archaisms, neologisms, and the like, nor his circumlocutions. Metaphor is absent here and rare in the rest of the *History;* when it does appear, it is more often than not borrowed from Bacon's sources, such as Polydore Vergil, Edward Hall, or John Speed. In contrast to Tacitus' considerable assonance and alliteration, Bacon seems unaware of any sound effects at all. In fact, except for occasional padding by means of doublets or near-doublets (by which Bacon makes some of his characteristic acute distinctions, for example, "accounted and chose") there is no poetic, rhetorical, or dramatic heightening at all. The tone and rhetorical structure is that of the Renaissance lawyer, quietly presenting the pros and cons of the situation in studied *antitheta*. This structure also characterizes the essays. Many of them, as the editions of Abbott and Wright show,[5] are themselves collections of *antitheta*. Henry is forever debating, coolly weighing pros and cons, as here, and like Bacon himself in the essays: "Certainly the fear of death . . . *but* the fear of it. . . . *Yet* in religious meditations. . . ." Long stretches of the *History* are nothing more than debates, with each side presenting long, lawyerly briefs. Tacitus, in common with ancient (and Elizabethan) historiography, often resorts to the framework of the debate. But Tacitus' debates are far removed from Bacon's businesslike marshaling of evidence pro and con. Again, by his seeming to be always coolly arguing a point without emotive language, Bacon is closer to the Restoration prose norm, with its separation of "Reason" and "The Passions," than to "Anti-Ciceronianism." Pathos, innuendo, and insinuation, Tacitean hallmarks, are lacking throughout. Speculation as to motives and causes is always spelled out and acutely analyzed rather than subtly suggested, as in Tacitus, by ambiguous words, violent asyndeton, or terse anaphora, or by the juxtaposition of events (for example, the heroic actions of Germanicus next to the crimes of Tiberius). Most of Bacon's *History* is taken up with this analysis of motives and causes. If we eliminate the analysis from our passage, we are left with the following:

He had given order that there should be nothing in his journey like unto a warlike march or manner, but rather like unto the progress of a King in full peace and assurance.
He entered the city upon a Saturday.
The mayor and companies of the City received him at Shoreditch; whence with great and honourable attendance, and troops of noblemen and persons of quality, he entered the City; himself not being on horseback, or in any open chair or throne, but in a close chariot.

35

He went first into St. Paul's Church, where he made offertory of his standards and had orizons and *Te Deum* sung; and he went to his lodging prepared in the Bishop of London's palace, where he stayed for a time.

During his abode there, he assembled his counsel and other principal persons, in presence of whom he did renew again his promise to marry with the Lady Elizabeth.

No such split between straightforward factual material and knottier analysis can be found in Tacitus. In his style fact, motive, and impression are inseparable.

For Tacitus, as for ancient historiography in general after Thucydides, history is a great drama as well as "the facts." All Tacitus' critics have praised his dramatic skill (see the Appendix). In Bacon, on the other hand, there is little of Tacitus' moral fervor or dramatic force. Comparing the *History of King Henry VII* to More's *Richard III*, Sister Mary Faith Schuster has shown us how Bacon's sentences

move from clause to clause without logical sequence. The non-dramatic quality of his actions is matched by the unemotional language void of figures of sound. Henry moves guardedly from one possible expedient action to another, rather than steadfastly adhering to fixed principles. . . . Here the sentence structure lacks the thought discipline, the rhythmic balance accentuating the thought climax, and the emotional power of structure which carried the more dramatic story of Richard III.[6]

Now the story of Henry VII, with its many broils, revolts, distressed ladies (including Elizabeth), palace intrigues, and folk heroes also had dramatic possibilities. Ford's *Perkin Warbeck*, with its Tacitean interest in abnormal psychology, attests to some of them. But except for Warbeck's speech to the Scottish king, lifted almost verbatim from Speed,[7] Bacon's account of the revolt focuses on military and political strategy rather than on dramatic action or character. The utterly undramatic character of Bacon's prose is the strongest possible evidence that Bacon was not Shakespeare; the man who wrote *Henry VII* could not have written *Henry*

IV. Any dramatic values in Bacon's account are dissipated by the intrusion of strategies and enumerations of laws. Unlike Tacitus, Bacon stays within his fragmentary and annalistic framework; he must bring in the digressions about Saturday, Henry's chariot, and the Bishop of London's palace.

In some respects, it is true, Bacon's *History* reminds us of the *Annals*. One figure dominates, affairs of state are analyzed, the common masses appear only in the role of rebels or attendants on celebrations, no social or economic background is given, and there are formal character portraits and invented speeches.[8] He follows the practices of ancient historiography in general, and of earlier English historians. What is distinctive in Tacitus' style is not to be found. In fact, I know of only one author in whom Tacitus' style is approximated in English, and that is the young Carlyle.[9]

The greatest difference between Tacitus and Bacon, and the one decisive for style, is in Bacon's amoral conception of history. Although Bacon, like Tacitus, praises and condemns his hero, it is not for his ethical qualities, or lack of them, but, as here, for his "great wisdom," or lack of it. Bacon is careful to tell us he means political wisdom; Henry is "not ignorant of the fears of the people," and he knows how to play upon them. Bacon praises Henry for that which Tacitus condemns in Tiberius: the "rising to great place . . . by a winding stair," notwithstanding that "it is sometimes base, and by indignities men come to dignities." [10] For Bacon, Tiberius is something of a hero because he dies "in dissimulation." In Tacitus' eyes this dissimulation is the working of an evil genius. In the Tacitean passage in the Appendix the "*consules, patres, eques*" rush into servitude and Tiberius conceals his misdeeds, with Tacitus' implicit moral condemnation. Bacon's "troops of noblemen and persons of quality" and King Henry do the same thing but receive no moral condemnation at all. On the contrary, the memory of Richard like Agrippa's still fresh, Bacon praises Henry for his wisdom here and later for his "dexterity" and "reputation for cunning and policy" (*Works*, XI, p. 363).

Comparing Bacon and Guicciardini, Vincent Luciani has shown that each of their historical writings "is distinguished by its acute analysis of the motives of princes (both secular and ecclesiastic) according to utilitarian passions. Patriotism, self-sacrifice, religious abnegation, and the other idealistic motives hardly exist. . . . Instead, calculation and intrigue are at the basis of all political events.[11] And according to Sister Mary Faith Schuster Bacon is the first Englishman "to treat man's civic life apart from its moral responsibility" ("Philosophy of Life" p. 481). When Bacon criticizes Henry, otherwise a "Salomon of England" (p. 354), it is for his avarice not because it is evil but because it is poor policy, since it instigates an uprising in Cornwall. Avarice is a psychological rather than a moral phenomenon. It is analyzed coldly rather than with Tacitus' moral fervor and insinuation: "Wherefore nature which many times is happily contained and refrained by some bands of fortune, began to take place in the King; carrying as with a strong tide his affection and thoughts unto the gathering and heaping up of treasure" (p. 324). A fact is a fact, with no Tacitean overtones. Given such a conception of history, there is no occasion for pathos (as in the death of the upright Germanicus), horror (the court of Nero), sensuality (Tiberius' villa at Capri), and so on. The *Annals* required an arsenal of rhetorical devices. Bacon's *History* is an unrhetorical monotone. Bacon thought history should be written this way. "And for all that concerns ornaments of speech, similitudes, treasury of eloquence, and such like emptinesses, let it be utterly dismissed. Also let all those things which are admitted be themselves set down briefly and concisely, so that they may be nothing less than words."[12]

A. A. Hill has said that, "Literary utterances can be

assumed to differ from other utterances by having character-istics of heightened symmetry and structure over and above the symmetry and structure inherent in all uses of lan-guage." [13] If so, then Bacon, as his practice and statement about history suggest, is trying to write a styleless or aliter-ary prose. Although Tacitus' prose is also lacking in "sym-metry," there are many elaborate "structures" in it. It is ob-viously a "literary utterance" whereas Bacon's is not. At any rate, Bacon's statement alone would disqualify Tacitus as his model of style for the new kind of historical writing.

Since, for Bacon, "History" includes not only our "his-tory" but also what we would now call "scientific" prose, and since we are directly concerned with scientific prose in this study, we would do well to turn to Bacon's theory of "History." It is both interesting and confusing, and has therefore prompted a good deal of study.[14] While a thor-ough examination of the theory is beyond our scope here, a consideration of its relevant aspects shows that Bacon could not possibly have chosen Tacitus for a stylistic model without succumbing to the famous Idols of the *Novum Organum.* "I consider history and experience to be the same thing," announces Bacon in his bold way (*De Aug-mentis, Works,* VIII, p. 408). For Bacon, however, "His-tory" embraces most of what we call "Science" ("Natural History"; the rest of our "Science" seems to be contained in "Physic" and "Medicine").[15] Under "History" Bacon also has our "History" ("Civil History"). He lumps science and history into the same category because they both are the function of "Memory," that is, they are, as Leonard Dean says, "a bare rehearsal of mentally recorded sense impression" ("Bacon's Theory," p. 163). Only History, in the broad Baconian sense, has the full status of truth. Poetry and Philosophy must rely, respectively, on Imagination and Reason, which are not as reliable, being further removed than Memory from "things." Under Civil History Bacon has Ecclesiastical History, History of Learning and the Arts, and, confusingly, Civil History, "which retains the name of the Genus" (*De Augmentis, Works,* VIII, p. 418). Under this lesser kind of Civil History Bacon divides and subdivides bewilderingly. The purpose of all these Histories is not moral edification but the Advancement of Learning. Not only is history (in our sense) a result of the same psychological process as science, but it has the same purpose and is just as amoral. History, therefore, is to be written in the same style as science, with all ornaments "utterly dismissed." Innuendo and insinuation are to be avoided, for history, like science, must be inductive. The events are to speak for themselves: "But for a man who is professedly writing a Perfect History to be everywhere introducing political reflexions, and thereby interrupting the narrative, is unseasonable and wearisome. For though every wise history is pregnant (as it were) with political precepts and warnings, yet the writer himself should not play the midwife" (*De Augmentis, Works,* VIII, p. 433).

This absence of generalization characterizes Bacon's own *History.* Like the essays and all of Bacon's writings, the *History* is part of the program for the Advancement of Learning,[16] and a methodological example for posterity. Bacon's theory does not describe Tacitus' practice. Tacitus did "play the midwife" at every turn. Bacon's model, by his own admission, is not Tacitus but Machiavelli: "And therefore the form of writing which of all the others is fittest for this variable argument of negotiation and occasions is that which Machiavel chose wisely and aptly for government; namely, *discourse upon histories or examples.* For knowledge drawn freshly and in our view out of particulars, knoweth the way best to particulars again." [17] "Particulars," concrete, real-life problems, rather than abstract moral virtues, should be the stuff of historical writing. "Whereas

History possesseth the mind of the conceits which are nearest allied unto action, and imprinteth them so; as it doth not alter the complexion of the mind neither to irresolution nor pertinacity" (*History, Works,* XI, p. 34).

Bacon was well aware of the distinction between idealistic morality and political wisdom. In a letter to King James urging him to call a Parliament, Bacon writes that, "The subject of the Parliament must have three properties. The first is that which I always begin with, that it be *de vero* good *bonum in se;* and not speculatively or common-place good, but *politicly* good; that is, apt and agreeable for the state of the King and Kingdom." [18] In the dedication of the *History* Bacon tells Charles, then Prince of Wales, of his treatment of Henry VII: "I have not flattered him, but took him to life as well as I could, sitting so far off, and having no better light. It is true, your Highness hath a living pattern, incomparable, of the King your father. But it is not amiss for you also to see one of these ancient pieces" (*History, Works,* XI, p. 43). Henry is not meant as a model of morality, since Charles has an incomparable one already and since Henry has his flaws. Rather, Charles is to learn from the events themselves the art, not the ethics, of ruling.

Bacon's references to Tacitus and his writings reveal no indebtedness to him either as a theoretician or stylist. Instead, Bacon seems to have regarded Tacitus as he regarded the events of King Henry's reign, as a mine of useful examples of "business." The last section of the *Advancement,* which deals with Civil Knowledge and the *faber fortunae,* is loaded with Tacitean citations. But the style is much closer to Machiavellian "discourse upon histories or examples" than to Tacitus. Tacitus is the best supplier of histories and examples. In particular, Tacitus was the standard authority on the crucial topic of dissimulation. For Bacon, however, dissimulation was a useful art (as the essay "On

Dissimulation" attests) rather than an example of moral depravity. As a result, most of Bacon's quotations from Tacitus are out of context. If, as appears from the *antitheta* which form the structure of most of the essays, he worked out of commonplace books, under the head of "Dissimulation" or its equivalent, he must have crowded *sententiae* and bits of scenes from the standard source, the *Annals* and *History* of Tacitus. References to dissimulation (such as the one we have already seen in connection with Tiberius in "Of Death") abound in the essays.[19]

When Bacon praises Tacitus, it is not for his style or even for his method as a historian. In a letter to Fulke Greville cited by Croll, Bacon says, "Of all stories, I think Tacitus simply the best, Livy very good, Thucydides above any of the writers of Greek matters." [20] The context of the praise is a discussion of the usefulness of history as a source of political examples for a statesman like Greville. It is the most useful study for one in Greville's position. "Of the choice (because you mean only study of humanity) I think story of most, and I had almost said of only use." Speaking to Greville in the same letter of a theoretical biography of Alexander, Bacon is explicit about the practical uses of "story" gathered into commonplaces (rather than epitomes, which provide only useless facts): "But he that will draw notes out of his life under heads will show, under the title of a Conqueror, That to begin in the strength and flower of his age; to have a way made to greatness by his father . . . are necessary helps to great conquests; Under the title of War, That the invader hath ever the advantage of the invaded. . . ." (Letter to Greville, p. 24).

Bacon is recommending Tacitus to Greville as the best source of practical wisdom. Tacitus is to be digested, not merely tasted. But nowhere does Bacon say Tacitus is to be imitated. The best books are "the Histories, for they will best instruct you in matters moral, military and politic by which and in which you must ripen and settle your judgement." [21]

Among the great Roman historians, Tacitus comes off better than Suetonius: "For as when I read in Tacitus the actions of Nero or Claudius, with circumstances of times, inducements, and occasions, I find them not so strange; but when I read them in Suetonius Tranquillus gathered into titles and bundles, and not in order of time, they seem more monstrous and incredible" (*Advancement, Works*, VI, p. 235). But the historian receiving the highest praise as historian rather than as a source of useful information is not Tacitus but the Ciceronian Livy. Writing at about the same time as the letter to Greville, Bacon notes in the *Advancement* "that the Romans never ascended to that height of empire till the time they had ascended to the height of other arts; for in the time of the two first Caesars, which had the art of government in greatest perfection, there lived the best poet, Virgilius Maro; the best historiographer, Titus Livius; the best antiquary, Marcus Varro: and the best, or second orator, Marcus Cicero, that to the memory of man are known" (p. 105). (Bacon's references to Cicero himself are all favorable, both with reference to content and style, for example, "But yet notwithstanding, it is a thing not hastily to be condemned, to clothe and adorn the obscurity even of philosophy itself with sensible and plausible elocution. For hereof we have great examples in Xenophon, Cicero, Seneca, Plutarch, and of Plato also in some degree; and hereof likewise there is great use." [22])

Bacon praises Tacitus even more extravagantly. He places Tacitus' works among "less famous writings that excel in usefulness" (my translation). "Many like the moral doctrines of Aristotle and Plato; but of Tacitus it may be said he utters the very morals of life itself." [23] Again, the context of this praise tells us that Bacon valued Tacitus for use; he does not mention imitation.

The context suggests that by *mores* (translated as "moral doctrines") Bacon means habits and customs rather than human conduct under the aspect of right and wrong, as in Tacitus and the Christian tradition. According to the OED the use of "moral" to designate "that kind of probable evidence which rests on a knowledge of character and of the general tendencies of human nature" was common in Bacon's time; this may well be the "moral" of *Essays or Counsels, Civil and Moral.* Bacon and Tacitus are "moralists" in entirely different senses of the word. For knowledge of the *mores* in which he is interested Bacon sends us to historians in general. In histories "we may find painted forth with great life, how affections are kindled and incited; and how pacified and refrained; and how again contained from act and further degree; and how they disclose themselves, how they work, how they vary, how they gather and fortify, how they are inwrapped one within another, and how they do fight and encounter one with another" (*Advancement, Works,* VI, p. 337).

It would be a serious misrepresentation to describe Bacon's attitude toward knowledge in general — and indeed his entire morality — as completely utilitarian. There are places in the *Advancement* and in the essays written at the same time in which an idealistic morality as well as a love of learning for its own sake jostles Bacon's prevalent tough-minded utilitarian ethic.[24] Such idealistic passages, though not uncharacteristic, are exceptional in Bacon.[25] His primary interest, especially whenever Tacitus comes up, is in practical rather than intellectual virtue. What little there is of Bacon's more idealistic ethics is quite conventional. It exerted little influence on his followers or, from the evidence of the bribery scandal and his treatment of Essex, on Bacon himself. What is "Baconian" and influential in the Restoration and beyond is Bacon's utilitarianism, which is remote from "Anti-Ciceronianism."

Imitation and Useful Prose

If there is one thread running through all Bacon's scattered comments on style, it is a distrust of all imitation. His one reference to Tacitus as a stylist counsels explicitly against it. Croll translates the passage as follows:

Somewhat sounder is another form of style, — yet neither is it innocent of some vain shows, — which is likely to follow in time upon this copious and luxuriant oratorical manner. It consists wholly in this: that the words be sharp and pointed; sentences concised; a style in short that may be called 'turned' rather than fused. Whence it happens that everything dealt with by this kind of art seems rather ingenious than lofty. *Such a style is found in Seneca very freely used, in Tacitus and the younger Pliny more moderately; and it is beginning to suit the ears of our age as never before.* And indeed it is pleasant to subtle and low-ranging minds (for by means of it they conciliate the honor due to letters); however better-trained judgements disapprove it; and it may be looked upon as a distemper of learning, in as far as it is accompanied by a taste for mere words and their concinnity.[26]

Croll and his followers also quote, as an instance of Bacon's Anti-Ciceronianism, what has become his best-known pronouncement on the relation between style and imitation. Early in the *Advancement* Bacon describes the renewal of ancient Latinity stemming from the controversies of the Reformation and culminating in such figures as Osorius, Car, and Ascham, who "with their lectures and writings almost deify Cicero and Demosthenes. . . . In sum, the whole inclination and bent of those times was rather towards style than weight. Here therefore [is] the first distemper of learning, when men study words and not matter." [27]

Bacon is condemning imitation of Cicero, not Cicero, just as he had condemned imitation of Seneca and Tacitus. He is much more aware than his critics that it is possible to use authors as sources of wisdom while rejecting them as stylis-

tic models. The Ciceronian and "Attic" styles are danger-
ously seductive, and he warns posterity not to imitate them.
The danger of imitation, as Bacon repeatedly states, is not
that it duplicates the style imitated — which would not be
so bad, for eloquence has its uses — but that it leads to abuses
of it, to "excess," as well as to perversions of truth. Although, as we have seen, "to clothe and adorn . . . even
philosophy itself" can be of "great use," yet, as Bacon
continues,

> surely to the severe inquisition of truth, and the deep progress
> into philosophy, it is some hinderance; because it is too early
> satisfactory to the mind of man, and quencheth the desire of
> further search, before we come to a just period; but then if a
> man be to have any use of such knowledge in civil occasions,
> of conference, counsel, persuasion, discourse, or the like; then
> shall he find it prepared to his hands in those authors which
> write in that manner. But the excess of this is so justly con-
> temptible, that as Hercules, when he saw the image of Adonis,
> Venus' minion, in a temple, said in disdain, *Nil sacri es,* [you
> are no divinity;] so there is none of Hercules' followers in learn-
> ing, that is, the more severe and laborious sort of inquirers into
> truth, but will despise those delicacies and affectations, as indeed
> capable of no divineness. And thus much of the first disease or
> distemper of learning. (pp. 120–121)

Bacon's new approach to knowledge requires a new approach
to style as well. Appropriateness demands that linguistic
cobwebs be swept away with intellectual Idols. Bacon
counsels against imitation in all things.

Function, rather than imitation, determines style for Bacon.
As Wallace and MacNamee have shown,[28] Bacon consistently holds that each particular rhetorical situation calls for
a special way of writing. His rhetorical theory is permeated
by what we could perhaps today call "form following function" or what Aristotle called "appropriateness."

Wallace has said that "Bacon's belief that the audience
ultimately governs communication and that the kinds of dis-

course have their own ends gives rise to the conviction that the form and structure of all utterance must be *functional*. His method manifestly indicates that order and arrangement in a composition must be adapted to the audience's knowledge and belief, to the subject matter, and to the purpose the speaker or writer intends to achieve" (*Communication and Rhetoric*, p. 24). Order and arrangement must also be adapted, as Croll and MacNamee[29] have pointed out, to the mind of the speaker as well. Appropriateness, then, looms large for Bacon's theory. Croll had implied as much by citing Aristotelian and Stoic theory, which also emphasized appropriateness, as necessary for Anti-Ciceronianism. But for Bacon brevity — the other *sine qua non* of Aristotelian and Stoic theory required by Anti-Ciceronianism — is really determined by appropriateness, too. For example, the *New Atlantis* and the later essays are not especially brief, but deliberately rambling and discursive. Brevity is desirable only in works designed for the "sons of science," as were the early essays. Thus it cannot be proven that Bacon followed Anti-Ciceronian theory, as embodied in Aristotle and the Stoics. All critics not concerned with establishing Bacon's Anti-Ciceronianism have noticed his diversity of styles. These styles are by no means restricted to the *genus humile* of the Anti-Ciceronians, as defined by Croll. They range from the extreme terseness of the early essays, to the courtly Euphuism of the letters written for the revels at Gray's Inn; the florid, almost Ciceronian flattery of King James at the beginning of the *Advancement*; the leisurely *New Atlantis*; the easygoing, almost colloquial slackness of the annalistic *History*; the later essays organized for popular appeal into topics and subtopics ("Methods"); the resonant praises of learning; the barren, utterly bloodless assemblages of observations. Bacon is un-Ciceronian, rather than Anti-Ciceronian.[30]

For these reasons Bacon's style, more than that of most

writers, resists influence-hunters. I think this may help to account for the relative neglect by scholars of his prose style, despite the reflex textbook praise of such expressions as "by common consent the best that the first quarter of the seventeenth century produced in England." [31] For all his huge erudition, Bacon was not likely to be influenced very easily. Zeitlin gives us some indication why:

That the man who took all knowledge to be his province, who at the age of sixteen conceived the idea of overthrowing Aristotle and renovating human science, who carried himself with an air of assured lordliness toward the greatest intellects of his day, who enjoyed invincible confidence in the originality and superiority of his genius, — that such a man should, in his maturity, during the busiest years of an active life, put himself to school in order to set down the results of personal observation is, on the face of it, unlikely. ("The Development of Bacon's Essays," p. 497)

Bacon's principle of utility governs not only his political, moral, and stylistic theory but also his style itself. There is no generalization in the studies on Bacon's thought repeated more often than that he was a utilitarian. Again and again, especially in the *Novum Organum* (1620), Bacon justifies what we would call "pure" research on largely utilitarian grounds: "Again there is another great and powerful cause why the sciences have made but little progress; which is this. It is not possible to run a course aright when the goal itself has not been rightly placed. Now the true and lawful goal of the sciences is none other than this: that human life be endowed with new discoveries and powers." Even the purest research, continues Bacon, has an end, the "new assurance" of useful "works" beyond itself.

But of this the great majority have no feeling, but are merely hireling and professorial. . . . And if any one out of all the multitude court science with honest affection and for her own sake, yet even with him the object will be found to be rather the variety of contemplations and doctrines than the severe and rigid

48

search for truth. And if by chance there be one who seeks after truth in earnest, yet even he will propose to himself such a kind of truth as shall yield satisfaction to the mind and understanding in rendering causes for things long since discovered, and not the truth which shall lead to new assurance of works and new light of axioms.[32]

For Bacon, as for the Royal Society later on, it is difficult to separate "pure" from "applied" research, since both are part of a grand program "that human life be endowed with new discoveries and powers":

At first and for a time I am seeking for experiments of light, not for experiments of fruit. . . . To suppose therefore that things like these are of no use is the same as to suppose that light is of no use, because it is not a thing solid or material. And the truth is that the knowledge of simple natures well examined and defined is as light; it gives entrance to all the secrets of nature's workshop, and virtually includes and draws after it whole bands and troops of works, and opens to us the sources of the noblest axioms; and yet in itself is of no great use. (*Novum*, I, cxxi, *Works*, VII, p. 152)

Bacon's word for experiments of light is "contemplation." It is a submission of the mind to things — the basis of Bacon's inductive method — ultimately for "profit": "For the wit and mind of man, if it work upon matter, which is the contemplation of the creatures of God, worketh according to the stuff, and is limited thereby; but if it work upon itself, as the spider worketh his web, then it is endless, and brings forth indeed cobwebs of learning, admirable for the fineness of thread and work, but of no substance or profit" (*Advancement, Works*, VI, p. 122). Here Bacon helps to inaugurate the happy alliance between Truth — divine and secular — and Utility adopted by his admirers in the Restoration. Only "fruitful" knowledge is true — a fundamental assumption of the century, and one crucial, as we shall see, for style: "As both heaven and earth do conspire and contribute to the use and benefit of man, so the end ought to

be, from both philosophies to separate and reject vain speculations and whatsoever is empty and void, and to preserve
and augment whatsoever is solid and fruitful; that knowledge
may not be as a curtesan, for pleasure and vanity only . . .
but as a spouse, for generation, fruit, and comfort" (*Advancement*, p. 135).

Bacon's utilitarianism here is exalted and humanitarian.
In the same paragraph he reminds us "When I speak of use
and action, [I do not mean] that end before-mentioned of
the applying of knowledge to lucre and profession: for I
am not ignorant how much that diverteth and interrupteth
the prosecution and advancement of knowledge. . . . Neither is my meaning . . . to leave natural philosophy aside,
and to apply knowledge only to manners and policy." But
knowledge is still for use, the "generation, fruit, and comfort" of everyone.

Turning to a central concern of this study, the relation
of style and science, I do not think it was our "science"
that determined the character of Bacon's prose. There is
little of the popular modern distinction in Bacon between
the "two cultures," science and the humanities. The word
"science" appears often in Bacon, but always in the old
sense of "Arts and Sciences," that is, with reference to any
systematic body of knowledge at all. We have already seen
Bacon's point of view in his placing of Natural and Civil
History (our "science" and "history") in one category,
with the same style assigned to both. Although he does
separate "history" from "poetry," Bacon does not seem to
separate utilitarian or scientific knowledge from "art" or the
"humanities" as we are inclined to do. Our coupling of
"cold" with "scientific" is not Baconian. His writing glows
warmest when he considers useful knowledge.

The important distinction for Bacon — and for later
Baconians — is between useful knowledge and useless. The

significance for style is crucial. Bacon's stylistic theory is chiefly concerned with the delivery of useful knowledge; useless knowledge is "mere words and their concinnity." Bacon understands "utility" in two senses, one with regard to the "matter" itself and the other with regard to the "method" in which it is delivered. Only "matter" useful in itself is to be considered at all. Therefore utility decrees the inclusion of aphorisms from the useful Tacitus, restricts the *History* to problems of practical statecraft, and requires that the early essays, as a kind of "history" of wise practice, be written in the aphoristic mode recommended for the bare recording of useful data in Natural and Civil History. Utility with regard to the "method" in which the useful matter is to be "delivered" dictates that, because these early essays are addressed to the "sons of science" they must be aphoristic, and the later essays, the *New Atlantis,* and the *Advancement,* written for popular consumption, must be in a freer, or more oratorical style. Eloquence is useful as a means for the propagation of useful knowledge if not for its advancement.

Bacon's philosophical utilitarianism, then, is of a piece with his strictly functional view of style. The various uses of knowledge determine the particular situation of author and reader, and this in turn determines the kind of prose. Appropriateness, which sets the style most useful for the particular occasion, is part of the stylistic creed of Anti-Ciceronianism as defined by Croll. The ultimate basis for it in Bacon, however, is not a borrowed rhetorical theory but his own utilitarianism.

Bacon sought a separate style for every purpose. Nevertheless there are certain stylistic features which appear in all his writings. One is his abstract vocabulary, surprising in one who advocated submitting his mind to "things," in the sense of physical objects. Utility itself is an abstraction and perhaps breeds others. Bacon even anticipates the emphasis on the abstract "primary qualities" of the Restoration thinkers:

To enquire the Form of a-lion, of an oak, of gold, nay of water, of air, is a vain pursuit: but to enquire the Forms of sense, of voluntary motion, of vegetation, of colours, of gravity and levity, of density, of tenuity, of heat, of cold, and all other natures and qualities, which like an alphabet are not many, and of which the essences (upheld by matter) of all creatures do consist; to enquire I say the *true forms* of these, is that part of Metaphysic which we now define of. (*Advancement*, pp. 220–221)

Such an inquiry is pretty remote from the dramatic, concrete immediacy of the "Anti-Ciceronians."

Closer to the present point in our study is the persistence in Bacon's prose of the "Anti-Ciceronian" period so ably described by Croll. Although utility dictated Bacon's style, we can nevertheless conjecture as to what literary influences affected Bacon's style other than, or in addition to, an "Anti-Ciceronian" writer such as Tacitus. Croll states that "in Bacon's case, the frequency of his quotation from Tacitus may be accepted as evidence of his preference of that author to all others" (*Style*, p. 193). But Bacon quotes from the Bible — especially from Ecclesiastes, the Proverbs, and the Pauline epistles — much more than from Tacitus. Following Croll's implicit principle that frequency of quotation indicates stylistic indebtedness, we would do well to turn to the Bible, in which Bacon was "saturated." [33] In the parts of it of which Bacon was fondest — that is, in which he found useful political and scientific aphorisms — there is a syntax not unlike Tacitus' and Bacon's. This is especially true in the parts attributed to Solomon. Bacon's reverence for Solomon far exceeds his reverence for any Greek or Roman writer. The citadel of science in the *New Atlantis* is Solomon's House, and the highest praise accorded

King Henry in the *History*, as we have seen, is that he is a Solomon. So overwhelmed is Bacon by the wisdom of Solomon that he interrupts his discussion of Civil Knowledge (a discussion, as we have observed, often dominated by Tacitus) to praise him and introduce a number of his "excellent cautions, precepts, positions, extending to much variety of occasions." [34] One of these, chosen at random, may serve to illustrate "Anti-Ciceronianism" in the Vulgate:

Erat civitas parva, et pauci in ea viri: venit contra eam rex magnus, et vadavit eam, intruxitque munitiones per gyrum, et perfecta est obsidio: inventusque est in ea vir pauper et sapiens, et liberavit eam per sapientiam suam; et nullus deinceps recordatus est hominis illius pauperis. [There was a little city and few men within it; and there came a great king against it and besieged it and raised great bulwarks round about it: and there was found in it a poor wise man, and he by his wisdom delivered the city; yet no man remembered that same poor man.] [35]

Brevity of members, the most important of Croll's characteristics of the curt style, is apparent. Most of the members are only four or five words long. There is hardly any syntactic connection between the members, other than those which "allow the mind to move straight on from the point it has reached" — the logically extraneous *et* and *que*. The characteristic "Anti-Ciceronian" movement is present. The first member makes a statement which is embroidered upon in the next two or three, with the consequent "trailing effect" — the beginning of the member discussing the last word of the previous one, rather than its main idea (for example, "*vir pauper et sapiens, et liberavit*"), the whole strung together loosely by *et* and *que*. Asymmetry is present in the sudden and expressive change of the position of the verb in the final member where we would expect it, as in the other members, to come first, and in the shifts in the mood of the verbs.

Another Biblical favorite of Bacon's was St. Paul, for whom Bacon, himself a kind of secular Apostle, must have felt a certain sympathy. St. Paul, as much as Tacitus, might well have influenced Bacon's style. In fact, Bacon cites Paul as something of an authority on style: "As substance of matter is better than beauty of words, so contrariwise vain matter is worse than vain words: wherein it seemeth the reprehension of St. Paul was not only proper for those times, but prophetical for the times following; and not only respective to divinity, but extensive to all knowledge: *Devita profanas vocum novitates, et oppositiones falsi nominis scientiae:* [shun novelties of terms and oppositions of science falsely so called.]" (*Advancement*, p. 121). St. Paul's abrupt, pithy, asymmetrical style resembles Bacon's practice and theory, which Croll would ascribe to "Anti-Ciceronianism."

Aside from the Bible, the list of authors quoted by Bacon whose aphoristic syntax resembles Croll's "Anti-Ciceronian" archetype includes Machiavelli, Guicciardini, and, on occasion, Cicero himself, whose aphorisms on "business" Bacon cites enthusiastically, as he does Virgil's and Livy's. These authors, as much as the alleged ancient fathers of "Anti-Ciceronianism," are entitled to consideration as influences on Bacon's style. Whenever he can, Bacon pays homage to the method and pithy wisdom of the Pre-Socratic philosophers, to the many proverbs from various folk traditions he is fond of quoting, and above all to the style of the civil law, in which he was immersed for so much of his life.[36]

For Bacon, all these disjointed styles or "methods" are aphoristic. Rather confusingly, he opposes this informal "delivery in Aphorisms," itself a "method," to "Methods," meaning the more formal mode:

Another diversity of Method, whereof the consequence is great, is the delivery of knowledge in Aphorisms, or in Methods; wherein we may observe that it hath been too much taken into custom, out of a few Axioms or observations upon any subject to make a solemn and formal art; filling it with some discourses, and illustrating it with examples, and digesting it into a sensible Method; but the writing in Aphorisms hath many excellent virtues, whereto the writing in Method doth not approach.

For first, it trieth the writer, whether he be superficial or solid: for Aphorisms, except they should be ridiculous, cannot be made but of the pith and heart of sciences; for discourse of illustration is cut off; recitals of examples are cut off; discourse of connexion and order is cut off; descriptions of practice are cut off; so there remaineth nothing to fill the Aphorisms but some good quantity of observation: and therefore no man can suffice, nor in reason will attempt, to write Aphorisms, but he that is sound and grounded. But in Methods . . . a man shall make a great shew of an art, which if it were disjointed would come to little. (*Advancement, Works*, VI, p. 291)

The earliest essays, some of the first book of the *Novum Organum*, the collections of scientific observations, and the *History* are aphoristic. It is the style for the advancement of learning; "Methods" (meaning the more formal styles) are for its "propagation" and "use": "Methods are more fit to win consent or belief, but less fit to point to action. . . . Methods, carrying the show of a total, do secure men, as if they were at furthest." [37] Therefore Bacon's persuasive efforts — political speeches, prefaces, dedications, reevaluations of mythology, and early popular writings on moral issues, such as the *Religious Meditations* — are predominantly in "Methods." So are some of the later essays, perhaps because, as MacNamee suggests, the earlier essays had proved unexpectedly popular.[38] The *Advancement* and parts of the *Novum Organum*, intended both for advancement and propagation, use both styles.

It is the aphoristic style, however, which is most frequently associated with Bacon. He felt that in aphorisms knowledge is delivered as it is induced. For him, therefore, aphorism is the most *natural* style, the closest to "matter," to thoughts as they really are as the outer world impinges on the mind unadulterated by Idols. (This is not true. Although thought as a whole is indeed disjointed, like the aphoristic style, individual thoughts are not polished aphorisms. No one ever thought in the antithetical constructions of the early essays, which are very aphoristic.)

For Bacon, the aphoristic style was also the *clearest*. In the *Novum Organum* it is Bacon's "design to set everything forth, as far as may be, plainly and perspicuously (for nakedness of the mind is still, as nakedness of the body once was, the companion of innocence and simplicity)" (*The Great Instauration, Works*, VIII, p. 38). Ultimately, though, a style which duplicates thought processes most closely is obscure — closer to *Ulysses* or *Finnegans Wake* (not to mention some "Anti-Ciceronian" prose) than to anything in Bacon.[39] For Bacon, the aphoristic style is also the most useful style. It "derives axioms from the senses and particulars, rising by a gradual and unbroken ascent, so that it arrives at the most general axioms last of all. This is the true way, as yet untried" (*Novum Organum, Works*, VIII, p. 71).

Although "Anti-Ciceronianism" is also aphoristic, it would appear that, because of Bacon's utilitarianism and resulting bias against imitation, he never "naturalized" any style at all, unless one speaks of an Aphoristic Tradition in literature of which Bacon is attempting a synthesis in English. Bacon himself was aware of such a tradition. Aphorisms are the Initiative or Probative style, the *Traditio Lampadis* or Handing-on-of-the-Lamp style, useful for the "progression" (as distinguished from the "use") of knowledge.[40] Rather than Anti-Ciceronian imitation, it is his program for collecting and inventing aphorisms that gives so many of his writings their abrupt, oracular impersonality. There is a certain paradox. The same Bacon who would throw off the chains of authority in learning as well as in style wrote the essay "Of Studies" and "The Wisdom of the Ancients." He favored assembling the best of what had been thought and said previously in aphorisms, aphorisms being the only "true way of searching into and discovering truth" (*Novum*, I, xix, *Works*, VIII, p. 71). Bacon had good precedent in the Renaissance for collecting pithy commonplaces;[41] the prevalence of the practice is reflected in Shakespeare's being able to put on the popular stage a Polonius, who is a caricature of aphorism collectors.

Croll's observations on the Aphoristic Tradition (specifically, on its brevity) are worth restatement. Brevity "is a quality almost necessarily involved in the attempt to portray exactly the immediate motions of the mind." Throughout the history of writing "those which have aimed at the expression of individual experience have tended to break up the long musical periods of public discourse into short, incisive members, each one carrying a stronger emphasis, conveying a sharper meaning than it would have if it were more strictly subordinated to the general effect of the whole" (*Style*, p. 87). Of ages of intellectual upheaval, such as the seventeenth century, Croll says acutely that, "The true literary modes are those that serve the purposes of criticism, protest, individual intelligence." The ideal mode for such a time is "the 'natural' style which expresses naïvely the candor of the soul. But in fact the style it demands for its self-expression is one that has been wrought upon with subtle art to reveal the secret experiences of arduous and solitary minds, to express, even in the intricacies and subtleties of its form, the difficulties of a soul exploring unfamiliar truth by the unaided exercise of its own faculties" (p. 95).

Everything in Croll's statements is true. But they contain a notion that contradicts Croll's theory that Bacon was an Anti-Ciceronian. For Croll seems to maintain here that there is a kind of universal mode for the expression of intellectual and spiritual independence. Surely we can include St. Paul, "Solomon," the Pre-Socratics, or, for that matter, Emerson, D. H. Lawrence, Ezra Pound, and Marshall Mc-

Luhan as practitioners of just such a prose style, as much as Seneca or Tacitus. It reflects a state of mind which would appear to embrace and account for much more in literary history than a movement as limited as Anti-Ciceronianism, or any conscious attempt to establish a *genus humile* along classical lines. The practice of Crollian critics, especially Williamson, of explaining any "brevity" or "curtness" or "asymmetry" as a result of the influence of "Anti-Ciceronianism" seems unwarranted.

Bacon, Montaigne, and Seneca

Before concluding this survey of Bacon and Anti-Ciceronianism we should discuss briefly two other writers, important for Anti-Ciceronianism, who have been cited as influences on Bacon. These are Montaigne and Seneca. The question of the influence of Montaigne on Bacon has been, as Bacon would say, so "excellently well-labored" that our knowledge is not "deficient." I pass over the problem with a summary of the literature on it, which has centered, as one might expect, on the *Essays*. Almost everyone who has gone into the problem in any depth agrees that, at least with regard to the earliest edition of the essays, Bacon owed only the name of the genre to Montaigne. As Villey, speaking of this edition, puts it: "Si nous regardons maintenant la forme, c'est une opposition radicale que nous constatons. Il n'y a rien de vivant, d'animé, de personnel comme un essai de Montaigne, au moins dans les deux dernières formes, celles des editions de 1588 et 1595" (*Revue de la Renaissance*, [1911], p. 122). In contrast to Montaigne, each essay in the first edition is "une collection des sentences pratiques, toutes nues, decharnées, depouillés de toutes les circonstances vivantes qui les ont suggerées a l'auteur, sans exemples, sans justifications" (p. 140). Villey does make an elaborate case for the influence of Montaigne on Bacon in the later editions of the essays. But he is soundly refuted by Zeitlin and Crane,[42] and on much the same basis as I have tried to refute the Tacitean influences: Bacon's conception of morality is so remote from Montaigne's that stylistic imitation would be unlikely. The instances, chiefly in the 1612 essays, when Bacon's morality is more oriented to conscience than to the needs of "business," Zeitlin attributes to the influence of Bacon's own ideas in the sections of the contemporaneous *Advancement* relating to "Moral" (idealistic) Philosophy as distinguished from "Civil Knowledge." Crane has shown that the style of the idealistic sections of the *Advancement* strongly resembles the essays in which idealism appears. To Crane, this indicates that for Bacon utility determines style: for this particular subject, a particular style was necessary. Another argument against Villey's insistence on the influence of Montaigne on the two later editions (1612 and 1625) is offered by Crane and Zeitlin. The style of these essays is not derived from the emerging awareness of Montaigne at that time since, in the *Religious Meditations,* the *Colours of Good and Evil, Certain Observations Made Upon a Libel, An Advertisement Touching the Controversies of the Church of England,* and the famous letter to Burleigh, Bacon shows "the habit of writing coherent, well-planned discourses, enriched with figures, 'sentences,' and 'examples,' so far from being a comparatively late development, the result of a psychological change or of the reading of Montaigne, was in reality an essential part of Bacon's literary equipment from the first" (Crane, p. 99). All these works, with the exception of the *Colours,* appeared before the first edition of 1597 (the *Colours* were published with this edition). Furthermore, as Zeitlin demonstrates, the discursive elements in the later essays are not distinctively Montaignesque. Indeed, there are certain stylistic features — especially the organization into headings and subheadings — that show a trend away from Montaigne. Again Bacon's style defies the influence-hunters. Bacon had read and appreciated Montaigne. But, as in the case of Tacitus and the Bible, he uses Montaigne in such a way as to change his spirit and true meaning, sacrificing these to the needs of utility. This holds for the very few direct allusions to Montaigne and for the conception of the essay itself. Rawley, Bacon's contemporary biographer saw truly that "though he was a great reader of books, yet he had not his knowledge from books, but from some grounds and notions within himself" (Bacon's *Works*, I, p. 47).

Those who argue against the influence of Montaigne on the essays usually replace him with Seneca. In the suppressed dedication to Prince Henry Bacon himself cites Seneca as an influence on the small pieces "which I have called Essays. The word is late, but the thing is ancient; for Seneca's epistles to Lucilius, if you mark them well, are but essays, that is, dispersed meditations, though conveyed in the form of epistles. . . . But my hope is, they may be as grains of salt, that will rather give you an appetite, than offend you with satiety" (*Essays*, ed. Wright, p. xii). It is to the *Epistles* that Bacon refers more than any other work of Seneca, and it is with them that the essays are to be compared. Since we have already looked at "Of Death," an examination of the Senecan epistles on death from which Bacon quotes naturally suggests itself. Epistle twenty-four (from which Bacon takes his observation that the trappings of death unnecessarily instill fear of it) is too long to quote in full. Seneca begins by chiding Lucilius for his fears over a pending lawsuit, and for expecting Seneca to tell him that everything will work out for the best. Seneca then goes on to discuss, by means of examples and *sententiae*, the futility of fear in general, and especially of death. Admittedly the subject is hackneyed. " 'Oh,' say you, 'those stories have been droned to death in all the schools; pretty soon, when you reach the topic "On Despising Death," you will be telling me about

Cato.' " Inevitably, Cato is indeed the next example, and
Despising Death the subject of the rest of the letter. The
remainder is taken up largely with an exegesis, in the manner of the schools of declamation, of a verse of Lucilius on
a commonplace about death, to which Seneca adds three
sententiae of Epicurus and a flood of his own, with considerable restatement of identical thoughts in different forms.
In the middle Seneca has an apostrophe to death, from which
Bacon apparently misquotes in his essay, and an observation
on philosophy which Bacon may well have had in mind in
his famous comment on hunting after words, not matter:

Quid mihi gladios et ignes ostendis et turbam carnificum circa
te frementem? Tolle istam pompam, sub qua lates et stultos
territas! Mors es, quam nuper servus meus, quam ancilla contempsit. Quid tu rursus mihi flagella et eculeos magno apparatu
explicas? Quid singulis articulis singula machinamenta, quibus
extorqueantur, aptata et mille alia instrumenta excarnificandi,
particulatim hominis? Pone ista, quae nos obstupefaciunt. Iube
contiscere gemitus et exclamationes et vocum inter lacerationem
elisarum acerbitatem! Nempe dolor es, quem podagricus ille
contemnit, quem stomachius ille in ipsis deliciis perfert, quem
in puerperio puella perpetitur. Levis es, si ferre possum, brevis
es, si ferre non possum.

Haec in animo voluta, quae saepe audisti, saepe dixisti. Sed an
vere audieris, an vere dixeris, effectu proba. Hoc enim turpissi-
mum est, quod nobis obici solet, verba nos philosophiae, non
opera tractare.

"Why dost thou hold up before my eyes swords, fires, and
a throng of executioners raging about thee? Take away all
that vain show, behind which thou lurkest and scarest fools! Ah,
thou art naught but Death, whom only yesterday a manservant
of mine and a maidservant did despise! Why dost thou again unfold and spread before me, with all that great display, the
whip and the rack? Why are those engines of torture made
ready, one for each several member of the body, and all the
other innumerable machines for tearing a man apart piecemeal?
Away with all such stuff, which makes us numb with terror!
And thou, silence the groans, the cries, and the bitter shrieks

ground out of the victim as he is torn on the rack! Forsooth thou art not but Pain, scorned by yonder gout-ridden wretch, endured by yonder dyspeptic in the midst of his dainties, borne bravely by the girl in travail. Slight thou art, if I can bear thee; short thou art, if I cannot bear thee!"

Ponder these words which you have often heard and often uttered. Moreover, prove by the result whether that which you have heard uttered is true. For there is a very disgraceful charge often brought against our school — that we deal with the words, and not with the deeds of philosophy.[43]

I think that this passage represents fairly the range of Seneca's epistolary style. Indeed, in it are found most of the elements which Summers, in his edition of selected Senecan epistles,[44] considers characteristic of Seneca's style. This way of writing "freely used by Seneca" Bacon and rhetorical tradition (beginning with Seneca's anonymous critics referred to in the passage) condemned and avoided as words rather than matter, *verba* rather than *opera*, and a means of seeming wise.[45] Bacon and the rhetoricians object to the same thing: the use of the figures of sound and elevated tone of the *genus grande* for the subject matter of the *genus humile*. The result is "mere words and their concinnity," declamation rather than eloquence. Above all, the spasmodic Seneca lacks an essential quality of eloquence, sustaining power. The *genus humile* will not tolerate elevation over a long stretch, although the figures used by Seneca require it. Seneca's style is at war with itself, now elevated, now intimate, seldom very settled.

The most striking quality of the apostrophe to death, as well as the following admonition to Lucilius, is its rhetorical extravagance in the framework of an intimate epistle. The bombastic rhetorical questions, personifications, apostrophes, and wealth of examples are deliberately contrived to rise to rhetorical climaxes (for example, at *"Pone ista"*). Bacon, on the other hand, is emotionally neutral in the essays, sacrificing sustained dramatic or rhetorical effect to individual aphorisms or examples. Croll, we have seen, associates figures of thought rather than figures of sound with Anti-Ciceronianism. Although Bacon, as in "Of Death," has his Euphuistic moments, he usually avoids schematic prose. But Seneca is laden with purely ornamental figures of sound. The result is a style organized much more closely than Bacon's (or Tacitus') by verbal echoes and antitheses. These are often antitheses of sound as well as thought: "qu*ae* s*ae*pe aud*isti*, *sae*pe dix*isti*. Sed an vere audi*eris*, an v*ere* dix*eris;* *puer*perio *puel*la *perpe*titur"; "*lacera*tionem *elisa*rum *acer*bitatem"; "*quam* nuper servus meus, *quam* ancilla contempsit . . . *quem* podagr*icus* ille . . . *quem* stoma*chius* ille . . . *quem*. . . ." Here is the "taste for mere words and their concinnity" which Bacon deplored, and generally avoided himself as a distemper of learning. Seneca's choice and arrangement of words also betrays his taste for concinnity: the rare "*excarnificandi*"; the strange "*podagricus*" (Seneca shares with Tacitus, though not with Bacon, the trick of turning little-used adjectives into odd substantives); two forms of the same word ("*carnificum*," "*excarnificandi*"); word-play ("*singulis articulis singula*"); elegant variation in the sounds of endings ("turb*am* carnific*um* te frement*em*"); and such powerful, mouth-filling verbs as "*extorqueantur*" and *obstupefaciunt*," with their clusters of consonants. Everywhere are figures of thought (for example, "*Levis es, si ferre possum, brevis es, si ferre non possum*"), but these are coupled with a parallelism of sound and thus are used in a more theatrical way, to point up a climax as well as to express a thought concisely, than in Bacon. The same is true of the other stylistic traits common to Bacon and Seneca, such as personification (compare Bacon's quiet "Death" with Seneca's strident "*Mors es*" and "*dolor es*"). In Seneca even brevity is lost, since thoughts are repeated when the dramatic effect requires it. As in Tacitus, it is the essentially dramatic character of Seneca's prose that is so remote from

Bacon. Nowhere is there in Bacon Seneca's attempt to ground each essay or epistle in a concrete situation. Bacon is speaking to a specific person — Buckingham in 1625, Prince Henry in 1612, and Anthony Bacon in 1597; the "you" in the Bacon essays is a real person, just as much as Seneca's Lucilius or Montaigne's la Boétie. But we are never really aware of him, any more than we are of Machiavelli's Prince Lorenzo. Unlike Montaigne, Bacon rejected Seneca's intimacy.

Bacon did retain something of Seneca's content and arrangement. From Seneca the Elder came the principle of the *antitheta* (*De Augmentis, Works,* IX, p. 155), which are also found in the epistles of Seneca the Younger. From the Senecan epistle Bacon, as he says himself, got the idea of the essay as a series of "dispersed meditations" fit for the leisure hours of a cultured gentleman. Some of these essays bear on moral cruxes of the kind Seneca and the schools of declamation discussed. As a result, both Bacon and Seneca are often giving advice. From Seneca, Bacon also appears to have picked up the idea of an essay as a literal "attempt," an incomplete covering of a topic, as opposed to a formal treatise — "grains of salt, that will rather give you an appetite, than offend you with satiety." Hence, most of the early essays are aphoristic or probative or initiative rather than magistral in method; the essays of the later editions, with their topics and sub-topics, look more and more like full discourses.

Of course, Seneca is not the only begetter of the form of Bacon's essays. E. N. S. Thompson and W. G. Crane have shown that there were other precedents for the predominantly aphoristic essay.[46] Furthermore, although the subjects of Bacon's essays are often Senecan, there is also a wealth of practical political advice which in its amorality recalls not Seneca so much as the Renaissance genre of books for the edification of princes and courtiers. It must not be forgotten that each edition of the essays, like the *History,* is written for someone immersed in "business."

Bacon also seems to have admired certain aspects of Seneca's theory of style. Bacon's preference for matter over words, as we have seen, may have derived from Seneca. "Seneca maketh the comparison well" of sophistry to juggling tricks (p. 274). "Seneca giveth an excellent check to eloquence: *Nocet illis eloquentia, quibus non rerum cupiditatem facit, sed sui:* [eloquence does mischief when it draws men's attention away from the matter to fix it on itself]" (*Advancement, Works,* VI, p. 310). Seneca has many pleas for plainness, brevity, and other Baconian desiderata.[47] In these, he is not especially original but is following traditional statements on the plain style and its suitability to the epistle.[48]

But Seneca is famous for the conflict between his theory and practice. Bacon seems to be aware of the discrepancy. He quotes Seneca's theory favorably while condemning his style. Williamson conjectures, with reason, that Bacon associated Senecan style with Euphuism, "mere words and their concinnity." [49] Summers describes Senecan style as anything but plain; it is the "kind of writing which, without sacrificing clearness or conciseness, regularly avoids, in thought or phrase or both, all that is obvious, direct and natural, seeking to be ingenious rather than true, neat rather than beautiful, exercising the wit but not rousing the emotions or appealing to the judgement of the reader" (*Select Letters,* p. xv). We have seen that Seneca does indeed rouse the emotions on occasion; but with these few exceptions Summers has accurately described Seneca's style or at least its epigrammatic quality. It is a quality, however, of the Aphoristic Tradition in general. Furthermore, for the most part Bacon is not seeking to be ingenious *rather* than true. It is this quality of Silver Latin which he generally avoids, and to which he objects in his censure of Seneca, Tacitus, and Pliny as stylistic models. Bacon seeks to be ingenious *and* true — which necessitates figures of thought rather than Senecan figures of sound. And, as we have seen in a work like the *History*, Bacon, with his loose-hung syntax that reminded Croll of Tacitus, is often "obvious, direct, and natural" rather than "ingenious," though still aphoristic. The one significant feature of Seneca's way of writing which accords with his theory of style — that writing should be familiarly personal — is lacking in Bacon. This lack, as I have tried to show, separates Bacon from Montaigne as well as from Seneca. Bacon did owe something to Seneca for the general idea of the Essay, and for his theory of style. But Bacon's prose itself is not Senecan. Croll maintains that Seneca was inadequate as a model for Bacon because he was "capable of becoming almost as transparently artificial" as a Ciceronian. Seneca "might *suggest* the ideal manner; but he was too superficial, too familiar, to furnish a complete model" (*Style*, pp. 191, 194–195).

Undoubtedly Bacon valued Seneca as he did Tacitus, more for his "matter" than his style. We can see this in the way he so often misquotes Seneca's words while retaining his thoughts. In "Of Death," *Pompa mortis magis terret, quam mors ipsa* reproduces only Seneca's idea, not his flood of examples or rhetorical padding. The antithesis is a figure of thought rather than sound, and the sharp asymmetry of length of the two parts of the sentence is in contrast to Seneca's balance or near-balance for purely rhetorical purposes.

Bacon distrusted at least one aspect of Seneca's matter as well. There is an addition to the *Valerius Terminus, or Interpretation of Nature* which is probably the most violent of Bacon's writings. It is a polemic against most of the revered names in science, especially Aristotle, and a eulogy of Bacon's favorites, especially the Pre-Socratics. Included among the corrupters of truth is Seneca, lumped together with Plutarch and, of all people, Cicero:

> For it is a slighter evil that thou [natural science] hast been the parent of philologers, and that under thy guidance, and the auspices of thy manifold genius, ensnared and satisfied with the fame and the popular and smooth jocundity of the knowledge of things, they did corrupt the severer investigation of truth. Among these were Marcus Cicero, and Annaeus Seneca, and Plutarch of Charonaea.[50]

Since the context of this attack is a survey of natural science (the "thou") and since Bacon generally quotes Seneca's moral writings with approval, the object of scorn here must be the *Quaestiones Naturales*, a work which, as a supplement to Aristotle, was important for the medieval science Bacon attacked. Although Seneca is a close observer of nature, the spirit of the *Quaestiones* is utterly un-Baconian. Instead of Bacon's ideal of an impersonal series of aphoristic observations on all manner of natural occurrences organized into "Forms," the *Quaestiones* is a series of epistolary speculations on spectacular and controversial events like earthquakes, comets, and thunderstorms. Few facts go uninterpreted. These interpretations are based not on observation but on hypothesis, a feature of scientific thinking infrequent in Bacon. Seneca intrudes not only scientific explanations but philosophical *sententiae* and moralized anecdotes as well. Lightning, for example, inspires the standard Stoic piece on fearing death. Worst of all, Seneca is forever arguing, agreeing and disagreeing with the "authorities." The *Quaestiones* is frankly controversial, much of it cast in the form of a debate reminiscent, like so much of Seneca's writings, of St. Paul, with whom Seneca was said to have corresponded. In short, Seneca's scientific style is supremely unlike the style recommended by Bacon for recording empirical knowledge. Seneca reverses the Baconian dicta, and uses "Methods" or the "Magistral" style where the "Initiative" or "Probative" aphoristic style is required. Seneca's aims are those of a controversialist rather than a severe investigator of truth. It is hard to imagine that Bacon, who would "admit nothing but on the faith of eyes,"[51] would look to such a figure as a model of style.

Bacon's antipathy to so much in the styles of Seneca and Tacitus may explain the total lack of favorable or significant reference to the great Renaissance champions of Seneca and Tacitus, Muret and Lipsius. Croll has shown that by the time Bacon was composing, or rather compiling, the first edition of the *Essays*, Lipsius was renowned as a leader of the Anti-Ciceronian cult. If Bacon, whose reading was prodigious, was also an Anti-Ciceronian, it is difficult to account for the absence. An examination of Lipsius' prose style reveals how remote it is from Bacon's, and how near to Tacitus' and Seneca's.[52]

I can only conclude that the influence of Tacitus and Seneca on Bacon is not sufficient to place him in the ranks of the Anti-Ciceronian movement, let alone as one of its founders.

Bacon and the Elizabethans

Not "Anti-Ciceronian" imitation, but the requirements of the program for the advancement of learning fixed Bacon's style. In the preceding discussion of Bacon and Anti-Ciceronianism, I have tried to show the influence of his utilitarian program by comparing Bacon's style and rhetorical theory with those of his alleged models. The utilitarianism of Bacon's style can be shown more dramatically by a comparison of his prose with that of his predecessors and contemporaries. Returning to the passage from the *History* (pp. 32–33), we may compare it briefly with some of its sources. The basic source is the sketchy and eulogistic account by

Bernard André, Henry VII's official panegyrist.[53] John Speed used André, and it is Speed's account (and his misreadings of André) that Bacon largely follows.[54] Bacon preferred his contemporary Speed because of Speed's interest in "business" and because of his (often gratuitous) interpretations of Henry's actions as Machiavellian Realpolitik.

Bacon also read and used Polydore Vergil's *Anglica Historia* (1534). The differences between Vergil and Bacon are instructive.

To such a marriage the girl had a singular aversion. Weighed down for this reason by her great grief she would repeatedly exclaim, saying, "I will not thus be married, but, unhappy creature that I am, will rather suffer all the torments which St. Catherine is said to have endured for the love of Christ than be united with a man who is the enemy of my family." This girl too, attended by noble ladies, was brought to her mother in London. Henry meanwhile made his way to London like a triumphing general, and in the places through which he passed was greeted with the greatest joy by all. Far and wide the people hastened to assemble by the roadside, saluting him as king and filling the length of his journey with laden tables and overflowing goblets, so that the weary victors might refresh themselves. But when he approached the capital, the chief magistrate (whom they call the 'mayor') and all the citizens came forth to meet him and accompanied him ceremoniously as he entered the city: trumpeters went in front with the spoils of the enemy, thundering forth martial sounds. In this way Henry came, after all his toils, to his kingdom, where he was most acceptable to all. After this he summoned a parliament, as was his custom, in which he might receive the crown by popular consent. His chief care was to regulate well affairs of State and, in order that the people of England should not be further torn by rival factions, he publicly proclaimed that (as he had already promised) he would take for his wife Elizabeth daughter of King Edward and that he would give complete pardon and forgiveness to all those who swore obedience to his name.[55]

Bacon has added the analysis of Henry's motives and omitted the dramatic and sensuous touches: Elizabeth's extravagant vow, the stage-prop "laden tables and overflowing goblets," and the sound effects.

Vergil's sensuousness is more pronounced in his imitator, Edward Hall. Hall must be quoted at length before any notion of his special quality can come through.

But God of his only goodness preserued ye christē mynde of that verteous & immaculate virgin, & from their flagicious & facinerous acte, did graciously protect and defende: The which lady not long after accōpanyed with a great nombre aswell of noblemē as honorable matrones was with good spede conueighed to London and brought to her mother.

In the meane ceason the kyng remoued forward by iorneyes toward London, and euen as he passed, the rusticall people on euery syde of the wayes assembled in great nombres & with great ioye clapped their hondes & showted, criying, kyng Henry, kyng Henry. But whē he approched nere the cytie, the Mayre, the Senate & the magistrates of thesame beyng all clothed in violet, met him at Shordiche, & not only saluted and welcomed him with one voyce in generall, but eurey person perticulerly preased and aduāced him selfe, gladly to touche and kysse that victorious hande which had overcome so monstruous & cruell a tyraunt, geuying laudes & praysynges to almightye God, and rendrynge immortall thankes to him, by whose meane and industry the cōmen wealth of the realme was preserued frō finall destruccion & perpetual calamite, and the aucthores of ye mischiefe sublated and plucked awaye. And with great pompe & triumphe he roade through the cytie to the cathedral churche of S. Paule wher he offred his iii. standardes. In the one was the ymage of S. George. in the secōd was a red firye dragō beaten vpō white and grene sarcenet, ye third was of yelowe tarterne, in the which was peinted a dōne kowe. After his praiers saide & Te deum song, he departed to the bishoppes palays & there sojourned a ceason, during whiche time, playes, pastymes & pleasures were shewed in euery parte of the cytie. And to thentent that their good mynd toward God should not put in obliuion, they caused general processiōs solemply to be celebrate to rendre and yelde to God their creator and redemer their hartye and humble thankes whiche had delivered them frō miserable captiuite & restored them to libertie and fredome. Besyde this, they that fauoured and loued the kyng were inwardly joyous to se & perceaue that their aduersaries and back frendes were all redy or like to be suppeditate & overthrowen.

When the solempnities & gratifications were done and passed: accordyng as other kynges had been accustomed, he cōgregated together the sage councelors of his realme, in which coūsail like a prince of iust faith and true of promes, detesting all intestine & cyuel hostilite, appointed a daye to joyne in matrimony ye lady Elizabeth heyre of the house of Yorke, with his noble personage heyre to ye lyne of Lancastre: which thyng not only reioysed and comforted the hartes of the noble and gentlemen of the realme. . . .[56]

Hall, unlike Bacon, is very much alive to the drama and splendor of the royal progress. Accordingly, he slows up the narrative flow to take in the magistrates "all clothed in violet," the descriptions of the three colorful standards, and the "playes, pastymes, and pleasures." To emphasize the formality of the occasion, and of history in general, Hall shamelessly pads his sentences by means of doublets, often baldly contrasted, to produce "concinnity": "verteous & immaculate," "flagicious & facinerous," "monstrous & cruell," and "laudes & praysynges." Hall's Latinate "inkhorn terms" (for example, "flagicious & facinerous") were later to bring down Ascham's wrath, but here they increase the melodrama and formality.

As objective history, Hall's chronicle (1542) is not very useful. It is moralistic, dramatic, and oratorical. Nor is Hall useful in the way in which history was useful for Bacon, for he does not add to our knowledge of statecraft. What we find in Hall is an awareness of the sensuous texture of both life and language as well as the moralizing strain. In Bacon these qualities are sacrificed to "business." Utility drives out pleasure.

For in a great work it is no less necessary that what is admitted should be written succinctly than that what is superfluous should be rejected; though no doubt this kind of chastity and brevity will give less pleasure both to the reader and the writer. But it is always to be remembered that this which we are now about is only a granary and storehouse of matters, not meant to be pleasant to stay or live in, but only to be entered as occasion requires, when anything is wanted for the work of the *Interpreter*, which follows.[57]

In historical writings, as in Natural History, values — aesthetic, moral, or otherwise — do not inhere in things themselves, but in their usefulness, a value imposed from the outside. Therefore Bacon, unlike Hall and Vergil, spends little time on the external appearance of solid objects, exploiting purely for their own sakes whatever values may inhere in these appearances. Bacon discusses their primary qualities or their relation to the "business" or the line of argument at hand. As a result his prose often has an abstract quality. Despite his emphasis on "things," few of Bacon's words refer to solid physical objects as they appear to the unaided senses, except in the collections of observations of natural phenomena. Here Bacon is closer to the Restoration Baconians than to the "Anti-Ciceronians." To put the matter another way, Hall's prose is "Elizabethan" (though Hall himself, like Vergil, technically is not), Bacon's is not. An abundance of utilitarian prose was written under Elizabeth. Such prose is written at all times. But the distinctive qualities of Elizabethan prose which readers have always felt — its exuberant artifice, its sensuousness, its moralizing cast — are largely lacking in Bacon, even when he is most rhetorical. This distinction between Bacon and Elizabethan prose is also valid for Bacon and Anti-Ciceronianism.

Bacon's subjects are often those that fired the imagination of his contemporaries, but he handled them in an entirely different spirit. For example, no one acquainted with the literature of Bacon's time is unaware of the impact that the theme of death had on the age. Donne's feverish broodings perhaps come first to mind. Bacon's essay on the subject is unlike contemporary writings, steeped as they are in Christianity and Stoicism. Though drawing on Christian writings, the essay is not especially Christian. Bacon reveals his characteristic use of writers who do not influence him. There is only one reference in the essay to the theme, all-important for Christianity, of life after death, and that not in a Christian context but on the excuse that the contemplation of the passing to another world is of more use than the "weak" fear of it. The passing itself, with its associations of hope, redemption, and victory, is ignored. Mortification, another Christian theme familiar in the literature on death, is barely mentioned. Bacon's chief interest in mortification is a scientific one, the inaccuracy of the friars' descriptions of painful physical sensations.

Nor is the essay Stoic, though laden with references to Stoic writings. Bacon sensibly observes that Stoicism is not very practical because it "bestowed too much cost upon death." Like the Stoics, Bacon advises us that death is not to be feared. Unlike the Stoics, however, Bacon thought well of the opportunities available for man in this life. "But above all, believe it, the sweetest canticle is, *Nunc dimittis*, when a man hath obtained worthy ends and expectations." Marjorie Walters has said rightly that for Bacon death was "the end of a natural process, not a test of mental endurance.[58] Death is an unemotional fact, reflected in Bacon's cool, neutral tone. His chief work on the subject is the *Historia Vitae et Mortis* — a purely scientific catalogue, as remote from the usual contemporary writing on death as possible, but not too far removed from the essay. Essentially the essay is what so much of Bacon's writing is: a concise, dispassionate survey of the available literature on the subject at hand (rhetorically presented in a work like the *Advancement*), with commonsensical observations from experience and recommendations for improvements thrown in.

A treatment of death more characteristic of the age is Jeremy Taylor's version of the passage from Seneca already analyzed (pp. 61–62), which Bacon used in "Of Death":

Take away but the pomps of death, the disguises and solemn bugbears, the tinsel, and the actings by candle-light, and proper and fantastic ceremonies, the minstrels and the noise-makers, the women and the weepers, the swoonings and the shriekings, the nurses and the physicians, the dark room and the ministers, the kindred and the watchers; and then to die is easy, ready and quitted from its troublesome circumstances. It is the same harmless thing that a shepherd suffered yesterday, or a maid-servant today; and at the same time in which you die, in that very night a thousand creatures die with you, some wise men, and many fools; and the wisdom of the first shall not quit him, and the folly of the latter does not make him unable to die.[59]

Taylor is closer to the usual early seventeenth-century feeling for death and to Seneca as well. The entire passage, in contrast to Bacon's, is grounded in particulars, giving a density and solidity to the experience of death. As in Seneca, there is an expressive combination of the sharp or colloquial ("bugbear," "candle-light," "noise-makers," "tinsel") and the suggestive, inexact formal ("pomps," "fantastic," "troublesome"). Nouns evoke images of sound ("minstrels and noise-makers," "the swoonings and the shriekings") as well as sight. In the first sentence, on the horror of death, the quick, breathless rhythm, free of the congestion of qualifiers, and the suggestive nouns act as a contrast to the loosely balanced slackness and unsuggestive vocabulary, with many adjectives and adverbs, of the second, with its theme of release and resignation. Rhetorical heightening of this kind is rare in Bacon, with his neutral, baldly enumerative lists (for example, "Groans, convulsions . . . and the like").

There are times when Bacon is not so neutral, times when one feels a suppressed, nonutilitarian sensitivity to things-in-themselves. Every once in a while we come across snatches that remind us of the sensuousness of a Sidney —

the *New Atlantis* has something of the opulence of the *Arcadia* — or a Nashe.

> The breath of flowers is far sweeter in the air (where it comes and goes like the warbling of music) than in the hand. ("Of Gardens," *Works*, XII, p. 238)
> The colours that shew best by candle-light, are white, carnation, and a kind of sea-water green. ("Of Masques and Triumphs," *Works*, XII, p. 210)

"We rejoice all the more," writes Douglas Bush, "when Machiavelli, or a Machiavellian Samuel Smiles, gives way to the Jacobean lover of beauty or royal magnificence in the loving particularity of the essays on gardens, buildings, or masques and triumphs" (*English Literature*, p. 197). Bacon is apologetic about these topics, or makes tenuous excuses on the grounds of utility. A prince should know about gardens and masques. "Of Gardens" opens with an apology, albeit a splendid one: "God almighty first planted a garden" (that is, so I am justified in writing about so seemingly useless a topic). The first sentence of "Of Masques and Triumphs" is more direct: "These things are but toys, to come amongst such serious observations. But yet, since princes will have such things, it is better they should be graced with elegancy, than daubed with cost."

The war between the sensuous element in Bacon and his prevalent utilitarianism was very one-sided. Bacon's main interest is not in things for their own sake, moral or physical, but in the advancement of learning for the benefit of man. His writings constitute a prolegomenon to all future knowledge. Bacon reviews previous literature, notes where knowledge is lacking, justifies and explains his method, and illustrates it by examples. Such a program calls for a concise, neutral style, except where the necessities of the rhetorical situation dictate the use of "Methods."

Though living amidst the great Elizabethan delight in language for its own sake, Bacon distrusted words. He felt they were not neutral enough for his purposes. His distrust appears in his preference for matter over words in his discussion of the Four Idols, in his plea for research into a universal grammar and a Real Character, and in his schemes for an "*abecedarium naturae*" and writing in ciphers. Naturally, he distrusted style, except for propaganda purposes, even more than bare words. As we have seen, he advocated a styleless Natural and Civil History, in which ornaments are "utterly dismissed." In contrast to earlier Renaissance rhetoricians like Coxe, Sherry, Wilson, Peacham, and Puttenham, Bacon pays almost no attention to style, in the sense of ornamentation. Bacon's rhetoric allies itself to logic rather than to a technique of tropes and figures. Here Bacon is closer to the ideal of the ancient *genus humile*, regarded as a philosophical style, than are his alleged "Anti-Ciceronian" models.

In his optimistic vision of an eventual reunion of rhetoric and logic Bacon differs from his Restoration followers, who were more inclined to separate them. Nevertheless, Bacon's stylistic legacy to his followers is great. First, Bacon articulated the notion of writers like Wilkins, Eachard, South, and at times, Glanvill and Sprat that the best style for prose is no style at all. The major "Anti-Ciceronians" made many statements on the virtues of "naturalness" as opposed to "art," but none of them went so far as Bacon did, or for the same reason. Lacking such "helps" as a Real Character or universal grammar, Bacon seems to have felt he was doing the best he could with aphorism, the style which he thought most closely approached no style. Second, and paradoxically, Bacon's advocacy and practice of aphorisms contributed to the notion of the Restoration that there is a Fit Style for all prose, especially for "expository" prose — an impersonal, concise, coolly argumentative style, good for almost any purpose. Third, the success of Bacon's own splendid rhetoric led his disciples in the

Restoration to advocate and attempt a similar mode when the occasion demanded.

Such a stylistic platform, as we shall see in the writings of such Baconians as Glanvill and Sprat, can owe nothing to "Anti-Ciceronianism," whose stylistic intentions are decidedly different from those of Baconian utilitarianism.

Glanvill, Sprat, and the Royal Society

A Controversial Writer

Of all the many disciples of Bacon, Joseph Glanvill, Protestant divine and defender of the new scientific faith, is the most interesting example of the influence of utilitarianism on prose style.[1] Consideration of Glanvill in this regard antedates the Croll-Jones controversy. From the start, this interest in Glanvill has centered on the revisions of *The Vanity of Dogmatizing*, first published in 1661. Ferris Greenslet began the discussion in 1900:

The reissue in 1665 of a revised version of *Vanity of Dogmatizing* as the *Scepsis Scientifica* marks the end of Glanvill's early manner. In the Epistle Dedicatory prefixed to the latter, he says of the style of the former, "For I must confess that the way of writing to be less agreeable to my present relish and genius, which is more gratified with manly sense flowing in natural and unaffected eloquence, than in the music and curiosity of fine metaphors and dancing periods." This, of course, is the customary feeling of any maturing writer toward the early work of his youth, when striving for effect is so natural and common. But in the present case, when we consider that this statement was addressed to the Royal Society, it seems to show receptivity to the changing ideals of his time. (*Joseph Glanvill*, p. 199)

Greenslet then collates the *Scepsis* with the *Vanity*. In "Science and English Prose Style" Jones repeats and elaborates Greenslet's thesis. For Jones, however, the contrast most significant for the history of prose style is between the *Vanity* and the *second* revision, published in 1676 and renamed "Against Confidence in Philosophy," the first of seven essays in a collection entitled *Essays on Several Important Subjects in Philosophy and Religion*. In this contrast Jones sees not the mild tendency noted by Greenslet toward the "simple, plain, and reasonable." There is a far more "profound change" in Glanvill under the influence of science.[2] By 1676 Glanvill was, in effect, writing in a new style altogether. Quoting from the manifesto on prose style in Sprat's *History of the Royal-Society*, Jones concludes from his collation that in Glanvill's second revision

gone is the Brownesque "swelling" sentence . . . and the touch of beauty . . . while the "vicious abundance of phrase" and "volubility of tongue" have given way to the "plain and familiar words" and the "close, naked, natural way of speaking" . . . there is an obvious change from "specious tropes" and "vicious abundance of phrase" to a "primitive purity and shortness" in which "positive expressions" and "native easiness" are manifest. The reduction of these "wide fetches and circumferences of speech" to a direct and "natural way of speaking" brings out in vivid relief not only the way in which the scientific spirit was destroying the sheer joy in language, but also how the definite linguistic stand taken by the Royal Society was producing results. (*Seventeenth Century*, pp. 93–94)

According to Jones, science also influenced Glanvill's theory of pulpit style decisively.

In his review of "Science and English Prose Style," Croll held that "Glanvill's later style is a *revision*" of his earlier style, rather than a different style altogether. To be sure, the shift is to be explained as part of "the scientific cult of unrhetorical speech from 1650 onward," but this cult

is a second, later stage in the history of the same naturalistic tendency that shows itself in the Anti-Ciceronian victory at the end of the preceding century. It did not create a new, a rival style to the Anti-Ciceronian; it only introduced certain changes within the cadres of that style. It was an attempt, a successful attempt, to take the heat and fever out of the imaginative naturalism of Montaigne, Bacon, and Browne, to prune their conceits and metaphors, to restrain the wild motions of their eloquence. But it did not change the form and structure of the prose of its time. Seventeenth century prose is and remains Anti-Ciceronian and predominantly Senecan.[3]

Croll's disciple Williamson goes even further, arguing that Glanvill as a stylist was not touched by science at all. Using a thesis suggested by Greenslet, Williamson holds that "Glanvill attributed his own rhetoric to youth. His growing distaste for that style he attributed to his 'humour,' but not to the influence of the Royal Society." The necessities of controversy were also a factor:

The *Vanity* had been written by a wit against the wits, and therefore in a brisker style than that of the 'Address,' which is quite formal. . . . There is no real evidence in the 'Address' that Glanvill was either adapting himself to or aware of a Royal Society programme for style. His 'address' is to their gravitas.[4]

Furthermore, notes Williamson, many other "wits" having nothing to do with the Society changed their styles as Glanvill did.

Something of a middle position between Jones and his opponents is taken by Jackson Cope.

The change which took place in Glanvill's practice after *The Vanity of Dogmatizing* may be summarized as a tendency within the "curt" style toward greater freedom of movement. But the flexibility of Glanvill's later prose is not achieved through an abuse of syntactic structure, as happens in the mid-century Senecanism which Croll labelled the "loose" style; rather its liberty is achieved by superimposing upon the basically antithetic member of the Senecan sentence a new respect for logical perspicuity. (*Anglican Apologist*, p. 159)

Cope, like Jones, would account for Glanvill's "new respect for logical perspicuity" by the influence of the Royal Society. Glanvill's "apology for the style is made with an eye toward pacifying the radical element in the Society's plans for linguistic reform: Wilkins, Ward, and Petty, with their sympathizers." In his stylistic practice Glanvill also reflected the ideals of the more moderate reformers in the Royal Society such as Sprat. According to Cope, Sprat followed Bacon, allowing for rhetorical prose outside the actual reporting of progress and discovery in science. Therefore, "In spite of his revising, there are a great many 'fine Metaphors and dancing periods' which Glanvill did *not* remove from the book which was now *Scepsis Scientifica*. And in spite of his casual 'apology' for a somewhat too rhetorical style, he later in the 'Address to the Royal Society' affirms that the style is fitted to his aim . . . 'not improper for the persons, for whom it was prepared'" (pp. 152–153).

More important, however, according to Cope, than either Anti-Ciceronianism or the scientific reformers as an influence on Glanvill is "the chief concern of Glanvill's life . . . Anglican anti-enthusiasm" (p. 146). Glanvill associated rhetoric with Catholic and Aristotelian error, with the type of preaching which emerged in the curious persistence of the style of Andrewes,[5] and with the "Enthusiastic" sects. At first Glanvill argues against any rhetorical speech; but later, following Bacon and Renaissance faculty-psychology, he allows for some rhetoric in sermons to help the "Affections" convey "Reason." Glanvill's feelings about sermon style carry over into the *Vanity* and its revisions. Cope understands these works to spring from a religious rather than a scientific impulse. Stylistically they represent Glanvill's Anglican quest for a *via media* between scholastic and enthusiastic rhetoric.

Cope's final position is eclectic. He seems to argue that, in the interests of Anglican antienthusiasm, Glanvill made his own mature theory and practice of style coincide with that of Sprat and, ultimately, Bacon, with their emphasis on decorum, while retaining a substrate of the fashionable Anti-Ciceronianism. But the real influence on Glanvill is neither Anti-Ciceronianism nor science. These merely suggest examples of stylistic practices which Glanvill finds similar to the kind of writing he has adopted because of its appropriateness to the calm, rational temper of Anglicanism. "It was his role as an Anglican apologist, not as a champion of the new scientific group at Gresham, that dictated Glanvill's outspoken prescription and practice of a new 'plain' style in prose after opening a career which bid well to flower in the gaudier meadows sown by Browne." [6]

Croll, Jones, and Cope agree that Glanvill's style changed after the first edition of the *Vanity*. The crux of the controversy is, Was the change merely a revision of an older Senecan style? Or was it an attempt at a new style altogether, directly influenced by science, and in conscious opposition to the earlier style? To put the matter another way, Is the style of the early Glanvill an example of the "literary and rhetorical expression of science" — the role Croll claims for Anti-Ciceronianism, especially Senecanism? Or is Glanvill's early style antithetical to the style desired and practiced by the scientists? Is Glanvill's early style Senecan in the first place? If it is not, then there is no connection at all, at least for Glanvill, between Senecanism and science under any circumstances. The question of Senecan influence on Glanvill, then, becomes our first concern.

Science and Senecan Prose

These questions may be answered by examining a passage from the first version of the *Vanity:*

Another thing, that engageth our *affections* to unwarrantable conclusions, and is therefore fatal to *Science;* is our doting on *Antiquity*, and the opinions of our Fathers. We look with a superstitious reverence upon the accounts of praeterlapsed ages: and with a supercilious severity, on the more deserving products of our own. A vanity, which hath possess'd all times as well as ours; and the *Golden Age* was never *present.* For as in *Statick* experiment, an inconsiderable weight by vertue of its distance from the Centre of the Ballance, will preponderate much greater magnitudes; so the most slight and chaffy opinion, if at a great remove from the present age, contracts such an esteem and veneration, that it out-weighs what is infinitly more ponderous and rational, of a modern date. And thus, in another sense, we realize what *Archimedes* had only in *Hypothesis;* weighing a single *grain* against the *Globe* of Earth. We reverence gray-headed Doctrines; though feeble, decrepit, and within a step of dust: and on this account maintain opinions, which have nothing but our *charity* to uphold them. While the *beauty* of a Truth, as of a *picture*, is not acknowledg'd but at a *distance*, and that wisdom is nothing worth, which is not fetcht from *afar:* wherein yet we oft deceive ourselves, as did that *Mariner*, who mistaking them for precious stones, brought home his ship fraught with common *Pebbles* from the remotest *Indies.* Thus our Eyes, like the *preposterous Animal's*, are behind us; and our Intellectual motions *retrograde.* We adhere to the determinations of our fathers, as if their *opinions* were entail'd on us as their *lands;* or (as some conceive) part of the Parents soul were portion'd out to his off-spring, and the conceptions of our minds were *ex traduce.* The Sages of old live again in us; and in opinions there is a *Metempsychosis.* We are our re-animated Ancestours, and antedate their *Resurrection.* And thus, while every age is but another shew of the former; 'tis no wonder, that Science hath not out-grown the dwarfishness of its *pristine stature*, and that the *Intellectual world* is such a *Microcosm.* For while we account of some admired Authours, as the *Seths Pillars,* on which all knowledge is engraven; and spend that time and study in defence of their Placits, which with more advantage to Science might have been employ'd upon the Books of the more ancient, and *universal Author:* 'Tis not to be admired, that Knowledge hath receiv'd so little improvement from the endeavours of many pretending promoters, through the continued series of so many successive ages. For while we are slaves to the *Dictates* of our *Progenitours;* our discoveries, like *water,* will not run higher than the *Fountains,* from which they own their derivation. And while we think it so piaculous, to go beyond the *Ancients;* we must necessarily come short of genuine *Antiquity,* Truth; unless we suppose them to have reach'd perfection of knowledge in spight of their acknowledgements of ignorance.[7]

Glanvill gives Seneca only two fleeting mentions in the first edition of the *Vanity* (pp. 142, 149), and there is no other evidence to indicate that Seneca influenced him directly. Yet Glanvill is closer stylistically to Seneca than Bacon is, although Bacon seems to have read Seneca more closely than Glanvill did. One who agreed with Williamson that Senecanism was the "most incisive pattern" in the prose of the age could argue reasonably that Glanvill was touched by the Senecan cult, if not by Seneca himself. For example, there is abundant evidence that Glanvill imitated Browne, often thought of as a Senecan. Surely in the preceding quotation Glanvill had in mind the passage from Browne that I shall quote (p. 154), with its "Metempsychosis" comparison.

Our quotation from the first edition of the *Vanity* has many of the salient characteristics of the "loose" kind of Senecan period described by Croll. The basic grammatical unit is the period rather than the sentence: "A vanity, which hath possess'd all times as well as ours; and the *Golden Age* was never *present.*" This period is "loose" in its abrupt ellipsis followed by the juxtaposition of long and short members; in its parenthetical, detachable character; in the weakly connective "and" carrying little logical force; and in the characteristic Senecan progression from a complete statement in the first member to a second member which is a "new apprehension of the truth expressed in the first," an "imaginative [moment] occurring in a logical pause or suspension" [8] the entire period culminating in a wistful suggestion rather than a rounded conclusion. Reminiscent of Seneca's Stoic diatribe is the steady accumulation of clauses and sentences beginning with, and controlled by, "we" followed by a verb in the present tense; these constructions rise to a Senecan climax in "The Sages of old live again in us, and in opinions there is a *Metempsychosis*" — effectively reversing, through the asymmetry, the we-plus-verb pattern. Like Seneca, Glanvill arranges his periods for rhetorical effect rather than logical progression, repeating himself many times. There is much doubling repetition purely for the sake of Latinate cadence: "our doting on *Antiquity*, and the opinions of our *Fathers*"; "though feeble, decrepit, and within a step of dust"; "contracts such an esteem and veneration." Throughout are Seneca's smart antitheses of thought, although these are not as obvious in Glanvill's "loose" style as in Seneca, for example, the pointed plays on "Author," "Ancients . . . Antiquity," and the "Metempsychosis" conceit. Glanvill regularly derives an antithetical effect from the placing of key words in grammatically parallel positions, usually at the end of clauses. "We look with a superstitious reverence upon the accounts of praeterlapsed ages: and with a supercilious severity, on the more deserving products of our own." Here in addition to the antithesis of thought in "praeterlapsed ages" and "our own," there is also a Senecan antithesis of sound between these terms, one Latinate, the other conversational. Senecan wordplay also appears in "superstitious reverence . . . supercilious severity." *Ingenium facile et copiosum* writes Quintilian of Seneca, having in mind the wealth of examples, unusual words, ceaseless pressure of "point," the flow of metaphors (often technical or colloquial), and the laboring of the subject. These features distinguish Glanvill's style as well.

This discussion by no means exhausts the features of the "rhetorical display" for which Glanvill apologizes in the preface to the *Vanity*. But it is clear (without granting Croll's and Williamson's insistence on the direct or indirect influence of Seneca himself or his imitators) that it is possible to describe this rhetorical display as "Senecan." In other words Glanvill, in contrast to Croll, does not associate a style like Seneca's with the *genus humile*. It seems, then, that even as early as the first edition of the *Vanity* Glanvill's heart is not in his Senecanism. If the revisions represent a turn against "rhetorical display" they represent a turn against Senecanism — a turn adumbrated in the apology to the preface. In the preface to the *Scepsis Scientifica* — the second edition of the *Vanity* — the "display" becomes a "dress, that possibly is not so suitable to the graver Geniuses, who have outgrown all gaieties of style and youthful relishes." [9] Glanvill's "present relish and genius," as we have seen, now "is more gratified with *manly sense,* flowing in a *natural* and *unaffected Eloquence,* then in the *musick* and *curiosity* of *fine metaphors* and dancing periods." But the actual stylistic changes in the *Scepsis* itself are minor. Jones is correct when he says that to see what reforms Glanvill might have had in mind, and whether or not they were Anti-Senecan, we should turn to the third edition of the *Vanity*. Here is Glanvill's revision of our passage:

But our *Affections* misguide us by the respect we have to *others,* as well as by that we bear to our selves: I mentioned the Instances of *Antiquity,* and *Authority.* We look with a superstitious Reverence upon the accounts of past Ages, and with a supercilious Severity on the more deserving products of our own: a vanity that hath possest all times as well as ours; and the *golden Age* was *never present.* For as an inconsiderable

Weight by vertue of it's distance from the Centre of the Ballance will out-weigh much heavier bodies that are nearer to it, so the most light, and vain things that are far off from the present Age, have more Esteem, and Veneration than the most considerable, and substantial that bear a modern date: and we account *that* nothing worth, that is not fetcht from a far off; in which we very often deceive our selves as that Mariner did, that brought home his Ship Fraught with common Pebbles from the Indies. We adhere to the Determinations of our Fathers as if their Opinions were *entail'd* on us; and our Conceptions were *ex Traduce*.

And thus while every Age is but an *other shew* of the *former*, 'tis no wonder that humane science is *no more* advanced above it's *ancient* Stature: For while we look on some admired Authors as the Oracles of all Knowledg, and spend that time, and those pains in the Study and Defence of their Doctrines, which should have been imploy'd in the search of Truth, and Nature; we must needs stint our own Improvements and hinder the Advancement of Science; Since while we are Slaves to the Opinions of those before us. Our Discoveries, like water will not rise higher then their Fountains; and while we think it such Presumption to endeavour beyond the *Ancients,* we fall short of *Genuine Antiquity,* Truth: unless we suppose them to have reach't perfection of Knowledg in spight of their own acknowledgements of Ignorance.[10]

The most obvious changes concern *copia.* Many illustrations are eliminated. One might attribute this condensation to the necessities of republication of a book as one of a collection of essays. Most of the other materials in the collection are also new issuings of previous work. These essays, some of them longer than the *Vanity,* are practically reprints. Certainly there is nothing comparable to the thoroughgoing stylistic revisions of the original *Vanity.* It was the *Vanity* — the only work for whose style Glanvill felt compelled to apologize — which stood out among all his writings for its style, and its revisions represent the mature Glanvill's reaction against his earlier way of writing. The final revision was difficult for Glanvill, but so strongly did he feel about the deficiencies of his earlier style that he persevered: "The FIRST Essay against *Confidence* in *Philosophy*, is quite changed in the way of Writing, and in the Order. Methought I was somewhat fetter'd and tied in doing it, and could not express my self with that ease, freedom, and fulness which possibly I might have commanded amid fresh thoughts: Yet 'tis so alter'd as to be in a manner new" (*Essays*, sig. a₃).

The revised passage retains some of the Senecan qualities. For example, Glanvill does not alter the syntax of the individual sentences I have analyzed for their Senecanisms. But all the revisions that he does make are Anti-Senecan. The omission of illustrations shows that he is driving his style away from the Senecan norm. He is curbing his earlier Senecan tendency to labor an argument. Examples from the exotic or learned — for example, Archimedes, the preposterous animal, Metempsychosis, Seths Pillars — Glanvill ruthlessly prunes. He tends to retain only those illustrations which are related step by step to the bare statement, and to do away with material which merely elaborates the idea allusively, for example, "The Sages of old live again in us; and in opinions there is a *Metempsychosis.*" He moves away from "Senecanism," the sacrifice of logical advancement for "a new apprehension of the truth expressed" previously, "successive flashes of a jewel or prism as it is turned about on its axis and takes the light in different ways" (Croll, *Style*, p. 212). Such jewellike flashes as "we reverence gray-headed Doctrines, though feeble, decrepit, and within a step of dust" are discarded. Glanvill retains almost solely those examples (most are also found in Bacon) related to physics, such as the image of the lever and the fulcrum, and the water which cannot rise higher than its source.

Glanvill drives his prose away from the wide range of Senecanism, which draws its examples from all experience. Furthermore, even his scientific images are not extended as far as in the first *Vanity*. They are metaphors, rather than conceits. His omissions weaken or destroy the excitement of the rhetorical suspension of the repeated clauses beginning with "we" in the first *Vanity*, with the climax at "The Sages of old" eliminated entirely. Glanvill also, as Greenslet and Jones have shown, moves his vocabulary away from the Latinate, and from the Senecan picturesque, learned, or metaphorical. He substitutes "past" for "praeterlapsed"; "out-weigh much heavier bodies" for "preponderate much greater magnitudes"; "most light and vain things" for "most slight and chaffy opinion"; "Science is *no more* advanced above it's *ancient* Stature" for "Science hath not out-grown the dwarfishness of its *pristine stature*"; "Oracles of all knowledg" for "the Seths Pillars, on which all Knowledg is engraven"; "Doctrines" for "Placits"; "Truth, and Nature" for "the Books of the more ancient, and *universal Author*"; and, "the Opinions of those before us" for "the *Dictates* of our *Progenitours*." Senecan antitheses, while still present, are less prominent. Glanvill has simply omitted what he would have called the "wittiest" parts of the original *Vanity*, and these are also the most antithetical. The total effect of the revision is now that of a settled discourse rather than a witty "Senecan" essay.

According to Croll, science introduced "an attempt, a successful attempt to take the heat and fever out of the imaginative naturalism" of the earlier Senecanism of the century; but "seventeenth century prose is, and remains, predominantly Senecan." This statement is difficult to accept, even assuming that "science" was responsible for the change in Glanvill. For once the heat and fever have been drained away, what remains is neither imaginative naturalism nor Senecanism but something else. By his own admission, Glanvill's revision is "so altered as to be in a manner new." While the syntax of the revised *Vanity* resembles that of the so-called Senecans, the total effect is not Senecan. Whatever it was that impelled him to revise his style drove him away from Senecanism rather than into a revision of it, as Croll maintains ("Glanvill's later style is a *revision* of Browne's"). Glanvill's praise of the style of Sprat's *History* is a condemnation of the style which Croll and his followers identify with Seneca.

It is writ in a way of so *judicious* a *gravity*, and so *prudent* and *modest* an *expression*, with so much *clearness* of *sense*, and such a *natural fluency* of *genuine Eloquence*, that I know it will both *profit* and entertain the Ingenious. And I say further, That the *Style* of that Book hath all the *Properties* that can recommend any thing to an *ingenious relish:* For 'tis *manly*, and yet *plain; natural*, and yet not *careless*; The *Epithets* are *genuine*, the *Words proper* and *familiar*, the *Periods smooth* and of *middle* proportion: It is not *broken* with *ends of Latin*, nor *impertinent Quotations;* nor made *harsh* by *hard* words, or *needless terms* of *Art:* Not rendred *intricate* by long *Parentheses*, nor *gaudy* by *flanting Metaphors*; not *tedious* by *wide fetches* and *circumferences* of *Speech*, nor *dark* by too much *curtness* of *Expression:* 'Tis not *loose* and *unjointed, rugged* and *uneven;* but as *polite* and *fast* as *Marble*; and briefly, avoids all the *notorious defects*, and wants none of the *proper Ornaments* of Language.[11]

Glanvill even distinguishes, in his condemnation, between the "curt" and the "loose" styles: Sprat is not "*dark* by too much *curtness* of Expression: 'Tis not *loose* and *unjointed, rugged* and *uneven.*" Glanvill thus allies himself with his model Sprat against the "*notorious defects*" of fashionable "Senecanism." But what he says about Sprat applies to his own revision of the *Vanity*. Glanvill has substituted "*Words proper* and *familiar*" for "ends of *Latin*" and "*Quotations,*" "*hard* words," and "*terms* of *Art.*" He has eliminated "long *Parentheses*" and his metaphors are not nearly as "flanting" as before. Nor are they "*wide fetches* and *circumferences* of Speech." In other words, he excises as not "proper" those expressions, such as "The Sages of old live again in us," in which the meaning in context is remote from the literal meaning. Above all, asymmetry — the prime criterion of

Senecan style for Croll — is brought under control: "the *Periods smooth* and of *middle* proportion . . . not *loose* and *unjointed, rugged* and *uneven.*"

Jones seems to be correct, at least as far as Glanvill is concerned, in regarding the dominant pattern of Restoration prose as a reaction against Senecan style rather than a revision of it. Is the reaction traceable to the direct, specific influence of science? Ultimately everything depends on what we mean by "science." No matter how the word is defined, its most tangible manifestation in England is the Royal Society, which Glanvill ardently defended. It is a natural inference that Glanvill followed the Society's stylistic platform, as outlined in the famous manifesto on style in Sprat's *History*. That Glanvill praised Sprat's style so highly is further evidence for a direct scientific influence on Glanvill's style. According to Jones, Glanvill is a fortunate example of one "whose style was radically changed under the pressure exerted by the Society." Jones sees the "Address to the Royal Society" prefixed to the *Scepsis Scientifica* as "a bid for an invitation to join the philosophers, and such an inference is borne out by the fact that on December 7, 1664, Lord Brereton presented the book to the Royal Society, and, after the 'Address' had been read, proposed the author as a candidate for membership." [12]

In the "Address," in the passage quoted above, Glanvill apologizes for the "fine Metaphors and dancing periods" of the first *Vanity* and, according to Jones, "swears allegiance to a stylistic creed that" would have assisted his application (*Seventeenth Century*, p. 90). Although Glanvill attributes his stylistic change to increasing maturity, Jones considers "immaturity" as an insincere excuse for his earlier rhetorical excesses. "When we remember that less than four years separated the two editions, the reference to the immaturity of youth provokes a smile. It is significant that a man seeking admission into the Society considered it

necessary to place himself in the proper position as to style."
Williamson accepts Glanvill's statements at face value:
"After he became a member of the Society he could only
continue to develop his new taste and genius, which carried
him away from Sir Thomas Browne, with no thanks from
the Society. . . . At best the statement that Glanvill's style
was altered by the influence of the Royal Society is only
an inference from Sprat's *History* to Glanvill's change"
(*Senecan Amble*, p. 282).

The controversy between Jones and Williamson turns on
the significance of terms like "immaturity" and "manly."
What both Jones and Williamson fail to point out is that
these words have reference, at least in the circle of the
Society, to style or ideas as much as to age or personal
qualities. "Maturity," "manly," and their synonyms are
familiar terms in Sprat's literary and philosophical criticism.
The pursuits of the Royal Society are for grown-ups only,
requiring a "masculine" style. "Nor is it impossible, but as
the *Feminine* Arts of *Pleasure*, and *Gallantry* have spread
some of our neighbouring Languages, to such a vast extent:
so the *English Tongue* may also in time be more enlarg'd,
by being the Instrument of conveying to the World the
Masculine Arts of *Knowledg*." [13] Pellisson's history of the
French Academy is praised for being "so masculinely . . .
done." Except for images of light and dark, the image of
children and the childish *versus* adults and maturity is the
most common of any in the *Vanity*, always with reference
to ideas or style rather than personal development.

And methinks the disputes of those assuming confidents [the
Aristotelians] . . . ignore the substantial realities; and like children make *babies*, for their fancies to play with, while their
useless subtilities afford but little intertain to the nobler
faculties. (pp. 14–15)

For since we live the life of *Brutes*, before we grow into
Man. . . . It cannot be that our Knowledg should be other,

than an heap of Mis-conception and Error, and conceits as impertinent as the toys we delight in. (p. 70)

Who can speak of such [Aristotelian] fooleries without a *Satyr*, to see aged Infants so quarrel at *put-pin, and* the *doating* world grown child *again?* How fond are men of a bundle of *opinions*, which are no more than a bagge of *Cherry-stones?*[14]

Glanvill used "childish" and "effeminate" to qualify "rhetorical," "dogmatic," "disputative," "Aristotelian," and the like. "Manly," "mature," and the like he applied to the experimental philosophy and the Royal Society. In the "Address to the Royal Society" he hails the "Society, that 'twill discredit that *toyishness* of *wanton fancy;* and pluck the misapplied name of the WITS, from those conceited *Humourists* that have assum'd it; to bestow it upon the more *manly spirit* and genius that playes not tricks with *words*, nor frolicks with *Caprices* of *froathy imagination:* But imployes a *severe reason* into the momentous concernments of the *Universe.*" [15] Glanvill apologizes to the Society for the rhetoric of the *Scepsis*, excusing himself on the grounds that the work, intended for "several ingenious persons" (the wits) "therefore wears a dress, that possibly is not so suitable to the graver Geniuses [members of the Society] who have outgrown all *gaities* of *style* and *youthful relishes.*" It is the style of the graver Geniuses, with its *"manly sense,"* that is more "agreeable to [Glanvill's] *present relish* and *Genius"* (sig. c₃). "Manly," opposed to "youthful," can only refer to style and ideas, not to Glanvill's own development. He is saying that he now finds that the style and "sense" of the experimental philosophers represent his ideal. He also indicates that in moving toward a more manly style he is moving away from the "Senecan" style, represented by its most characteristic form, the informal essay of Seneca himself. The *Scepsis* "can pride itself in no higher title, then that of an *ESSAY*, or imperfect offer of a subject, to which it could not do right but by discoursing all things. On

93

which consideration, I had once resolv'd to suffer this trifle to pass both out of *Print* and *Memory*" (sig. c₃). But Glanvill changed his mind about repressing the essay, even though the prose of "manly sense" had become more agreeable than "that way of writing . . . the *musick* and curiosity of *fine metaphors* and *dancing periods*" of the Senecan essay style of the *Vanity*.

It would be impossible to prove that the Society was entirely responsible for Glanvill's change. But at least there is no doubt that he found the Society's style congenial and planned to model his own style on the Society's mature and manly ideal, in opposition to the childish and effeminate rhetoric of the "Senecans." Thus Williamson's account is misleading when he says that "Glanvill attributed his own rhetoric to his youth," since the principal contrast for Glanvill is not between his own maturity and immaturity but between two different ways of thinking and writing which he calls by such terms as "manly" and "childish." In "Modern Improvements of Useful Knowledge" (formerly the *Plus Ultra* of 1668) Glanvill himself attests to the importance of the manly Society for his own stylistic as well as personal development:

And for my *own* part, I must confess, That while I was a Youth in the Unversity, I was much delighted with those *subtilties* that exercise the Brain in the *Nicities* of *Notion* and *Distinctions,* and afford a great deal of *idle Imployment* for the Tongue in the *Combates* of *Disputation.* . . . I was by degrees taken off from the *implicit Veneration* I had for *that Learning,* upon the account of the great name of *Aristotle* which it bore. And thus the great *impediment* was removed, and the prejudice of *Education* overcome; when I thought further, That *useful* Knowledge was to be look'd for in *God's great Book* the *Universe,* and among those *generous* men that had convers'd with *real* Nature, *undisguised* with *Art* and *Notion.*[16]

Jones is right to describe Glanvill's shift as a conscious effort to write according to the stylistic platform of the

Royal Society, in opposition to the so-called "Senecan" style. If Jones' assertion that Glanvill was influenced by the Society is, as Williamson claims, "at best . . . only an inference from Sprat's History to Glanvill's change" (*Senecan Amble*, p. 282); it is certainly a very plausible inference, since Glanvill and Sprat use the same critical vocabulary to describe the same literary and cultural phenomena. Furthermore, there is the evidence of Glanvill's praise, in "Modern Improvements," of Sprat's "manly, and yet plain" style. For Glanvill, Sprat's style is the ideal persuasive style, having "all the *properties* that can recommend anything to an *ingenious relish.*" Glanvill's ideal has some striking resemblances to the famous manifesto on style of the very author he is praising. The Royal Society, according to Sprat, has exhibited

a constant Resolution, to reject all the amplifications, digressions, and swellings of style: to return back to the primitive purity, and shortness, when men delivered so many *things*, almost in an equal number of *words*. They have exacted from all their members, a close, naked, natural way of speaking; positive expressions; clear senses; a native easiness: bringing all things as near the Mathematicall plainness, as they can: and preferring the language of Artizans, Countrymen, and Merchants, before that of Wits, or Scholars. (*History*, p. 113)

Sprat's "Mathematicall plainness" and "close, naked, natural way of speaking" correspond to Glanvill's "natural fluency" and "plain, natural, and yet not careless" ideal. Sprat and the Royal Society would abolish "amplifications, digressions, and swellings of style"; Glanvill opposes *"wide fetches," "long Parentheses,"* and *"circumferences of Speech."* Sprat favors "a native easiness," Glanvill favors *"Words . . . familiar."* Sprat prefers "the language of Artizans, Countrymen, and Merchants, before that of Wits, or Scholars"; Glanvill seeks a style which "is not *broken* with *ends* of *Latin*, nor *impertinent Quotations;* nor made *harsh* by *hard* words, or *needless terms* of *Art*." Glanvill opts, if not necessarily in favor of artisans, countrymen, and merchants, then certainly against wits and scholars. The *Plus Ultra* was commissioned by the Society as a companion piece, of equal weight and importance, to Sprat's *History*.[17] (It was intended to remedy the *History's* insufficient accounts of the actual discoveries of the Society.) Glanvill's remarks on Sprat must therefore be as official a statement of the Society's stylistic platform as the better-known passage of the *History*. Glanvill's stylistic theory, and actual practice as exemplified in the revisions of the *Vanity*, reflect the views of the Society, and the evidence suggests that Glanvill consciously modeled his style to suit the Society's ideal in reaction against the style which Croll and Williamson consider Senecan.

An Ardent Utilitarian

The Royal Society influenced, or was congenial to, Glanvill's style. But what influenced the Royal Society? Or what group in it might have affected Glanvill and the reformers of style? Can we speak with Jones of something called "Science" of which the Society was the embodiment, and which affected other aspects of culture, such as prose style? After the first *Vanity* Glanvill is not a Senecan, and he is affected by the Society; but is his style a result of the direct influence of science, as Jones maintains? Or of religion, as Cope holds? Or of something else?

The question of the intellectual and sociological roots of the Royal Society is, of course, very complicated, and has been the subject of much recent attention. As is true of all other significant moments in the history of ideas, there is no completely satisfactory way to explain why so much scientific talent appeared at the same time. Nevertheless there is general agreement that the early Society is to be understood not only as an isolated and self-propelled phenomenon acting decisively on other aspects of culture but equally as a specialized manifestation of, to use Glanvill's one enduring phrase, the "climate of opinion." [18] Scholars of a sociological bent, especially R. K. Merton and Christopher Hill,[19] have enumerated the many forces which made "the cultural soil of seventeenth century England . . . particularly fertile for the growth and spread of science" (Merton, "Science, Technology, and Society," p. 597). After the civil wars, the calmness and tolerance of the scientists was identified and defended as an instance of the universally stated desire to avoid more disputes. This desire was predominant, of course, among the members of the victorious Establishment, whether Fellows of the Royal Society or opponents of the New Philosophy. Technological and industrial advancement allied with Anglican Latitudinarianism and (though to a lesser degree than Merton and Hill suggest) moderate Puritanism often inspired the serious experimenters in the Society. For artisans and industrialists, the Society held out an obvious promise of useful inventions; for the Anglican, the Society's investigations into nature were equally useful as proofs of God's handiwork. Merged in the Protestant Ethic, with its exaltation of the mundane *Beruf*, religion and industry were not only congenial to the activities of the Society but in many ways were responsible for it. Protestantism, technology, and the experimental investigations of the Society all emphasize empiricism, pragmatism, diligence, industry, choice of the most profitable vocation, good sense as opposed to "useless" speculation, the individual instance regarded as part of a crucial experiment, useful education as a "good work," and a faith that nature is rationally conceived.

In sum, the Protestant Ethic and experimental investigation are related in two ways: they had a similar outlook, grounded in utilitarianism and a faith that the universe is rational, and each exploited the other for its own purposes. In this way they were characteristic of the culture of mid-seventeenth-century England. "This culture rested securely on a substratum of utilitarian norms which identified the useful and the true. Puritanism itself had imputed a threefold unity to science. Natural philosophy was instrumental first, in establishing practical proofs of the scientist's state of grace; second, in enlarging control of nature and third, in glorifying God. Science was enlisted in the service of the individual, society, and deity" (Merton, p. 444). In seventeenth-century utilitarianism, everything is useful for something else, rather than valuable in its own right. The method of the Royal Society necessitates

a neglect of the qualitatively unique, the individually variable aspects of phenomena with the focus of attention upon the recurrent, quantitatively comparable aspects. Utilitarianism has thus penetrated the very core of the scientific assumptions of the age. The individual event in all its uniqueness, which may be of interest to the aesthete or the moralist as an "end," as a completed object which is attended to precisely because of its individual characteristics, is regarded by the scientist as an instance of a universal, as being instrumental to the establishment of law and regularity if its immediacy is ignored. It is regarded in terms of what it makes possible rather than in intrinsic terms. (pp. 587–588)

Utilitarianism is responsible, not only for the famous schemes of Ward, Beck, Dalgarno, Parker, Wilkins, Hooke, and others to construct a language of mathematical signs, but also for such utterances as Sprat's and Glanvill's pleas for a "Mathematicall plainness" in language.

Language was to become an instrument of precision, rather than a blunted and inexact tool. The attitudes which were basic to these attempts at linguistic invention permeated the field of literature proper, so that the decline of poverty and the ascent of prose becomes quite comprehensible. These implicit norms of utilitarianism (literature as a means of concrete description and exposition) and instrumentalism . . . constituted the values about which the culture of that period was integrated. (pp. 380–381)

In the light of Merton's discussion, it is possible to resolve the controversy between Jones, who understands Glanvill primarily as an apologist for the Royal Society, and Cope, for whom Glanvill is the "Anglican Apologist" *par excellence*. The truth of the matter is that the mid-seventeenth century, for the most part, did not distinguish as emphatically as we do between something called "science" and something else which was nonscientific and included "religion." For Glanvill's age, the crucial distinction was between the useful and the useless, not between the "scientific" and the "nonscientific." What is more, there is every reason to believe that Glanvill and his age identified "plain" not necessarily with "science" alone but with "useful," while the ornate was within the province of the "useless." The opponents in the controversies in which Glanvill immersed himself are not "science" and "religion" but on the one hand, the useful — the Royal Society, Skepticism, and Anglicanism — and on the other the useless — Aristotelianism, dogmatism, and the "Enthusiastick" sects.

Glanvill, of course, never clearly defines "utility" or the "use" to which the New Philosophy, skepticism, and Anglicanism are to be directed. My guess is that Glanvill's ultimate "use" is to avoid more civil wars. He seems to blame both the earlier conflicts and potential future ones on the passionate rhetoric of dogmatism and Enthusiasm, and perhaps even Aristotelianism. What is clear is that what we would today call "Science" — a skeptical, empirical, inductive habit of mind, as well as the specific discoveries and techniques of the "experimental way" — is significant for Glanvill chiefly as a means to some larger "use." The utilitarian and nonutilitarian wings of the Royal Society and Anglicans like Glanvill thought of themselves as allies engaged in essentially the same endeavor — the investigation of God's universe, its accessible rationality an assumption of the experimental philosophy since Bacon, and of Anglicanism at least since Hooker. Now we see as through a glass darkly, but once we see the rational system of the universe through the new telescopes and microscopes all religious disputes will end as everyone comes to see the Light. In this way the Royal Society answered the charge that it fostered atheism. It is impossible and, to invoke the seventeenth-century criterion, useless to distinguish between "scientific" and "religious" influences on prose style when the real struggle is between the utilitarians and their opponents, real or imagined.

Glanvill, at any rate, understands the intellectual conflict of the age in this way: The *Vanity* and its revisions are a defense of the same "Natural Philosophy" as that espoused by the Royal Society, as skepticism and rational Latitudinarian Anglicanism. Glanvill's enemies are dogmatism in general and Aristotelianism in particular, and there are observations on the role of reason and the passions which anticipate the later Glanvill's attacks on the "Enthusiasticks." There is no need here to summarize the *Vanity* in detail. After a lively resumé of unsolved philosophical cruxes, and an attack on Aristotelianism, Glanvill concludes with a summary of "considerations against Dogmatizing." It is these considerations (and the flamboyant "Apology for Philosophy" which follows, in the first edition) to which all his arguments have been leading. Glanvill, in the end, must justify his attack on dogmatizing on utilitarian grounds: "Considerations against Dogmatizing: (1) Tis the effect of Ignorance. (2) It inhabits with untamed passions, and an ungovern'd Spirit. (3) It is the great Disturber of the World. (4) It is ill manners, and immodesty. (5) It holds men captive in Error. (6) It betrayes a narrowness of Spirit" (p. 224). Dogmatizing is bad not in itself but in the effects it produces.

Margaret Wiley has shown how Glanvill's antidogmatic skepticism is utilitarian, "instrumental, and not terminal," "a way, and not a port of destination." [20] Writes Glanvill, "I have no design against *Science;* my indeavour is to promote it. *Confidence* in uncertainties is the greatest enemy to what is certain; and were I a *Sceptick,* I'de plead for *Dogmatizing*" (sig. A₃). Thomas White, a Catholic and Aristotelian contemporary, misunderstood the *Vanity* and attacked Glanvill for making an end, rather than a means, of skepticism. The main thrust of Glanvill's defense of the *Vanity* in his *Scir$\frac{e}{i}$ Tuum Nihil Est* (1665) is directed against White's misinterpretation[21] of his skepticism. Again and again Glanvill asserts that he is a skeptic largely because skepticism is useful to arrive at the certainties of religion.

I am not the *Sceptick* you suppose me. And that the Author of *Sciri* hath no Antagonist in *him* that writ against the *Dogmatists.* For if I understand *yours,* our ends are so far from being *repugnant,* that they are *coincident;* only we differ in the *Means,* and *Method.* The *End* of *both* is the *Advance* of *Knowledge;* which you think is best promoted by pressing a perswasion, that *Science* is not *uncertainty.* And I suppose that the quarrelsome World needs to be convinc't, That *uncertainties* are not *Science.* . . . For to believe that *every thing* is *certain,* is as great a disinterest to *Science,* as to conceive that *nothing* is *so; Opinion of fulness being,* as my Lord *Bacon* notes, *among the causes want.*[22]

For Glanvill's tolerant Latitudinarianism skepticism is useful as a counter to the fierce dogmatism of religious and political disputes. "Unreasonable *confidence* in *doubtful* matters is the *raging Plague* of our times. . . . Which *sad affirmation* is too easie to be read in those *black* and *fatal* Characters, the *Rents* and *Schisms* of the *Church,* and the *Ruins* and *devastations* of *States* and *Kingdoms,* that have derived from this *root* of *evil*" (sig. a₂). Glanvill follows the Anglican *via media* between the Enthusiastic sects and Aristotelian Rome. Dogmatizing "mischievously corrupts them, sowring Mens spirits with *Envy, ill Nature,* and *Moroseness:* and mingling their Religion with *Schism, bitter Zeal,* and *Sedition.* . . . There's a *Medium* between being *Blind* and *Infallible*" (p. 4). Against White's charge of atheism, Glanvill quotes his own observation, in the *Vanity,* on confidence in uncertainties as the greatest enemy to what is certain. Glanvill then works a variant of the familiar teleological argument that the careful investigation into nature glorifies God. This Baconian position controls the *Vanity.* Fortified with the mass of evidence obtained by the skeptical inquirer (as opposed to the often inaccurate assertions of the dogmatist), we will have more grounds for belief than ever before. Therefore to White he says,

my opinion of your ingenuity deceives me, if you think not you have been too liberal to me, when you consider, that *Sceptick* is but a more civil term for *Infidel* and *Atheist* (sig. A₄)

I have professedly attacqued the *disputing way* of Inquiry, and the *verbal emptiness* of the *Philosophy* of the Schools. . . . And while the Schools of Learning are under the regency of that kind of Spirit, I fear little is to be expected from *Philosophy* but *bold* talk; and endless disputes and quarrels. For what else can be the fruit of a *Philosophy* made up of *occult Qualities, Sympathies, Entelechia's, Elements, Celestial Influences,* and abundance of other *hard words* and *lazy generalities,* but an arrest of all ingenious and practical indeavour; and a *Wilderness* of *Opinions* instead of *certainty* and *Science?* But thanks be to Providence, the World begins to emerge from this state of things, and to imploy it self in more deep and concerning Disquisitions; the issue of which, we hope, will be a *Philosophy* fruitful in *works,* not in *words,* and such as may accommodate the use of *Life,* both *natural* and *moral.* (p. 49)

The model for the useful sort of skepticism Glanvill advocates and opposes to the "deadly *Pyrrhonical* contagion" is the Royal Society. "I have nought to do with that shuffling Sect, that love to doubt eternally, and to question all things.

My profession is *freedom* of *enquiry*, and I own no more *Skepticism* than what is concluded in the *Motto* which the ROYAL SOCIETY have now adopted for theirs, NULLIUS IN VERBA" (p. 3).

The *Vanity* and Glanvill's defense of it contain the germs of these ideas, developed later at much greater length in the *Essays*. In "Of Scepticism and Certainty" Glanvill, again answering White, discusses further the crucial distinction between his own instrumental skepticism, derived from Sextus Empiricus, and skepticism considered as an end in itself, as in Pyrrho. The fourth essay in Glanvill's collection, "The Usefulness of Real Philosophy to Religion," is an elaborate exposition of the Protestant utilitarian attitudes toward the activities of the Royal Society. Not only does the knowledge of God's works reveal his glory, so that it "promotes the *end* of *Religion*" (p. 5), but the Society battles against the enemies of religion — "Atheism, Sadducism, Superstition, Enthusiasm, and the Humour of Disputing" (p. 6). Against atheists Glanvill argues that "the more we understand the *Laws* of *Matter* and *Motion*, the more shall we discern the *necessity* of a *wise* mind to order the blind and insensible *Matter* and to direct the *original* Motions" (p. 8). Against the first step to atheism, "Sadducism" (the denial of the existence of spirits and the immortality of the soul), the patient and careful researches of the Society are the only weapon; Glanvill's inquiries into the occurrences of witchcraft form his own contribution, in the manner of the Society, for the use of religion.[23] Superstition (heretical belief in evil spirits and the like) Glanvill regards as a form of madness impossible for one who has habituated himself to the sanity of the experimental philosophers. Religious Enthusiasm also withers away in the Society's dry light, as do religious and political disputes. How closely skepticism, the emphasis of the Anglican Protestant Ethic on the holiness of patient and careful industry, and the Royal Society were intertwined may be suggested by the following paragraphs from a long section in which Glanvill is advocating *"that the Ministers and Professors of Religion ought not to discourage but promote the knowledge of Nature, and the Works of its Author"* (p. 30):

Of ATHEISM. . . . Philosophy is one of the best Weapons in the World to defend Religion against it; and my whole Discourse is a confutation of this envious and foolish charge.

Concerning it I take notice, That *Philosophical* Men are usually dealt with by the *Zealous*, as the greatest Patrons of the *Protestant* Cause are by the *Sects*. For as the *Bishops* and other Learned Persons, who have *most strongly* oppugned the *Romish Faith*, have had the ill luck to be accused of *Popery* themselves; in like manner it happens to the *humblest* and *deepest Inquisitors* into the *Works* of God, who have the most and fullest *Arguments* of his *Existence*, have raised *impregnable Ramparts*, with much *industry* and *pious pains* against the *Atheists*, and are the *only Men* that can with success serve *Religion* against the *Godless Rout*. . . . And the certain way to be esteemed an *Atheist* by the *fierce* and *ignorant Devoto's*, is to study to lay the *Foundations* of *Religion sure*, and to be able to speak *groundedly* and to *purpose* against the *desperate* Cause of the *black Conspirators* against *Heaven*. (p. 31)

Earlier, Glanvill had argued that the New Philosophy

helps *Religion* against the HUMOUR OF DISPUTING. . . . The *Real Philosophy* brings Men in love with the *Practical Knowledge:* The more we have imployed our selves in *Notion* and *Theory*, the more we shall be acquainted with the *uncertainty* of Speculation; and our esteem, and love of Opinions will abate, as that sense increaseth; By the same degrees our respect and kindness for *Operative* knowledge will advance and grow; which disposition will incline us also to have less regard to *Nicities* in *Religion*, and teach us to lay out our chief Cares and Endeavours about *Practical* and *certain Knowledge*, which will assist and promote our *Vertue*, and our *Happiness*. (pp. 24–25)

Glanvill, author of a defense of the Royal Society entitled "Modern Improvements of Useful Knowledge" as well as

"The Usefulness of Natural Philosophy to Religion," thought of the Society as embarked on a religious as well as technological mission. Its use was "the improving the minds of Men in *solid* and *useful notices* of things, helping them to such theories as may be serviceable to *common life;* and the searching out of the true *laws* of *Matter* and *Motion,* in order to the securing of the *Foundations* of *Religion* against all attempts of *Mechanical Atheism*" (*Scepsis,* sig. a$_2$).

In his reworking in the *Essays* of Bacon's *New Atlantis,* "Anti-Fanatick Theologie and Free Philosophy" (the running title is "Anti-Fanatical Religion and Free Philosophy"), the Royal Society is seen as one aspect of an immense program conducted by the Latitudinarian clergy against the Enthusiastic sects to bring a war-weary populace to the plain and simple truths of fundamental Christianity. Nowhere does Glanvill posit something called "Science" pursued by the Society for its own sake. In a striking anticipation of Hume's critique of induction, Glanvill does not even regard the experimental method as a means of acquiring absolute Truth but only a useful approach to it.

Utility is therefore the only significant excuse for the activities of the Society. Glanvill understands the methods and discoveries of the Society as instrumental to the religious and political ends of the Latitudinarians. The experimental method assists the Anglican bishops in their religious work.

They read, and consider'd all sorts of *late* improvements in *Anatomy, Mathematicks, Natural History,* and *Mechanicks,* and acquainted themselves with the *Experimental Philosophy* of *Solomon's House,* and the other Promoters of it. So that there was not any valuable Discovery made, or Notion started in any part of *Real Learning,* but they got considerable knowledge of it. And by this *Universal* way of proceeding, They furnish'd their Minds with great *variety* of *Conceptions,* and rendred themselves more capable of judging the *Truth,* or *likelyhood* of any propos'd *Hypothesis.* . . . Being thus prepared, They addrest themselves to the more *close*, particular, and thorow study of *Divinity*. . . . (*Essays*, p. 9)

On the other hand, the ultimate justification of the Society is its contribution to technology. Even in "Anti-Fanatick Theologie and Free Philosophy" the goals of technology insensibly displace, at times, those of religion. The "Bensalemites"

thought, with much reason, that the best *Foundation* for *Natural Philosophy* would be a good *History of Nature*. . . . From its *inlargement*, *more*, and *surer* Light might be expected, and the uses of Life, and Empire of man over the Creatures, might be greatly promoted, and advanc'd. For These ends the Foundation of *Solomon's House*, about that time, was laid; and *This* divers of them thought the best design that ever was for *increasing* Natural Knowledge, and the advantages of Humane Life, and infinitely beyond all the *disputing*, *notional* ways, from which nothing could arise, but *dispute*, and *notion:* They consider'd this method of joint endeavours, in such a royal, and noble Assembly, about the *Phaenomena*, and effects of Nature, to be the way to make *Philosophy operative*, and *useful* . . . and to make it an *Instrument* of *Action*, and profitable works. (*Essays*, p. 49)

For Glanvill, at least, the vital intellectual conflict of the age is not between "science" and "religion" but between whatever is useful and whatever is not. His works indicate that he did not understand the Royal Society as the embodiment of a great X, Modern Science, emerging full-blown in the middle of the seventeenth century and altering everything else. He saw the Society as one of the many expressions of the quest for the useful which formed so much of the climate of opinion of his world. Jones must be at least partly right when he attributes the change in Glanvill's style to the influence of the Royal Society, rather than to Glanvill's age, as Williamson suggests, or to a revision of Senecanism under the impact of Cartesianism, as Croll maintains. Jones errs, however, in his implicit equation of the Royal Society with modern "science" and in his assertion that this science itself acted directly upon other aspects of culture over-whelmingly. Cope acts as a valuable corrective to Jones by showing the extent of Glanvill's concern with Anglican apologetics, and the impact on Glanvill of the stylistic theory and practice of other Protestant divines. Following Merton, it is possible to reconcile Cope and Jones by understanding that neither "science" nor "religion" was Glanvill's controlling concern. Rather, he was occupied with anything that he considered useful for man's purposes, whether technological, philosophical, political, moral, or theological.

Recent studies have shown how hard it is to isolate any movement within the Society itself dedicated to "pure" research. Robert Boyle is drawn to what he called the "Invisible College" — the informal meetings at Gresham College which, according to one theory, led to the forming of the Society — because of its utilitarianism: "The other humane studies I apply myself to are natural philosophy, the mechanics and husbandry, according to the principles of our new philosophical college, that values no knowledge but as it has a tendency to use." [24] In 1661 the "College" commissioned Christopher Wren to draw up a preamble to the Charter of Incorporation of what was to become the Royal Society. Wren's preamble explicitly rejects knowledge for its own sake. Even knowledge of "the hidden causes of things" is subservient to the uses of man:

We, therefore, out of paternal care for our people, resolve . . . that obedience may be manifest by not only the public but the private felicity of every subject and the great concern of his satisfactions and enjoyments in this life. The way to so happy a government we are sensible is in no manner more facilitated than by promoting of useful arts and sciences, which upon mature inspection are found to be the basis of civil communities and free governments, and which gather multitudes by an Orphean charm into cities, and connect them in companies; that so by laying in a stock as it were of several arts and methods of industry, the whole body may be supplied by a mutual commerce of each other's particular faculties, and consequently, that the various miseries and toils of this frail life may be, by as many various expedients ready at hand, remedied or alleviated, and wealth and plenty diffused in just proportion to every one's industry, that is to every one's deserts.

And whereas we are well informed that a competent number of persons, of eminent learning, ingenuity, and honour, concording in their inclinations and studies towards this employment, have for some time accustomed themselves to meet weekly, and orderly, to confer about the hidden causes of things, with a design to establish certain and correct uncertain theories in philosophy, and by their labours in the disquisition of nature, to prove themselves real benefactors to mankind; and that they have already made a considerable progress by divers useful and remarkable discoveries, inventions and experiments . . . we have determined to grant our Royal favour, patronage, and all due encouragement to this illustrious assembly, and so beneficial and laudable an enterprize.[25]

Wren's emphasis on practical, and especially political, achievement may be in accordance with the preferences of the king. Then as now, we may assume, requests for aid from governments must emphasize "results." Except in such extraordinary fields as atomic physics, scientists nowadays are not much interested in the practical applications of their work, and it would be hard to believe that the scientists and virtuosi of the seventeenth century were completely different. From the records of the early Society in Birch's *History*, Merton (p. 526) finds that 41 per cent of the Society's research was "pure."

At any rate, a somewhat less utilitarian note is sounded by Sprat. The purpose of the Society

is, in short, to make faithful *Records*, of all the Works of *Nature*, or *Art*, which can come within their reach: that so the present Age, and posterity, may be able to put a mark on the Errors, which have been strengthened by long prescription: to restore the Truths, that have been neglected: to push on those, which are already known, to more various uses: and to make the way more passable, to what remains unreveal'd.

This is the compass of their Design. And to accomplish this, they have indeavour'd, to separate the knowledge of *Nature,* from the colours of *Rhetorick,* the devices of Fancy, or the delightful deceit of the *Fables.* (*History,* pp. 61–62)

Although a utilitarian, Sprat acknowledges that experimental investigation is pleasurable in its own right. At one point he outlandishly suggests that the delights of research will seduce the lecherous wits of the Restoration court into the greater pleasures of philosophy (p. 344). Even Glanvill mentions the "pleasure" of experiment in the "Address to the Royal Society": " 'Tis however a *pleasant* spectacle to behold the *shifts, windings,* and *unexpected Caprichios* of distressed *Nature,* when pursued by a *close* and *well managed Experiment*" (*Scepsis,* sig. b₂). The "Address," by Glanvill's own admission, is to the wits as well as the Society; Glanvill may well be appealing, like Sprat, to their voluptuousness. For the most part Glanvill is an ardent utilitarian. The *Plus Ultra* was intended as an improvement on Sprat's *History,* which, it was felt, did not hymn sufficiently the useful achievements of the Society. Glanvill's book is based on the successes of the archutilitarian Boyle, author of a famous tract on the usefulness of natural philosophy. In page after page of the *Plus Ultra* Glanvill celebrates the usefulness for technology of the Society.

The *Modern Experimenters* think, That the *Philosophers* of elder Times, though their *Wits* were excellent, yet the way they took was not like to bring much *advantage* to *Knowledge,* or any of the *Uses* of *humane Life;* being for the most part *that* of *Notion* and *Dispute,* which still runs round in a *Labyrinth* of Talk, but *advanceth nothing:* And the *unfruitfulness* of those *disputing Methods,* which directly and by themselves never brought so much *practical, beneficial Knowledge,* as would help towards the *Cure* of a *Cut Finger,* or the *Cooling* of an *Hot Head,* is a palpable Argument, That they were *fundamental Mistakes,* and that the *Way* was not right.

For, as my Lord Bacon observes well, Philosophy, as well

as *Faith,* must be *shewn* by its Works. . . . ("Modern Improvements," pp. 47–48)

Although the disinterested quest for truth for its own sake must have motivated the founders of the Society, especially the mathematicians at Oxford, to some extent — probably more than they were willing to admit to potential sponsors and a skeptical public — the main impulse, or at least the one that affected their ideals of prose style, was the advancement of knowledge for utility. Lyons has shown that only half of the original thirty-five members of the Society were "men of science": "Nineteen may be considered as men of science, while the other sixteen included statesmen, soldiers, antiquaries, administrators, and one or two literary men. Medical men, of whom there were fourteen, formed the largest group" (*The Royal Society,* p. 22). Even the "men of science" had other interests; Boyle, to cite the most prominent example, was something of a theologian, and, like Glanvill and most of the other "men of science," placed science at the service of divinity, as well as technology. The early Society persistently justified even its most seemingly "pure" researches on the grounds that they would someday find a practical application.

Ironically the Society came under attack from the start for a lack of utility. The story of these attacks, culminating in Swift's satire, has been discussed many times, and need not be rehearsed here. Glanvill found himself in the thick of the controversies. Glanvill associates his opponents, Thomas White and Henry Stubbe among them, with the enemies of Anglicanism, Catholicism (White) and Enthusiasm (Stubbe). White and Stubbe are also Aristotelians; Glanvill fights his wars on many fronts at once, but the enemies are always the same. The surly and acrimonious Stubbe,[26] a Greek scholar and sublibrarian at the Bodleian, was an experimental philosopher himself. His main quarrel with the Society is, first, the scholar's objection to its rejection of antiquity, especially Aristotle and Galen. Stubbe also opposes Sprat's and Glanvill's proposals for a scientific education. Although favorable to the experimental philosophy, he belittles the achievements of Boyle and other modern experimenters, in particular those recorded in detail in Sprat's *History*. Stubbe inveighs against the Society, especially Sprat, for implying that knowledge of nature, rather than the Bible, will lead one to God. He reads in Sprat's tolerant Latitudinarianism a plot to bring back Popery into England.

What is striking is that Glanvill and his opponents are agreed at least on the surface as to *ends*, although Glanvill suspects Stubbe of secretly favoring the aims of Enthusiasm; their quarrel, if we disregard the personal attacks, turns on the question of the usefulness of the *means* advocated by the Royal Society to advance practical knowledge, and of the actual discoveries of the Society. Neither Stubbe nor Glanvill favors anything for its own sake. Each accuses the other of antiutilitarianism — of supporting worthless or impractical or dangerous activities — for personal gain or prejudice. Each accuses the other of hypocritically pretending to support worthy ends. Glanvill accurately outlines Stubbe's professed aims, which, apart from making "the Virtuousi really ridiculous," are also Glanvill's:

His Designs; of *these* I shall briefly give his *own* Account of his *latest* Books. They were (if we may *believe* him) the securing and promoting the *Interest* of the present Monarchy [Pref. against *Plus Ultra*, p. 4] Protestant Religion [ibid.] and the Church of England [Title, Pref. &c. against Dr. *Sprat*.] School-Divinity [p. 1, against *Plus Ultra*] Universities [pp. 1, 2, 13.] In order to the carrying on these *great* Intendments, He design'd further to make the *Virtuousi really* ridiculous and odious to the Kingdom, [Pref. p. 4] to avenge *his Faculty upon M. Glanvill*, and by Sacrificing that *Virtuouso to publick Obloquy to establish general Repose and Tranquillity*.[27]

Glanvill goes on to show that Stubbe is at heart an Enthusiast who is now trimming with the Royalist and Anglican tide, that he does not really believe in his alleged goals, that his suggested means of achieving them (especially his vilification of the Royal Society) run counter to them, or that Stubbe is caviling to no useful end. Glanvill's arguments show that neither he nor Stubbe regards the activities of the Royal Society as "science," different from everything else and isolated from it. For both men these activities are intimately connected with, and judged by their use to, the culture of which the Society is a part, a culture whose values, as Merton has shown, are integrated around utilitarianism. Glanvill is defending the Royal Society against Stubbe and White. But the argument is not "science" against "religion," since both Glanville and his opponents are in favor of both. The real antagonists, as Glanvill sees the matter, are Anglicanism and skepticism against Enthusiasm, Aristotelianism, Catholicism, and dogmatism, and everyone claims to have utility, as well as God, on his side.

Utility and Prose Style

Even in the Society's earliest days, and contrary to its own official declarations, there must have been considerable "pure" science. But it was the Society's over-all utilitarianism that determined its theory and practice of prose style. This conclusion is evident in the works of the official spokesmen, Glanvill and Sprat. Sprat's appeal for a "close, naked, natural way of speaking" unquestionably represents the official view of the Society. But the manifesto is hedged about with problems, mostly arising from its context in the *History*.

There is one thing more, about which the *Society* has been most sollicitous; and that is, the manner of their *Discourse*: which unless they had been very watchful to keep in due temper, the whole spirit and vigour of their *Design*, had been soon eaten out, by the luxury and redundance of *speech*. The ill effects of this superfluity of talking, have already overwhelm'd most other *Arts* and *Professions;* insomuch, that when I consider the means of *happy living,* and the causes of their corruption, I can hardly forbear recanting what I said before; and concluding, that *eloquence* ought to be banished out of all *civil Societies,* as a thing fatal to Peace and good Manners. To this opinion I should wholly incline; if I did not find, that it is a Weapon, which may be as fully prouv'd by *bad* man, as *good:* and that, if these should onely cast it away, and those retain it; the *naked Innocence* of vertue, would be upon all occasions expos'd to the *armed Malice* of the wicked. This is the chief reason, that should now keep up the Ornaments of speaking, in any request: since they are so much degenerated from their original usefulness. They were at first, no doubt, an admirable Instrument in the hands of *Wise Men:* when they were onely employ'd to describe *Goodness, Honesty, Obedience;* in larger, fairer, and more moving Images; to represent *Truth,* cloak'd with Bodies; and to bring *Knowledg* back again to our very sense, from whence it was at first deriv'd to our understandings. But now they are generally chang'd to worse uses: They make the *Fancy* disgust the best things, if they come sound, and unadorn'd: they are in open defiance against *Reason;* professing, not to hold much correspondence with that; but with its Slaves, *the Passions;* they give the mind a motion too changeable and bewitching, to consist with *right practice.* Who can behold, without indignation, how many mists and uncertainties, these specious *Tropes* and *Figures* have brought on our Knowledg? How many rewards, which are due to more profitable, and difficult *Arts,* have been still snatch'd away by the easie vanity of *fine speaking?* For now I am warm'd with this just Anger, I cannot with-hold my self, from betraying the shallowness of all these seeming Mysteries; upon which *we Writers,* and *Speakers,* look so bigg. And, in few words, I dare say, that of all the Studies of men, nothing may be sooner obtain'd, than this vicious abundance of *Phrase,* this trick of *Metaphors,* this volubility of *Tongue,* which makes so great a noise in the World. But I spend words in vain; for the evil is now so inveterate, that is hard to know whom to *blame,* or where to begin to *reform.* We all value one another so much, upon this beautiful deceipt; and labour so long after it, in the years of our education: that we cannot but ever after think kinder of it, than it deserves. And indeed, in most other parts of Learning, I look on it to be a thing almost utterly desperate in its cure; and I think, it may be placed among those *general mischiefs;* such, as the *dissention* of Christian Princes, the *want of practice* in Religion, and the like, which have been so long spoken against, that men are become insensible about them; every one shifting off the fault from himself to others; and so they are only made bare common places of complaint. It will suffice my present purpose, to point out, what has been done by the *Royal Society,* towards the correcting of its excesses in *Natural Philosophy,* to which it is, of all others, a most profest enemy.

They have therefore been most rigorous in putting in execution, the only Remedy, that can be found for this *extravagance:* and that has been, a constant resolution, to reject all the amplifications, digressions, and swellings of style: to return back to the primitive purity, and shortness, when men delivered so many *things,* almost in an equal number of *words.* They have exacted from all their members, a close, naked, natural way of speaking; positive expressions; clear senses; a native easiness: bringing all things as near the Mathematicall plainness, as they can: and preferring the language of Artizans, Countrymen, and Merchants, before that of Wits, or Scholars. (pp. 111-113)

First, there is some question as to whether Sprat is discussing oral or written discourse. "Redundance of *speech,*" "superfluity of talking," "Ornaments of speaking," "*fine speaking,*" "volubility of *Tongue,*" and "natural way of speaking" would seem to indicate that Sprat means the spoken language. But words like "speech" and "talking" can refer to either type of "discourse" in Sprat's critical vocabulary. For example, in the *Life and Writings of Mr. Abraham Cowley* Sprat refers to the poems of Horace as "speeches" and to his own written prose as "speech." "I might, Sir, have made a longer Discourse of his Writings, but that I think it fit to direct my speech concerning him by the same rule by which he was wont to judge of others." [28] (Similarly Glanvill, in the *Plus Ultra,* praises the written prose of the *History* for avoiding "*wide fetches* and *circumferences* of Speech.") Sprat seems explicitly to include written as well as oral discourse in his discussion when he scorns the "seeming mysteries upon which we writers, and speakers, look so bigg." Both written and oral prose are "speech." In the piece on Cowley Sprat says prose is "certainly the most useful kind of writing of all others, for it is the style of all business and conversation" (p. 132). Sprat is concerned with the usefulness of prose, not with the distinction between spoken and written discourse.

Second, there is some doubt as to whether Sprat meant to restrict the "close, naked, natural way of speaking" of the Royal Society to "scientific" discourse, or to apply it to prose that was not "scientific" as well. I think it is clear from the context of the manifesto on style and from Sprat's understanding of prose as the medium of utility in general that he intended the style practiced by the Society to serve as a model of what all prose which advanced useful knowledge should be, not only prose useful to advance knowledge unearthed by the experimenters. The important contrast for Sprat is not between one style for natural philosophy and one style for everything else but between a useful style and a useless style. He praises the style of the Society not only for its usefulness for natural philosophy, but as an example for others to follow to prevent disputes, chiefly religious and political. In fact, Sprat understands the manner of discourse of the Society as the best way for all the "other *Arts* and *Professions*," "the other parts of Learning." "And indeed, in most other parts of Learning, I look on it [rhetorical excess] to be a thing almost utterly desperate in its cure. . . . It will suffice my present purpose, to point out, what has been done by the Royal Society, towards the correcting of its excesses in Natural Philosophy, to which it is, of all others, a most profest enemy." Sprat's "present purpose" restricts him to what the Royal Society has done about style. He is indicating the correct style for the Society's discourse. He is also defining an all-purpose utilitarian style "which is the only Remedy, that can be found for this *extravagance*," the "abundance of Phrase, this trick of *Metaphors*, this volubility of *Tongue*" described above, which "in Religion, and the like" has so disrupted society.

Of course, "eloquence" is not bad in itself, provided it is put to the right use and not abused. If the times were not so degenerate, then eloquence would be appropriate for the discourses of natural philosophy, for, by Sprat's Baconian psychology, it would "bring knowledge back again to our very sense, from whence it was first derived to our understandings." Contemporary science is just as susceptible to "superfluity of talking" as the other arts and professions, and is, as Marjorie Nicolson has reminded us in our own time, a source of eloquence and imagery. The Society has learned from experience, though, that eloquence in these degenerate times leads to useless controversy. It is the good sense of the Society's members, not "science," which has led the Society to adopt a "plain" style, for "unless they had been very watchful to keep in due temper, the whole spirit and vigour of their Design, had been soon eaten out, by the luxury and redundance of speech." Jones' contention that "science" itself led to a plain style is not borne out by Sprat's manifesto. Sprat describes the style which he thinks will promote the general welfare — "happy Living" — and does not regard it as peculiarly "scientific." Like Glanvill, Sprat reveals himself here and elsewhere as a Latitudinarian and antienthusiastic Anglican, disturbed by the recent religious and political upheavals, and infected by the utilitarianism of the bourgeois Protestantism of the "Artizans, Countrymen, and Merchants" he admires throughout the *History*.[29]

A great problem remains, however, for the utilitarian. A "close, naked, natural way of speaking" will suffice for fellow seekers of useful knowledge in commerce, religion, politics, and natural philosophy. "Useful relations" are bound by the "purity and shortness which are the chief beauties of

Historical writings" — the same "primitive purity and shortness" of the manifesto on the style of the Royal Society.
But how does one convince the corrupted wits? Obviously,
by being "witty" one's self. "Objections and Cavils" against
the Society "did make it necessary for me to write of it
not altogether in the way of a plain History, but sometimes
of an Apology." [30] To avoid sinking to the level of the wits,
however, one must be witty in a special way. So argues
Sprat at the end of the *History*.

> Their is in the *Works of Nature*, an inexhaustible Treasure of
> *Fancy* and *Invention*. . . .
> To this purpose I must premise, that it is requir'd in the
> best and most delightful *Wit*; that it be founded on such
> Images which are generally known, and are able to bring a
> strong, and a sensible Impression on the *mind*. The several Sub-
> jects from which it has been rays'd in all Times, are the *Fables*,
> and *Religions* of the *Antients*, the *Civil Histories* of all *Countries*,
> the *Customs* of *Nations*, the *Bible*, the *Sciences* and *Manners* of
> *Men*, the several *Arts* of their hands, and Works of *Nature*. In
> all these, there may be a resemblance of one thing to another, as
> there may be in all, there is a sufficient Foundation for *Wit*.
> This in all its kinds has its increases, heigths, and decays, as
> well as all other human things: Let us then examine what Parts
> of it are already exhausted, and what remain new and untouch'd,
> and are still likely to be farther advanc'd (p. 413)

Here is Sprat's "eloquence," employed to describe "in larger,
fairer, and more moving Images; to represent Truth, cloak'd
with Bodies; and to bring *Knowledge* back again to our very
sense, from whence it was at first deriv'd to our understandings." Natural philosophy, which supplied Glanvill with so
many images in the *Vanity*, and the useful arts, which deal
with the works of nature, the manners of men, and the arts
of men's hands, are sources of both the "close, naked, natural
way of speaking" and of eloquence for the propagation of
useful knowledge. Bacon himself "was abundantly recom-
pens'd for his noble Labours in that *Philosophy*, by a vast
treasure of admirable *Imaginations* which it afforded him,

wherein to express and adorn his Thoughts about other Matters." For Sprat as for Bacon there appear to be two useful styles, one for the advancement of knowledge, the other for its propagation. The word for the special type of eloquence required to convince the wits is "proper." Sprat has in this quotation catalogued some of the proper "ornaments of speech . . . so much degenerated from their original usefulness."

Sprat's list describes the style of the apologetic parts of the History itself, which are clearly aimed at the wits, better than the much more famous analysis of the "close, naked, natural way of speaking." Here, by way of example for stylistic analysis, is Sprat's elaborate appeal for an international community of natural philosophers:

Whoever shall soberly profess, to be willing to put their shoulders, under the burthen of so great an enterprise, as to represent to mankind, the whole Fabrick, the parts, the causes, the effects, of Nature: ought to have their eyes in all parts, and to receive information from every quarter of the earth: they ought to have a constant universall intelligence: all discoveries should be brought to them: the Treasuries of all former times should be laid open before them: the assistance of the present should be allow'd them: so farr are the narrow conceptions of a few private Writers, in a dark Age, from being equall to so vast a design. There are indeed some operations of the mind, which may be best perform'd by the simple strength of mens own particular thoughts; such are invention, and judgement, and disposition: For in them a security from noise, leaves the Soul at more liberty, to bring forth, order, and fashion the heap of matter, which had been before supply'd to its use. But there are other works also, which require as much aid, and as many hands, as can be found. And such is this of observation: Which is the great Foundation of Knowledge: Some must gather, some must bring, some separate, some examine; and (to use a Similitude, which the present time of the year, and the ripe fields, that lye before my eyes, suggest to me) it is in *Philosophy*, as in *Husbandry*: wherein we see, that a few hands will serve to measure out, and fill into sacks, that Corn, which requires a very many more laborers, to sow, and reap, and bind, and bring it into the Barn. (pp. 20–21)

The agricultural images are drawn from what is "generally known" to all — "the Arts of their hands." The elaborate image is also a digression and an amplification, however, and it occurs at the end of a considerable rhetorical swelling, despite the counsel of the manifesto against all three. Here is Sprat on "Criticks and Philologists":

For methinks, that wisdom, which they fetch'd from the ashes of the dead, is something of the same nature, with Ashes themselves: which, if they are kept up in heaps together, will be useless: But if they are scattred upon Living ground, they will make it fertile, in the bringing forth of various sorts of Fruits. To these men then we are beholding, that we have a fairer prospect about us: to them we owe, that we are not ignorant of the times that are gone before us: which to be is (as *Tully* says) *to be always Children*. All this, and much more, is to be acknowledg'd: But we shall also desire of them, that they would content themselves, with what is their due: that by what they have discover'd, amongst the rubbish of the *Ancients*, they would not contemn the Treasures, either lately found out, or still unknown: and that they would not prefer the *Gold* of *Ophir*, of which now there is no mention, but in Books, before the present Mountains of the *West-Indies*. (pp. 24–25)

Again Sprat swells and amplifies. More elaborate images (though from husbandry, in accordance with Sprat's rules for rhetoric), a classical tag, and a Biblical allusion recall "Wits and Scholars" more than "Artizans, Countrymen, and Merchants." The carefully unbalanced sentences, with a firmly stopped falling-off in the final clause, is reminiscent of Browne, though Sprat lacks Browne's wistful reflectiveness, resonant music, Latinity, suggestiveness, and intimacy. Thus the *History* oscillates between moderately witty apologetics and the "plain History" of the activities of the Royal Society.

It is not at all certain that Sprat clearly distinguished, in either his practice or theory of style, between one "plain" style for the advancement of knowledge and a less "plain" style for the use or propagation of knowledge. Sprat praises Pellisson's history of the French Academy for being "so masculinely, so chastly, and so unaffectedly done" — for having qualities which answer to the "manly" style and "native easiness" of the "close, naked, natural way of speaking." But Sprat also regards Pellisson as a model of elegance, as opposed to his own history, which is "without any ornament of *Eloquence*."

I can hardly forbear envying the *French Nation* this honour: that while the *English Royal Society* has so much out-gone their *Illustrious* Academy, in the greatness of its undertaking, it should be so far short of them in the abilities of its *Historian*. I have onely this to allege in my excuse; that as they undertook the advancement of the Elegance of Speech, so it became their *History*, to have some resemblance to their enterprize: Whereas the intention of ours, being not the Artifice of Words, but a bare knowledge of things; my fault may be esteem'd the less, that I have written of *Philosophers*, without any ornament of *Eloquence*. (p. 40)

Bacon is also a stylistic model for Sprat's history, allegedly devoid of any "ornament of Eloquence." Yet Sprat praises Bacon for his "Art" and "Wit."

Nowhere is Sprat's uncertainty as to the direction in which the English language should reform itself more apparent than in his famous "proposal for erecting an English Academy." Echoing the familiar English prejudice about the frivolous French, Sprat praises the contrasting manly "English genius": "I hope now, it will not be thought a vain digression, if I step a little aside to recommend the forming of such an *Assembly*, to the Gentlemen of our Nation. I know, indeed, that the *English Genius* is not so airy, and discoursive, as that of some of our neighbours, but that we generally love to have Reason set out in plain, undeceiving expressions; as much, as they to have it deliver'd with colour, and beauty" (p. 40). But Sprat yearns for some of the French polish in English. "But besides, if we observe well the *English Language;* we shall find, that it seems at this time more than others, to require some such aid, to bring it to its last perfection. The Truth is, it has been hitherto a little too carelessly handled; and I think, has had less labor spent about its polishing, then it deserves" (pp. 41–42). Whereas later in the *History* the stormy disputes of the civil wars lead Sprat to advocate the "close, naked, natural way of speaking" of "Artizans, Countrymen, and Merchants" (pp. 112–114), here the same conditions, recounted in a historical sketch, suggest to Sprat the need for reforms of an *opposite* nature — toward "smoothness," "colour and beauty," "Humour and Wit and Elegance." He labels these qualities French and contrasts them to "the rough German." In the wars, English, because of the controversies

receiv'd many fantastical terms, which were introduc'd by our *Religious Sects;* and many outlandish phrases, which several *Writers,* and *Translators,* in that great hurry, brought in, and made free as they pleas'd, and with all it was inlarg'd by many sound, and necessary Forms, and Idioms, which it before wanted. And now . . . if some sober and judicious Men, would take the whole Mass of our Language into their hands, as they find it, and would set a mark on the ill Words; correct those, which are to be retain'd; admit, and establish the good; and make some emendations in the Accent, and Grammar: I dare pronounce, that our Speech would quickly arrive at as much plenty as it is capable to receive; and at the greatest smoothness, which its derivation from the rough *German* will allow it. (p. 44)

Sprat then tells us that the Society itself is reforming English in the direction of French elegance: "The *Royal Society* is so far from being like to put a stop to such a business, that I know many of its members, who are as able as any others, to assist in the bringing it into practice."

Elsewhere Sprat indicates that an all-purpose English Style will come, not from "Artizans, Countrymen, and

Merchants," but from their exact antitheses, the "Wits" (the exquisite and Francophile court of King Charles) and "Scholars." From these two sources came the language of that paragon of good style and eulogist of the new philosophy, Abraham Cowley. "We have many things that he writ in two very unlike conditions, in the University and the Court. But in his Poetry as well as his Life, he mingled with excellent skill what was good in both states. In his life he join'd the innocence and sincerity of the Scholar with the humanity and good behaviour of the Courtier. In his Poems he united the Solidity and Art of the one with the Gentility and Gracefulness of the other. . . . He forsook the Conversation, but never the Language, of the City and Court." [31] There is every indication, then, that Sprat admired, advocated, and practiced, perhaps knowingly, two styles at the same time.

Glanvill echoes Sprat's ambivalence, supporting Jones's thesis that the Royal Society, as exemplified by Sprat, influenced Glanvill directly. The praise of Sprat's style in the *Plus Ultra*, as we have seen, has much in common with Sprat's appeal for a close, naked, natural style. But Glanvill also praises Sprat for writing in a "proper" style of "so judicious a *gravity*, and so prudent . . . an expression," with "*Words* proper . . . the *Periods smooth* and of *middle* proportion . . . as *polite* and as *fast* as Marble," wanting "none of the *proper Ornaments* of Language." Here judiciousness, prudence, smoothness, polish, and, above all and including all, propriety, become the criteria for an ideal Style to "*profit* and entertain the Ingenious." Glanvill sees no conflict between the "proper" style and manly and plain style. Indeed, he seems to understand Sprat's writing as a happy compromise between two opposed styles. The tension between the polished courtly and down-to-earth bourgeois is lurking beneath Glanvill's careful antitheses: "manly, and yet plain, natural and yet not careless . . . *proper* and

familiar. . . . Not rendred *intricate* . . . nor *gaudy* . . .
not *tedious* . . . nor *dark* . . . not *loose* and *unjointed*,
rugged and *uneven,* but as *polite* and *fast* as *Marble."* Like
Sprat, Glanvill blurs the distinction between the "natural"
style of the artisans, countrymen, and merchants, and the
"proper" style of the polite court. Although Glanvill speci-
fies that the *History* is addressed to the wits of "ingenious
relish," the criteria of the artisans, countrymen, and merchants creep into the definition of the ideal Style of "genuine
Eloquence."

Much the same confusion prevails in Glanvill's theory and
practice of sermon style. In the essay "Anti-Fanatick Theologie and Free Philosophy," Glanvill condemns Enthusiastic and witty preaching in the same language that he and
Sprat use in condemning the kind of writing the Royal
Society opposed. Against the Enthusiasts, "those that dealt
most in jingles, and *chiming* of words, in *Metaphors* and
vulgar *Similitudes,* in *Fanatic* phrases, and *Fanciful* schemes
of speech" (p. 42), the best preachers are, once acquainted
with the Experimental Philosophy,

Plain both in opposition to, First, *Obscurity,* and Secondly, *Affectation.* First, They preach'd no *dark,* or *obscure* notions. . . .
Their great aim was the edification, and instruction of those to
whom they spoke; and therefore they were so far from preaching the *heights* of *speculation.* . . . They did not involve their
discourses in *needless words* of *Art,* or *subtile distinctions;* but
spoke in the plainest, and most intelligible Terms: and distinguished things in the most easie and familiar manner that the
matter of discourse would bear. . . . They affected not to osten-
tate Learning, by high-flown expressions, or ends of *Greek,* and
Latine: They did not stuff their Sermons with numerous needless *Quotations.* . . . (pp. 42–43)

Here the sober criteria of Sprat's artisans, countrymen, and
merchants predominate. The goal is frankly utilitarian; even
the plain style is a rhetorical device. Preachers must try "by
the *weight* of their sense, and the *reason* of their *perswa-*

sions, endeavouring by their *understanding,* to gain the affections and so to work on the will." In Glanvill's later
sermon manual, *An Essay Concerning Preaching* (1678), he
repeats himself and the usual admonitions of the Royal Society and other Anglican divines, to be plain by avoiding
"hard terms," "finery, flourishes, metaphors, and cadencies,"
"scraps of *Greek* and *Latin*," [32] and so on. But now the
utilitarian Glanvill reluctantly admits "terms of art" from
formal philosophy and divinity, as well as English words of
Latin derivation. Some "hard words" are now "proper."
The preacher must now be "Affectionate" as well as "Plain,"
"Practical," and "Methodical" (pp. 54–56). Throughout his
discussion of affectionateness Glanvill oscillates, as in his
judgments on Sprat's style, between an ideal of "proper" or
allowable rhetoric and an ideal of plainness. Beyond these
two limits lie the extremes of "words metaphorical and ambiguous" and the like, and "rude and blunt allusions" and
other features "accommodated to the humor of the vulgar."
Affections

we must endeavour to excite; they are the springs of the
Soul, that move the Will, and put our Powers into Action.
Now the best, and most lasting Affections, are such as are
raised by the Understanding, and the knowledg of our Duties,
and our Interest: so that we should represent the influencing
truths of the Gospel, in plainness, and power, to beget due,
and deep conviction in the Mind. But generally 'tis only the
wisest sort whose Affections are stirred in this noblest, and
most regular way: The common People are incapable of much
Theory . . . their Affections are raised by figures, and earnest-
ness and passionate representations. . . . God himself doth so
condescend; he speaks in our Language, and in such Schemes of
Speech as are apt to excite the Affections of the most Vulgar,
and Illiterate. . . . Milk must be given, as well as strong Meat.
(pp. 54–56)

But propriety must be observed. Glanvill's rhetorical pen-
dulum swings back and forth nervously to accommodate the

"vulgar" as well as the "ingenious" as he seeks a mean between "Enthusiasm" and dullness.

There are indeed a sort of conceited weak that are not mov'd but by vain phancies and senseless phrases, and unintelligible notions, by a rude loudness and apish gestures and boisterous violence. . . . To such humours, and follies as these, we must not accommodate: for this is a debasing of the Gospel. . . . But this we ought to indeavour, *viz.*, to give our matter its proper colours . . . to study all the warrantable ways by which Men use to be awakened, and excited; and to press the Truths, and Duties we teach, with a Zeal and Warmth proportionable to the concernment of them, taking care to avoid all indecency, and extravagance. (pp. 56–59)

As in his description of the ideal style represented in Sprat's *History* — and as in Sprat's manifesto — Glanvill implies that there is one "plain" style for simple communication of knowledge, another "proper" style for its propagation. Glanvill opposes both these styles, and especially the plainer one, to the style identified by Croll and his followers as Senecan. Glanvill may well have the "Senecan" vogue in mind when he condemns, as a mere passing fad, "a certain stiffness in the composition of many Sermons, in the which Words are set and Period measur'd, and Cadences turn'd all which argue a vain endeavour to entertain, and please conceited Hearers. . . . This way is painful, but the effects of it are harsh, and forced, and unnatural. . . . This is like *fashions* that will not last, the modes of it vary continually; and what is rare Language in one time, is foolish and ridiculous in another: But what is natural and proper, lasts always" (p. 63). Glanvill probably is referring to "Senecans" like Andrewes when he condemns sermons which "lose their efficacy and force by being too full and close": he even quotes, in this connection, Quintilian's famous criticism of Seneca, *Divisionum minutiis rerum franguntur pondera*. The spasmodic and aphoristic quality of the "Senecan" writer comes under fire: "Another fault I have observ'd in some Sermons is *difformity:* Heights, and falls; Eloquence, and Sordidness; Wit, and no Sense; this is the fault of Collectors, that make Nosegays, and pick a piece out of one Author, and a piece out of another." Glanvill's preacher must not digress or ramble in the intimate and witty manner of Seneca.

A Man in a Journey will not run over Hedges to gather Flowers; and the Preacher is much to blame that forsakes the direct course of his matter to fetch in notions, and elegancies; such as are grave and pertinent, and lie in his way he may use, but to set his fancy a ranging, and beating abroad after them, is folly, and affectation. . . . Another fault to be noted is a desultory sort of skipping from one thing to another, without following anything home. The Sermons of some consist altogether in little Remarks, and pretty Notes, and strain'd Observations. These propose no main business to pursue, but touch abundance of things superficially and slightly: so that no body is taught, none edified. (pp. 73–76)

Glanvill prefers rigid adherence to "Methods," a formal outline.

In his theory of sermon style Glanvill is demonstrably un-Senecan. But Jones is hasty when he attributes Glanvill's reaction against Senecanism in preaching to "science," even though Glanvill advocates the same styles for the advancement and propagation of knowledge as for preaching, and suggests (in "Anti-Fanatick Theologie and Free Philosophy") that a good plain style will come out of a scientific education. Rather Glanvill justifies his stylistic theory, as he justifies everything else, on the ground of utility. Utilitarian concerns drive Glanvill into formulating his "proper" sermon style, suitable to the purposes of his amiable Latitudinarianism, with its hatred of disputing.

It would be a Felicity, not only to the Clergy, but even to the People, that are to be instructed by them: were Men brought to judge by one, and the right measure: For then the Preachers would not have the temptation of complying with the phancies of their hearers; Nor these the occasion of quarrelling [with] their Teachers, and vilifying their Doctrine, because it is not dres'd up according to their capricious humours, and uncertain imaginations.

Now the Rule whereby the People are to judge ought also to be the measure by which the Divine should Preach; and the measure no doubt ought to be taken from the *End:* This one thing considered, would reduce the Rules of Preaching to a narrower compass: and if Men would but ask themselves the question, *What is the End of Sermons;* they would easily see the folly and extravagance of their measures. . . . When it is proper for the promoting these ends, it is good Preaching; when it is not so aim'd though the Discourse be never so Elaborate, Witty, Eloquent, or Learned, it is not *Preaching:* It may have its proper commendation as a Speech, but ought not to be reckon'd as a good Sermon. (pp. 8–11)

Glanvill's concern here is not with "science" but with the problems connected with composing useful sermons — a concern which at times in the essay on preaching leads him, as we have seen, away from a strictly "plain" style.

Glanvill's actual sermon practice follows his theory closely insofar as there is an oscillation between "plainness" and an appeal to the "affections." Following contemporary theory for the construction of sermons into "methods," Glanvill thinks the sermon should consist of "First, The choice of the *Text.* Secondly, the *Preface.* Thirdly, The *Body* of the Sermon. And Fourthly The *Application*" (p. 41). Glanvill divides the "Application" into various "Uses," the "Inference, Advice, and Motives" (p. 52). Since "the *Motives* afford those considerations whereby our duties are inforc'd, and our indeavours are incouraged and excited" (p. 52), this final section of the sermon is consistently the most rhetorical, in Glanvill's practice. For the modern reader, these "motives" come as a welcome relief after a tiresome train of "uses." Despite Glanvill's theoretical bias against the "Senecan" style, these passages represent a return to a "proper" version of the florid "Senecanism" of the first *Vanity.* After reading them, we can understand why Glanvill, who is known as an apostle of plainness, had in his own time a reputation as a "romantick" preacher.[33]

Thus Glanvill throughout his career and Sprat in his *History* illustrate the unstable position to which contemporary utilitarianism drove prose style, which wavered between two ideals of plainness, one of decorous expression of feeling, the other of "manliness." To determine what the seventeenth century meant by "plain" — in relation to science and Anti-Ciceronianism — is our next problem.

CHAPTER FOUR

Res et Verba, *Things and Words:* *The Classical Plain Style*

Some Versions of Plainness

In "Anti-Fanatick Theologie and Free Philosophy" Glanvill distinguishes between two "plain" styles. Before the Restoration, preachers

saw, they did but please with their *sound*, without conveying any sense into the minds of those that were so much delighted with them. So that the pretended *plain preaching* of those days, was really *not at all understood;* nor as much as *intelligible.* Therefore instead of such phrases, They [post-Restoration preachers] us'd the most proper, and natural expressions, and such as most easily opened the mind to the things they taught.[1]

For Glanvill only one of these "plain" styles deserves the epithet, the new style practiced by the Anti-Fanatick religion, that is, the Latitudinarians, and the Free Philosophy, that is, the Royal Society. The other style, commonly but erroneously labeled "plain," is everything to which the Anglican and scientific reformers object. As we have seen, this "pretended plain" style has many affinities with Croll's "Senecanism." Glanvill, perhaps because he moved self-consciously from "Senecanism" to the new plain style himself, shows a more acute awareness of the ambiguities of the word "plain" than many modern critics. The same word is used to refer to opposed styles. This failure to understand what "plain" (and its close relations, such as "precise") meant to the seventeenth century is responsible for the Crollians' identification of "Senecan" style with its opposite, the prevailing plain style of the Restoration. It is clear from stylistic theory and practice that as the seventeenth century ran its course, and especially after the Restoration, "plain" came to describe what we shall call for now an impersonal style in which the emotional attitudes of the observer did not appear. As Glanvill's statement suggests, the new style had the utilitarian intention of presenting "things" plainly to the reader or listener. The revelation of the inmost thoughts and feelings of the writer was not sought. Before the Restoration the style called plain was personal, a style "that portrays the process of acquiring the truth rather than the secure possession of it . . . a vivid and acute portrayal of individual experience rather than . . . the histrionic and sensuous expression of general ideas." [2] So-called Senecanism and its extension, the "libertine" style, represent an extreme variety of the personal plain style, another style altogether.

As examples of the confusion for literary history resulting from the failure to distinguish the two meanings of "plain," I cite the following remarks from *The Senecan Amble* and the introduction to the edition of Sprat's *History* by Jackson Cope and H. W. Jones:

One begins to wonder why the Royal Society was so afraid of being "eaten out by the luxury and redundance of speech," how the English could have become so debauched by the general mischief of eloquence, or why any reform was necessary. It is to be remembered that Sprat speaks of this reform of style as directed primarily toward the requirements of natural philosophy. But when he devotes a short section at the end of his book to the consideration of possible benefits from experiments to wits and writers, his chief standard of value for wit is whether the comparisons derive from things apparent to the senses. Here his standard for style may reflect that requirement, 'so many things, almost in an equal number of *words*' — not 'things and notions,' as Wilkins puts it. For Sprat's antipathy to the abstractions of the schoolmen colours his definition, preferring the language of those who deal in things before the language of those who deal in notion. Viewed in the light of his discussion of wit, this would only be another aspect of the doctrine of plainness as perspicuity. . . . Seneca (*Ep.* 114) had found in Sallust more thoughts than words, or still greater brevity. Thus Sprat's remark would associate the Royal Society programme with Senecan brevity rather than Ciceronian copiousness.[3]

Discussing Sprat's ideal of "Mathematical plainness," Cope and H. W. Jones, citing the same text from Seneca, also uphold the Crollian identification of scientific style with Senecanism:

I have called the mathematical analogy a *metaphor* in Sprat's usage, because it does not seem to suggest anything like the rigidly organized language of signs created in Wilkins' "real Character," a system with which Sprat was certainly familiar during his writing of the *History*. Rather, the conjunction of the mathematical analogy with the phrase "so many *things*, almost in an equal number of words" might suggest that Sprat is placing the Society in the long tradition from Cicero to Cowley which exhorted, in Cato's phrase, "*Rem tene, verba sequentur.*" The key authority in this tradition for the seventeenth century was certainly Seneca, whose influence spread both wider and deeper than that of any classical rival for prestige. He adopted the ideal of significant words in a favorite comparison of Sallust's style with that of Arruntius. . . . But Seneca in the same epistle (114) had spoken of all sorts of stylistic faults, including obscure brevity, which result from exceeding the proper limits (*plus justo*) of decorum. And the "criterion that lies at the foundation of all his ideas about writing . . . is the principle that excellence of style . . . results from employing language according to nature." Sprat speaks of the same qualities: clarity, ease, and a "natural way of speaking" as well as "so many *things*, almost in an equal number of *words*." And if we agree that

Seneca was chiefly interested in distinguishing a proper philosophical style, we are able to see that Sprat was perhaps closer
to Seneca's aim than were more obvious Senecan imitators in
the tradition of curt style.[4]

For Croll, Williamson, Cope, and H. W. Jones, a "plain"
style is one in which words approximate things. Williamson
points out correctly that for Sprat "things" are physical
substances as opposed to Wilkins' "notions." Did Seneca
mean "things" in this sense, as Williamson seems to assume?
And would Seneca's "notions" have been the same as Wilkins'? R. F. Jones, as we might expect, has objected to such
assumptions:

There are, to be sure, certain resemblances between the two
stylistic attitudes. In both "reality" is emphasized, but with the
scientists the term generally means a material reality, while the
Anti-Ciceronians used it to refer much more widely to rationalistic explanations of human experience. Though in both "things"
are preferred to "words," the experimental philosophers had
concrete objects in mind, while the others were thinking of
intellectual or moral conceptions.[5]

I think Jones's position is correct here. Wesley Trimpi, to
whom the ensuing discussion of the classical plain style is
heavily indebted, has stated the distinctions most acutely:

The difference between the plainness sought by the Royal Society and that of the classical plain style is that the former was
a style in which the writer himself intruded as little as possible
in the description of the physical world, a language as near to
mathematics as possible. The classical plain style was developed
to reveal the writer himself, to analyze and to portray the individual personality. The difference is not simply between philosophy and "natural philosophy," but between the methods of
analysis that each subject matter imposes. The conscious ex-
clusion of the writer's personality — even his mind if that were
possible — in the language of mathematics is directly opposed
to the cultivation of the individual and psychological search for
philosophic truth, as it is described by Morris Croll.[6]

The Classical Plain Style
and Anti-Ciceronianism
in Antiquity

I have quoted the critics at such length to show that a great controversy turns on the classical and Renaissance definitions of "plain" — invariably expressed as the relation of *res* to *verba* — and the corresponding seventeenth-century notions. What did the ancients mean by a "plain" style? Is the classical plain style the same as Croll's original, ancient "Anti-Ciceronianism?" Was this ancient style the model for the new "plain" style of the Renaissance "Anti-Ciceronians" and later for the Royal Society and the Restoration? What follows is a survey of some of the more important of the innumerable statements that in a plain style words should approximate, or be subordinate to, things. My discussion should be read as a commentary on Croll's, summarized in Chapter One (pp. 10–18), of the history of the *genus humile*.

Rhetorical tradition almost unanimously assigns the first significant awareness of a plain style, as distinct from an ornate one, to Plato's *Phaedrus*. Plato assigns persuasion to lofty rhetoric, philosophical truth to the plain style. The audiences of the rhetoricians receive "the representation of knowledge without the reality." Rhetoric and rhetoricians are impersonal and soulless. "You would imagine that they had an intelligence, but if you want to know anything and put a question to one of them, the speaker always gives one unvarying answer." But to Plato the "reality" of knowledge is in the soul, and its language is an "image" of the soul: "*Soc.* May we not imagine another kind of writing or speaking far better than this is, and having far greater power, — which is one of the same family, but lawfully begotten? . . . I am speaking of intelligent writing which is graven in the soul of him who is learned, and can defend himself, and knows when to speak and be silent." [7] Words exactly describe things, or are a sort of image of them. "Truth" is in the Ideal Soul, not in Sprat's physical world. The plain style is nobler than oratory because it reproduces this Truth: "Only in principles of justice and goodness and nobility taught and communicated orally and written in the soul which is the true way of writing, is there clearness and perfection and seriousness . . . being, in the first place, that which the man finds in his own bosom." [8]

It is in Roman theory, however, that we find the most detailed discussions of the plain style. Cicero is well aware of the distinction between the philosophical and oratorical styles: "If style, then, makes so much difference in philosophy, where the attention is concentrated in the meaning, and words as such are not weighed, what must we think of the importance of style in suits at law which are wholly swayed by oratorical skill?" [9] Like all theorists on the plain style, with its roots in the Platonic dialogue, Cicero holds that it is decorously conversational. It "is gentle and academic; it has no equipment of words or phrases that catch the popular fancy; it is not arranged in rhythmical periods, but is loose in structure; there is no anger in it, no hatred, no ferocity, no pathos, no shrewdness; it might be called a chaste, pure, and modest virgin. Consequently it is called conversation rather than oratory." [10] Like the philosopher, Cicero's "restrained and plain" (*summissus et humilis*) Attic orator pays more attention to things or thoughts than to words: "He should also avoid, so to speak, cementing his words together too smoothly, for the hiatus and clash of vowels has something agreeable about it and shows a not unpleasant carelessness on the part of a man paying more attention to thought than to words" (*Orator*, 77, p. 363). In all speech, in fact, "the words we employ, then, are . . . the proper and definite designations of things, which are almost born at the same time as the things themselves." In lofty, non-Attic oratory the speaker adds "rare words, new coinages, and words used metaphorically." [11] In the plain Attic tradition, and in the nonoratorical philosophical style as well, words remain "the proper and definite designations of things," that is, the "things" in the head of the speaker rather than the "things" of Sprat's physical reality. The plain or Attic style is to teach, the grand style to move, another "middle" style to delight. In the *Rhetorica Ad Herennium* these three become the "characters" of style.[12] Both Cicero and the author of the *Ad Herennium* assume that the style in which words are closest to things will be conversational, the supreme example being, of course, the dialogues of Plato.

With the formulation of the three "characters," the plain style becomes identified with four genres: comedy, satire, epigram, and epistle. Wesley Trimpi has shown that "the intention common to all four genres . . . is to reveal with the greatest possible candidness and accuracy what men actually do. Since the satirist hopes that when they see themselves objectively reflected, as if in a mirror, they will be inclined to reform, the speculum becomes the central symbol of the didactic writer" (*Ben Jonson's Poems*, p. 14). The theory of language as *speculum* implies that words shall approximate things, that is, be a mirror of the soul. The epistle is even closer than satire to the Socratic origins of the plain style. More than any other form, letters emphasize self-knowledge: "The epistle was concerned chiefly with self-examination. Originating in the Socratic reform of style, whose intention was to help one know one's self, the *sermo* most effectively served the purpose of self-revelation and self-analysis by expressing most directly what the writer had to say about himself and even to reveal the very process of his thought. For this reason Seneca, in his letters and the treatises on letter writing, advocates the plain style" (pp. 14–15). Seneca's pronouncements on the epistle follow the orthodox view of the plain style, from Plato through Cicero and through Horace, who, as Grant and Fiske have shown, is directly indebted to Cicero. Both Cicero and Horace describe the plain style as exactly reflecting and being subordinate to things, meaning mental and largely moral concepts rather than Sprat's physical things or Wilkins' notions of them. Both agree that if words do describe the things in the mind, the result is chaste and urbane conversation.[13]

Horace's intimate style, which he describes as "now grave, often gay, in keeping with the role, now of orator or poet, at times of the wit," [14] enlarges the province of the plain style beyond Cicero's rather abstract moral discourse in a way which, as we shall see, is significant for the seventeenth century, especially for "libertine" prose. Words still mirror the things of the mind for Horace, but the *speculum* now turns in all directions, like the syntax of Croll's "curt" period: "Successive flashes of a jewel or prism as it is turned about on its axis and takes the light in different ways" (*Style*, p. 212). For Horace's successor Juvenal the *sermo* also embraces *quicquid agunt homines* — "all the doings of mankind, their vows, their fears, their angers and their pleasures, their joys and goings to and fro." [15] Juvenal agrees with Horace that only in the plain style do words equal real life in all its variety. Persius echoes Juvenal; the conversational flow of satire is the equivalent of life as it impinges on our consciousness, and as we reflect it back in the *speculum* of language. All human folly — certainly not Sprat's physical world — is the subject of satire for Persius: *O curas hominum, o quantum est in rebus inane!* [16]

It is not the satirists and letter-writers, but Quintilian who has the most extended discussion of the relationship of words and things. Although he clearly accepts the traditional division of the three "characters" of style, Quintilian seems to have in mind, throughout most of the sections on style in the *Institutio*, one all-purpose style for eloquence in general which often conforms to the conventions of the traditional plain style. He lays "the failure of the orators of the Asiatic and other decadent schools" [17] to their hunting more for words than for matter. Significantly for our purposes, Quintilian follows Cicero rather than Seneca: "Cicero holds that, while invention and arrangement are within the reach of any man of good sense, eloquence belongs to the orator alone, and consequently it was on the rules for the cultivation of eloquence that he expended the greatest care. That he was justified in so doing is shown clearly by the actual name of the art of which I am speaking. For the verb *eloqui* means the production and communication to the audience of all that the speaker has conceived in his mind." However, continues Quintilian, in a passage to become a *locus classicus* for the "Anti-Ciceronians" of the Renaissance,

this does not mean that we should devote ourselves to the study of words alone. . . . A translucent and irridescent style merely serves to emasculate the subject which it arrays with such pomp of words. Therefore I would have the orator, while careful in his choice of words, be even more concerned about his subject matter. For, as a rule, the best words are essentially suggested by and are discovered by their own intrinsic light. But to-day we hunt for these words as though they were always hiding themselves and striving to elude our grasp. (Preface, VIII; Loeb Library, III, pp. 185–189)

Following the orthodox theory of the plain style, Quintilian implies that if words follow or are subordinate to things (the character of the speaker), a direct, conversational style results. The standard authority for this style is the golden Cicero.[18]

Its enemies are clearly Quintilian's brilliant but empty Silver contemporaries. Ideally, "words will yield us ready service, not merely turning up when we search for them, but dwelling in our thoughts and following them as the shadow follows the body. . . . And yet," adds Quintilian, doubtless with Seneca in mind, there are some who are never weary of morbid self-criticism, who throw themselves into an agony of mind over separate syllables, and even when they have discovered the best words for their purpose look for some word that is older, less familiar, and less obvious, since they cannot bring themselves to realize that when a speech is praised for its words, it implies that it is inadequate. While, then, style calls for the utmost attention, we must always bear in mind that nothing should be done for the sake of words only, since words were invented merely to give expression to things; and those words are the most satisfactory which give the best expression to the thoughts of our mind and produce the effect which we desire upon the minds of the judges.[19]

Quintilian's model of fashionable vulgarity is indeed Seneca himself, whose unconversational words do not relate to his "matter":

It is true that I had occasion to pass censure upon him when I was endeavouring to recall students from a depraved style, weakened by every kind of error, to a severer standard of taste. But at that time Seneca's works were in the hands of every young man. . . . His style is for the most part corrupt and exceedingly dangerous, for the very reason that its vices are so many and attractive. One could wish that, while he relied on his own intelligence, he had allowed himself to be guided by the taste of others. For if he had only despised all unnatural expressions and had not been so passionately fond of all that was incorrect, if he had not felt such affection for all that was his own and had not impaired the solidity of his matter by striving after epigrammatic brevity [si rerum pondera minutissimus sententiis non fregisset], he would have won the approval of the learned instead of the admiration of boys. (X, i; Loeb Library, IV, pp. 71–73)

For Quintilian Seneca is everything the plain style is not, because his words are not appropriate to his matter. If Quintilian were advising Sprat to seek a style which fulfilled the Royal Society's requirement of "mathematical plainness" and "so many things, almost in an equal number of words," it seems likely he would have gone to Cicero rather than to

Seneca. At any rate Quintilian would not have connected the "Anti-Ciceronianism" of Silver Latin with any sort of plain style.

Yet Seneca, like Quintilian and the other writers on the plain style, also wanted words to equal things. The crucial passage, as we have seen, is in Epistle 114. This letter is a long series of variations on the theme of words approximating things. It places Seneca as a theorist squarely in the tradition of the plain style, from Plato through Cicero and Quintilian. Seneca emphasizes that style is an index of character, as in the comparison noted by Williamson, Cope, and H. W. Jones, of Sallust to his imitator Arruntius, who reveals himself by his shameless copying. "Sallust used the words as they occurred to his mind, while the other writers went afield in search of them." Seneca clearly means here as elsewhere that language reflects moral and psychological "matter," not ideas of concrete objects.[20] In keeping with the tradition, Seneca identifies the decorous plain style with the epistle. He also sees it as the style for philosophy: "A meticulous manner of writing does not suit the philosopher; if he is timid as to words, when will he ever be brave and steadfast, when will he ever show his worth? Fabianus's style was not careless, it was assured. That is why you will find nothing shoddy in his work; his words are well chosen and yet not hunted for." [21] Here Seneca follows Plato's and Cicero's stylistic theory in his assumption that good style is a reflection of an ethical ideal rather than merely a useful means of persuasion. In fact, Cicero is one of Seneca's models, for his "style has unity; it moves with a modulated pace, and is gentle without being degenerate. . . . Mention someone whom you may rank ahead of Fabianus. Cicero, let us say. . . . Or Asinius Pollio. . . . You may also include Livy. . . . But consider how many writers Fabianus outranks, if he is surpassed by these only — and these three the greatest masters of eloquence!" (Ep. c, pp. 153–155). Seneca again identifies with the usual views on the plain style, from Cato's *Rem tene, verba sequentur* on down, even though Croll, Williamson, Cope, and H. W. Jones place him outside it, as an "Anti-Ciceronian." Seneca himself has little but praise for Cicero. Like Quintilian, Seneca proclaims his allegiance to the "Anti-Ciceronian" virtues of the *genus humile*, but the model for both is Cicero! For them Cicero illustrated the Attic graces as well as the "rhetorical excellence" for which, as Croll admits (p. 51), even the Anti-Ciceronians praised him.

While Croll rightly understands the history of ancient style as a struggle between oratory and the *genus humile*, his treatment of that history is oversimplified, as his recent editors demonstrate (p. 46). Croll's placing of Virgil, Cicero, Livy, Catullus, Horace, and St. Augustine as the chief exemplars of oratory, and Lucan, Seneca, Juvenal, Persius, Tacitus, Plutarch, and Epictetus of Atticism, is open to question. Cicero could serve as a model for both styles, and even Livy was admired by all. Horace embodied the *genus humile*. Virgil and Catullus were epic and lyric poets; could they really have affected prose style significantly? Certainly St. Augustine's prose often recalls the rounded periods of Cicero's oratory; but at least the *Confessions* are also intensely intimate in a sort of Christian *genus humile*. In fact, in Book III Augustine tells us how important it was for him to break away from Ciceronian oratory in order to appreciate the sublimity of the lowly Biblical mode. On the other hand, Persius and Martial would appear to be more in the *genus humile* than Tacitus, who has many of the characteristics of the *genus grande*, as does Juvenal on occasion. Seneca, although his theory favored the *genus humile*, did not consistently practice it; he regarded Cicero as a model of good style in general. Seneca is usually intimate and conversational, but is sometimes quite florid, forsaking his own injunctions. Like Bacon, Quintilian agrees with much of Seneca's theory of style but criticizes his practice.

The outlines of ancient "Anti-Ciceronianism" are more confused than Croll realized. The main difficulty comes from Croll's equation of "Anti-Ciceronianism" with the classical plain style. They are not at all the same. Long before Cicero the classical plain style was the customary vehicle for philosophy, comedy, epigram, satire, and epistle. There is little reason to call it "Anti-Ciceronian," since Cicero, at least in his philosophical writings and letters, was one of its foremost practitioners. To be sure, Seneca and Tacitus, Croll's chief "Anti-Ciceronian" prototypes, do not write Ciceronian oratory; but Seneca, after all, is writing epistles and Tacitus history. In fact, apart from a few debatable instances such as Tacitus' *Dialogus* (an attack, like Quintilian's, on slavish Ciceronian imitation, but certainly not on Cicero), one wonders whether there ever was a significant "Anti-Ciceronian" movement in prose style, conscious or unconscious, in antiquity after Cicero's death.

The Classical Plain Style and Anti-Ciceronianism in the Renaissance

I think one can ask the same question about the Renaissance, if not on the continent, then at least in England. Trimpi concedes that if there was Anti-Ciceronianism in the Renaissance, it did not find its models in the literature actually written in antiquity: "If Cicero's features and attitudes are reflected in Ciceronianism, they are barely recognizable, and the same thing may be said of Seneca in the anti-Ciceronian reaction. . . . Throughout the Renaissance the terms [Ciceronian and Senecan] developed an autonomous history of their own which was, for the most part, unrelatable to antiquity" (*Ben Jonson's Poems*, p. 28). Is "Anti-Ciceronian-ism" related to anything that was actually happening in the literature of the Renaissance? If not, the term is meaning-less, an invention of modern scholars with no relation to stylistic history itself, and cannot seriously be considered as the decisive influence on Restoration style.

I think such a position is too extreme. There was an Anti-Ciceronian, and especially Senecan, vogue in England, but far too much has been claimed for it. It was not nearly so intense as its continental counterpart, and I do not think it influenced the English scientists and the Restoration at all. Again we look to the *res-verba* opposition. It is true that at times "Ciceronian" acquires in the Renaissance and later a meaning — an excess of words over things — which re-flected a widespread view of both Cicero and Ciceronians. Erasmus, who of course was influential in England, attacks the Ciceronian in this vein: "Let your first and chief care be to know the subject which you undertake to present. This will furnish you with a wealth of speech and true, natural emotions. Your language will live, breathe, persuade, convince, and fully express yourself." [22] Erasmus' *Cicero-nianus* of 1528 was followed in 1577 by Gabriel Harvey's. Ralph Lever speaks in 1573 of "Ciceronians and sugar tongued fellowes, which labour more for fineness of speach, then for a knowledge of good matter, they speake much to small purpose, and shaking foorth a number of choise words, and picked sentences, they hinder good learning, with their fond chatte." [23] By 1580 Sidney found "Ciceronianisme the chiefe abuse of Oxford, *Qui dum verba sectantur, res ipsas negligunt.*" [24] Then there is Bacon's famous history of Cic-eronian imitation and Montaigne's praise of Seneca's letters, which are better than Cicero's "eloquence, which leaves us with a desire for it, and not of things." [25] The pedant of the Overburian characters "never had meaning in his life, for he travelled only for words. His ambition is criticism, and his example Tully." [26] Williamson lists many more instances.

But Cicero — apparently Cicero as philosopher and letter-writer — is often thought of as a model for an unrhetorical plain style, and more often than Seneca. Such leading Anti-Ciceronians as Vives, Muret (in his later works), and, in England, Jonson cite Cicero himself, and the Ciceronian Horace, as models of plainness. Cicero is certainly an authority on philosophical style for Vives: "If an author expresses his subject matter sufficiently clearly, he has done his job well no matter what words he uses. If one should bring eloquence as an addition to a philosopher, Cicero said, I should not reject it; if one should not bring it, I should not require it, for in all philosophy the art is concerned with meaning and not with expression, and it is better that a philosopher err in words than in truth." [27] Ascham, whose Ciceronian prose is plainer than most "Anti-Ciceronianism," wonders why "Caesar and Cicero's talk is so natural and plain, and Salust's writing so artificial and dark, when they all three lived in one time?" [28] Even as he fights the pedantry of contemporary Ciceronians Muret invokes almost the entire tradition of the classical plain style, including Cicero: "Would I improve your eloquence more if I recommended examples of tropes and schemes and chanted these dictations of the schoolmasters everyday . . . than when I explain the books of Plato's *Republic* or of Cicero's philosophy? True and substantial eloquence is posited not only in words but in subject matter. Moreover, Horace declares: Scribendi recte sapere est in principium et fons./rem tibi Socraticae poterunt ostendere chartae,/verbaque provisam rem non invita sequentur." [29] Jonson is indebted to Cicero, too: "The conceits of the mind are Pictures of things, and the tongue is the Interpreter of those Pictures. . . . He who could apprehend the consequence of things in their truth, and utter his apprehensions as truly, were the best Writer, or Speaker. Therefore *Cicero* said much, when hee said, *Dicere rectè nemo potest, nisi qui prudenter intellegit.*" [30]

Although Seneca's theory is certainly thought of as authoritative for the plain style, the revival of the various genres of the *genus humile* must be attributed in large part to a classical tradition which embraces Cicero as well. Vives' description of epistolary style, for example, is based on Cicero's favorable description of the Attic orator. Vives, well aware of the Ciceronian tradition in descriptions of the plain style, tells us that "most of the ancients" agree with Cicero. Like Cicero, he assumes that in the plain style words equal things, and are an index of character, with the inevitable concomitant that such a style will be conversational. The conversation must be polite and urbane. Epistolary style

ought to be most effective when it expresses, as nearly as possible, conversation and familiar discourse . . . of prudent and learned men. . . . Therefore, most of the ancients considered that a letter should be graced by simplicity and be very refined without adornment, except meanness was to be absent. . . . The ancients, therefore, thought the one rule for writing letters was that *no rule should be applied,* provided first that stupid and muddled sense and a too confusing order be absent, and second that the words of the language be pure in which it was written; for grandiose, finicky, tumid, and affected words they thought did not make a letter graceful but ridiculous, *as peacock plumes on a military helmet.*[31]

Lipsius, the most formidable Anti-Ciceronian of all, quotes freely from the descriptions of the plain style in Demetrius, Horace, and Cicero as well as Seneca. A letter "sets forth clearly myself and those things which concern me . . . even those which are deeper and closed off by walls. *Speculum animi liber* is the old saying: but it is spoken most truly about letters in which our feelings and almost our very thoughts *Are exposed as if engraved on a votive tablet.* . . . In a similar spirit may my familiar conversations and opinions reveal myself and my concerns." [32] Lipsius also uses Cicero's image (in the description of the Attic orator) comparing epistolary style to a simply dressed woman:

Concerning style: certainly . . . it ought to be simple, without careful refinement, and similar to daily speech. Thus Demetrius wished a letter to be writen as if it were a dialogue, & Cicero himself says, *I have concealed it in daily words.* Seneca appropriately says *as my conversation is unlabored and casual, as if we were sitting together or strolling, so do I wish my letters to be.* That which is said to adorn women is not to be adorned ornately; so the letter.[33]

Trimpi has demonstrated that not the avowed Senecans but Ben Jonson, more than any other major English writer, exemplified the classical plain style in its four closely related genres of comedy, satire, epigram, and epistle, as well as in his criticism. The *Discoveries* is completely dominated by the classical tradition of the plain style, from Plato through Cicero and Horace, Seneca, and Quintilian, and their Renaissance counterparts, such as Vives, Lipsius, and Hoskyns. Much of the *Discoveries* is little more than translations of these authorities. The words-things equation controls Jonson's thinking just as it controlled the tradition: "*Language* most shewes a man: speake that I may see thee. It springs out of the most retired, and inmost parts of us, and is the Image of the Parent of it, the mind. No glasse renders a man's forme, or likenesse, so true as his speech." [34]

Yet in his stylistic theory Jonson repeatedly opposed any style which only duplicated the processes of the mind. Fearing the sloppy prose which such a doctrine could lead to, Jonson held for the gentlemanly "pure and neat" style which Trimpi traces through Jonson's original, Vives, to Cicero's Attic orator. Trimpi is struck by "how far Jonson and Vives are, in general attitude, from the extreme Senecans of the sixteenth and seventeenth centuries" (*Ben Jonson's Poems*, p. 48). Barish observes that even in the prose of the comedies, "Where the other baroque writers explicitly dramatize their tensions, in Jonson the tensions remain buried." [35] Like Seneca Jonson, of course, favored asyndeton. Nevertheless Jonson continually warns against excessive abruptness and brevity, qualities which he associates with Seneca's style,

> which hath many breaches, and doth not seem to end, but fall. For Order helpes much to Perspicuity, as Confusion hurts. We should therefore speake what wee can, the nearest way, so as wee keepe our gage, not leape; for too short may as well be not let into our memory, as too long kept in. Whatsoever loseth the grace, and clearenesse, converts into a Riddle; the obscurity is mark'd, but not the valew. (*Discoveries*, pp. 623-642)

Translating Hoskyns' censure of Lipsius, Jonson accuses the Senecans — and perhaps Seneca himself — of prolixity, too many words for the thing:

> As *Quintilian* saith, there is a briefnesse of the parts sometimes, that makes the whole long, as, *I came to the staires, I tooke a paire of oares, they launch'd out, rowed a pace, I landed at the Court-gate, I paid my fayre, went up to the Presence, ask'd for my Lord, I was admitted.* All this is but, *I went to the Court, and spake with my Lord.* This is the fault of some Latine Writers, within these last hundred years, of my reading, and perhaps *Seneca* may be appeacht of it; I accuse him not. (p. 631)

Jonson is defending the main tradition of the classical plain style against its partial corruption at the hands of those who have taken too literally the admonition to let words follow things, or the wanderings of the mind. Such language is without the check of clear-sighted urbanity (Attic, Roman, or London) that distinguishes the true classical plain style, and Jonson's own style. As Barish has shown in *Ben Jonson and the Language of Prose Comedy*, the language of the comedies is indeed asymmetrical and "baroque," rather than "plain and neat." At the same time, though, it is regulated by the classical canons of decorum in a way that "libertine" prose is not. "The triumph of prose as the language of [Jonsonian] comedy, and its convergence with realism, seem by hindsight an almost inevitable outcome of the history of the genre, perhaps the final issue of Aristotle's identification of comic style and comic characters as 'low'" (Barish, p. 273). Jonson, then, understands stylistic theory in terms of the traditional *genera dicendi*, in which comedy was one of the four "plain" or intimate genres. But he does not think in terms of "Ciceronian" versus "Anti-Ciceronian." In fact Jonson, who put Sidney and Livy before Donne and Sallust, regards the arch-Ciceronian Hooker as an excellent stylistic model: "Sir *Philip Sidney*, and Mr. *Hooker* (in different matter) grew great Masters of wit, and language; and in whom all vigour of Invention, and strength of judgement meet" (*Discoveries*, p. 591). This criticism puts Jonson in the Anti-Senecan camp.

The most important Anti-Senecan document is Bacon's, also expressed in the words-things relationship (Senecan style "is nothing else but a hunting after words, and fine placing of them"). For Bacon as well as Jonson Senecan style is opposed to the classical plain style, in which words equal things. Like Quintilian, neither Jonson nor Bacon would recommend Seneca to Sprat as a writer of "so many *things*, almost in an equal number of *words*." Bacon in fact repeats Quintilian's famous censure of Seneca, *Verborum minutiis rerum frangit pondera.*[36]

Although critics commonly speak of the "Senecan" Bacon's reversal of the "Ciceronian" Ascham's favoring of words over things, Ascham and Bacon are criticizing the same kind of writing, though not in quite the same way. Ascham is writing in 1570 before the age assigned by Croll to full-blown "Anti-Ciceronian" imitation, but his criticism of Stoics and libertines evidently is directed at the authors designated by Croll as the precursors of the movement:

For Stoics, Anabaptists, and friars, with epicures, libertines, and monks, being most like in learning and life, are no fonder and pernicious in their opinions, than they be rude and barbarous in their writings. They be not wise, therefore, that say, What care I for man's words and utterance, if his matter and reasons be good? . . . Ye know not what hurt ye do to learning, that care not for words, but for matter; and so make a divorce betwixt the tongue and the heart.[37]

The theorists on the plain style also fear a divorce betwixt the tongue and the heart. What is unusual here is Ascham's attribution of the divorce to overmuch attention to matter, and not enough to words, thus reversing the usual formula. I think Ascham has discovered that the familiar doctrine of things over words logically leads to obscurity and mannerism, rather than a clear revelation of the soul in language. Ascham's writing itself is an instance of his theory — pure English undefiled, intimate, and winning, but kept dignified and elegant by balanced syntax and euphuistic touches. In its engaging polish it embodies the *urbanitas* of the classical plain style, contradicting the Crollian equation of the plain style with "Anti-Ciceronianism." [38]

Some of the rude and barbarous Stoics and libertines of the later Renaissance who strove to end the divorce betwixt heart and tongue by ignoring the usual arrangements of words may illustrate what Ascham had in mind. Jonson, the master of the plain style, censures one Stoic and libertine "Senecan" archetype, Montaigne:

Some, that turne over all bookes, and are equally searching in all papers, that write out of what they presently find or meet, without choice; by which meanes it happens, that what they have discredited, and impugned in one work, they have before, or after, extolled the same in another. Such are all the *Essayists*, even their Master, *Mountaigne*. These, in all they write, confesse still what bookes they have read last; and therein their owne folly, so much, that they bring it to the *Stake* raw and undigested; not that the place did need it neither; but that they thought themselves furnished, and would vent it. (*Discoveries*, pp. 585–586)

The criticism, though aimed only at a specific type of inconsistency, challenges the basis of Montaigne's entire method. As Montaigne never tires of reminding us, he is attempting — literally *essaying* — to give his readers a picture of the writer's inmost being, with no regard for logical consistency. "I ayme at nothing but to display my selfe, who peradventure (if a new prentiship change me) shall be another tomorrow." [39]

Montaigne has some affinities with the classical plain style. But, as Jonson seems to sense instinctively, Montaigne is apart from the main line of the *genus humile*. He is approaching the extreme of the impulse to bare the soul in prose. When this happens, urbanity begins to disappear. *Urbanitas* does not mean stripping off your clothes and rolling up the blinds. Auerbach has observed how far Montaigne is from the intention of the classical plain style in his psychological profundity. As in St. Augustine's *Confessions*, the content of the *Essais*

is the *humaine condition* with all its burdens, pitfalls, and problems, with all its essential insecurity, with all the creatural bonds which confine it. . . . All this is serious and fundamental enough; it is much too high for the *sermo humilis* as understood in antique theory, and yet it could not be expressed in an elevated rhetorical style, without any concrete portrayal of the everyday.[40]

In *The Anatomy of Melancholy*, Burton reminds us almost as often as Montaigne of his indebtedness to the general intention and actual sources of the classical plain style. Burton "respects matter" but accuses his literary opponents of being "wholly for words." [41] Like some of his Roman predecessors, he enlarges the province of the plain style as far as the mind itself. This is understandable, since the style seeks to represent the mind as a whole:

I am therefore in this point a professed disciple of Apollonius, a scholar of *Socrates*, I neglect phrases and labour wholly to inform my reader's understanding, not to please his ear; 'tis not my study or intent to compose neatly, which an Orator requires, but to express myself readily and plainly as it happens. So that, as a river runs sometimes precipitate and swift, then dull and slow, now direct, then *per ambages,* now deep, then shallow, now muddy, then clear, now broad, then narrow, doth my style flow; now serious, then light, now comical, then satirical, now more elaborate, then remiss, as the present subject required or as at that time I was affected. (*Anatomy*, I, p. 32)

What Burton produces, however, is not the urbane, familiar utterance of the classical plain style, but one of the queerest and most private works of the age. The demand of "libertines" like Montaigne and Burton for complete freedom of subject matter is, to be sure, an extension of the theory of *res et verba* of the classical plain style. If words can equal things, they can equal any thing in the mind at all; hence Juvenal's *quicquid agunt homines* as the explicit subject of Burton's *Anatomy* as well as Horace's and Pliny's emphasis on rapidly shifting moods and subjects. But the libertine associationism of a Montaigne or a Burton is not really in the tradition of the classical plain style, even though that style is its point of departure. Suppose we take the dogma of self-revelation literally, as Montaigne and Burton do. The ultimate result is, to use the inevitable example, something along the order of the monologues revealing the unconscious minds of the characters in *Ulysses* or *Finnegans Wake* or, for that matter, the disjointed oddities of the ultimate in self-revelation, the psychoanalytic interview. Such writing and talking, of course, is not what the classical tradition had in mind. It is at the opposite extreme from the easy conversational clarity the ancients sought. The assumption of the classical plain style, that well-bred conversation would be the mirror of the mind, we now see is inadequate. Burton and Montaigne are part of the way toward Joyce. In other words, the theory of the *genus humile* is, if taken literally, ultimately contradictory. The prose after a while is not plain at all.

The paradoxical tendency of the "plain" style to evolve into mannerisms, associationism, queerness, and obscurity is recognized in Croll's comment that "Anti-Ciceronian" prose "is no more a bare, unadorned, unimaginative style than the oratorical style is" (*Style*, p. 89). And Williamson demonstrates how "Senecanism" ancient and modern imbibed the devices of Euphuism, and that these are the very Gorgian-Isocratic-Ciceronian devices that "Anti-Ciceronianism" supposedly reacted against. One can only concur with R. F. Jones that it is hard to believe such a style could serve as a model for the likes of a Sprat or a Dryden.

Richard Whitlock's *Zootomia* (1654) illustrates as well as anything else how self-conscious, mannered, obscure, and private libertine prose could become. Whitlock extravagantly admires all the libertine favorites, including Seneca, Plutarch, Montaigne, and Hall. But Whitlock insists that he does not *imitate* them. His proud motto is *"to let the World know I think not as shee thinketh."* [42] He is trying not to imitate anyone, but to write in his own distinctive way, even for himself alone.

Instructions (Courteous *Reader*) that render the *Designe* and Purpose of the *Work*, may well be stiled an *Essay* upon the *Author*, and as it were *Contents*, of *him*, no lesse than the *Book*; and so may well supply the room of a *Dedicatory Epistle* to some protecting *Eminence*, or of courting *Apologies*, like *forlorne hopes* first sent out to set *upon* the *Benevolence* of Readers. . . . Instead of other kindes of *Epistles*, take therefore this *Anatomy* of the *Anatomy*, (the Book it self) by way of a *Preface*; and so not tied to the shortness usual of *Epistles*; it may serve for an *Essay* on Mens *Publications* of Themselves by *Writing*, and more especially on mine. (p. 3)

The ultimate origins of this bizarre and self-conscious mode in the classical plain style, and especially in the epistolary

genre, are apparent from the start. But the coy little jokes
(Anatomy of the Anatomy); the playful, offhand Euphu-
isms (forlorne hopes first sent out to set upon); the many
parenthetical expressions; and the capitalization and italiciza-
tion, more whimsical than even the loose standards of the
age allowed, all call attention to self-revelation more than
in the usual classical plain style. Significantly, though Whitlock carefully tells us that he is aware of the traditions
governing epistolary form, he is at great pains to let us
know that his epistle is unlike the "other kindes." Finally,
and perhaps most important for this study because of the
total contrast to the ideals of the Restoration and the Royal
Society, Whitlock's *dulce* takes precedence over systematic
utile. His teacher is Montaigne:

Je aime en generall les liures, qui usent les sciences, non ceux
qui les dressent. *I love, saith he, books that make use of* Sciences,
not compile *them into their* Geneticall, *or* Analyticall *Parcels.*
Authors (to say true) are more Thumb'd *that are* variously usefull, *than those* Embodyers *of* Arts *in* Cancellos suae Methodi,
into the limits *of their* proper Method: usefull *I confesse they
are, but wanting the* Dulce, Pleasure *of* variety, *and convenience
of more* contracted brevity: *the* paines *of* reading *them is seldom
bestowed on them, especially if they* swell *into* Tomes *of that*
bignesse, *that he that can have no* leisure, *dareth not look on
them.* (pp. 8-9)

The most readable style reproduces the contours of thought
processes. "*As* Montaigne *saith of himselfe,* Tracts *of a* continued Thread *are* tedious *to most* fancies, *which of it selfe
indeed is of that* desultory *nature, that it is pleased with*
Writings *like* Irish Bogs, *that it may* leap *from one* variety
to another, than tread *any* beaten Path" (p. 9). *Zootomia* is
like those modern Irish Bogs, *Ulysses* and *Finnegans Wake,*
in that these associations, rather than a standardized grammar, determine the syntax. Always we hear the "voice" of
the author:

Would you know . . . my manner of writing? it is a kind of
voluntary Tiding of, *not* Pumping for; Notions flowing, *not*
forced; *like* Poets unconstrained Heats *and* Raptures: *such is*
mine, *rather* a running Discourse *than a* Grave-paced Exactness;
having in them this Formality *of* Essayes (as *Sir* W. Cornwallyes
saith of his) *that they are* Tryals *of bringing my* hand *and*
Fancy acquainted *in this using my* Paper, *as the* Painters Boy
a Board *he blurs with* Tryals (p. 17).

A famous example of a more artfully controlled libertinism[43] is the *Religio Medici* (1642). As an instance of the
striving of libertine prose toward its ideal of illuminating a
wide but very personal range of mental experience in a
way foreign to the Restoration and the Royal Society, and
as one of the supreme examples of the "Anti-Ciceronianism"
to which the age after Browne objected, we would do well
to examine it.

It is a justified commonplace of criticism that Browne as
an essayist is closer to the continental tradition of Montaigne
than to Bacon. In the preface to the *Religio* Browne repeats
Montaigne's desire that language follow mental associations.
But Browne holds that *rhetoric* best illustrates his special
intention, which is self-revelation rather than reasoned exposition.

This, I confess, about seven years past, with some others, of
affinity thereto, for my private exercise and salvation, I had at
leisurable hours composed. . . . He that shall peruse that work,
and shall take notice of sundry particularities and personal expressions therein, will easily discern the intention was not publick; and, being a private Exercise directed to my self, what is
delivered therein, was rather a memorial unto *me*, than an Example or Rule unto any other; and therefore, if there be any
singularity therein correspondent with the private conceptions
of any man, it doth not advantage them. . . . It was set down
many years past, and was the sense of my conceptions at that
time, not an immutable law unto my advancing judgement at
all times; and therefore there might be many things therein
plausible unto my passed apprehension, which are not agreeable
unto my present self. There are many things delivered Rhetori-

cally, many expressions therein merely Tropical, and as they best illustrate my intention; and therefore also there are many things to be taken in a soft and flexible sense, and not to be called unto the rigid test of Reason.[44]

What distinguishes Browne from the Restoration theorists — and perhaps barred him from the Royal Society — is the high value he places on "things" delivered Rhetorically to illustrate his private conceptions. Even though merely Tropical, the language best suited to them is of value. What we find here is not a flight into an aesthetic hedonism but an Elizabethan respect for rhetoric. The Restoration and the Royal Society chose to ignore mannered self-revelation on the utilitarian grounds, conceded by Browne in his disarming way, that "it doth not advantage anyone." A passage from the *Religio* illustrates how rhetoric serves Browne's intention:

By this means I leave no gap for Heresies, Schisms, or Errors, of which at present I hope I shall not injure Truth to say I have no taint or tincture. I must confess my greener studies have been polluted with two or three; not any begotten in the latter Centuries, but old and obsolete, such as could never have been revived, but by such extravagant and irregular heads as mine: for indeed Heresies perish not with their Authors, but, like the river Arethusa, though they lose their currents in one place, they rise up again in another. One General Counsel is not able to extirpate one single Heresie: it may be cancell'd for the present; but revolution of time, and the like aspects from Heaven, will restore it, when it will flourish till it be condemned again. For it is as though there were a Metempsychosis, and the soul of one man passed into another. Opinions do find, after certain Revolutions, men and minds like those that first begat them. To see ourselves again, we need not look for Plato's year; every man is not only himself; there hath been many Diogenes, and as many Timons, though but few of that name; men are liv'd over again; the world is now as it was in Ages past; there was none then, but there hath been some one since that parallels him, and is, as it were, his revived self. (pp. 6–7)

Browne's chief interest is not in the logic or clarification of his argument, which would have been the concern of a Restoration writer, but rather in his own attitude and relationship to heresies and to the feelings and associations that heresies evoke in his own extravagant and irregular head. Browne spins out his associations for us as they come to him in what Croll called the "trailing effect" of Anti-Ciceronianism. The revival of "old and obsolete" heresies reminds Browne that ideas never perish; this, in turn, recalls the attempts of unsuccessful Councils to stamp out heresy; then Browne is reminded of the effects of time on ideas, the precedence of our entire character or fate in the past, and finally the wistful conclusion to the effect that there is nothing new under the sun. From the experience of one among many — the experience of the single extravagant and irregular head himself — Browne moves to The One, the revolutions of Time and our collective Pythagorean and Platonic immortality. Not that Browne necessarily believes in such an immortality — "it is as though there were" one — but the metaphor, with its touch of Pythagorean mysticism, suggests the remoteness and wonder in which Browne envelops the bare fact of recurring heresies. The remoteness and wonder are part of the idea itself. Metaphor is idea rather than, as in the Restoration or "scientific" prose, an explanation of ideas.

Rather than explanation, Browne seeks a series of impressions or associations, closer to the way in which mental experience actually takes place. In Browne there is little of the Restoration's attempt to separate tenor from vehicle, referent from reference, with the intention of making the logic of the argument clearer. Such separation would be impossible in Browne's richly analogical world. Heresy, because it returns, is like a revolution or circle (the controlling image of the entire *Religio*). Everything we can reckon time by, including the advent of ideas, comes back; so time itself is like a circle, too. Heresies are repeated, then, in the "revolutions of time." Ideas are "begotten," die, and are resurrected, and so it is with all things: "the world is now as it was in Ages past." The mingling of the cozily subjective concrete with the objective abstract naturally suggests the climactic parts of the passage, "As though there were a Metempsychosis, and the soul of one man passed into another," and "the world is now as it was in Ages past." Other comparisons enrich the meaning; for example, Browne uses the "river Arethusa" to exploit the natural connotation of any river's seemingly eternal current, and the creative, regenerative significance of this one in particular, the maiden renewed by Artemis eternally as water, appearing intermittently like the "Metempsychosis" of the heresies of history. Above all, Browne suggests the "revolutions of time" in the circular balance of his periods, with their careful alternation of tenses, working against the inexorable straight line of the forward thrust of his associations until they dissolve, in the end, into vistas of eternity and an "O altitudo!" The progression from the slack, chatty intimacy of "I must confess my greener studies" and "my extravagant and irregular head" to the austere, stately cadences of Browne's meditation on eternity at the end illustrates the wide stylistic range, abhorrent to the Restoration, of libertine prose. All the while Browne never lets us forget the concrete, intimate experience — the "hope" of Browne "at present" — which is inseparable from the eternal Idea. Words describe thoughts, in the fullest sense of the word, and it is rhetoric which best illustrates Browne's intention, in a sort of colloidal suspension of associations.

It was exactly this type of prose that the Royal Society and the Restoration rejected.

The Classical Plain Style and Christianity in the Seventeenth Century

Neither Browne's rhetoric nor Whitlock's seeming art-lessness reflects the ideals of the classical plain style, despite certain resemblances. All classical literature depends on assumptions about *mimesis*, the imitation or representation of reality. In classical *mimesis* words do not equal things, in the sense either of Sprat's physical substances or Whitlock's subjective self. Rather the ideal artist is a "maker," a creator of objects beyond observed nature and corresponding as much as possible to a Platonic Ideal of Truth.[45] The *loci critici* for classical *mimesis* in English are Sidney's *Apologie* and Jonson's *Discoveries*. For Jonson a poet

is that which by the *Greeks* is call'd . . . a Maker or fainer; His art, an Art of imitation or faining; expressing the life of man in fit measure, numbers, and harmony; according to *Aristotle*. . . . Hence he is call'd a *Poet*, not hee which writeth in measure only; but that fayneth and formeth a fable and writes like the Truth. For the Fable and Fiction is (as it were) the forme and Soule of any Poeticall worke. (*Discoveries*, Herford and Simpson, VIII, p. 635)

Although the emphasis in the theory of the classical plain style on *verba* following *res* might suggest (and did, to some of the libertines) an abandonment of the standard devices of "Art" in favor of such eccentric modes as Whitlock's or Browne's associationism, in fact the classical plain style demanded an artificial copy of an Ideal Soul, the Self of an ideal Attic or Roman or London gentleman or, in Jonson's comedies, the Typical Gull or Mistress. Jonson's emphasis, for all his realism and asymmetry, is on the creation of an artificial thing. The representation of an Ideal Soul requires an Ideal Style, subject to its own rules of "Art" and decorum. Thus Jonson, following in the tradition of the *Apologie*, preferred "Sidney before Donne," conscious artifice before feigned artlessness, the classical plain style before libertine self-revelation. Jonson's "maker" carries this doctrine to its extreme form, for he must imitate or copy other writers already in possession of the Ideal. This is Jonson's procedure in that extraordinary anthology, the *Discoveries*. *Mimesis* is then imitation of an imitation.

The libertine writer, on the other hand, reflects a different ideal of *mimesis*. Its roots, as Auerbach's *Mimesis* shows, lie in the Judeo-Christian experience. Auerbach distinguishes between the two principal modes of "the literary representation of reality in European culture":

The two styles, in their opposition, represent basic types: on the one hand, fully externalized description, uniform illumination, uninterrupted connection, free expression, all events in the foreground, displaying unmistakable meanings, few elements of historical development and of psychological perspective; on the other hand certain parts brought into high relief, others left obscure, abruptness, suggestive influence of the unexpressed, "background" quality, multiplicity of meanings and the need for interpretation, universal-historical claims, development of the concept of the historically becoming, and preoccupation with the problematic. (p. 19)

The plain style, of all the three classical "characters" which together comprise the first of these two modes, comes closest to Auerbach's Judeo-Christian "paratactic" mode, the second described in the preceding quotation. Parataxis in the form of asyndeton is one of the main distinguishing traits of "Anti-Ciceronianism." As Horace, Pliny, and Juvenal expanded the *res* of the plain style to include all subject matter and emotional attitudes, including those formerly reserved for the *genus nobile*, so the realism of Judeo-Christian *mimesis* uses a plain style for all things and effects, including the sublime. But what the theorists and practitioners of the classical plain style actually sought was not what Croll calls "the attempt to portray the immediate motions of the mind" or "the process of acquiring the truth rather than the secure possession of it" (*Style*, p. 89).

Rather, they wanted an all-purpose Good Style which would never go out of fashion or seem merely idiosyncratic and which would reveal the Ideal Urbane Soul. Of Jonson's "true artificer"

an other Age, or juster men, will acknowledge the vertues of his studies: his wisdome, in dividing: his subtilty, in arguing; with what strength hee doth inspire his Readers; with what sweetnesse hee strokes them; in inveighing, what sharpenesse; in Jest, what urbanity hee uses. How he doth raigne in mens affections; how invade, and breake in upon them; and makes their minds like the thing he writes. (*Discoveries*, pp. 587–588)

This is an Ideal, not an ideal of self-revelation. Trimpi rightly sees a conflict not between Ciceronians and Anti-Ciceronians, but between two contradictory tendencies in the classical plain style:

The Socratic and Stoic attitude toward experience and the literary analysis and expression of personal experience in the *sermo* remain the same for Jonson and Vives as for the Senecans. But whereas the Senecans, especially those of the Libertine movement, tended more and more to use the *sermo* to reveal personal idiosyncrasy until the plain style itself became eccentrically mannered, Vives and Jonson retained, as an idea, the *sermo* as described by Cicero in his discussion of the Attic orator. (*Ben Jonson's Poems*, p. 53)

Cause-and-effect relations in such large matters are all but impossible to prove. I think it could be shown, though, that Judeo-Christian realism, more than Senecan imitation, pulled all plain styles toward extreme and often eccentric self-revelation. These styles ranged from Browne's stately cadences to the confessions of the "Enthusiasts." The same impulse figures in a work as early as Erasmus' *Ciceronianus*, which is for Williamson the best possible introduction to Anti-Ciceronianism. The style which Erasmus opposes to

Cicero's is not Williamson's Senecan Amble, however, but a specifically Christian way of writing: "If Cicero's style was lacking in manly vigor, do you think it appropriate for Christians, whose every plan looks rather to living virtuously than to speaking ornately and elegantly, from whose lives all paint and theatrical effects ought to be far removed?" [46] In Christian, as opposed to classical imitation, words designate the immediate motions of the inmost soul rather than an elegant and ornate ideal. "What conclusion, then, except that we may learn from Cicero himself how to imitate Cicero? Let us imitate him as he imitated others" (p. 81). What Erasmus means is that Cicero, unlike contemporary Ciceronians, did not copy pedantically. To be true Ciceronians,

Let us care first for thoughts, then for words; let us adapt the words to the subjects, not subjects to words. . . . Thus, in short, will the oration be alive only when it is born in the heart and does not float on the lips. The precepts of art let us not ignore, for they contribute most to the invention, disposition, and handling of arguments . . . but, when a serious case is to be handled, let wisdom hold the first place. . . . Cicero has written that the soul of Laelius breathed forth in his writings; but it is stupid for you to try to write with the taste of another and to take pains that the soul of Cicero may breathe forth from your writings. (p. 81)

For "Nature too who intended speech to be a mirror of the mind rebels against that effort" (p. 121) to imitate slavishly the tricks of another writer. The Christian should favor "imitation that aids rather than hinders nature," that is, a culling of writers not antagonistic to one's own native genius, "not just adding to your speech all the beautiful things that you find, but digesting them and making them your own, so that they may seem to have been born from your mind" (p 123).

The *Ciceronianus*, then, is not an attack on Cicero, whom Erasmus defends whenever he can, but on a pedantic corruption of classical *mimesis* foreign to the methods of Cicero himself. As Izora Scott shows in her essay on the sixteenth-century controversies on Cicero, Erasmus' many followers agreed with his statement in a letter to his friend de Brie: "In my *Ciceronianus* I do not condemn the style of Cicero. I have always attributed to him so much that others, compared to him however eloquent, grow dumb. But I have condemned the foolish affectation of Ciceronian diction" (*Controversies*, p. 26). The nearest approximation in antiquity to Christian candor is not Seneca but that model of the classical plain style, Horace. "As soon as I became more familiar with Horace, all others, in comparison to him, began to offend. What do you think was the reason for this . . . ? This genuine, native quality does not breathe out in the language of those who express nothing but Cicero" (*Ciceronianus*, p. 122). Seneca, in fact, hardly appears at all in the dialogue, and then merely as another rhetorician, not to be copied any more than Cicero.

Thus for Erasmus as for Bacon nearly a century later, both Cicero and Seneca are in the category of authors whom we must not copy slavishly because such imitation is foreign to our special situations. Many other "Anti-Ciceronians" are Anti-Senecan as well, and for similar reasons. We have already encountered this Anti-Senecanism in Bacon and Jonson, and they are not alone. For example, in Sir Henry Savile's translation of Tacitus in 1591 we find Silver Latin condemened as "that bastard Rhetorick" and "a kind of Sophisticate Eloquence, and Rhyming Harmony of Words, whereunder was small matter in Sense, when there seemed to be most in appearance." It is "that Heresie of Style begun by *Seneca, Quintilian, the Plinies*, and *Tacitus*." [47] For Jonson, Bacon, Savile, and others, the important division is between the plain style and oratory not between Seneca or Tacitus and Cicero. As Williamson's documentation in *The Senecan Amble* shows, Cicero and Seneca are often compared as examples of contrasting types of *eloquence*. The comparison has been standard at least since Quintilian. What Williamson does not observe is that only rarely (a possible example is Cornwallis' essay "Of Vanity" [48]) do we find a comparison of "eloquent" Cicero with "plain" or "philosophical" Seneca. Seneca was not ordinarily a model for authors seeking to write in a "plain" style. It would be hard to believe, then, that the stylistic platform of the Royal Society is, as Croll contends, a "revision" of a pervasive Senecan imitation. Most Restoration and "scientific" prose, as I shall try to show, represents an attempt to avoid imitation, classical or Christian, altogether.

Before going on, however, it is worth while noting that in the Renaissance the desire for plainness — for words to approximate mental things — comes from many sources other than those we have been describing. Some of these influences have been suggested in the scholarship on the Croll-Jones controversy, as can be seen in the long footnote at the end of my first chapter. So numerous are these influences, in fact, that Senecan imitation — if it ever was a force for plainness at all — seems insignificant by comparison. Except for a few essayists and character-writers Williamson's description of Senecanism as the "most incisive pattern" (p. 9) in the prose of the seventeenth century seems an exaggeration. The force of Williamson's vast documentation is reduced by his attributing almost every instance of brevity, plainness, or sententiousness to a variety of direct Senecan imitation.

Similarly, too much has been explained by the "scientific" influence. "The notion that prose writing before 1660 was largely ornate and poetical, and that a plain, workaday, modern style was first inaugurated after the Restoration, chiefly through the efforts of the Royal Society to develop this along with other elements of its Baconian heritage" Douglas Bush, who has read as much seventeenth-century prose as anyone, regards as a "vulgar error" for the correction of which "we have only to think of the vast bulk of plain writing in books of travel, history, biography, politics, economics, science, education, religion, and much popular literature. Plain prose was the natural medium for most kinds of utilitarian writing, and most writing was utilitarian. . . . Dryden and his fellows represented a culmination rather than a beginning." [49] Many of the voluminous Puritan writings of the first part of the century, to take the chief example of a plain style outside both "Senecanism" and "science," represent a far more widespread movement toward a plain style. They also illustrate our chief present interest, the effects of the Christian mode of expression on a plain style. These plain Puritans, unlike Milton, ignored classical writers as stylistic models; in fact, as Jones has shown in *The Triumph of the English Language*, the movement is anticlassical and closely allied to the general revival of the vernacular as well as to the new anti-Aristotelian Ramist logic. The Puritan "upholders of plainness are far removed from classical model or classical authorities, and they do not develop any suggestion of the particular stylistic ideal demanded by the Anti-Ciceronians. Furthermore, their ascetic and utilitarian spirit possessed little in common with the literary spirit animating Anti-Ciceronianism." [50]

The plain sermon is also in part a reaction to the unfettered libertinism of preachers like Andrewes, Adams, and Donne. Some of these Anglican preachers, following the fathers of the church, cultivated a kind of third-hand Senecanism. But these were neither numerous nor influential despite their invariable inclusion in modern anthologies. Miller and Haller have told us how in old and New England Puritan plain style reflected not classical urbanity or libertine self-revelation but the utilitarian necessities of teaching the unlettered.[51] Bunyan and Baxter, in their different ways, are the later culmination of Puritan plain style.

Its utilitarian emphasis foreshadows the theory of style in the Restoration; its passionate austerity is profoundly Christian, and especially Protestant. The connection between moderate Puritan and Restoration plain style is best seen in Glanvill's admiration for Baxter and his style, which has at once a "sweet kind of irresistible violence" and a "smartness" and "coherence" which "overpowers opposition." [52]

Among the Enthusiasts, of course, an Augustinian introspection — another characteristic of Protestantism — overpowers the utilitarian virtues of smartness and coherence. Eventually this emphasis drives some Puritan prose into the "Enthusiasm" condemned by men like Glanvill and Sprat. Throughout the Restoration the attack on Enthusiasm is closely connected with the attack on libertine prose, for both are guilty, in the eyes of a Restoration Anglican like Glanvill, of the rhetorical individualism and appeal to the "affections" through figurative language which the Anti-Fanatick Theologie and the Free Philosophy sought to correct. [53]

Res et Verba, *Things and Words: Seventeenth-Century Plain Style*

The New Plain Style and the New Philosophy

The attitudes of the Royal Society and the Restoration toward things and words were adumbrated half a century earlier in Bacon. As we saw in Chapter Two, he rejects Senecan imitation because, like Ciceronianism, it leads to useless verbal notions and disputes. But he does accept, in some ways, the ideals of the classical plain style as defined (if not always practiced) by Seneca. Jonson, the style's chief contemporary spokesman and practitioner, lauded Bacon for condemning the study of words as the first distemper of learning. Jonson's famous praise of Bacon was adapted from a passage in Seneca the Elder:

Yet there hapn'd, in my time, one noble *Speaker*, who was full of gravity in his speaking. His language, (where hee could spare, or passe by a jest) was nobly *censorious*. No man ever spake more neatly, more pres[t]ly, more weightily, or suffer'd less emptinesse, lesse idlenesse, in what hee utter'd. No member of his speech, but consisted of [his] owne graces: His hearers could not cough, or looke aside from him, without losse. Hee commanded where hee spoke; and had his Judges angry, and pleased at his devotion. No man had their affections more in his power. The feare of every man that heard him, was, lest hee should make an end.[1]

Although Jonson is describing Bacon the orator, the praise applies to Bacon's aphoristic prose as well. In the tradition of the classical plain style, Bacon, like Jonson, defines a desirable prose style in terms of the relation of words and things:

So that these four causes concurring, the admiration of ancient authors, the hate of the schoolmen, the exact study of languages, and the efficacy of preaching, did bring in an affectionate study of eloquence and copie of speech, which then began to flourish. This grew speedily to an excess; for men began to hunt more after words than matter. . . . Here therefore is the first distemper of learning, when men study words and not matter. . . . It seems to me that Pygmalion's frenzy is a good emblem or portraiture of this vanity: for words are but the images of matter; and except they have life of reason and invention, to fall in love with them is all one as to fall in love with a picture.[2]

The basis of the classical plain style is the Socratic distinction between, on the one hand, oratory, in which words are a remote copy of reality, and, on the other, the "essay" or "philosophical" style, in which words signify "matter" or "things." Similarly, for Bacon true philosophical method ("the life of reason and invention") deals directly with "matter." As such, it must be inductive rather than syllogistic: "The syllogism is not applied to the first principles of sciences, and is applied in vain to intermediate axioms; being no match for the subtlety of nature. It commands assent therefore to the proposition, but does not take hold of the things." If words are to take hold of things, then philosophical language must represent the course of inductive reasoning. "Knowledge that is delivered as a thread to be spun on, ought to be delivered and intimated, if it were possible, *in the same method wherein it was invented;* and so it is possible of knowledge induced . . . A man may re-

visit and descend unto the foundations of his knowledge
and consent; and so transplant it into another as it grew in
his own mind (*Advancement*, pp. 289–290). As in the conventional theory of the classical plain style, a "philosophical"
mode, which comprises Bacon's "Probative," "Initiative,"
and "Aphoristic" styles, duplicates the motions of the
writer's mind. Both the classical plain style and Baconian
plain style start from observations of concrete particulars
and move to precepts and generalizations. Both styles are
adaptable to a wide range of subject matter. Both oppose a
plain, truthful, inductive style to an oratorical style for
persuasion, deceit, aesthetic pleasure, or individual glory.
Both understand good writing as an index of thought, rather
than as a bag of showy tricks or mannerisms.

For as knowledges are now delivered, there is a kind of contract
of error between the deliverer and the receiver: for he that
delivereth knowledge desireth to deliver it in such form as may
be best believed, and not as may be best examined; and he that
receiveth knowledge desireth rather present satisfaction than
expectant inquiry; and so rather not to doubt than not to err:
glory making the author not to lay open his weakness, and sloth
making the disciple not to know his strength. (p. 289)

Despite these apparent similarities in theory of style, however, Bacon's stylistic practice is unlike the classical plain
style. Bacon himself thought his Probative Style was, if not
entirely new, at least quite rare, a "via deserta et interclusa"
(p. 289). It is the impersonality of Bacon's plain style — in
fact, of all his styles — which distinguishes him most obviously from the tradition of the classical plain style. As we
have seen, the contrast is most obvious between Bacon's
essays and Montaigne's. Bacon's essays are more impersonal
than even the chilly ones — scarcely Jonson's at all —
incorporated into the *Discoveries*. Bacon's letters are similarly cool and unrevealing, as are most of his aphorisms
on natural phenomena and collections of epigrams, apo-

thegms, and the like. Bacon never resorts, in his philosophical writings, to the Montaignesque monologue or the Platonic dialogue of the tradition of the classical plain style;
instead he uses austere aphorisms or, more commonly,
the formal "Methods" of the "Magistral" style. Of the
four genres of the classical plain style — comedy, satire,
epistle, and epigram — Bacon practiced only the last two,
and these in a way fundamentally unlike his alleged predecessors.

There is, then, an apparent contradiction between Bacon's
actual stylistic impersonality in his plain style and his
ideal of words as the record of the gradual growth of
"knowledge and consent" in the mind. The contradiction
can be resolved once we understand what Bacon means by
the kind of "matter" or "things" which are to be recorded.
Unlike all the theoreticians of the classical plain style, Bacon
means by "things" objective physical reality and its causes,
existing before and after the writer's perception of them
and independent of him. The Baconian writer, like his ideal
researcher, submits his mind to these things, rather than
constructing a mental edifice of his own according to some
ideal pattern or looking within himself to relate the physical
world to his own private concerns. But in the classical plain
style "things" are intellectual and subjective, not physical
and objective. In Croll's words, the *res* are "the candor of
the soul. . . . the secret experiences of arduous and solitary
minds . . . exploring unfamiliar truth by the unaided exercise of its [the soul's] own faculties." [3] Baconian theory,
with its emphasis on the passivity of the faculties, and its
distrust of their unguided exercise, is in effect a denial of
the classical plain style, as well as Christian *mimesis*. Well
might Bacon have regarded his new style as a "via deserta
et interclusa!"

Bacon's equivalence of "things" to objective physical
reality and the consequences for his philosophical or plain

style are apparent throughout his works but nowhere more unequivocally than in the famous discussion of the four Idols in the first book of the *Novum Organum*. Much of that work is an attack on the notion that the unguided exercise of our faculties can take us to the truth. The mind fails, says Bacon, because it mistakes mental constructions (which would include the *res* of the classical plain style) for reality, which for Bacon is seen in the behavior of physical things. We are deceived because we put our faith in the words our faculties, unassisted by "helps," produce.

There is no soundness in our notions whether logical or physical. Substance, Quality, Action, Passion, Essence itself, are not sound notions: much less are Heavy, Light, Dense, Rare, Moist, Dry, Generation, Corruption, Attraction, Repulsion, Element, Matter, Form, and the like; but all are fantastical and ill defined.

Our notions of less general species, as Man, Dog, Dove, and of the immediate perceptions of the sense, as Hot, Cold, Black, White, do not materially mislead us; yet even these are sometimes confused by the flux and alteration of matter and the mixing of one thing with another. All the others which men have hitherto adopted are but wanderings, not being abstracted and formed from things by proper methods. (*Works*, VIII, p. 70, Aphorisms xv–xvi)

This nominalistic position dominates Bacon's discussion of "the most troublesome" (p. 86, Aphorism lix) of the Idols, that of the Market-place.

Let us take for example such a word as *humid;* and see how far the several things which the word is used to signify agree with each other; and we shall find the word *humid* to be nothing else than a mark loosely and confusedly applied to denote a variety of actions which will not bear to be reduced to any constant meaning. For it both signifies that which easily spreads itself round any other body; and that which in itself is indeterminate and cannot solidise; and that which readily yields in every direction; and that which easily divides and scatters itself; and that which easily unites and collects itself; and that which readily flows and is put into motion; and that which readily clings to another body and wets it; and that which is easily reduced to a liquid, or which being solid easily melts. Accordingly when you come to apply the word, — if you take it in one sense, flame is humid; if in another, air is not humid; if in another, fine dust is humid; if in another, glass is humid. So that it is easy to see that the notion is taken by abstraction only from water and common and ordinary liquids, without any due verification. (p. 88, Aphorism lx)

If we reduce words as near to things as possible — to marks or arbitrarily designed counters which are univocal representations of equally arbitrarily marked-off chunks or qualities or causes of physical reality — we shall have arrived at a true understanding of nature. For Bacon holds that words which imply value judgments (for example, Final Cause, Natural Desire), because they depend on personal opinions rather than exist as arbitrary signs of things, are meaningless when applied to objective physical reality.

"Utility," however, is an exception — the one value-word applicable to physical reality which does not refer to our understanding of the physical bodies themselves. Therefore "utility" is a legitimate term for Bacon. If, as he says, it is dangerous to call something "humid," it is incomparably more dangerous to call it by such appallingly subjective terms as "good" or "sad" or "beautiful," or to talk about its Final Cause. But for Bacon there is no harm in calling it "useful" since that adjective does not refer to our understanding of the thing itself or to one of its causes but only to the end to which we can put it once we understand what it is. Once we have rid ourselves of all subjective interpretations of nature — the same subjective interpretations which are the very essence of the classical plain style — all that will be left are truths about things and utility. Indeed, Bacon goes further, in saying that utility is "the very same thing" as truth, divine as well as secular. In fact, knowledge is even more valuable as a revelation of God's "exquisite" handiwork ("truth") than as "contributions to the comforts of life":

Again, it will be thought, no doubt, that the goal and mark of knowledge which I myself set up (the very point which I object to in others) is not the true or the best; for that the contemplation of truth is a thing worthier and loftier than all utility and magnitude of works; and that this long and anxious dwelling with experience and matter and the fluctuations of individual things, drags the mind down to earth. . . . Now to this I readily assent. . . . For I am building in the human understanding a true model of the world, such as it is in fact, not such as a man's own reason would have it to be; a thing which cannot be done without a very diligent dissection and anatomy of the world. But I say that those foolish and apish images of worlds which the fancies of men have created in philosophical systems, must be utterly scattered to the winds. Be it known then how vast a difference there is . . . between the Idols of the human mind and the Ideas of the divine. The former are nothing more than arbitrary abstractions; the latter are the Creator's own stamp upon creation, impressed and defined in matter by true and exquisite lines. Truth therefore and utility are here the very same things: and works themselves are of greater value as pledges of truth than as contributing to the comforts of life. (pp. 156–157, Aphorism cxxiv)

Actually Bacon seeks a certain kind of truth. "Truth" itself is as much an abstraction as the scholastical terms Bacon attacked. "What we should doubtless have liked to get from Bacon," writes Basil Willey, "is a classification of the meanings of such words as 'Truth.' " [4] Willey argues well that for the most part "Truth" is the "satisfying explanations" or descriptions demanded by each age. Theological and some moral dogma excepted, for Bacon the only true or satisfying explanations or descriptions were useful ones. These would lead to "works" for the "comforts of life" instead of wordy, useless debates. Only in the "diligent dissection and anatomy of the world" of Bacon's inductive "contemplation" was there freedom from "foolish and apish" verbosity, as well as the possibility of future "works." Bacon was thus able to provide the age with a satisfying kind of argument from design for the skill and glory of the Creator and arrived at a pious justification of Baconian investigation.

This marriage of utility and truth, rather than the moral force and urbanity of the classical plain style or the individualism of libertinism, fixes the character of Bacon's plain style. Bacon's "Probative" and "Aphoristic" style is the record of the passive apprehension of sense data. The writer does not indicate his own attitudes. It is, as we have seen, a most useful style, and to be useful a style must be clear. Otherwise no one will benefit since no one will understand. The criterion of Good Style is no longer its ability to reproduce the immediate motions of the mind as it shapes the world around it. Now the emphasis has shifted from the speaker's or writer's mind to the listener's or reader's. Good Style is Public Style, a style easy to read because accessible and appropriate to the group for which it is intended. Hence Bacon's rhetorical theory and practice are strictly functional. Utility regarded as an *end* (the acquisition or "progression" of useful knowledge) and as a *means* (the propagation or "use" of this knowledge) determines style.

The Probative and Aphoristic kind of style, because it claims to deliver and intimate knowledge "in the same method wherein it was invented," seems to come close to the ideals of the classical plain style and libertine prose. But Bacon tells us "the method of the mathematiques" furnishes the only "shadow" of what he has in mind. Only a style as bloodless as that of mathematics could serve as the equivalent of the calm passivity of the mind absorbing sense data — the first step of Baconian induction. Furthermore, it is the style best suited to the dissemination of knowledge among the "sons of science." The method of the mathematiques is completely unlike that of self-revelation.

Evidently Bacon seeks a style stripped of connotations, associations, and the like so that there will no longer be "a kind of contract of error between the deliverer and the receiver," the legal image perhaps indicating the kind of language Bacon wants.

Bacon's utilitarian attitude toward style in general is also illustrated in his statements about, and practice of, the opposite of the classical plain style, the *genus grande* — "a science excellent" (*Advancement, Works*, VI, p. 296). In almost all classical and Renaissance theories of the plain style the Socratic association of moral edification with the plain style and deceit with the pragmatic *genus grande* is always present. Bacon thought of the *genus grande* as the best style for moral discourse. Against a familiar Platonic comparison Bacon uses another saying of Plato:

And therefore it was a great injustice in Plato, though springing out of a just hatred of the rhetoricians of his time, to esteem of Rhetoric but as a voluptuary art, resembling it to cookery. . . . Plato said elegantly *That virtue, if she could be seen, would move great love and affection;* so seeing that she cannot be shewed to the Sense by corporeal shape, the next degree is to shew her to the Imagination in lively representation. (p. 298)

This shewing is, of course, the office of Rhetoric. "Reason would become captive and servile, if Eloquence of Persuasions did not practice and win the Imagination from the Affection's part, and contract a confederacy between the Reason and the Imagination against the Affections" (p. 299). Here Bacon goes directly against the classical theory of the plain style in an attack on one of its sacred texts, the *Gorgias* of Plato. Bacon asserts that no style is inherently immoral or moral, and that, indeed, the style usually described as most immoral or deceitful is more useful for morality than the severer plain style. As we have seen, Bacon himself is most rhetorical when moralizing. The moral ends justify the rhetorical means. To be sure, not all Bacon's followers were to agree that Rhetoric had any use at all or that it could possibly win the Imagination *away from* the Affections; most of the critics were convinced that Rhetoric worked *in alliance with* the Affections. But for everyone the Affections are to be handled carefully because of their potential to enhance or interfere with the propagation of useful truth, the prime concern of language. This utilitarian or functional view of language is contrary to the earnest spirit of the classical plain style, which eschews any sort of rhetorical art, even for a good cause, if it means a sacrifice of candor.

Bacon's position on the function of the *genera dicendi* shows the effects of the new criterion of utility on prose style. He finds it useful and true to consider "things" as objective physical reality. Since his plain style deals with "things," this way of writing is not for moral edification but for the progression of knowledge about the physical world, which knowledge eventually will be turned to useful ends. Language is therefore for clear communication, not self-revelation or revelation of an Ideal Self. The goal is now that "a man may . . . [transplant] knowledge into another" (*Advancement*, p. 290). The writer in the plain style no longer asks, Am I revealing my ideal soul? but rather, as Bacon asked Rawley, Am I understood? (*Works*, I, p. 11).

The "Progression" of knowledge is best served by the "Real Character," the "Alphabet of Nature," or any of the other schemes to substitute marks for words which fascinated Bacon and his followers. The Real Character has certain advantages over words, which are relatively so equivocal. Words are inferior to arbitrary marks for portraying Baconian "things," the objects of the "simple, sensuous perception" on which all knowledge depends. It is in Bacon's suspicion of language itself as a vehicle for the expression of true statements about the real world that his antipathy to the candid but often highly wrought art of the classical plain style most profoundly reveals itself.

Behind such a suspicion and the program derived from it L. C. Knights sees the seventeenth-century "dissociation of sensibility." The dissociation Knights charges up to the effects of Baconian utilitarianism. The effect on style of the dissociation arising from the split between thought and feeling is that "in the *Advancement* and the *Essays* the function of the images is not to intensify the meaning, to make it richer or deeper, but simply to make more effective a meaning that was already fully formed before the application of the illustrative device." [5] By and large, as I shall try to show, images work exactly the same way in Restoration prose, including the prose of an apologist for "science" like Sprat.

However one feels about Eliot's much disputed dictum, there is little doubt that Bacon's views on language lurk behind Sprat's "Mathematical plainness" of "so many things, almost in an equal number of words." Sprat's manifesto was influenced by Wilkins' proposal to set up a language based on a Real Character along the lines originally suggested by Bacon. Sprat was also influenced directly by Bacon himself. At times Sprat practically plagiarized.[6] Under the influence of Bacon Sprat's rhetorical theory and practice in the *History* oscillated, as we have seen, between one "close, naked, natural" style for the "progression" of all useful knowledge, and another rhetorical one for the propagation or "use" of knowledge; these two modes correspond to Bacon's "Probative" or "Aphoristic" style on the one hand, and the "Magistral" on the other. Like Bacon, Sprat goes against Plato, Seneca, and the classical plain style in defending the *genus grande*, assigning to it a useful moral function. Rhetoric "is a Weapon, which may be as fully prouv'd by *bad* men, as good. . . . This is the chief reason,

that should now keep up the Ornaments of speaking, in
any request: since they are now so much degenerated from
their original usefulness." [7] Sprat sees natural philosophy
itself as a fruitful source for rhetoric. Bacon is a good model,
being "abundantly recompenc'd for his Noble Labours in
that *Philosophy*, by a vast Treasure of admirable *Imaginations*, which it afforded him, wherewith to express and adorn
his thoughts about other matters" (p. 416). This rhetoric,
unlike Montaigne's, Browne's, or any other "Anti-Ciceronian's," is not intended to reveal the motions of the
mind in its difficult quest to define itself. Its aim is the
Baconian one of persuasively making things easier for the
reader, for "it is requir'd in the best and most delightful
Wit; that it be founded on such Images which are generally
known, and are able to bring a strong and sensible impression
on the *Mind*" (p. 413). Sprat's new rhetoric is a Public
Style, grasping the "generally known" rather than the
private and individualistic. Its utilitarian goals fix its character; if the reader understands, then he will profit, technologi-
cally, politically, or even morally.

The rhetoric of a Whitlock or a Browne, on the other
hand, is not much concerned with the reader's ease of comprehension. It is moral edification through self-revelation
that is the object of classical and libertine plain styles. Moral
teaching is to be found not only in detachable disquisitions
but in the specific dramatic situation which the author in-
vites the reader to share intimately. Here is the concrete
res of the tradition. Now, in Sprat's proposed close, naked,
natural style, men delivered so many things almost in an
equal number of words.

Such an aim, as we have seen, has suggested to Crollian
critics the influence of Seneca on Sprat. In contrast to the
theory of words and things of Seneca and the classical plain
style, Sprat nowhere says that the goal of his style is self-
revelation. And we certainly do not find out very much

about his soul in the *History*. In, say, *The Anatomy of Melancholy* or the *Pseudodoxia Epidemica* — like the *History*, a review of natural investigations — we learn a great deal about Burton's and Browne's extravagant and irregular heads. It is clear that, as in Bacon, "things" for Sprat are the physical objects of the world of artisans, countrymen, and merchants, not the motions of the witty and scholarly minds of the libertines:

The solitary imaginations of *Speculative Men* are of all others the most easy: there a man meets with little stubbornness of matter: he may choose his subject where he likes: he may fashion and turn it as he pleases: whereas when he comes abroad into the world, he must indure more *contradiction:* more *difficulties* are to be overcome; and he cannot always follow his own *Genius:* so that it is not to be wonder'd, that so many *great Wits* have despis'd the labor of a practical cours; and have rather chosen to shut themselves up from the *nois* and *preferments* of the *World*, to convers in the shadow with the pleasant *productions* of their own *fancies.* (pp. 335–336)

Even in Sprat's more rhetorical mode the images are to be drawn, as we have seen, from "the Arts of Men's Hands and the Works of Nature" because "the *Sciences* of Mens Brains are none of the best Materials for this kind of *Wit.* Very few have happily succeeded in *Logical, Metaphysical, Grammatical,* nay even scarce in *Mathematical Comparisons;* and the reason is, because they are most of them conversant about Things remov'd from the Senses, and so cannot surprize the *fancy* with very obvious, or quick, or sensible Delights" (p. 415).

This contempt for "Things remov'd from the Senses" expresses the "modern" position in the quarrel with the "ancients," whose "Defects" in "natural Knowledge" "did also straiten their Fancies." Now, however, the "comparisons" afforded by experiments

will be intelligible to all, because they proceed from Things that enter into all mens Senses. These will make the most vigorous Impressions on Mens *Fancies,* because they do even touch their *Eyes,* and are nearest to their *Nature.* Of these the variety will be infinite, for the particulars are so, from whence they may be deduc'd: These may be always new and unsullied, seeing there is such a vast Number of *Natural* and *Mechanical* things, not yet fully known or improv'd, and by Consequence not yet sufficiently apply'd. (p. 416)

Seneca is merely another of the "ancients." Sprat's citation of the old chestnut out of Quintilian suggests that the Bishop thought Seneca exemplified the useless and unintelligible style of antiquity devoid of "Practice":

[Learning] does neither practice nor cherish this humor of disputing, which breaks the force of things by the subtility of words; as *Seneca* was said to do by his style: It weakens mens arms, and slackens all the sinews of action: For so it commonly happens, that such earnest disputers evaporate all the strength of their minds in arguing, questioning, and debating; and tire themselves out before they come to the *Practice.*[8]

Sprat's impulse, in the end, is utilitarian and Baconian: If we reduce the semantic range of each word as much as possible to one unalterable referent in the physical world ("proper" terms) then everything "will be intelligible to all" and we shall avoid disputes and advance knowledge for profit. The assumptions that have crept in are that what is useful is also clear as well as true, that is, a copy of physical "Things." In effect, Sprat continues Bacon's denial of classical *mimesis* in any form.

Up to now I have been arguing that Sprat represents a Baconian reaction against "Senecan" style as well as the entire classical plain style. There is another side of Sprat which emerges in his proposals to establish an English Academy. Sprat admires Pellisson's history of the French Academy even though it is an "Artifice of Words" rather than "a bare knowledge of things" (p. 40). Pellisson is, in fact, a model for English prose as well. Sprat would like to see some "airy and discursive" French polish and smoothness grafted onto the "plain, undeceiving" English genius. This combination of discursive ease and polish is, of course, a hallmark of the classical plain style. The ideal Sprat must have had in mind appears in his description of Cowley. To Sprat Cowley is a model Horatian. On his English Sabine farm Cowley "forsook the Conversation, but never the Language, of the City and Court." [9] Cowley also imitated all four genres of the classical plain style. In these Cowley's words equaled the things of his urbane mind. "In all the several shapes of his Style there is still very much of the likeness and impression of the same mind: the same unaffected modesty, and natural freedom, and easie vigour, and cheerful passions, and innocent mirth, that appear'd in all his Manners" (Spingarn, *Essays*, II, p. 128). Cowley's letters are models of the classical ideal of intimate but polite self-revelation. They "always express'd the Native tenderness and Innocent gaiety of his mind" without descending into libertine mannerisms:

They should not consist of fulsom Complements, or tedious Politicks, or elaborate Elegancies, or general Fancies. But they should have a Native clearness and shortness, a Domestical plainnes, and a peculiar kind of Familiarity, which can only affect the humour of those to whom they were intended. . . . In such Letters the Souls of Men should appear undress'd: And in that negligent habit they may be fit to be seen by one or two in a Chamber, but not to go abroad into the Streets. (Spingarn, II, p. 137)

Cowley himself — whose own prose style evolved, like Glanvill's, from "Senecan" to "scientific" — understood quite well the linguistic theory of Bacon and its application to the Royal Society and prose in general. In the exuberant *Ode to the Royal Society* affixed to Sprat's *History*, Cowley hails the new positivism:

From words, which are but Pictures of the Thought
(Though we our Thoughts from them perversely drew)

To Things, the Minds right Object, he [Bacon] it brought,
Like foolish Birds to painted Grapes we flew;
He sought and gather'd for our use the Tru;
And when on heaps the chosen Bunches lay,
He pressed them wisely the Mechanic way,
Till all their juyce did in one Vessel joyn,
Ferment into a Nourishment Divine,
   The thirsty Souls refreshing Wine.
Who to the life an exact Piece would make,
Must not from others Work a Copy take;
   No, not from *Rubens* or *Vandike;*
Much less content himself to make it like
Th' Ideas and the Images which ly
In his own Fancy, or his Memory.
   No, he before his sight must place
   The Natural and Living Face;
   The real Object must command
Each Judgement of his Eye, and Motion of his Hand. (sig. B$_2$)

Here is the familiar unity of utility and truth (Bacon "gather'd for our use the Tru") with the "real Object" understood as physical reality, all contained in a "proper" conceit of wine-making out of "the Arts of Men's Hands and the works of Nature." *Mimesis* is no more. Other artists, "Fancy," and "Memory" are not to be imitated. Instead of "perversely" relying on our own creative Faculties, we are to submit ourselves passively to Things — "the real Object must command." Such a program renounces every traditional theory of artistic expression and argues, in the Baconian tradition, against all imitation, Senecan or otherwise.

Sprat's and Cowley's inconsistent theory of rhetoric is a mirror of the confusion of the age with regard to the two ideals of "plainness," classical and Baconian. Long after Bacon — most notably in the Horatian aspects of the eighteenth century — the classical ideal flourishes. The example of Sprat shows that it was not the classical plain style as a whole but its "Senecan" libertine offshoots that were especially distressing to the reformers of the Royal Society. To take the foremost example: Dryden, a sometime member of the Society, is, as we shall see, an Anti-Senecan sympathetic to the classical plain style.

For the most part, though, and despite the persistence of florid rhetoric among the Fellows, Bacon's "Probative" style is the one associated with the New Philosophy. We have already seen this aspect of Bacon's influence on Sprat's and Glanvill's stylistic programs. Its influence is also felt in the first of the three major mid-century defenses of the New Philosophy, John Webster's *Academiarum Examen* (1654). Webster follows the usual seventeenth-century division of all knowledge into the useful ("Practick") and the useless ("Speculative"): "Those Sciences that the *Schools* usually comprehend under the title of Humane, are by them divided divers and sundry waies, according to several fancies or Authors; but most usually into two sorts, *Speculative* and *Practick:* wherein their greatest crime lies in making some meerly Speculative, that are of no use or benefit to mankind unless they be reduced into practice, and then of all other most profitable, excellent, and usefull; and these are, natural *Philosophy* and *Mathematicks*, both of which will clearly appear to be practical." [10] Webster, who is attacking the universities, disagrees further with their placing of natural philosophy in the category of the useless:

Can the Science of natural things, whose subject they hold to be *Corpus naturale mobile*, be only speculative, and not practical? is there no further end nor consideration in *Physicks* but onely to search, discuss, understand, and dispute of a natural movable body, with all the affections, accidents, and circumstances thereto belonging? . . . Surely natural *Philosophy* hath a more noble, sublime, and ultimate end, than to rest in speculation, abstractive notions, mentall operations, and verball disputes . . . but . . . to see and behold *the eternal power and God-head* of him, who hath set all these things as so many significant and lively characters, or *Hieroglyphicks* of his invisible power, providence and divine wisdom. . . . And secondly, not onely to know natures power in the causes and effects, but further to make use of them for the general good and benefit of mankind. (pp. 18–19)

The Baconian version of the words-things relationship provides the philosophical background of the entire *Examen*. Webster's ideal of "Natural Philosophy" is the practical "science of natural things" as opposed to mere words — the "speculation, abstractive notions, mentall operations, and verball disputes" unhinged from material stuff of those who do not make natural philosophy a useful art. As in Bacon, Truth and Utility are one. Hence Webster's desiderata of prose style are not the self-revelation of Senecanism and the classical plain style, but "perspicuity, certainty, and utility" (sig. a₂). Like Bacon, Webster declares against words altogether. To represent the "*Hieroglyphicks* of his invisible power" Webster would prefer the near-hieroglyphics of the projected Real Character.

Webster replaces the universities' classifications of learning with his own, according to utility: first, sciences "instrumental, subordinate, and subservient to other Sciences" (Grammar, Logic, Mathematics); second, "Sciences that confer knowledge of themselves and are not instrumental or subservient to others" (Natural Philosophy, Metaphysics, Politics, Ethics, Economics); and third, sciences that "conferre some knowledg, and have some peculiar uses, so they seem necessary as ornamental, and such I account *Oratory* and *Poesie*" (pp. 20–21). Oratory and Poesie are condemned for their lack of utility, which in turn goes back to their severance of words from things. Here Webster foreshadows the Restoration dissociation of Ornament from Sense: "Lastly, for *Rhetorick*, or *Oratory*, *Poesie* and the like, which serve for adornation and are as it were the outward dress, and attire of more solid sciences. . . ." (p. 88). Webster's ideal plain style excels not because it reveals the mind of the author, but because it is clear to the reader: "Both Eloquence and *Poesie* seem rather to be numbered among the gifts of nature, than amongst the disciplines, for those which excell much in reason, and do dispose those things which they excogitate in a most easie method, that they may be clearly, and distinctly understood, are most apt to perswade, although they did use the language of the *Goths*, and had never learned *Rhetorick*" (pp. 88–89). As might be expected in such a forbidding program, there is no indication of any indebtedness on Webster's part to classical plain style or to Seneca. There is a laudatory reference to Seneca's "writings about vertue, tranquillity, and curing the minds diseases, infinitely beyond all those needless, fruitless, vain and impertinent discourses of the proud *Stagyrite*" (p. 88), but the context is a discussion of ethics, not style. It is Aristotle, not Cicero, with whom Seneca is compared.

Reading Webster we can easily understand how the controversy between what Glanvill called the "pretended plain" style of the earlier part of the century and the new utilitarian plain style of the scientists became an expression of the quarrel between the ancients, represented by the humanistic scholarship and outlook of the universities, and the moderns.[11] The positivistic urges of the moderns reach a climax in Wilkins' proposal, originating with Bacon, for a Real Character, the theory of which Webster supported. The universities were not entirely against the moderns. The *Examen* was attacked immediately by Seth Ward, the Oxford astronomer and one of the original members of the Royal Society, as well as the chief inspiration, after Bacon, for Wilkins' scheme. Ward assails Webster for holding that the universities are barren of scientific and mathematical progress. Though allied with the Society's less empirical and utilitarian wing, Ward has approximately the same theory of language as Webster. "It is very well known to the youth of the University," he admonishes, "that the avoiding of confusion or perturbation of the fancy made by words, or preventing the loss of sight of the generall reason of things, by the disguise of particular numbers, having passed through severall formes of operation, was the end and motive of inventing Mathematicall Symbols; so that it was a design perfectly intended against Language and its servant Grammar." [12] Utility through clarity is the object of the scheme, as it was for Bacon's original proposals:

If ever there be a speedy way made to the attainment of Knowledge, it must be by making a shorter, and clearer cut to the understanding (by the way of signification) than that which is travailed now by words; which advancement of Learning and Knowledge, will bring (not an advance, as this man innocently supposes but) an elevation and uselessenesse upon Language and Grammar. For this effect is what is intended by the *Universall Character.* (p. 20)

A Baconian distrust of words to represent things drives Ward to reduce words themselves to things. Sharing Bacon's vision of a grand international community of scholars, Ward is sure that the Real Character would end the language barrier. "An Universall Character might easily be made wherein all Nations might communicate together, just as they do in numbers and in species" (p. 21).

Like John Locke a generation later, Ward finds that he must manufacture a new set of designs for abstractions. Ward's task is simpler, since his abstractions are mathematical while Locke must invent a new system of "mixed modes." But the linguistic intentions are the same.

The thing thus proposed is feasible, but the number of severall Characters would be almost infinite. . . . So that the tradition of Learning, or facilitation of it would be but little advanced. . . . But it did presently occur to me, that by the help of Logick and Mathematicks this might soone receive a mighty advantage, for all Discourses being resolved in sentences, those into words, words signifying either simple notions or being resolvible into simple notions, it is manifest that, if all the sorts of simple notions be found out, and have Symboles assigned to them, those will be extreamly few. . . . This design if perfected, would be of very great concernment to the advancement of Learning. . . . Such a Language as this (where every word were a definition and contain'd the nature of the thing) might not unjustly be termed a naturall Language. (pp. 21–22)

Again Truth and Utility kiss as Sprat's "mathematical plainness" is carried to its logical extreme. The mode useful for the Advancement of Learning (Ward's Baconian echo is intentional) is true and "naturall," that is, it enables the reader "to fetch the notions of things with ease and celerity" (p. 26). Like Bacon and the Baconians, Ward's criterion for communication is ease for the reader, not Senecan self-revelation. Ward, in fact, is an Anti-Senecan, explicitly associating Seneca not with the new plain style but with the old oratory, as Webster had neglected to do:

Supposing those *Morall* Authours which even now he [Webster] mentioned, *Zeno, Seneca, Epictetus*, or those *Politick* writers or *Rhetoritians*, did conteine things better in their kind than *Aristotle*, yet they are not so fit to be read in Universities by way of Institution, as he. They have written diffusedly *stilo oratorio*, or use by way of Dialogues, but have not given a briefe Methodicall body of the things they handle. (p. 39)

Ward, as we have noted, was a major source of inspiration for Wilkins' *Essay Towards a Real Character* (1668). Wilkins "had frequent occasion of conferring with him, concerning the various *Desiderata* proposed by Learned men, or such things as were conceived, yet wanting the advancement of several parts of Learning; amongst which, this of the *Universal Character*, was one of the principal." [13] Wilkins goes beyond Bacon by designating the system of mathematical symbols not only for "facilitating mutual *Commerce*, amongst the several Nations of the World, and the improving of the Natural knowledge," but as the vehicle for "the clearing of some of our Modern differences in

Religion, by unmasking many wild errors, that shelter themselves under the design of affected phrases" ("Epistle Dedicatory," p. 5). Fortunately the useful style is also the one which best reproduces the truth, that is, the way in which things — physical objects — impinge on our senses. Like the others, Wilkins describes the happy marriage of Right Reason and Utility:

As men do generally agree in the same Principle of Reason, so do they likewise agree in the same *Internal Notion* or *Apprehensions of Things.*

The *External Expression* of these Mental notions, whereby men communicate their thoughts to one another, is either to the *Ear,* or to the *Eye.*

To the *Ear* by *Sounds,* and more particularly by Articulate *Voice* and *Words.*

To the *Eye* by any thing that is *visible,* Motion, Light, Colour, Figure; and more particularly by *Writing.*

That *conceit* which men have in their minds concerning a Horse or Tree, is the Notion or *mental image* of that *Beast,* or natural thing, of such a nature, shape, and use. The *Names* given to these in several Languages, are such arbitrary *sounds* or *words,* as Nations of men have agreed upon, either casually or designedly, to express their Mental notions of them. The *Written word* is the figure or picture of that Sound.

So that if men should generally consent upon the same way or manner of *Expression,* as they do agree in the same *Notion,* we should then be freed from that Curse in the Confusion of Tongues, with all the unhappy consequences of it.

Now this can only be done, either by *enjoyning* some one Language or Character to be universally learnt and practised, (which is not to be expected . . .) or else by *proposing* some such way as, by its facility and usefulness, (without the imposition of Authority) might *invite* and ingage men to the learning of it; which is the thing here attempted. (p. 20)

Wilkins here looks backward to Bacon and ahead to Locke. But Wilkins' more radical nominalism pushes beyond both philosophers to assert that no words at all, only the unequivocal signs of his system, can represent unalterable

"Mental notions." What is perhaps most significant is Wilkins' intention to create a universally intelligible mode. The un-"Senecan" assumption is that there is only *one* proper mode of discourse for truthful statements.

Another religious scientist, Robert Boyle — a formidable utilitarian and theologian as well as the Father of Chemistry — fights a two-front war in *Some Considerations Touching the Style of the Holy Scriptures* (1663) against those who object that the Bible is plain and therefore dull and those who say it is prolix and therefore deceitful. Boyle replies by making God a utilitarian. God wanted the Bible to be useful, so he made it plain, and intelligible to all. To be sure, the Bible at times is disjointed and unmethodical, but so are the things of nature, such as the stars. St. Paul digresses, but the best and most spirited horses dart off the path. Boyle blames most of the seeming breaches of Decorum in the Bible on our own linguistic ignorance: the Bible seems hard because we do not know Hebrew and Greek; the Bible would be quite plain if we knew the original tongues. There are critics who protest that the Bible should avoid repetitions, so that "more of usefull matter is deliver'd in fewer words." [14] But morality is good; God wisely repeats it. Of the books of the Bible as a whole, "We may find this difference between Them and Human Writings, That those first mention'd contain more Matter than Words, and the Other more Words than Matter. Nay, many of the very Flowers of Rhetorick growing there, have (like the Marygold that in hot Countries points at the Sun) a virtue of hitting the usefullest and sublimest Truths" (p. 131).

For the pious chemist, Truth is utility, utility Truth, that is all we need to know. The opposite of the useful Biblical plain style, in which words are close to things, is associated with Seneca, for those who think the Bible too rhetorical give it "the Title, *Nero* gave *Seneca's* style, of *Arena sine calce* [sand without lime]" (p. 62). To those who object because the Bible, unlike Seneca, is too plain, Boyle argues that if Machiavelli, that most coldly pragmatic of all authors, wrote plainly, why cannot the Bible be plain, too? "If a meer Statesman, writing to a Prince, upon a meer civil Theme, could reasonably talk thus: with how much more Reason may God expect a welcoming Entertainment for the least Adorn'd parts of a Book, of the Truth is a direct Emanation from the Essential and Supreme Truth . . . ?" (pp. 152–153).

It is Boyle, Sprat, Glanvill, Webster, Ward, and Wilkins that we must rely upon for the formal exposition of the new philosophy's theory of style. But almost every defender of the Baconian ideals has something to say about style along the lines of the authors we have discussed. Comments embedded among the reports of the investigators themselves are even more revealing of the extent to which Baconian assumptions about the plain style had routed Senecan and other classical assumptions. There is inexhaustible material to choose from here; it seems at times that almost every scientific work in the Restoration begins with an apology for the author's "plainness" on the grounds of utility. Francis Glisson's *Treatise of the Rickets* (1651) can even summon up classical authority for a "scientific" style: "Finally expect no flashes of Rhetorick and Courtly-Language; Nobis licet esse tam dicertis,/Musas qui colimus severiores. And indeed the conditions of the matter forbids all such painting; in such a manner, Ornari res ipsa negat, contenti doceri." [15] But Glisson's *res* are not personal feelings or ideas. "Matter," not the inmost stirrings of the soul, dictate the style. Another investigator, Robert Plot, in his *Natural History of Oxfordshire* (1676), explicitly associates his words with the things of physical reality, assuring us that the local natural phenomena he intends "to deliver as succinctly as may be, in a plain, easie, unartificial Stile, studiously avoiding all ornaments of Language, it being my purpose to treat of Things, and therefore would have the Reader expect nothing less than Words." [16] Plot is at one with Bacon's empiricism and utilitarianism, in which "plain" means submission to concrete physical objects and little work for the reader (Plot's "easie").

One of the most ardent of these Baconians is Joshua Childrey, author of a geographical survey called *Britania Baconica* (1661). Childrey says,

> [I have] endeavoured to tell my tale as plainly as might be, both that I might be understood of all, and that I might not disfigure the face of Truth by daubing it over with the paint of Language. *Renatus Des Cartes* hath told us, not without reason, how hard it is either to tell what we have seen, or what we have heard, or to understand a related theory exactly, according to the Relatours sense. So much difference there is between seeing and speaking, and between hearing and apprehending.[17]

Childrey seizes upon the common ground shared by Descartes and Bacon — their skepticism and faith in experiment — and ignores or dismisses Cartesianism's tremendous epistemological difficulties and Descartes' attempts to solve them. A good Baconian, Childrey is apologizing for imitating someone, here authors of English rarities which he has not seen himself. His words, he fears, are at a greater remove from things, the physical reality, than the words of his sources. Firsthand observation would impel Childrey to use a "harsh and ungrateful" style, but one that would be closer to "things": "If the places and things themselves were visited, they would tell us as much, and appear different from what they are said to be. And peradventure by examining the particulars of them, we should find some one that would discover, or give a light unto the cause of them" (sig. B4). Undoubtedly Swift, attempting to restore the classical plain style and the reputation of the word in general, had "projectors" like Childrey in mind when he satirized the Royal Society as the Grand Academy of Lagado.

The other project was a scheme for entirely abolishing all words whatsoever; and this was urged as a great advantage in point of health as well as brevity. . . . An expedient was therefore offered, that since words are only names for things, it would be more convenient for all men to carry about them such things as were necessary to express the particular business they are to discourse on."

The assumptions of the Baconians parodied by Swift are at the opposite extreme from those of earlier "Anti-Ciceronian" investigators, such as Burton or Browne, who make a point of filtering the stubborn facts through their own sensibilities.

The New Plain Style and the Sermon

At first this sampling of stylistic theories by writers obviously associated with the New Philosophy suggests that as Jones contends, "Science" itself directly and profoundly altered the course of English prose as a whole, driving it away from "Anti-Ciceronianism" into utilitarian modes. Such an inference, I think, is largely unjustified. As good a case could be made (and has been made, by Jackson Cope in his book on Glanvill) for the influence of contemporary religion on the Royal Society's stylistic platform. Since almost all members of the Society who expressed themselves at length on style were also clergymen, why not speak of the influence of contemporary religion on scientific style rather than the other way around? Certainly the sects closest to the "scientific" spirit, Anglican Latitudinarianism and moderate Puritanism, included virtually the entire membership of the Society. However, other religious writers, untouched by or hostile to the New Philosophy and the

Society, are advocating identical stylistic programs using identical arguments. These writers are also Anglicans and moderate Puritans. The same holds for philosophers and literary men (insofar as such distinctions are possible in the seventeenth century), some of whom, like Hobbes, earned the wrath of both the Baconian scientists and their religious apologists.

One must agree with Mitchell that, "The pulpit, consequently, which for long had been the last refuge of antiquated modes of rhetorical expression, and a prime corruptor of style, not only assented to a reform too frequently attributed solely to the Court acting under French influence and the growing exigencies of natural science, but was itself a pioneer in the movement for a simplification of style." [18] But to discuss "influences" in terms of "religion" or "science" is to be caught in a fruitless chicken-or-egg controversy. The decisive "influence" is whatever can be found to impel consciously or unconsciously all or most of our theorists, who are all advocating and writing more or less the same style. I have been arguing throughout that rather than "science" or "religion" the controlling assumption of the age, or at least the one decisive for Restoration prose style, was the identification of one ill-defined abstraction, Truth, with another, Utility. The strange libertinism of the "Anti-Ciceronians," or of the "Enthusiasts," was associated by the Restoration as a whole — not only the scientists — with the kind of barren and divisive controversies of scholastics and sectarians which helped to bring about the civil war. Against the individualism, candor, and accompanying rhetorical excitement of such authors the scientists and nonscientists of the Restoration outlined a few useful styles. In these the emphasis is shifted away from the author and toward "things" and the reader. "Wit," in the sense of the free play of the mind as it reveals itself, making up allegories, similes, metaphors, and so forth as it rambles along, becomes distrusted. "Judgement" — the impersonal, inexorable, and very prudent rules of Right Reason — drives out such dangerous and useless stuff. "Judgement" either replaces "wit," or else "wit" — *true* "wit" — is redefined as "judgement." Utility underlies not only "Judgement" but also "Decorum." If he is to be useful, the writer must be sure that his words are exactly suited to himself, his audience, and the "matter" at hand.

The Elizabethans had a similar theory of "Decorum." But the "self" of the new prose of utility is an abstract "Gentleman," the "audience" is appealed to only through objective argumentation, and the "matter" is logical. The prose, therefore, is uniformly "polite," "smooth," "civil," and "fashionable." No style could possibly fulfill all these qualifications perfectly. But Boyle's recommendation for the utilitarian style of *The Sceptical Chymist* (1661) defines much of the total complex and, in particular, how the requirements of argumentation underlie "neoclassic" Decorum:

I have almost all along written these dialogues in a style more Fashionable than That of meer scholars is wont to be. I hope I shall be excus'd by them that shall consider, that to keep a due *decorum* in the Discourses, it was fit that in a book written by a Gentleman, and wherein only Gentlemen are introduced as Speakers, the Language should be more Smooth, and the Expressions more civil than is usual in the more Scholastick way of writing. And indeed, I am not sorry to have this Opportunity of giving an example how to manage even Disputes with Civility; whence perhaps some Readers will be assisted to discern a Difference betwixt Bluntness of speech and Strength of reason.[19]

Here Boyle the scientist speaks; in the essay on Biblical style we hear Boyle the theologian. For scriptural and scientific truth — each amiably coexisting for Boyle, as for the other Baconians — utility determines the character of the style in which it is to be conveyed. Although in general there is one "fashionable," "smooth" style for civilized discourses, the specific situation of the writer and the nature of his "matter," rather than his own attitudes toward it, fix his style. There is one kind of style for each type of knowledge as opposed to Anti-Ciceronian and libertine "bluntness of speech" for all matters — *quicquid agunt homines.*

The Restoration theorists do not always explicitly trace Decorum to the demands of argumentation. Sometimes it seems that to have words approximate things is an end in itself. Much the same could be said of any other part of the complex of ideas we have been discussing, such as the striving for "judgement" or the attack on metaphor. For example, Restoration "Decorum" does owe something to classical imitation. As with most Restoration clichés, it is risky to imply that "Decorum" meant only one kind of thing. Who can say for sure whether the reaction against "Wit" after the civil wars comes from a practical need to avoid further rhetorically inspired conflicts or from a "neoclassic" dislike of whatever is unreliable, irrational, and impermanent? Do preachers emphasize "Reason" because they feel that rational approaches convince more people, or because they like being reasonable? Such questions are all but unanswerable, but Utility, much more than anything else, hovers in the background as the ultimate basis of the new ideals. Furthermore Utility is almost always placed in opposition to self-revelation, the goal of the older plain styles.

As I have indicated, the utilitarian stylistic theories of the scientists are indistinguishable from those of the preachers. As with Glanvill and Boyle, the same writer may prescribe identical styles for preaching and for "science" — in fact, for all useful knowledge. The scientist Wilkins wrote a renowned manual on preaching as well as the *Essay Towards a Real Character.* In its general tendencies, if not in its fantastic schematizations, Wilkins' *Ecclesiastes* (1646) is the precursor of all the later Restoration tracts on preaching style. Wilkins wants divinity "distinctly treated of in one plain Method, with that strength and perspicuity as the nature of Things would bear; this might in many Respects be of singular Use, both for Teachers and Learners." [20] Again we hear the cry for the useful style in which words are subordinated to things. Wilkins rejects the ramblings of libertinism and the older plain style: "An immethodical Discourse (though the materials of it may be precious) is but as a *Heap*, full of Confusion and Deformity; the other as a *Fabrick* or Building, much more excellent, both for *Beauty* and *Use*" (p. 5). Utility is not only Beauty but also standardized Decorum: "There is a particular *Art of Preaching*, to which, if Ministers did more seriously apply themselves, it would extreamly facilitate that Service, making it more easie to them, and more profitable to their Hearers" (p. 1).

Wilkins' understanding of "plain" at first seems to recall the emphasis of the classical and libertine theorists on things as mind rather than matter. The discourse "must be plain and natural, not being darkened with the affectation of *Scholastical* harshness, or *Rhetorical* flourishes. Obscurity in the Discourse, is an Argument of Ignorance in the mind. The greatest learning is to be seen in the greatest plainness. The more clearly we understand any thing our selves, the more easily we can expound it to others" (p. 251). But Wilkins really has utility rather than self-revelation in mind. The preacher is to reveal his thought not as a libertine exhibition of personality but because his own soul is filled with the Holy Spirit. What the preacher says, in fact, transcends personality and "Man's wisdom": "When the notion itself is good, the best way to set it off, is in the most obvious plain expression. St. Paul does often glory in this, that his Preaching *was not in wisdom of words, or excellency of speech; not with inticing words of Mans wisdom, not as*

194

pleasing Men, but God who trieth the heart. A Minister should speak *as the Oracles of God.*" [21]

Unlike Wilkins some of the major theorists on sermon style had no connection with the New Philosophy or the Royal Society and some, like South, opposed both. Others were members of the Society, but there is no evidence that their membership, or "Science," had anything at all to do with their ideas about style. Yet the theories of all these men are similar to those of Sprat and Glanvill — and to those preachers who were also serious about the New Philosophy — thus calling into question Jones' inference of "scientific" influence on pulpit oratory. Like the scientists, but usually with no reference to them, the reformers of sermons distinguished, not between scientific and unscientific, but between different kinds of "plain" styles, Glanvill's useless "pretended plain" style and the new authentically plain variety.

In the influential *Friendly Debate Between a Conformist and a Non-Conformist* (1669) of Bishop Symon Patrick — a nonmember but well acquainted with the Society's works — the Non-Conformist assures his opponent that the dissenting preachers "love to preach very plainly." He is answered:

C[onformist]. Now I understand what you mean by *plain preaching*, (which you so much talk of), *viz.* To use rude and broad expressions. . . . Have I not hit your meaning?
N[on]. C[onformist]. No.
C. Then it is very hard to know what it is. And indeed, the Assembly of Divines, when they direct men how to perform their Ministry, and among other things tell them they must preach *plainly*, do not speak plainly themselves in the Directory, *i.e.*, not so as to be understood.[22]

The contrast here is between the new style of the Restoration against the "canting" of the sects, rather than Restoration style versus the classical plain style or "Senecan" libertinism. But Patrick's objections could also apply to "Anti-Ciceronianism." Like Senecanism, the Enthusiasts' style was introspective and emphasized self-revelation; Patrick would make the criterion for "plain" the ease with which the listener understands. Rather than using a "plain and proper language" the Non-Conformists "seek to please their itching Ears, and gratifie the longings of their fancies with new-found words, affected expressions, and odd Phrases" (p. 69). Patrick attacks stylistic individualism in general and in particular colloquialism, asymmetry, and obscurity, qualities which Croll assigns to "Anti-Ciceronianism." The Non-Conformists "hack in an unseemly manner, or make a stop, or use such words as are too rude and slovenly, or speak broken and imperfect language, or at the best such as is too hard and obscure, and unintelligible by the Vulgar" (p. 69). Therefore Patrick, like Sprat, would impose a "prescribed Form of words" to replace the libertinism of the other "plain" style which Patrick, like the Royal Society, blames on the language of wits and scholars and justifies on the grounds of "profit": "The Assembly told you (if you would have observ'd) what *plain preaching* is . . . where they require Ministers to forbear unprofitable use of unknown Tongues, strange Phrases, Cadences of Sounds and Words, and to cite Sentences out of Writers sparingly, though never so elegant" (pp. 147–148). Although Patrick here adopts the same stylistic stance as the reformers of the Royal Society and although he commended the Latitudinarians for embracing the discoveries of the scientists, there is no evidence of the influence of the Society or of "Science." Rather Patrick is responding to the general utilitarianism. The very title of Patrick's manual for preachers, *A Discourse of Profiting by Sermons*, is illuminating. Anglicanism, not the New Philosophy (which is not mentioned at all), is responsible for the new profitable style, with its emphasis on the listener rather than the speaker:

Now if the *composition* [of sermons] be faulty, it is because their *Method* is not clear and perspicuous: or the *Language* not plain enough to convey the Sense of them to the mind of the Hearers. Neither of which, I am confident can be truly charged upon them. For never did men more indeavour orderly discourse and aim at plain, unaffected Speech, than they do now in the Church of *England:* where good Sense, in the most easie and familiar Words, is now lookt upon as the principal Commendation of Sermons.[23]

None of the reforming tracts was as utilitarian as John Eachard's lively and often-imitated *Grounds and Occasions of the Contempt of the Clergy and Religion* (1670). Eachard tells us directly that the new plain style does not necessarily emanate from the New Philosophy: "Neither shall I here examine which Philosophy the Old or New, makes the best Sermons: It is hard to say that Exhortations can be to no purpose, if the Preacher believes that the Earth turns round: Or, that his Reproofs can take no effect, unless he will suppose a *Vacuum*. There have been good Sermons, no question, made in the days of *Materia Prima,* and *Occult Qualities:* and there are doubtless still good Discourses now under the Reign of Atoms." [24] With a certain prophetic philosophical acuity Eachard sees that it is possible to consider "Atoms" as mere symbols or words, like *Materia Prima,* rather than things. For all his cavalier dismissal of the New Philosophy, Eachard shares the general prejudice against wits and scholars compared to artisans, countrymen, and merchants. "An ordinary *Chees-monger,* or *Plumb-seller,* that scarce ever heard of an University, shall write much better Sense, and more to the purpose than these young Philosophers, who injudiciously hunting only for great Words, make themselves learnedly ridiculous" (p. 25). A Franklinesque Protestant Ethic creeps into

Eachard's counsel, with its ironic equation of the market-place with virtue: "If the Minister's words be such as the Constable uses, his Matter Plain and Practical, such as come to the common Market, he may pass possibly for an Honest, Well-Meaning Man, but by no means for any Scholar" (p. 33). For the no-nonsense Eachard "things" are not "atoms" but concrete objects like the cheeses and plums of the market. Like Bacon, Eachard would have us hunt for these rather than "great Words"; again, like Bacon, Eachard inveighs against the inexperienced assemblage of aphorisms removed from "things": "I'll but suppose an Academick Youngster to be put upon a *Latin* Oration: Away he goes presently to his Magazine of collected *Phrases:* he picks out all the *Glitterings* he can find; he hales out all the *Proverbs, Flowers, Poetical Snaps, Tales* out of the Dictionary" (p. 26).

The antihumanistic Eachard joins the moderns against the ancients. As the preceding quotation suggests, the discussion of sermon style occurs in the context of a proposal to reform the conventional curriculum of the universities in which Eachard goes against the entire humanistic tradition in favor of the useful arts. The "Ridiculousness, Phantastical Phrases, harsh, and sometimes blasphemous Metaphors, abundantly foppish similitudes, childish and empty Transitions, and the like, so commonly uttered out of Pulpits" (p. 27) he charges up to contemporary education. Despite a considerable difference in general temper, Eachard follows Sprat's and Webster's division of all knowledge into the useful and the useless, with the new plain style associated with the useful and with material "things." Utility is the arbiter of style. "Certainly what is most undoubtedly Useless and Empty, or what is judg'd absolutely ridiculous, not by this or that curious or squeamish *Auditor*, but by every Man in the *Corporation* that understands but plain *English* and Common Sense, ought to be avoided" (p. 37). Again, the useful style is not only plain but true because nearest to material things. Rhetoricians "do so weaken and enfeeble their Judgment by contenting themselves to understand by Colours, Features, and Glimpses, that they perfectly omit all the more profitable searching into the Nature and Causes of things themselves" (p. 41). "Colours, Features, and Glimpses," of course, are the very essence of the older plain style, and "Anti-Ciceronianism," with its tentativeness and allusive immediacy.

The point of view shared by Wilkins, Patrick, and Eachard is typical of the age. And practice followed theory; the styles of even the greatest Restoration divines can be identified only by experts like Mitchell. In the history of the evolution of a uniformly "modern" style this sameness is of immense significance, for the sermon was by far the most important and influential literary prose form of the century. It is significant then that with the possible — and considerable — exception of Tillotson, none of the four greatest preachers of the Restoration — South, Barrow, Stillingfleet, and Tillotson — shows the influence of "Science" in general, or of the Royal Society in particular.

Certainly none of these pillars of the Establishment can be found using the language of artisans, merchants, and countrymen. Even so, Robert South, though more hostile to the Royal Society and the new philosophy than Eachard,[25] unwittingly agrees with Sprat and Bacon, rather than Seneca and the classical plain style, on the relation of words, things, and utility. South's invective against the style of Jeremy Taylor is notorious, and his sermons on "The Fatal Imposture and Force of Words" comprise the most elaborate discussion of the problem by any preacher. South begins with a Lockean nominalism: "The way in which good and evil generally operate upon the mind of man, is by those words or names by which they are notified and conveyed to the mind. Words are the signs and symbols of things;

and as in accompts, ciphers and figures pass for real sums, so in the course of human affairs, words and names pass for things themselves." [26] The image of the cipher and figures is reminiscent of Sprat and the Real Character of Bacon and Wilkins. All these men make the nominalistic division between words and material things. Words represent only "notions," which are merely signs for arbitrary slices of matter, or qualities abstracted out of matter. Moral qualities require larger, more complex abstractions — what Locke was to call "mixed modes." "In most things good and evil lie shuffled and thrust up together in a confused heap; and it is study and intention of thought which must draw them forth, and range them under their distinct heads" (p. 456). This is simply Wilkins' program for the Real Character without the Real Character; South hopes that words themselves can have the same unalterable referents as mathematical symbols. Such words exist not among wits and scholars but in the marketplace. The Protestant Ethic bobs up again. In the market words are of most "practice and design," and morality in commerce is South's analogy for morality in general.

This therefore is certain, that in human life, or conversation, words stand for things; the common business of the world not being capable of being managed otherwise. For by these, men come to know one another's minds. By these they covenant and confederate. By these they buy and sell, they deal and traffick. In short, words are the great instruments both of practice and design; which, for the most part, move wholly in the strength of them. Forasmuch as it is the nature of man both to will and to do, according to the persuasion he has of the good and evil of those things that come before him; and to take up his persuasions according to the representations made to him of those qualities, by their respective names or appellations. (pp. 449–450)

What separates notions as well as words from things is the Imagination. "For things, or objects, cannot enter into the mind, as they subsist in themselves, and by their own natural bulk pass into apprehension; but they are taken in by their ideas, their notions, or resemblances; which imprinting themselves after a spirited immaterial manner in the imagination, and from thence, under a further refinement, passing into the intellect, are by that expressed by certain words or names, found out and invented by the mind, for the communication of its conceptions, or thoughts, to others" (p. 449). Agreeing with the entire Baconian tradition, South holds that trouble comes when words, after being imprinted in a spirited immaterial manner, are taken for exact designations of real, material things. The result is that "the generality of mankind is wholly and absolutely governed by words or names; without, nay, for the most part, even against the knowledge men have of things. The multitude, or common rout, like a drove of sheep, or an herd of oxen, may be managed by any noise or cry which their drivers shall accustom them to" (p. 450). Words perversely persist in acquiring connotations, associations, and overtones, refusing to limit themselves to one specific referent, one solitary Thing. "As for the meaning of the word itself, that may shift for itself: and as for the sense and reason of it, that has little or nothing to do here; only let it sound full and round, and chime right to the humour, which is at present agog. . . . For a plausible, insignificant word, in the mouth of an expert demagogue, is a dangerous and a dreadful weapon" (p. 450).

South again is thoroughly in accord with the Baconian spirit, with its merger of the true, the good, and the useful, where words are things and there are no more demagogues. (South, like Sprat, is recovering from the effects of the civil wars.) There would be no more "Anti-Ciceronians" either, since their way of writing depends on the very qualities of language which South would banish. South's attacks on the "vain, luxurious allegories, [and] rhyming cadencies of similar words" of preaching like Adams' and Andrewes' are Anti-Senecan. Such traits are described in another sermon as "the plastering of marble, or the painting of gold." [27] In South's citation, immediately following, of Quintilian's well-worn jibe at Seneca, "that he did *rerum pondera minutissimis sententis frangere,* break, and, as it were, emasculate the weight of his subject by the little affected sentences," South reveals an awareness of the origin of this language in Senecan imitation. Like Sprat and Glanvill, South is an Anti-Senecan; but his new plainness does not proceed from the new philosophy (against which South preached), but is, according to Mitchell, "part of a larger national movement which was demanding that prose style in general should conform to these standards" (p. 377).

Thus Isaac Barrow, one of the few men who could equal South in the pulpit and second to none as a mathematician, was a member of the Royal Society, which South attacked. But "Barrow cannot be classed as a 'Royal Society divine,' meaning by that term a clerical member of that Society whose work exemplifies the stylistic ideals set out by Sprat" (Mitchell, p. 322). That Barrow's style was on the outer limits of what the Restoration permitted is demonstrated by the fact that Barrow's editor, Tillotson, felt compelled to simplify and "improve" the original text. Barrow's ideas on style do agree with South's — and so many others' — utilitarian Protestant Ethic, with its own variety of Decorum. The very titles of Barrow's sermons are revealing: "The Profitableness of Godliness," "The Fruitlessness of Sin," and five discourses on "Industry" in general, in "our general calling, as Christians," "in our particular calling, as gentlemen" and "as scholars." In "Against Foolish Talking and Jesting," the useful style must be humorless, like the language of "the shop and the exchange" and "business" for "profit." Never, though, has so sober a doctrine been enunciated with such grandeur. Even the following passage on stylistic theory illustrates Barrow's plain splendor through great piles of balanced, though not antithetical, phrases, usually in settled triplets:

> In deliberations and debates about affairs of great importance, the simple manner of speaking to the point is the proper, easy, clear, and compendious way: facetious speech there serves only to obstruct and entangle business, to lose time, and protract the result. The shop and the exchange will scarce endure jesting in their lower transactions: the senate, the court of justice, the church do much more exclude it from their more weighty consultations. Whenever it justleth out, or hindereth the despatch of other serious business, taking up the room or swallowing the time due to it, or indisposing the minds of the audience to attend it, then it is unseasonable and pestilent. . . . He that for his sport neglects his business, deserves indeed to be reckoned among children; and children's fortune will be to attend him, to be pleased with toys; and to fail of substantial profit.[28]

Against the self-revelation and libertinism of the older plain style, "the casual hits and emergencies of roving fancy; for stumbling on an odd conceit or phrase, which signifieth nothing" (p. 413), Barrow opposes Right Reason, Virtue, and Utility, which, by the familiar equation, are the same. The question-and-answer form of the passage here illustrates the influence of the magniloquent patristic authors, especially Barrow's favorite, Chrysostom:

> It is these two, reason and virtue, in conjunction, which produce all that is considerably good and great in the world. Fancy can do little; doeth never anything well, except as directed and wielded by them. Do pretty conceits or humorous talk carry on any business, or perform any work? No; they are ineffectual and fruitless: often they disturb, but they never despatch any thing with good success. It is simple reason, as dull and dry as it seemeth, which expediteth all the grand affairs, which accomplisheth all the mighty works that we see done in the world. (p. 411)

Exactly the same ideal of utilitarian decorum emerges in the theory of the "perspicuous," "equable," and "noble"

Edward Stillingfleet (Mitchell, p. 307), who had nothing whatever to do with the Royal Society or "Science." The most popular London preacher of the Restoration, he attacked

all fine Harangues in the Pulpit, *i.e.* Words well put together without suitable Matter; All dry, flat insipid Discourses, about things of so great consequence to Men's Salvation; All affectations of Jingling Sentences; Far-fetched Allusions, Elaborate Trifles; All impertinent Disputes about needless, vain, intricate Controversies; All Enthusiastick unintelligible Talk, which tend to confound Men's Notions of Religion, and to evaporate the true Spirit of it into Fansies and Eastern Modes of speaking. . . .

But setting all these aside, there remains a Grave, Serious, Pious, Affectionate, Convincing way of Preaching; which is profitable, in its degree, for the same ends for which the holy Scripture is useful, viz. *for Doctrine, for reproof, for Correction, for Instruction in Righteousness,* i.e for the best purposes in the World. . . .

It is very easie to shoot over the People's heads, and to spend an hour to little or no purpose; but it requires all our skill to Preach plainly without flatness; and to set the matters of Religion in the best light, and to recommend them to the minds of People, with the greatest force of Persuasion. . . .

And it is hardly possible to mistake, as to the best Method of Preaching, if men do but judge aright concerning the End and Design of it.[29]

If Stillingfleet was the most popular of the great Restoration divines, Archbishop John Tillotson was probably the most influential. "All the nation proposed him as a pattern, and studied to copy after him," wrote Burnet.[30] There is some hard evidence that Tillotson was influenced by the stylistic program of the Royal Society. Not only was he a member, but Wilkins himself was his father-in-law. What is more important, we are told in Bishop Burnet's funeral sermon in 1692 for Tillotson:

His joining with Bishop *Wilkins* in pursuing the scheme of the Universal Character, led him to consider exactly the Truth of Language and Stile, in which no man was happier, and knew better the Art of preserving the Majesty of things under a Simplicity of Words; tempering these so equally together, that neither did his Thoughts sink, nor his Stile swell: keeping always the due Mean between a low Flatness and the Dresses of false Rhetorick. . . . He cut off both the Luxuriances of Stile, and the Length of Sermons; and he concluded them with some Thoughts of such Gravity and Use, that he generally dismissed his Hearers with somewhat that stuck to them.[31]

On the other hand, in the large corpus of Tillotson's works, there is not a single reference to the Royal Society or the New Philosophy. These writings, however, are shot through with a utilitarianism of near-Hobbesian tough-mindedness, and it is this, rather than "Science," to which Tillotson attributes his method of persuasion:

All human actions have an order and reference to some end, and consequently suppose some knowledge of the end, and of the means whereby it may be attained. So that unless a man do believe and be persuaded that such a thing is some way or other good for him, and consequently desirable and fit to be propounded as an end, and that this end is attainable, and the means which he useth are profitable and likely for the attaining of this end, he will sit still and do nothing at all about it. So that without faith it is impossible to do any thing: he that believes nothing will do nothing.[32]

Almost all men can be reasoned into faith, continues Tillotson, and therefore into their own self-interest; therefore a sermon must be rational:

Now, there needs no more to be done to put a man upon any thing, but to satisfy him of these two things: that the action you persuade him to is reasonable; that is, possible and fit to be done: and that it is highly in his interest to do it; that is, if he do it, it will be eminently for his advantage. . . . If you can once possess a man, that is any degree sober and considerate, with these persuasions, you may make him do any thing of which he is thus persuaded. (p. 257)

The end dictates the style:

This may correct the irregular humour and itch in many people, who are not contented with this plain and wholesome food, but must be gratified with sublime notions and unintelligible mysteries, with pleasant passages of wit, and artificial strains of rhetoric, and nice and unprofitable disputes, with bold interpretations of dark prophecies, and peremptory determinations of what will happen next year, and a punctual stating of the time when antichrist shall be thrown down, and Babylon shall fall, and who shall be employed in this work. Or, if their humour lies another way, you must apply yourself to it, by making sharp reflections upon matters in present controversy and debate; you must dip your style in gall and vinegar, and be all satire and invective against those that differ from you, and teach people to hate one another, and to fall together by the ears; and this men call gospel preaching, and speaking of seasonable truths. ("The Necessity of Repentance and Faith," *Works*, VII, p. 223)

All of which is about as far as the doctrine of plain and useful Decorum in preaching style can go, except perhaps for Bishop Samuel Parker's proposal in 1670 for "an Act of Parliament to abridge Preachers the use of fulsom and lushious Metaphors . . . an effectual Cure of our present Distempers" of preachers who have "affected phrases and Forms of Speech . . . without having any Notion of the Things they signifie." [33]

Toward the end of the century, understandably, a mild reaction against plainness in favor of "Rhetorick" — mere words without specific referents — set in. We have seen this reaction already in Glanvill's *Essay on Preaching*; similar statements appear in the sermon manuals of Arderne, Fowler, and Burnet, all of whom allow for "Eloquence" at least in the concluding "Motives" of the sermon.[34] Eloquence is justified reluctantly on the usual utilitarian grounds as a concession to the necessity for rousing the laity. This kind of language is the preachers' equivalent of Sprat's rhetorical apologetic style in the *History* designed to stir the "wits" or to Bacon's "methods" for the "use" of knowledge. Its model, according to Burnet's *Discourse of the Pastoral*

Care (1692), is not the "vain Eloquence" of the Senecan tradition but Ciceronianism. "He that has a Taste and Genius for Eloquence, must improve it by reading *Quintilian*, and *Tully's* books of *Oratory;* and by observing the spirit and method of *Tully's* Orations" (p. 225). The views of Burnet, a member of the Royal Society who preached Boyle's funeral sermon as well as Tillotson's, correspond to Bacon's with respect to Seneca. Seneca is useful for his "matter," but Burnet indicates that his manner holds perils for the young writer, who "is also to make a Collection of all such Thoughts, as he finds either in the Books of the Ancient Philosophers (where *Seneca* will be of great use to him) or of Christian Authors: he is to separate such Thoughts as are forced, and that do become rather a strained Declamation made only to please, than a solid Discourse designed to persuade" (p. 234).

The Christian authors given to strained Declamations are the early imitators of Seneca who found their echoes in the seventeenth century in the school of Andrewes. These early Christians, "disgusted" at the "Plainness" of a Basil or Chrysostom,

brought in a great deal of Art into the Composition of Sermons: Mystical Applications of Scripture grew to be better liked than clear Texts; an Accumulation of Figures, a Cadence in the Periods, a playing upon the Sounds of Words, a Loftiness of Epithets, and often an Obscurity of Expression, were according to the different tastes of the several Ages run into. Preaching has past through many different forms among us since the Reformation. But without flattering the present Age, or any person now alive, too much, it must be considered, that it is brought of late to a much greater Perfection than it ever was before among us. It is certainly brought nearer the Pattern that S. *Chrysostom* has set, or perhaps carried beyond it. Our Language is much refined, and we have returned to the plain Notions of simple and genuine Rhetorick. (pp. 215–216)

For Burnet Senecan imitation leads to debased oratory not "Plainness."

Anglican plain style, like the style advocated by the Royal Society, should be viewed then as a reaction against, rather than a "revision" of, the earlier libertinism. But it is difficult to regard the style advocated by the Society's reformers as simply stemming from a "scientific" — as distinct from a "religious" — influence when so many of its principal advocates and practitioners are clergymen themselves, and when the identical style is advocated and practiced by other clergymen — most notably Eachard, Stillingfleet, South, and Ferguson — who are indifferent or hostile to the Society and "Science." The scientists and divines in the Society "were not so much originating a movement as seeking to emphasize a possibility already achieved" (Mitchell, p. 332). Surely so vast a linguistic event as the shift of an entire prose style, "the movement towards the simplification of style, away from conceits, incessant and unnecessary quotations, and phonic ingenuities imitated from ancient rhetorical practice, was not due to the sudden whim of Court or the fiat of a Society" (p. 311).

There is considerable evidence, as Haller, Miller, and Fisch have suggested, that the earlier Puritan reaction against the "Senecanism" of the school of Andrewes and Adams had at least as much to do with the later Anglican reforms as any "scientific" influence. In the Calvinist William Perkins' extremely influential *Art of Prophecying* (1592), preaching is regarded as a branch of rhetoric, with set systems of tropes and figures. Even so, utilitarian considerations dictate an impersonal plain style:

Humane Wisdome must be concealed, whether it be in the matter of the sermon, or in the setting forth of the words:. . . . He ought in publike to conceale all these from the people, and not make the least ostentation. . . . Wherefore neither the words of arts, [nor] Greeke and Latin phrases must be intermingled in the sermon. 1. They disturbe the minds of the auditours, that they cannot fit these things which went afore with those that follow. 2. A strange work hindreth the understanding of those things that are spoken. 3. It drawes the mind away from the purpose to some other matter.[35]

Richard Baxter, the great Puritan whose style the Anglican Glanvill admired, voices in 1656 the identification, familar to Anglicans and scientists alike, of truth, utility, and a close, naked, natural way of speaking:

All our teaching must be as Plain and Evident as we can make it. For this doth most suit to a Teachers ends. He that would be understood must speak to the capacity of his hearers, and make it his business to make himself understood. Truth loves the light, and is most beautiful when most naked. . . . Truth overcomes prejudice by meer Light of Evidence, and there is no better way to make a good cause prevail, then to make it as plain, and commonly and thoroughly known as we can; and it is this Light that will dispose an unprepared mind.[36]

And in 1659 a gentle divine, John Geree, in a pastiche of allusions to St. Paul, describes the Puritans' style as plain, useful, and impersonal, similar to that of the later Anglicans. The Old English Puritan

esteemed that preaching best wherein was most of God, least of man, when vain flourishes to wit and words were declined, and the demonstration of Gods Spirit and Power studied: yet could he distinguish between studied plainness, and negligent rudeness. He accounted perspicuity the best grace of a Preacher; And that method best which was most helpful to understanding, affection, and memory. To which ordinarily he esteemed none so conducible as that by Doctrine, Reason, and Use.[37]

Finally, even in the heyday of Andrewes and Adams the necessities of controversy were compelling certain Anglicans to adopt a plain style. Archbishop Ussher himself, "notwithstanding the Learnedness of most of his Hearers . . . rather chose a plain and substantial way of Preaching, for the promoting of Piety and Vertue, than studied Eloquence, or a vain ostentation of Learning: so that he quite put out of countenance that windy, affected sort of Oratory, which was then much in use, called *floride* preaching, or strong lines." [38] His decision was not without its effect. Ussher's biographer Parr reports, "Observing how plain, and yet moving [his sermons] were, and being sufficiently satisfied that it was not for want of Wit, or learning, that he did not do otherwise, he was soon convinced, that this was not the most ready way of gaining Souls, and therefore quitting his affected Style, and studied Periods, took up a more plain and profitable way of preaching" (p. 49).

Thus from sources remote from, opposed to, or antedating the Royal Society came similar stylistic ideals. There is as much evidence that the reform of the sermon influenced the Society's view of style as that "science" affected the preachers.

The New Plain Style and Intellectual Prose in General

Not only the religious writers but philosophers and literary critics — such distinctions, it cannot be repeated often enough, are arbitrary indeed for the seventeenth century — developed a theory of style which was indistinguishable from that of the Royal Society in its understanding of "things" as material reality, its division of expression ("Ornament") and content ("Sense" or "Matter"), and its attack on the ideals of the older plain style, including "Anti-Ciceronianism." Again the influences on these theorists are to be found not so much in "science" but in the general feeling that prose should exist primarily for purposes of useful communication.

Meric Casaubon, son of the great classical scholar, illustrates the transition from Renaissance humanism to the new ideals. One of Glanvill's foremost opponents, he attacks the Society for its utilitarianism.[39] In this he is untypical of his age; the Society was not usually attacked on *that* score. Glanvill's failure to reply to Casaubon is perhaps significant.

Was a reply possible? As we might expect from such an upholder of the old virtues, Casaubon writes in an intimate manner reminiscent of the ancient epistolary form. Yet Casaubon's ideas about rhetoric, if not his own stylistic practice, are indistinguishable from the Society's.[40] On the subject of rhetoric Casaubon writes in his *Treatise Concerning Enthusiasme* (1655), "Seneca is very copious, and in my judgement hath done very well." [41] He realizes that Seneca's practice does not follow his theory. After quoting the end of the piece on tranquillity, in which Seneca hails enthusiasm as a source of oratory, Casaubon allows us to follow his own speculations. The rambling but generous scholar is charmingly present: "Here is a perfect *Enthusiasme*, with allusion to the *Sibylls*, and such others as were generally conceived to be possest. Yet whether *Seneca* himself did believe so much, as his words seem to import, is a question: it being his manner, to be very high and tumid in his expressions; which nevertheless a sober reader will not allwayes take to the utmost of what they will bear" (p. 145). Casaubon then discusses Seneca's fury, which seems to contradict his Stoic philosophy. "We must therefore conclude, that *Seneca* in this place was, against his own reason, overswayed by his own *genius*, being a man of violent spirit naturally, as appears by him in many places; and would have appeared much more, had not Reason and Philosophy moderated it" (p. 146). Here is the standard Restoration antithesis between Reason and Passion, with their respective allies plainness and rhetoric. Casaubon knows all the other right things to say about style. What is most important for our purposes is his identification, in this *Treatise Concerning Enthusiasme*, of the "high and tumid" Senecan style with Enthusiastic rhetoric. Both come under the same attack not only from the Royal Society but from a writer such as Casaubon who is antagonistic to it. Again, "science" is not responsible for an attack on oratory and the older plain style.

Another enemy of the Society, though remote in style
and temperament from Casaubon, is the blunt Hobbes. He is
a special case. He shares many of the assumptions of the Society but carries them much farther than it was willing to
allow. In the relentless materialism of *Leviathan* (1651)
there is nothing except physical bodies in motion. Our
"fancies" themselves are "Motions within us, reliques of
those made in the Sense." [42] Words are, or should be, signs
of these physical motions: "The generall use of Speech, is
to transferre our Mentall Discourse, into Verball; or the
Trayne of our Thoughts, into a Trayne of Words. . . .
So that the first use of names, is to serve for *Markes*, or
Notes of remembrance. Another is, when many use the same
words, to signifie (by their connexion and order) one to
another, what they conceive, or think of each matter; and
also what they desire, feare, or have any other passion for.
And for this use they are called Signes."

Hobbes reveals more psychological perception than his
contemporaries by refusing to acquiesce in their assumption
that the rigorous or methodical kind of discourse necessarily
best reveals the immediate motions of the author's mind.
Rather Hobbes recognizes that the mind left to itself rambles
about in swift and almost inexplicable associations.

This Trayne of Thoughts, or Mentall Discourse, is of two
sorts. The first is *Unguided, without Design,* and inconstant;
Wherein there is no Passionate Thought, to govern and direct
those that follow, to it self, as the end and scope of some desire,
or other passion: In which case the thoughts are said to wander,
and seem impertinent one to another, as in a Dream. Such are
Commonly the thoughts of men, that are not onely without
company, but also without care of any thing. (pp. 16–17)

Such a "Trayne" could serve as a manifesto for Montaigne
or Browne or any other of the lonely "Senecans" and other
aloof Stoics of the earlier part of the century not only without company but also without care of any thing. The other

kind of mental discourse transferred into verbal is restricted by its function:

> The second is more constant; as being *regulated* by some desire, and designe. For the impression made by such things as wee desire, or feare, is strong, and permanent, or, (if it cease for a time) of quick return: so strong it is sometimes, as to hinder and break our sleep. From Desire, ariseth the Thought of some means we have seen produce the like of that which we ayme at; and from the thought of that, the thought of means to that mean; and so continually, till we come to some beginning within our own power. And because the End, by the greatnesse of the impression, comes often to mind, in case our thoughts begin to wander, they are quickly again reduced into the way: which observed by one of the seven wise men, made him give men this praecept, which is now borne out, *Respice finem*; that is to say, in all your actions, look often upon what you would have, as the thing that directs your thoughts in the way to attain it. (pp. 17–18)

There is little question that Hobbes prefers the style which looks toward utility, "the End," as the means of acquiring any sort of knowledge. After this paragraph we hear nothing more about the first mode of discourse but a great deal about the second. For it Hobbes, like Sprat, seeks a mathematical plainness, but Hobbes goes further and would have prose follow not the discursive motions of the mind Unguided without Design but the impersonality of geometric proofs, in which all terms are defined. His source is Cicero: "For it is most true that *Cicero* sayth of them somewhere; that there can be nothing so absurd, but may be found in the books of the Philosophers. And the reason is manifest. For there is not one of them that begins his ratiocination from the Definitions, or Explications of the names they are to use; which is a method that hath been used onely in Geometry; whose Conclusions have thereby been made indisputable" (pp. 34–35). Like Bacon, Wilkins, and South, the nominalist and positivist Hobbes would have each word a "sign" equivalent to one hard, unchanging nugget of meaning, which in turn has been abstracted not from our random thought processes but from the Real World Out There. "And therefore in reasoning, a man must take heed of words; which besides the signification of what we imagine of their nature, have a signification also of the nature, disposition, and interest of the speaker; such as are the names of Vertues, and Vices; For one calleth *Wisdome*, what another calleth *feare;* and one *cruelty*, what another *justice.* . . . And therefore such names can never be true grounds of any ratiocination. No more can Metaphors, and Tropes of speech" (pp. 30–31).

Hobbes' linguistic theory is more sophisticated than Bacon's. But both philosophers drive in the same direction, toward the elimination of the nature, disposition, and interest of the speaker, as revealed in metaphors and tropes. Such a stylistic intention is the opposite of "Anti-Ciceronianism" and the classical plain style in general; the words of an allusive, suggestive, and designedly intimate author like Browne, who deliberately delivers thoughts rhetorically, would be totally unacceptable as true grounds for any ratiocination. Ratiocination is simply the collecting of things like Bacon's aphorisms or ciphers, now understood more philosophically as well-defined tokens or counters of discrete units of meaning. "REASON, in this sense, is nothing but *Reckoning* (that is, Adding and Subtracting) of the Consequences of generall names agreed upon, for the *marking* and *signifying* of our thoughts; I say *marking* them, when we reckon by our selves; and *signifying*, when we demonstrate, or approve our reckonings to other men" (p. 32). The mathematical imagery is uppermost: "When a man *Reasoneth*, hee does nothing else but conceive a summe totall, from *Addition* of parcels; or conceive a Remainder, from *Subtraction* of one summe from another" (p. 31). Significant discourse is a matter of objective argumentation — of demonstration or approval — and is as impersonal as geometry. Metaphor and rhetoric in general are an abuse of truthful language because they intrude a distinctive, particular, personal observation between words and physical matter. Suggestive and inexact, they defy arithmetical "reckoning"; "To the use of Metaphors, Tropes, and other Rhetoricall figures, instead of words proper. For though it be lawfull to say (for example) in common speech, *the way goeth, or leadeth hither or thither, The Proverb says this or that* (whereas wayes cannot go, nor Proverbs speak;) yet in reckoning, and seeking of truth, such speeches are not to be admitted" (p. 211). In metaphors the one-to-one relationship between token and bit of meaning is lost, and "reckoning" is impossible. The results are disastrous. With Sprat and South, Hobbes believes that metaphor and rhetoric keep existence solitary, poor, nasty, brutish, and short; as a case in point, they caused the controversies leading to the civil wars. Hobbes' entire thesis, with the inevitable equation of Truth and Utility, is summarized in one of his violently straightforward paragraphs:

To conclude, The Light of humane minds is Perspicuous Words, but by exact definitions first snuffed, and purged from ambiguity; *Reason* is the *pace;* Encrease of *Science,* the *way;* and the Benefit of man-kind, the *end.* And on the contary, Metaphors, and senselesse and ambiguous words, are like *ignes fatui;* and reasoning upon them, is wandering amongst innumerable absurdities; and their end, contention, and sedition, or contempt. (pp. 37–38)

Even Hobbes, attacked so frequently for his general philosophy, hews closely to the orthodox theory of Restoration plain style. He is responding not to the new philosophy or the Royal Society, which *Leviathan* antedates, but to the intellectual climate which itself produced the Society as well as contemporary Anglicanism. (Undoubtedly he is helping to create this climate, too.) *Leviathan* is a book on political theory, not on our "science." The nominalism underlying all contemporary theories of the plain style pulls Hobbes into the extreme position that metaphor is not to be admitted in reckoning and seeking of truth.

How impossible such a program would be is apparent in the use of metaphor to deny metaphor, for truth is "sought" and speeches "admitted." What Hobbes is willing to "admit," it seems, is a certain kind of unobtrusive or played out, and hence impersonal, metaphor. It is a metaphor sanctioned by general usage and Decorum rather than individual whim or quirk, a metaphor, in other words, agreeable to current notions of useful Truth. Of course, Hobbes does not put it this way, since he claims to exclude all metaphor in the first place.

The difficulties of so radical a position are seen in Robert Ferguson's *The Interest of Reason in Religion* (1675), the century's most extensive discussion of metaphor (the only tract at all comparable is to be found in 1696 in John Sargeant's *The Method to Science*). Like everyone else we have encountered in the Restoration, Ferguson is opposed to metaphors for their being untruthful to "things." The difficulty is that God uses them in the Bible. By resorting to the famous "accommodation" theory of Scriptural interpretation — that is, that Biblical metaphors are God's accommodation to our lesser intellects — Ferguson attempts a resolution of the problem:

I can very well allow that in Philosophy, where the Quality and Nature of things do not transcend and over-match words, the less Rhetorical ornaments, especially the fewer Metaphors, providing still that the phrase be pure and easie, the better. But in Divinity, where no expressions come fully up to the Mysteries of Faith, and where the things themselves are not capable of being declared in *Logical* and *Metaphysical* Terms; Metaphors may not only be allowed, but are most accomodated to the assisting us in our conceptions of Gospel mysteries.[43]

God, in other words, almost tells lies. But God is doing it for good Ends. All of which, of course, is thoroughly

Baconian, though I have no evidence that Bacon influenced Ferguson directly. There is nothing in Bacon to restrict the use of rhetoric for practical purposes, and Divinity is no exception: "For we see that, in matters of Faith and Religion, we raise our Imagination above our Reason; which is the cause why Religion sought ever access to the mind by similitude, types, parables, visions, dreams" (*Advancement, Works*, VI, pp. 258–259).

Unlike the excessive allegorizing of rabbis, nonconformists, friars, Socinians, Quakers, and other such rabble, divine metaphors are, according to Ferguson, "proper." Like Hobbes, Ferguson finds a certain kind of metaphor attractive:

However as the Phantastical trifling with Words and Syllables, and the Boyish affectation of Cadencies is wholly grown to disuse and distast, as unbecoming the Sanctity of the Mysteries we treat of . . . so I hope a care will likewise possess us in reference to the other, *viz.*, that we coyn no Metaphors of our own to express things by, but what are modest, cleanly, and carry a due Proportion, Analogy, and Similitude to the things they are brought to illustrate. But our adversaries must in the mean time pardon us if we be not so fond of their Effeminate, amorous stile, as to introduce it into the Pulpit: For indeed it savours more of the style of the *Grand-Cyrus, Cleopatra, Parthenissa*, &c. than any style that the Doctrines of Faith, and Precepts of Morality have been heretofore delivered in. (pp. 296–297)

The ideal metaphor has a referent as similar as possible to its reference; Ferguson instances such categories of similarity as "Quality, Affection, Property, Operation, or Adjunct" (p. 302). Metaphor *"is the traduction of a Word from its immediate and proper sense, and the extending it to the denotation of some other thing, upon the account of some similitude or proportion betwixt the one and the other"* (p. 299). The ideal metaphor is as close to a "proper" expression as possible in that a word is traduced as little as possible from the unalterable nugget of sense data it sup-posedly denotes. Such metaphors are desirable because "ob-vious and pertinent" (p. 312). They are "not obscure and unintelligible, but accommodated to the Understandings of those we address them to" (p. 369). Thus the criterion for good metaphor is not its truth to experience. Its usefulness for discourse, that is, its ease for the reader, is what matters.

Glanvill, for example, in his revision of *The Vanity of Dogmatizing,* cut out "The Sages of old live again in us, and in opinions there is a Metempsychosis." The metaphor was undesirable for three reasons. First, the exact relation between tenor and vehicle is not spelled out; the reader is left to work it out for himself. Second, "Sages" and "Me-tempsychosis" are not the same sort of thing as recurring ideas, and again the reader must work to figure out the connection. The word "Sages" is traduced too much from its immediate and proper sense. Finally, if the reader does not know about "Metempsychosis," he must work some more and perhaps do some research. Decorum decrees that figures must be accommodated to the audience, and God is the ultimate — but most decorous — accommodator.

God is not the only one who can accommodate. As Fer-guson confesses, with what for the Restoration is refresh-ing candor, it is current fashion, rather than the desire for a way of framing truthful statements, that determines sty-listic practice in his own time; like the "Phantastical trifling with words and Syllables" of a Senecan preacher, the wrong kind of metaphor "is wholly grown to disuse and distast." Just as the Restoration found certain truths more satisfying, it found a certain kind of discourse more palatable than other kinds. It called these truths Truth, this style the only Proper Style. In the unfashionable style metaphor is "empty" and "vain" when, as in "Senecan" or libertine style, it inter-poses between words and material things the immaterial things of the unreliable and useless individual soul. What

Ferguson says of the Quakers could apply to the "Anti-Ciceronians": "*Quakers*, who by turning the whole Scripture into Allusions, have wrested the Revelations of the Word to justifie their own wilde Phantasm's, and fram'd the Words of Scripture *to their own private Notions,* and thereby evacuated the sublimest Doctrines and most Glorious Actions into empty Metaphors and vain Similitudes" (p. 310).

Like the other theorists Ferguson's interest is in argumentation rather than revelation of one's own private Notions. To serve the purposes of argument metaphors must be "unfolded," revealed as a patently ornamental, purely rhetorical commentary on the serious business of the discourse, the Argument. Their relation to the Argument must be seen as clearly as possible. This kind of "clarity" is a major goal of Restoration style. To achieve it, tenor and vehicle are separated in a one-to-one relationship of figure to "things." "The best and most ornate as well as the most usual Similitudes are where one thing is compared with another in some adjunct, affection, &c. wherein they resemble one the other, and are alike; and that to which the other is compared, is disposed and put first, and that which is compared to it, is put last" (p. 304). Ferguson devotes many pages to the proper techniques for "unfolding a Metaphor." It involves a rigorous submission of individual feeling and experience to the demands of argumentation: "In the Unfolding and explicating of Metaphors, great Sobriety as well as Diligence is to be observed, lest mistaking the Quality, Affection, Property, Operation, or Adjunct why any Word is transferred from what it originally signifies, we misapply it to intimate something else" (p. 302). "Things" for Ferguson are the same as for Sprat. The Real World is the solid one of everyday utility:

Seeing the Scripture expresseth somewhat of Religion by all the parts of the Creation, by the Imployments of the very

utensils of Human Life, and by the usages and customs of Mankind: Metaphors are not a subject for any undertaker to
exercise upon who hath not more than a tincture of knowledge
in all those. . . . It cannot otherwise be, but that to persons
ignorant of natural Philosophy, Agriculture, &c. . . . many
Texts will seem obscure which are not at all so to such as are
imbued with true *Ideas* of the Natures and properties of things.
(pp. 345–346)

In Ferguson appears the final stylistic result of the Baconian
complex of clarity, impersonality, the submission of the
mind to concrete physical things, and, above all, utility. Yet
there is no evidence of any "scientific" influence on this
author.

Ferguson is a theorist. The practice of metaphor in the
Restoration is better illustrated by a famous contribution to
theory in 1667 of John Dryden. Sometime Anglican, occasional fellow of the Royal Society, and versatile literary
man, Dryden is a microcosm of the groups interested in the
new prose of utility. In the preface to the *Annus Mirabilis*
Dryden says he "endeavored to adorn" the poem

with noble thoughts, so much more to express those thoughts
with elocution. The composition of all poems is, or ought to
be, of wit; and wit in the poet, or wit writing (if you will
give me leave to use a school-distinction) is no other than
the faculty of imagination in the writer, which, like a nimble
spaniel, beats over and ranges thro' the field of memory, till it
springs the quarry it hunted after; or, without metaphor, which
searches over all the memory for the species or ideas of those
things which it designs to represent. Wit written is that which
is well defin'd, the happy result of thought, or product of
imagination. But to proceeed from wit, in the general notion of
it, to the proper wit of an heroic or historical poem, I judge it
chiefly to consist in the delightful imaging of persons, actions,
passions, or things. 'Tis not the jerk or sting of an epigram,
nor the seeming contradiction of a poor antithesis, (the delight
of an ill-judging audience in a play of rhyme) nor the jingle
of a mere poor *paranomasia;* neither is it so much the morality
of a grave sentence, affected by Lucan, but more sparingly

us'd by Virgil; but it is some lively and apt description, dress'd in such colors of speech that it sets before your eyes the absent object as perfectly and more delightfully than nature.[44]

Dryden is complicated, and generalizations about him are dangerous. In many ways this urbane satirist, writer of comedies, and translator of Juvenal and Persius is in the main tradition of the classical plain style. To set before the eyes of the reader as truthful statement images more delightful than nature is an ideal reminiscent of classical *mimesis*, not Baconian passivity. His notion of the "things" which language is supposed to reproduce seems to include the intimate and specifically personal — "persons, actions, passions" — as well as the concrete "things" of the useful, material world. If his baffling definition of "wit" in the *Author's Apology* prefixed to *The State of Innocence* as "a propriety of thoughts and words; or, in other terms, thoughts and words elegantly adapted to the subject" means anything, it includes the notion, crucial to the classical plain style, of language as an index of character.

But in his conception of language as a means of persuasion easily accessible to all, Dryden is a utilitarian. (Although he is discussing metaphor in the preface to a poem, like the other theorists he seems to make no distinction between metaphors in poetry and those in prose.) Like Ferguson, he admits metaphor cautiously and apologetically. Its ultimate status as Ornament rather than Truth is apparent in the "unfolding" in "proper" language ("without metaphor") of the metaphor. Vehicle and tenor are carefully separated and analytically compared so that every physical detail in the figure is related to one specific idea. Such a procedure is exactly what Dryden is advising in the tenor of the very metaphor under discussion: proper wit is a submission of the Imagination to things (in the vehicle, the things are the spaniel, field, and quarry) which are exact equivalents of individual ideas (in the tenor, respectively, the search of the imagination, the memory, the ideas of things). The result, as here, is that this kind of Restoration metaphor, surrounded by apology and explication, stands out conspicuously — and paradoxically — in so antimetaphorical a time. Wanning has characterized Restoration metaphor aptly as having "the quality of self-consciousness about it that a reformed drunkard has in taking a drink." [45]

Dryden contrasts his type of figure, in which things are delightfully imaged, with improper wit. In his condemnation of epigram, antithesis, figures of sound, puns, and *sententiae* Dryden's description is an attack on the salient qualities of "Senecan" style, which Dryden must have recalled as the drunkenness of the preceding age.[46] All these devices are undesirable because they derive from the associative patterns of the mind, not from an orderly arrangement of Things, with "thought" and "elocution" clearly differentiated.

This differentiation gives Restoration prose its air of "precision" or "clarity" or "plainness," the critical terms most frequently applied to it then and now. More exactly, it has a certain kind of "precision" — an avoidance of the striking disjunctions of the earlier writers in favor of a systematic arrangement of abstract nouns — which the Restoration thought was the only kind. As an example we can do no better than to follow Dryden further:

So then, the first happiness of the poet's imagination is properly *invention*, or finding of the thought; the second is fancy, or the variation, deriving, or molding of that thought, as the judgement represents it proper to the subject; the third is elocution, or the art of clothing and adorning this thought, so found and varied, in apt, significant, and sounding words: the quickness of the imagination is seen in the invention, the fertility in the fancy, and the accuracy in the expression. For the two first of these, Ovid is famous amongst the poets; for the latter, Virgil. Ovid images more often the movements and affections of the mind, either combating between two contrary passions, or extremely discompos'd by one: his words therefore are the least part of his care; for he pictures nature in disorder, with which the study and choice of words is inconsistent. This is the proper wit of dialogue or discourse, and consequently of the *drama*, where all that is said is suppos'd to be the effect of sudden thought; which, tho' it excludes not the quickness of wit and repartees, yet admits not a too curious election of words, too frequent allusions or use of tropes, or in fine anything that shews remoteness of thought or labor in the writer. On the other side, Virgil speaks not so often in the person of another, like Ovid, but in his own: he relates almost all things as from himself, and thereby gains more liberty than the other, to express his thoughts with all the graces of elocution, to write more figuratively, and to confess as well the labor as the force of his imagination.

Dryden has just told us that wit written is well defined (the phrase itself is a definition). So we are greeted at the outset with a clutch of definitions; and definitions, as we have seen, are essential in the new plain style, with its effort to give words the solidity of things, as in mathematics and the Real Character. But Dryden's definitions obviously depend on other, undefined abstract nouns. For example, Fancy is the variation, deriving, or molding of individual thought, as the judgement represents it proper to the subject. Now what is Judgement? or Proper? And how are thoughts derived? One verbal puzzle has replaced another in this supposedly "precise" prose. The answer, of course, is that Judgement is what Fashion says it is, and Fashion is not determined by "Science" or the fiat of a Society, but by the total Baconian complex we have been examining up to now. Needless to say, terms defined by Fashion are, as Eachard seems to have seen, as arbitrary as the jargon of the despised schoolmen (from whom Dryden admittedly borrows his distinction about "wit" and "wit written") and not nearly as constant. It is assumed we all know the Things which fashionable words stand for, which is quite flattering to us readers; and when we are flattered, when we feel we are at one with the Best Critics, we feel we have been reminded of the Precise Truth. Actually we have been *told* we have learned, or already know, what the Best Critics think about Fancy, Judgement, and the rest, but no hard information has been supplied. Rather we have been assured by the method of definitions and Dryden's careful, exquisitely varied antitheses that concepts like Fancy and Judgement are as solidly and sharply defined as the Things from the worlds of Hobbes' mathematicians, Sprat's artisans, merchants, countrymen, and experimenters, Eachard's cheesemongers and plum-sellers, Barrow's marketplace, and so on.

Nothing, however, is very clearly shown us. For example, we do not find out very much about that exciting and subtle operation, the creative process, despite Dryden's announced intention to tell us of the nature of the happiness of the poet's imagination. Instead of an attempt to indicate the rich associative complexities of the imagination leaping after its quarry in the field of memory, we have an analytical breakdown of the first term, the happiness of the poet's imagination, into three other terms: Invention, Fancy, and Elocution. Where a Montaigne or a Browne presents us, as much as possible, with an actual experience as it is felt on the particular pulse of a particular author, a Dryden — and the whole Baconian tradition — gives us definitions dependent ultimately on Fashion.

Similarly, Dryden does not give us a "precise" picture of Ovid and Virgil, who emerge as constellations of abstractions, such as Passions, Affections, Accuracy, or Elocution. These authors are seen not in their individuality, in their specific historical setting, but as examples of degrees of adherence to Restoration norms. Ovid, in fact, is for Dryden a model of the Restoration idea of the classical plain style, for Ovid images more often the movements and affections of the mind and cares less for words than nature in disorder. Dryden correctly associates this mode with the drama, the dialogue, and an easy style in general, which has nothing that shows remoteness of thought or labor in the writer. By his admiring citation of Ovid's refusal to admit a too curious election of words, too frequent allusions, or the use of tropes, Dryden again seems to distinguish between "Senecanism" and the classical plain style, to the detriment of the former. Thus to the Best Critic of the Restoration it is in the classical plain style, not Senecan imitation, that words equal the things of the mind. Of the particular qualities of Ovid's mind, however, we learn nothing. Nor does Dryden himself follow Ovid's method and reveal his own self. The Restoration understanding of the words-things relationship forbids it. In a very real sense the style of an Ovid or a "Senecan" is more "precise" than Dryden's in that it provides us with precise equivalents of what is going on in the writer's mind. Of course, this is not the kind of "precision" the Restoration found useful.

As the Restoration demanded a certain kind of "precision," it also demanded a certain kind of figurative language. As we have seen, Restoration metaphors, despite the universal distrust of them, protrude obviously. They are usually elaborate, yoking a chain of causal relations into one scheme, for Restoration writers want to be explaining a process or arguing a proposition coolly and objectively rather than presenting states of mind. Mixed metaphor presents no problem in the densely figurative Elizabethan or "Senecan" language; no one is upset when Hamlet takes arms against his sea of troubles. But it becomes the *bête noire* of practice and theory in the Restoration, with its goal of purposeful argument rather than exploration of the vagaries of the inmost soul. As little as possible is left for the reader to work out on his own. The tenor is of the same order of existence as the vehicle. Dryden tells us immediately how the spaniel is like the imagination; in the "Senecan" antithesis or the metaphysical conceit the relation of reference to referent is deliberately not obvious at first until we watch the author solve the seeming incongruity, thereby telling us something about the processes of his mind. Dryden and the Baconians would eliminate, as much as possible, this subjective and revealing play of the mind and substitute an impersonal recital of cause and effect. A Montaigne or a Browne portrays the spaniel leaping about in the field of memory, while a Dryden reveals only the captured quarry, carefully arranged.

This constant suggestion that an explanation or argument is in progress is another aspect of Restoration prose which gives the reader a sense that it is "precise." In the passage I have quoted, Dryden seems to be taking pains to tell us exactly where he is going ("But to proceed from wit, in the general notion of it. . . . 'T is not so much in the jerk or sting . . . but it is some lively and apt description. . . . So then, the first happiness . . . the second . . . the third. . . ."). Actually, Dryden is not arguing anything, but retailing Fashion. But there is a feeling that he is arguing something, even when he is only reckoning up counters of Things, defined according to Fashion, and therefore clear to all. Such a method is an updating of Bacon's writing in Methods, which has its origins in the utilitarian requirement of persuasive and useful discourse.

The utilitarian emphasis on "precise" argument over self-revelation is prevalent in all areas of discourse. In the preface to the *Annus Mirabilis* Dryden is postulating for poetry the same criteria everyone else has been postulating for prose. His own prose illustrates the effect of these criteria. The classics of Elizabethan prose strike us as "poetic," while Restoration poetry at its best has the virtues we associate with good prose. What Dryden says is good for poetry Eachard says is good for the sermon, too:

Another thing, Sir, that brings great disrespect and mischief upon the Clergy, and that differs not much from what went

226

immediately before, is their packing their Sermons so full of *similitudes;* which, all the World know, carry with them but very small force of Argument, unless there be an exact agreement, with that which is compared; of which there is very seldom any sufficient care taken. Besides, those that are addicted to this way of discourse, for the most part, do so weaken and enfeeble their judgment by contenting themselves to understand the colours, features, and glimpses . . . that the conviction or persuasion will last no longer in the Parishioners minds, than the warmth of their Similitudes shall glow in their Phansie. (*Grounds and Occasions*, p. 41)

Of this statement Wanning (who has written better than anyone else on these matters) finds that "the interesting thing in it, apart from its explanation of the terms upon which similitudes *are* admissible, is its apparent assumption that sermons should not *describe* religious effects, or religious states of mind, but should expound Arguments" ("Some Changes," p. 176). Like his age, Eachard rejected the intimate pulpit oratory of a Donne or an Andrewes as useless. Here is one of the many points where the attack on Enthusiasm merges with an assault such as Dryden's on "Senecan" imitation, for Dryden, Eachard, and Sprat all reject self-revelation on the same utilitarian grounds. Similarly, Symon Patrick warns against the expression of deeply felt religious experience in sermons. Why could the nonconformist "not as well have said, that he had a long time thought of the efficacy and virtue of the Bloud of *Christ;* or, that he was much acquainted with the love of Christ in dying for us? But to say that he had *lain long a-soke* in his blood, is as absurd as if he had told us that he had *lain long baking himself* in the Beams of the Sun of Righteousness" (*A Friendly Debate*, p. 25). The trouble with the intimate style is that it necessitates extravagant images, which are not Precise and therefore not useful since incomprehensible. Rather than present his own state of mind, Patrick would have his speaker argue in favor of abstractions like Efficacy and Virtue. These immutable counters are easily reckoned by "Reason and Judgement." Such at any rate is the current fashion, to which Patrick wholeheartedly subscribes:

There are two ways to come at the Affections: One by the Senses and Imagination; and so we see people mightily affected with a Puppet-play. . . . The other is by the Reason and Judgement; when the evidence of any Truth convincing the Mind, engages the affections to its side, and makes them move according to its direction. Now, I believe your Affections are moved in the first way very often; by melting Tones, pretty Similitudes, riming Sentences, kind and loving Smiles. . . . The better sort of Hearers are now out of love with these things. (*Debate*, p. 11)

If the Restoration emphasized hard, material "things," it seems strange that it also emphasized the processes of argumentation at the expense of the representation of sensuous experience, the abstract word for the concrete, "Quality, Affection, Property, Operation, or Adjunct" for the Elizabethans' "direct sensuous apprehension" of the totality of experience, which is so much greater than the sum of such arbitrarily designated parts. John Locke asks the same question and offers an answer: "All things that exist being particulars, it may perhaps be thought reasonable that words, which ought to be conformed to things, should be so too, I mean in their signification, but yet we find quite the contrary. The far *greatest part of words* that make all languages *are general terms:* which has not been the effect of neglect or chance, but of reason and necessity." [47] Everyone agrees that Locke's *Essay Concerning Human Understanding* (1690) is not so much an original work as a weaving together of the generally accepted assumptions and theories of the age. Locke himself, physician, fellow of the Royal Society, statesman, skeptic, and liberal Christian, is, like Dryden, the embodiment of the many forces pressing for a new plain style along the lines originally advocated by Bacon. Book III, "Of Words," is the century's longest and most profound exposition of the words-things relation, and does indeed summarize most contemporary religious, scientific, literary, and philosophical thinking on the subject. Locke therefore may suitably conclude this section.

In the passage quoted, Locke joins "reason," the process of attaining Truth, with "necessity," the problem of useful communication. Words, if they are to conform to reason and be useful as well, must have some relation to things. But *"it is impossible that every particular thing should have a distinct peculiar name"* (III, iii, 2). Because our memory is limited we must make abstractions out of the discrete bits of sense-data constantly being impressed on us in experience. Even if our memories could store up each discrete bit of data,

it would yet be useless, because it would not serve to the chief end of language. Men would in vain heap up names of particular things, that would not serve them to communicate their thoughts. Men learn names and use them in talk with others only that they may be understood: which is then only done when, by use or consent, the sound I make by the organs of speech excites, in another man's mind who hears it, the *idea* I apply it to in mine when I speak it. This cannot be done by names applied to particular things, whereof I alone having the *ideas* in my mind, the names of them could not be significant or intelligible to another who was not acquainted with all those very particular things which had fallen under my notice. . . . *A distinct name for every particular thing would not be of any great use for the improvement of knowledge,* which, though founded in particular things, enlarges itself by general views, to which things reduced into sorts, under general names, are properly subservient. (III, iii, 3–4)

In Locke as in the Baconian Anti-Senecans, utility makes the goal of language easy reading or listening, rather than self-revelation. The language of Reason and Necessity shuns the subjectivity of the sensuous and concrete "names applied to particular things" which delighted Elizabethan and "Senecan" alike. Instead, language is a kind of map of physical reality, easier to understand than an exact duplication of things themselves. Words are not signs of things but of ideas of things. "*Words, in their primary or immediate signification, stand for nothing but the* ideas *in the mind of him that uses them,* however imperfectly soever or carelessly those *ideas* are collected from the things they are supposed to represent" (III, ii, 2). However, "because *men* would not be thought to talk *barely* of their own imaginations, but of things as really they are, therefore they *often suppose their words to stand also for the reality of things. . . . Men,* even when they would apply themselves to an attentive consideration, do *set their thoughts more on words than things*" (III, ii, 5, 7). Words relate only to secondary qualities. The "real essences" of things are evidently their primary qualities, inaccessible to ordinary language.

Nor indeed *can we* rank and *sort things,* and consequently (which is the end of sorting) denominate them, *by their real essences,* because we know them not. Our faculties carry us no further towards the knowledge and distinction of substances than a collection of those sensible *ideas* which we observe in them; which, however made with the greatest diligence and exactness we are capable of, yet is more remote from the true internal constitution from which these qualities flow than, as I said, a countryman's *idea* is from the inward contrivance of that famous clock at *Strasbourg,* whereof he only sees the outward figure and motions. (III, vi, 9)

Nevertheless, "proper" language aspires to describe the primary qualities or real essences of things, which are themselves abstractions albeit very definite ones. The seventeenth century, as Whitehead showed us, somehow persuaded everyone to believe in the objective reality of the odd notion of concrete abstractions. But what the Elizabethan or "Senecan" thought he saw with his eyes were not abstractions at all, and the language he used to describe them was not "proper," in the Restoration sense.

Communicating intelligibly the new view of the physical

world requires a new kind of language. Like Hobbes, Locke distinguishes between two kinds of discourse,

> One for the recording of our own thoughts. . . . The other for the communicating of our thoughts to others. As to the first of these, *for the recording of our own thoughts* for the help of our own memories, whereby, as it were, we talk to ourselves, any words will serve the turn. For since sounds are voluntary and indifferent signs of any *ideas*, a man may use what words he pleases to signify his own *ideas* to himself; and there will be no imperfection in them if he constantly use the same sign for the same *idea*, for then he cannot fail of having his meaning understood; wherein consists the right use and perfection of language. (III, ix, 1–2)

"Communication of words" has "a double use," civil and philosophical:

> By their *civil use*, I mean such a communication of thoughts and *ideas* by words as may serve for the upholding common conversation and commerce about the ordinary affairs and conveniences of civil life in the societies of men one amongst the other. *Secondly, By the philosophical use* of words, I mean such an use of them as may serve to convey the precise notions of things, and to express in general propositions certain and undoubted truths which the mind may rest upon and be satisfied with in its search after true knowledge. These two uses are very distinct; and a great deal less exactness will serve in the one than in the other. (III, ix, 2)

Locke of course is almost wholly absorbed in the philosophical use of words as they serve to convey the precise notions of things. But "Anti-Ciceronianism" and the classical plain style in general exist for the recording of our own thoughts. Locke's dismissal of this mode of discourse as a means of useful or truthful statement, like Hobbes', is a dismissal of the earlier plain styles as well. The key word again is "precise." The former, more personal style is rejected for its imprecision, that is, the imprecise relation of words to things.

At first one might think that Locke's program for a

philosophical style was inspired by the "clear and distinct ideas" of Descartes.[48] In at least one place in the chapter on the abuses of words Locke, otherwise an avowed anti-Cartesian, suggests Cartesian influence. "The first and most palpable abuse is the using of words without clear and distinct *ideas*, or, which is worse, signs without anything signified" (III, x, 2). But what Locke, like Dryden and at times Sprat, really means by words with clear and distinct ideas is something like "the Best Diction, agreed upon by Fashion, or Authority." It is all very well to have words as precise equivalents of ideas of things. But what words are we to choose? Things themselves do not automatically suggest their own names. The problem is especially desperate with regard to "mixed modes," names abstracted arbitrarily from other, simpler ideas of things. And it is on mixed modes (Locke's examples include "justice," "murder," "obligation") that morality and religion depend. The thrust of the large section on the remedies for the abuses of words is that we submit ourselves for guidance to the Best Authors.

Propriety of speech is that which gives our thoughts entrance into other men's minds with the greatest ease and advantage, and therefore deserves some part of our care and study, especially in the names of moral words. The proper signification and use of terms is best to be learned from those who in their writings and discourses appear to have had the clearest notions and applied to them their terms with the exactest choice and fitness. (III, xi, 11)

Here is the familiar identification of decorum with ease and precision, and the justification of all of them on grounds of utility, best served through a submission to the model of the Best Authors. In a similar vein, and recalling the efforts of some in the Royal Society to establish an English Academy, Locke also wants a new dictionary to standardize the language. For this work we are to rely on the scientists rather than the moralists:

It were therefore to be wished that men, versed in physical inquiries and acquainted with the several sorts of natural bodies, would set down those simple *ideas* wherein they observe the individuals of each sort constantly to agree. This would remedy a great deal of that confusion which comes from several persons applying the same name to a collection of smaller or greater number of sensible qualities, proportionably as they have been more or less acquainted with or accurate in examining the qualities of any sort of things which come under one denomination. (III, xi, 25)

Again Locke's desire for an impersonal public mode of discourse places him in reaction against the ideals of the older plain style. He spoke for his age as a whole. In *The Problem of Style*, Middleton Murry has observed that, "It would demand much more skill and learning than most of us possess to pronounce positively on the authorship of an unfamiliar piece of English prose written at the end of the seventeenth century. The *sermo communis* of those days had a limpidity which makes it hard to be sure of the personal nuance." [49] As his contribution to the theory of the *sermo communis* Locke suggests a program by which each word signifies one discrete nugget of meaning, accessible to all; apparently he feels that the Best Authors wrote this way. From this ideal come the proposals not only of Locke but of Sprat, Parker, and others to establish dictionaries, academies, or even acts of Parliament to narrow the range of fashionable words, and to give those that are accepted into the canon the narrowest possible semantic range in the form of lexical meanings that will not be affected by their context. Such a procedure is exactly opposite to that of the Elizabethans and of "Anti-Ciceronians." It is, in effect, a negation of the value of emotive language as true statement.

As we have seen, the impulse toward a public mode of discourse is inseparable from the preoccupation with definitions, which figures so prominently in Bacon, Hobbes,

Dryden, and Locke. The age sought a language made up of what we should call "technical terminology," that is, with all important words well defined. By the usual nominalist presuppositions, these words need not be signs of real things but of ideas of things. Definitions and well-defined terms are purely utilitarian; they make the going easier for the reader rather than reveal the individuality of the author or even the truth about the "things" of reality. Eventually the truth-utility equation begins to break down. Bishop Parker is even blunter than Locke on this score: "I conclude that the office of Definitions is not to explain the Nature of Things, but to fix and circumscribe the signification of Words; for they being Notes of Things, unless their signification be settled, their meaning must needs be Equivocal and uncertain." [50]

Locke would not have included "Senecans" and libertines in his list of Best Authors but would have condemned them for their nontechnical imprecision. Except in extremely specialized discourse, however, which is not the only kind that Locke had in mind, language cluttered with technical terms is neither plain, precise, nor useful. To the despair of his commentators, Locke himself is guilty of six or seven indiscriminate uses of his favorite word "idea." The appalling effect on modern English of this kind of "precision" is too well known to be discussed here. Our fascination with jargon is often foreshadowed in the theory and practice of the Restoration; our concern about it appears as early as the dramatists' satires on the "Virtuosi." One wonders at times whether the fruits of the Restoration reforms were "plain" in any sense of the word. While these reforms were essential if prose was not to lapse into anarchy, and if Learning was to Advance, a style with more technical terms is not necessarily plainer or more precise. Coleridge saw that when words are asked to stand alone without any aid from their context they are likely to be less precise, and he associated this kind of imprecision with the Restoration. He found that in writing before the Restoration, "the precise intended meaning of a word can never be mistaken; whereas in the later writers, as especially in Pope, the use of words is for the most part purely arbitrary, so that the context will rarely show the true specific sense, but only that something of the sort is desired." [51]

If precision and plainness are defined as "Anti-Ciceronian" and the theorists of the classical plain style as a whole defined them — as the accurate representation of a mind — then such devices as metaphor are an *aid* to precision and plainness as well as a delight in themselves. So says Aristotle, in a crucial section of the *Rhetoric:*

All men take a natural pleasure in learning quickly; words denote something; and so those words are pleasantest which give us *new* knowledge. Strange words have no meaning for us; common terms we know already; it is *metaphor* which gives us most of the pleasure. Thus, when the poet calls old age 'a dried stalk,' he gives us a new perception by means of a common *genus;* for both the things have lost their bloom. . . . It follows that a smart style, and a smart enthymeme, are those, which give us a new and rapid perception in either those which convey knowledge, as soon as they are uttered, though this knowledge was not possessed before; or those, behind which intelligence lags only a little; for here is a sort of acquisition. [52]

In contrast to the usual Restoration views Aristotle regards metaphor as inseparable from Sense rather than as mere Ornament, calculated Deceit, uncalculated carelessness, or the offspring of the Passions. Furthermore, by enlarging the context metaphor makes the meaning more precise and communication more effective and useful. Metaphor is successful, in other words, on the Restoration's own grounds of utility. Middleton Murry, going further than Aristotle, finds in metaphor "the man himself":

In the development of a great master of metaphor like Shake-speare we can watch the gradual overriding of the act of com-parison. Metaphor becomes almost a mode of apprehension. Only by regarding metaphor in this light can we really account for the indescribable impression made by Shakespeare's later manner, in which metaphors tumble over one another, yet the effect is not one of confusion, but of swift and constant illumination. . . . How impossible it really is to conceive metaphor as a kind of ornament. Metaphor is the unique expression of a writer's indi-vidual vision. . . . In all the famous definitions of style by writers who knew what they were talking about, the emphasis infallibly falls on what we may call the organic nature of style. The most famous of all Buffon's definitions sweeps away the whole mechanism of expression. Style is the man himself. (*Prob-lem of Style*, pp. 11–12)

Metaphor adds to clarity and precision and is a form of truth-ful statement in that it is an imitation of the soul of "the man." In this imitation is pleasure, the pleasure that Murry obtains from Shakespeare or that Aristotle gets from the comparison of age to a dried stalk. Both Murry and Aristotle are speak-ing in the tradition of classical *mimesis*. Although Aristotle nowhere says that the style is the man himself, he would agree that precision and truth are not separable from pleasure, and that pleasure (as well as utility) is a legitimate justification of metaphor: "Again, since learning and ad-miring are pleasant, it follows that pleasure is given by acts of imitation, such as painting, sculpture, poetry, and by every skillful copy even though the original be un-pleasant; for one's joy is not in the thing itself; rather, there is a syllogism — '*this is that*': and so it comes that one learns something" (1371b, pp. 49–50). The Restoration division between, on the one hand, ornament, words, false-hood, and pleasure, and on the other, sense, things, truth, and utility, does not exist in the *mimesis* of the classical plain style. It is surmounted in metaphor, and in the sur-mounting is pleasure and truth as well as clarity and there-fore utility. The syllogism "this is that" creates something in the mind more delightful even than the physical thing itself.

The classical plain style and seventeenth-century "Anti-Ciceronianism" do condemn "rhetoric," but not for the same reason the Restoration did. The theorists of the earlier plain style, all the way from Socrates, who attacks the Sophists who persuade rather than reveal the "things" of the inmost soul, down to Jonson, who appeals for a "plain and neat" language which "springs out of the most retired and inmost parts of us," all distrust rhetoric because it does not reveal candidly the inmost motions of the Ideal Self. The animus of people like Locke against rhetoric derives from a feeling that it reveals the mind of its author too much and at the expense of the real purpose of language, which is clear, useful discourse. The arguments of ancients and moderns against rhetoric spring from completely unrelated and in fact opposed motivations; consequently the kinds of "plain" styles desired and achieved are completely opposed.

Much of the distinction between the two plain styles turns on the venerable question of universals. Bacon, Hobbes, and Locke represent the theory of the new plain style best, and all are "Nominalists"; that is, they distrust words, since even the simplest of them are our ideas of things rather than representations of the order of things themselves. This would seem to restrict the legitimate uses of language to utilitarian persuasion rather than truthful statements. Only a few theorists, such as Wilkins, Parker, and Bacon occasionally were willing to go that far. Instead, the age invented a compromise, Restoration English; this, it felt, was closest to physical things and therefore to true statement, and in addition it was most useful. In the seventeenth century, as the classic works of Burtt, Whitehead, Willey, Spencer and others have shown, the universe loses its inner analogical correspondences, its heritage from Christian humanism.[53] Metaphor then ceases to be a legitimate way of making true statements and becomes instead merely a handy persuasive device.

It is not only the scientists who feel this way. We may look to Bishop Parker, for example, for the stylistic implications in 1666 of the new world view:

Now to Discourse of the Natures of Things in Metaphors and Allegories is nothing else but to sport and trifle with empty words, because these Schems do not express the Natures of Things but only their Similitudes and Resemblances, for Metaphors are only words, which properly signifying one thing, are apply'd to signify another by Reason of some Resemblance between them. When therefore any thing is expressed by Metaphor or Allegory, the thing it self is not expressed, but only some similitude observ'd or made by Fancy. So that Metaphors being only the sportings of Fancy comparing things with things, and not marks or signes of Things. All these Theories in Philosophie which are expressed only in metaphorical Termes, are not real Truths, but the meer Products of Imagination, dress'd up (like Children's *babies*) in a few spangled empty words . . . empty Phraseologies that have not Notion & Thing enough to fill them out. Thus their wanton & luxuriant fancies climbing up into the Bed of Reason, do not only defile it by unchast and illegitimate Embraces, but instead of real conceptions and notices of Things, impregnate the mind with nothing but Ayerie and Subventaneous Phantasmes.

But 'tis still more fantastick and absurd to talke metaphorically concerning these things, of whose Ideas we are utterly ignorant, & of which we are not able to discourse in Proper Terms, for such Discourse must needs be Non-sense, and the matter of it must needs be nothing; because they treat of they know not what. For Metaphors not signifying things, and things being always signified by proper Termes, what can be more evident than that meer Metaphors without proper Terms are employed about nothing at all, or only an imaginary something. And they that talk thus, do but first imagine a subject, and then imagine in it some Resemblances to something else, that is in effect, they make a bauble, and then play with it. Of this nature (to give you one instance) are the greatest part of their discourses concerning the Soul, in discoursing of which, they draw Metaphors from all the Senses, Members, and Functions of the Body, from all the General Hypotheses of Nature; from all the Phaenomena of the Heavens and the Earth, from all the several Properties and Operations of the several species of Creatures, and apply them to the Nature, Faculties, and operations of the Soul; But because they are altogether ignorant of the nature and substance of the Soul, and are not able to express the greatest part of these things by proper terms; all these Metaphors must pass for idle and insignificant Non-sense. (*A Free and Impartial Censure*, pp. 75–77)

Parker's statement is a good summary of what the Restoration as a whole regarded as common sense about language. The style of this selection from *A Free and Impartial Censure of the Platonick Philosophie* is also thoroughly representative. Even the title is characteristic of the age in its objectively argumentative quality. Although Parker denies metaphor as a vehicle for truthful statement, it is quite all right as ornamental reinforcement, as witness the extraordinary figure of wanton and luxuriant fancies climbing into the bed of Reason to impregnate the mind. Like most Restoration metaphors, this one is explanatory rather than sharply visualized or descriptive, and therefore quite conspicuous and elaborate, even threatening to spill over into the next paragraph as the author attempts to tie as many thoughts together as possible. Of great interest also are the metaphors that Parker specifically excludes. Here he negates the standard humanistic vision of the world, with its analogies between the microcosm and the macrocosm, the psychological order and the order of nature, and so on, on the grounds that the analogies are purely metaphorical. The decline of such comfortable correspondences terrified a Donne or a Pascal, but the Restoration was not disturbed at all. Once the truth of the analogical world view was questioned, Bacon willingly conceded the point with his positivistic injunction to hunt for matter rather than words. What took the terror out of the Baconian world view was the appeal to utility, for Bacon promised that once we sweep away metaphysical cobwebs we will be able to control nature for practical benefit, and in addition find out the real order of things, if not in words then through Real Characters or mathematics. These are more or less the nominalist and utilitarian assumptions of Restoration style. *Mimesis,* on the other hand, requires an "Anti-Nominalistic" or "Conceptualistic" point of view, in which words do represent the structure and shape of things. Hence the assumption in the theory of *mimesis* that the mind unassisted by Baconian "helps" can describe and even improve on physical reality. We are not passive spectators before a blank, neutral world of primary qualities. The seventeenth century eventually found the nominalistic conceptions more to its liking and called them "true" and "precise."

We are fortunate to have, in Thomas Baker's *Reflections Upon Learning,* a document published in the convenient year 1700 which summarizes the entire history of prose style in the seventeenth century. Baker understands the mid-century shift in prose style to come from the general realization that words are nothing more than "Conceptions in our minds." Cicero is condemned for his Conceptualism, which renders his oratory "of no Use": "His *Orator* is too great and inimitable an Example, perfectly imaginary, and consequently of no Use in Human Life, for which Eloquence is design'd. He himself gives him only an Ideal Being, and owns that he is no where to be found but in the Conceptions of our Mind." [54] Seneca fares no better, representing merely another form of useless oratory: "There are few that read *Seneca,* that do not imagine he writes with great force and Strength, his Thoughts are lofty, almost every Line in him is a Sentence, and every Sentence does seem a Reason; and yet it has been well observ'd . . . that there is little more in him, at the bottom, than a Pomp of Words" (p. 52). Nor does "Science."

Of the scheme for the Universal Character, Baker writes: "Bishop Wilkins was an extraordinary person, but very Projecting, and I doubt this Design may go along with his *Daedalus* and *Archimedes*, and be ranked with his *flying Chariot* and *Voyage to the Moon*" (p. 102). "Use," not "Science," is responsible for the downfall of Ciceronianism and its "fantastick" successor. Here, in a paragraph, is a history of prose style in the seventeenth century before it became of "Use in Human Life":

In Queen *Elizabeth's* Reign, the Writers of that Age seem to have affected a *Ciceronian* Stile in *English*, both in the length of their Periods, and often by throwing the Verb to the End of the Sentence: The succeeding Reign degenerated rather than improv'd, when the Generality ran into an affected way of Writing, and nothing would please, without a fantastick Dress and Jingle of Words. And tho in the following Reign, this way of Writing was much laid aside, yet even then they larded their Discourse so thick with Sentences of Greek and Latin, that as things now are, it would be a hard matter to excuse them from Pedantry. What sort of Oratory obtain'd in the late Times of Confusion, is well known, especially in the Pulpit: As if the Observation of our Neighbours had been Calculated for them; little Similitudes and Odd examples, and a worse sort of Cant, was the Eloquence of these Times; which notwithstanding charm'd the People to that degree, that it hurried them besides themselves, and almost out of their Wits. (pp. 60–61)

Some Notes on the New Prose of Utility

Introduction

I have been arguing up to now that the two explanations most frequently offered to account for the rise of modern prose style in the seventeenth century — the Anti-Ciceronian movement and the "New Philosophy" — are both unsatisfactory. Because of limits of space and time I have centered my discussion on those writers who have been claimed by both sides of the controversy, showing that in many instances a sort of *tertium quid*, a nebulously conceived but prevalent utilitarian ethic, determined the new style. I have tried to show that the extent and influence of Anti-Ciceronianism have been much exaggerated. Furthermore, though it is doubtless wrong to deny any causal role to science in the evolution of the new prose, in the seventeenth century "scientific" prose and to some extent "science" itself are an expression of other cultural forces, integrated around a utilitarian ethic, rather than an influence on them or an initiator of them.

Of course I have not shown that this "utilitarian ethic" alone explains the rise of modern prose style. No single explanation could possibly account for so complicated a thing as the normal literary prose style of an age. All I can claim is that, for those writers traditionally regarded as important in the development of prose style in the later seventeenth century, the utilitarian ethic is very important. I use "utilitarian" the way the seventeenth century did, in a very broad and quite unphilosophical way to refer to that outlook which values things as means to ultimate ends rather than things (excluding the ultimate ends themselves) for their own sakes. Thus, for example, in *The Virtuoso* Shadwell ridicules the scientist, Sir Nicholas Gimcrack, for being interested in learning for its own sake rather than for its ultimate end, the good of humanity. Similarly, the substance of Swift's attack on the "projectors" at Lagado is that, though claiming to be utilitarian, they spend all their time on hairbrained projects of no use to anyone. The proponents of the new plain style in the Restoration attack the earlier styles for being too much delighted with language itself, rather than the ends to which language should be directed. And so on.

The best examination of the rise of modern prose style is Andrews Wanning's unpublished dissertation.[1] Since I am now to go over much the same ground he covers, now and then using his method of comparative translations and at times recapitulating his remarkable insights, I should justify my own efforts. First of all, Wanning discussed various aspects of style (vocabulary, metaphor, syntax) separately. This procedure is perhaps valid for an analysis of prose style in general. But each of the different kinds of prose, such as fiction or biography, has its own special stylistic dimensions. After a preliminary section on the new prose style in general, I have, therefore, included separate sections on those genres of prose written in the seventeenth century and still of chief interest to us today: biography, fiction, and drama.

Second, Wanning's method, more than any other I know, allows for valid generalizations about style and culture. Wanning is, however, primarily concerned with demonstrating the influence of science on seventeenth-century style. The results of my use of certain of Wanning's methods demonstrate to me the large extent to which the utilitarian ethic, rather than "science" or "Anti-Ciceronianism," accounted for the new prose style. Again I do not claim it was the only factor, if for no other reason than that no style can be traced to any single "influence." But I do think it was very important.

To be sure, the predominance of a detached point of view, causal explanations, syntax like mathematical ratios, technical terms, and the series of balanced progressions that we find in Restoration prose we also find characteristic of the scientific method. They all make for an impersonal style, and Wanning has traced this impersonality to "that desire of the scientific mentality to base its generalizations upon objective procedure divorced from the variable of individual subjectivity" (p. 431). Certainly the Restoration writers wanted to divorce themselves from the variable of individual subjectivity. But is such a divorce limited to the "scientific method?" Or are the "scientific" aspects of Restoration prose really a result of larger causes? There is a chicken-or-egg problem here, to which Wanning refers: "Whether the specific material achievements which are known as the sciences encouraged through their success the general background of the scientific habit of thought; or whether the sciences themselves are made possible by some obscure prior movement . . . is a problem in ultimate history with which one would have to be very brave indeed to meddle" (p. 435).

Throughout this book I have been bravely meddling. I have held that Restoration prose represents the general neglect of the "qualitatively unique" (p. 98) in favor of some more quantitative and useful end. Especially as it came under the influence of the spirit (if not often the method) of Bacon, "Science" in the latter part of the seventeenth century — or at least, that part of "Science" which affected prose style — is but one aspect of this "obscure prior movement." The same neglect, as I have tried to show in the previous chapters, is taking place in all other areas as well, including those indifferent or hostile to science. I can see no reason to single out the New Philosophy or any impossibly broad definition of "Science" as the influence on everything else. The escape from subjectivity is universal.

My intention in this chapter is to go beyond the scholarly controversies of the first five chapters to isolate the specific linguistic elements which distinguish the new styles from the old. I make no claim to cover the topic completely. For this we need a more systematic way of comparing styles than any we now have. Here our best hope seems to be the recent efforts to unite traditional stylistic criticism with linguistics. Until this effort has proceeded much further than it now has, I find myself restricted to what I concede at the outset is a sketchy survey.

From the Restoration on, normal literary prose is, to use McLuhan's terms, a "linear" product of the "print culture." The chief aim of such prose is useful public communication. Therefore it is made to seem "rational" or "precise" or "neoclassic," terms of which the Restoration would have approved but which are not inclusive or accurate enough to describe the prose itself.

Of course performance is never as exclusive as theory. In the various kinds of imaginative literature, and especially in as oral and relatively private a medium as the comedies of King Charles's court, the prose is less impersonally utilitarian and more intimate. Even so, the language of prose comedy in *The Man of Mode* is unlike that of *Much*

Ado About Nothing. For much the same reasons, Bunyan's and Defoe's austere narratives are worlds apart stylistically from Elizabethan fiction, as are the lean Burnet and the rotund Clarendon from the earlier biographers and character-writers.

Prose in General

Let us begin by comparing two translations of an identical passage in Plutarch. The first is Philemon Holland's (1603) and the second P. Lancaster's (1684):

It seemeth at the first sight, that there is no difference betweene envie and hatred, but they be both one. For vice (to speake in generall) having (as it were) many hookes or crotchets, by means thereof as it stirreth to and fro, it yeeldeth unto those passions which hang thereto many occasions and opportunities to catch holde one of another, and so to be knit and enterlaced one within the other; and the same verily (like unto diseases of the body) have a sympathie and fellow-feeling one of anothers distemperature and inflammation: for thus it commeth to passe, that a malicious and spightful man is as much grieved and offended at the prosperitie of another, as the envious person: and so we holde, that benevolence and good-will is opposite unto them both, for that it is an affection of a man, wishing good unto his neighbour: and envie in this respect resembleth hatred, for that they have both a will and intention quite contrary unto love: but forasmuch as no things like to the same, and the resemblances betweene them be not so effectual as to make them all one, as the differences to distinguish them asunder; let us search and examine the said differences, beginning at the very source and original of these passions.

Envy and Hatred are passions so like each other, that they are often taken for the same; and generally all the vices are so confusedly twisted and entangled, that they are not easily to be distinguished: for, as differing diseases of the Body agree in many the like causes and effects; so do the disturbances of the Mind. He who is in Prosperity, is equally an occasion of grief both to the Envious, and Malicious Man: therefore we look upon Benevolence, which is a Willing our Neighbours good, as an opposite to both Envy and Hatred; and fancy these two to be the same, because they have a contrary purpose to that of Love. But their Resemblances make them not so much One, as their Unlikeness, distinct: therefore we endeavour to describe each of them apart, beginning at the Original of either Passion.[2]

Mild and straightforward, Philemon Holland is no racy and eccentric "Elizabethan" like Greene or Dekker. Nevertheless he is writing in another world from Lancaster's. Why do we read Holland one way and Lancaster another when they are both "saying the same thing?" I think we can answer this question by comparing the vocabulary, figurative language, and syntax of the two texts.

Vocabulary. Linguists distinguish "nominal" from "verbal" styles.[3] Nominal style is more impersonal, more esoteric or technical, and has fewer clauses and complex sentences and less variety of sentence patterns. I think it is clear that Holland's style is more verbal than Lancaster's. This is not because Holland has more verbs. A statistical comparison would be meaningless. What is decisive for style is what the verbs and nouns are doing. In a nominal style the verbs are chiefly operative, mere markers to indicate distinctions and logical processes to the reader. They are the pale, well-behaved verbs whose meaning is not affected by their subject or context. In their invariability they have the virtues of well-defined nouns. In the verbal style, on the other hand, verbs are descriptive or, more rarely, evaluative, imperative, or interjections.[4] They are affected by their contexts. For example, we can compare Holland's "it *stirreth* to and fro, it *yeeldeth* unto those passions which *hang* thereto many occasions and opportunities to *catch holde* one of another, and so to be *knit* and *enterlaced* one within the other" with Lancaster's "all the vices *are* so confusedly *twisted* and *entangled*, that they are not easily to be *distinguished*." Holland's verbs are more descriptive both of the subject matter and Holland's attitude to it than Lancaster's.

Let us name one vocabulary "verbal descriptive" and the other "nominal operative." Where the former records the observations and attitudes of the speaker, the latter merely indicates the processes of abstract logic. The verbal descriptive style will contain more complex sentences and subordinate qualifying elements expressing the point of view of the speaker. Thus Holland has more syntactic variety than Lancaster's series of ratios.

Nouns and adjectives, as well as verbs, are operative in the Restoration, descriptive in the earlier prose. In the Restoration nouns are very important, frequently doing the jobs that verbs or verbal constructions performed previously. The Restoration habit of capitalizing nouns is significant. Adjectives, which frequently merely fill out a description in the early prose, more often point out a distinction in the Restoration. For example, in Holland's "for it commeth to passe, that malicious and spightfull man is as much grieved and offended at the prosperitie of another, as the envious person," "malicious and spightfull" and "grieved and offended" are in part merely rhetorical doublets. In Lancaster's "he who is in Prosperity, is equally an occasion of grief both to the Envious, and Malicious Man" there is no such padding. A substantive, "occasion of grief," has replaced Holland's verbal construction, while the adjectives ("Envious, and Malicious") now only point out a logical distinction.

In nominal operative prose, nouns appear to have unique, invariable meanings unaffected by their contexts. "We look upon Benevolence," writes Lancaster, "which is a Willing our Neighbours good, as an opposite to both Envy and Hatred," making "Benevolence" operate as a token or counter neatly parallel to Envy and Hatred in a sort of definition.

This neatness — "precision," the Restoration would have

called it — is not present in Holland's tangle of subordinate clauses. One has the feeling in reading Restoration prose that ordinary nouns such as Envy, Benevolence, and Hatred actually stand for fixed, technical concepts, of which everyone has a clear and distinct idea, and which have already been defined. The nominal operative style is, in other words, an expression of the nominalistic philosophy of the age — and of *our* age — with its distrust of "ordinary language." Nouns and adjectives in the verbal descriptive style, on the other hand, have the characteristics of verbs in that style. Often they seem brought in on the spur of the moment and therefore not clearly defined. They may reveal what the author felt at a given moment about the subject matter, but the function of language in the Restoration was to argue or explain purposefully. If Lancaster read Holland's translation he would not have regarded "hookes" and "crotchets" as suitable for serious discourse. They are too idiosyncratic, not impersonal enough. They describe, but they do not advance the Argument.

There is a more dramatic contrast between the old and new vocabulary in a comparison of the versions of Montaigne by that robust Elizabethan John Florio (1603) and Charles Cotton (1686):

& au lieu de m'esguiser l'appetit par ces preparatoires & avantieux, on me le lasse & affadit.

And whereas with these preparatives and flourishes, or preambles, they think to sharpen my taste, or stirre my stomacke, they cloy and make it wallowish.

Instead of whetting my Appetite by these Preparatives, they tire, and pall it.[5]

The Elizabethan adds synonyms ("preparatives and flourishes, or preambles") and extra phrases ("sharpen my taste, or stirre my stomacke") not to define the application of the first word or phrase but to make everything more rhetorically or dramatically emphatic. He is more interested

in giving us his own feelings about the text than in translating with "accuracy." He is delighted with language
for its own sake. A juicy, homey word like "wallowish" is
not to be found in Cotton, who would keep the diction
on the impersonal level of objective argumentation. Florio's
boisterous inaccuracy and his promiscuous heaping-up of
words from all sorts of experience goes against Decorum
and would have been offensive to Cotton. In fact, Cotton
goes in exactly the opposite direction by eliminating Montaigne's "avant-ieux."

Translations of another passage from the *Essais* illustrate
the transition from descriptive to operative language:

Ce sont les pieds de paon, qui abbatent son orgeuil. (III, v)
It is the fouleness of the peacocks feete, which doth abate his
pride, and stoope his gloating-eyed tayle. (Florio, p. 527)
They are the Peacocks Feet that abate his pride. (Cotton, III,
p. 155)

An expression like Florio's sudden "gloating-eyed" is too
casual, too unexpected, and too whimsical to serve in the
Argument for Cotton and, indeed, Montaigne himself. In
this spendid image Florio adds to Montaigne the sensuous
"fouleness" and, what is the most outstanding visual feature
of the peacock, his tail. Montaigne's simple "orgeuil" is too
abstract for Florio, who must provide a visual equivalent
for everything. He must get across the exact appearance of
the peacock's tail, with its little circular whorls like gloating
eyes; but Cotton is concerned only with the Sense of the
Argument.

In general then the earlier prose, though quite lively, is
static, but intimate and descriptive, while in the Restoration
prose always seems to be moving toward a goal or indicating
a causal process. Lancaster writes, "As differing diseases of
the Body agree in many the like causes and effects; so do
the disturbances of the Mind," while Holland knows not

"causes and effects" but has "and the same verily (like unto diseases of the body) have a sympathy and fellow-feeling one of anothers distemperature and inflammation." In effect we have a metaphorical and padded description for Lancaster's progression of causal relations and disinctions.

Figurative language. We saw in Chapter Five that, despite its manifestos the Restoration did use figurative language. It is a special kind, however, one in which the relation of "figure" to "sense" is clearly spelled out. Each figure is long, linking together a chain of causal relationships. Where the Elizabethan figure is casual, as in the Florio extracts above, startling, and suggestive, the later ones are more formal and restrictive. Where the earlier prose has clusters of similes or metaphors with referents drawn from areas remote from the subject at hand, the Restoration prefers isolated metaphors with vehicle and tenor closely related to each other and to the discourse.

We can compare the treatments of Plutarch's disease simile. In Holland the simile ("like unto diseases of the body") is tossed off casually in a parenthesis. Holland gives much more attention to the figure itself, with its two doublets ("sympathie and fellow-feeling one of anothers distemperature and inflammation"). The primary meaning is: Certain vices are like certain diseases in that they are hard to distinguish. But there are at least two submerged metaphors in Holland: first, vice is morbid, like a disease; second, vices and diseases are like two friends drawn together by common suffering. Like so many Elizabethan figures, this conglomeration is "mixed." Friends are not the same kind of thing as diseases. But we are not conscious of this in the fairly dense metaphorical texture of Holland's prose.

With Lancaster, on the other hand, all the relationships are spelled out formally, in a sort of ratio: certain diseases are similar in their causes and effects, just as certain vices are. There is never any witty attempt to say that vices are like diseases themselves. Lancaster says only that vices have the same relation to each other that diseases have. Unlike things — vices and diseases — are kept in separate compartments. The figure is not "mixed." The elements of the comparison are hauled out not, as is chiefly the case with Holland, for their intrinsic interest, but for whatever contribution they make to useful argumentation. Where Holland's figures fuse disparate concepts together, Lancaster analyzes them apart into causal relations. Therefore Holland's figures turn on verbs ("stirreth," "yeeldeth," "hang," "catch holde") — the most suggestive, fusing element of language — and Lancaster's on nouns, sharply set off and balanced. Where Holland has interlocking clusters of figures Lancaster has hardly any at all. Lancaster's vices "tangled and entwined" has almost no metaphorical value. As metaphors these words are completely played out or "adequated." They are therefore safe to use since their meanings are invariable and they express no individual quirk of an author comparing unlike things. They have the virtues of well-defined nouns.

Holland wants us to experience his own "direct sensuous apprehension" of thought. So he gives us several quick metaphors: vices are like things with hooks and crotchets which wiggle about, catching up neighboring passions, which are then somehow knit together. It is more an impressionistic blur, the way we understand things when emotional or relaxed, than a sharply focused, isolated image. Essentially Holland's translation, like so much early prose, is a series of alternative ways of describing one thing. Gustav Stern has described metaphor as a "verbal shorthand" saving periphrasis. "It gives the emotion directly, instead of talking about it; it does not describe, but makes us experience." [6] His account only holds for the earlier metaphor not the Restoration variety. Restoration metaphor does not save periphrasis, it is periphrasis. It does not make us experience but assists in the argument or is merely ornamental.

Syntax. We have spent so much time on syntax in the first five chapters that there is not much more to be said here. We should note, though, that while Lancaster's syntax is almost a set of mathematical ratios, these are not balanced rigidly or even antithetically. Where balance in much Elizabethan prose and in the asymmetrical "Anti-Ciceronianism" is obtrusive and often obviously antithetical, in the Restoration it is quieter. This is because it is subsumed under the progress of The Argument. In Holland, as in "Anti-Ciceronianism," parenthetical elements (for example, "like unto diseases of the body") remain parenthetical; in Lancaster they are incorporated into The Argument — even when not necessary for it — and of course into the balanced syntax.

Before going on to the various prose genres, I would like to mention a concept in linguistics which may provide us with a way of ordering these observations on the inseparable concerns of vocabulary, figurative language, and syntax. In "Patterns and Ranges" Angus MacIntosh says, "The meanings a given word has (however we may define meaning) are in some direct way associated with our experience of that word in a variety of contexts, our association of that word with other words which have, in our experience, a somewhat similar range, and our association of the word with other words of similar shape, but not always etymologically related." [7] There are a limited number of words with which any given word may cohabit. Words, as MacIntosh puts it, "have only a certain potential of collocability" (pp. 327–328). When confronted with an unusual collocation — "molten feather" is MacIntosh's example — we can write it off as meaningless, search about for some unexperienced meaning (for example, a new, little-known meaning for "feather"), or "seek to read into one or the other of the words some plausible extension of a familiar meaning" by "postulating an extension of range for which we can find reasonably close parallels" (p. 331). Much of the time when we read Elizabethan prose we are performing this last task; we almost never are when we read Restoration prose. Florio's "stoope his gloating-eyed tayle" is certainly an unusual collocation for which we must imagine "some plausible extension of a familiar meaning." This means, first of all, more work for the reader, and, as we have seen, more work for the reader means less "precision" or "clarity," in the Restoration sense. Now, Truth for the Restoration is always Clear and Distinct. Therefore prose such as Florio's must be banished utterly. Since the serious purpose of prose is the presentation of The Argument, Cotton has only "They are the Peacocks Feet that abate his pride." One metaphor is still there, but the other, with its unusual collocation, has disappeared.

For the Restoration, metaphor in general is suspect since all metaphors are, in a sense, unusual collocations. In the Restoration metaphor, however, the collocation is made less unusual because the reader's work is done for him. The extension of the meaning is "unfolded" chiefly by the balanced syntax with its implicit ratios. The dominant and contrasted position of the substantives ("they," "Feet," "pride") gives the effect of a ratio. The reader's work is made easier because, as in a well-constructed mathematical problem, the solution for the unknown X follows logically from what has gone before. Cotton (as well as Montaigne) has given us the answer a few ratios earlier: "Nature has ordered the most troubles of Actions to be the most common, by that to make us equal, and to parallel Fools and wise Men, Beasts and us. Even the most contemplative and prudent man, when I imagine him in this posture, I hold him an impudent Fellow to pretend to be prudent and contemplative. They are the Peacocks Feet that abate his pride." X equals Troublesome Actions. But what does Florio's "gloating-eyed Tayle" equal? This expression is from another "range" (in MacIntosh's terminology) altogether. The Restoration woud have said the figure was not "proper." We come upon it utterly unprepared. It is not part of a logical progression but seems struck off in the first heat of composition. The intention of a style like Florio's seems to be the articulation of the mind of the writer or "speaker" himself in contrast to the impersonal, "precise" Restoration vein.

Just as Restoration syntax and figurative language offer few surprises compared to the Elizabethan, so the later vocabulary has fewer unusual collocations. Following MacIntosh (p. 333) we may classify style into four categories:

1. Normal collocations, normal grammar,
2. Unusual collocations, normal grammar,
3. Normal collocations, unusual grammar,
4. Unusual collocations, unusual grammar.

Elizabethan prose tends to head down toward number four, Restoration prose up to number one. If all prose were in style number one there would be no difference between language as a system of fixed norms and language in actual practice. All language would be "correct."

What we have come upon here is a facet of the famous — and vexed — distinction in linguistics between language and speech, *langue* and *parole*.[8] *Langue* is the way the linguistic code "ought" to be used by everybody; *parole* is the way it actually is used by different people. Saussure's point, of course, was that, although *langue* underlies *parole*, no one ever does use *langue* pure and simple. The Restoration, with its passion for a universal, impersonal, "proper," and "correct" language, sought to abolish the distinction between *langue* and *parole*. Only in this way could prose be understood by all, and thereby become able to fulfill its main function of utilitarian communication.

Character and Biography

One of the most curious events in the literary history of the seventeenth century is the outbreak of "Characters" in the sixty years before the Restoration. Written as a separate genre, they also infiltrated all the major forms of literature, especially the essay and the drama. Even more curious is their virtual disappearance — only Butler, Tom Brown, and Flecknoe remain to carry on the tradition — after the Restoration, when they are replaced with a new kind of biography. One naturally suspects a connection between the general change in prose style after 1660 and the decline of the character. Boyce traces the decline to the characters' being written in Bacon's "magistral" mode rather than in the "method referred to progression" favored, according to Boyce, by the decisively influential Restoration scientists:

Instead . . . of examining separate cases statistically and scientifically to see into the complex and variable roots of men's behavior, the Characterist assembles and blends in a Character all the data from many individual and necessarily dissimilar men and thus makes one typical figure out of a man who never lived. . . . That is why . . . the polemic writers of the midcentury made so much use of it and why, after 1660, it was kept alive by the satirists and moralists . . . rather than by John Evelyn, Bishop Sprat, or John Locke. It could not be hospitable to the "method referred to progression." [9]

I think this view is mistaken. If anything, the character, with its ceaseless "point," is closer to the "delivery of knowledge in Aphorisms" which Bacon opposed to the "Methods" of the "magistral" mode "referred to progression." Here, by way of example, is the beginning of an "Overbury" character:

A Meere Scholler

A meere Scholler is an intelligible Asse: Or a silly fellow in black, that speaks Sentences more familiarly than Sense. The Antiquity of his University is his Creede, and the excellency of his Colledge (though but for a match at Foot-ball) an Article of his faith. He speaks Latine better than his Mother-tongue; and is a stranger in no part of the World, but his owne Countrey. Hee do's usually tel great Stories of himselfe to small purpose, for they are commonly ridiculous, be they true or false. His Ambition is, that he eyther is, or shall be a Graduate: but if ever he get a Fellowship, hee ha's then no fellow.[10]

Bacon's description of his Aphoristic mode is a good description of the style of "Overbury": "Discourse of illustration is cut off, descriptions of practice are cut off; so there remaineth nothing to fill the Aphorisms but some good quantity of observation. . . . But in Methods . . . a man shall make a great show of art, which if it were disjointed would come to little." [11] In "Overbury," as in Bacon's aphoristic prose, any sentence could be put anywhere else, and it would make no difference. Like Bacon's "knowledge induced," the characterist's knowledge seems to be "delivered and intimated in the same method where it was invented," a "good quality of observation" huddled together rather than in the settled order of "Methods." In its syntax, this typical character with its curt asymmetry is "Anti-Ciceronian."

The character all but disappears after the Restoration, in the heyday of Baconian and "scientific" influence. This would indicate what we have been saying all along, that the "Anti-Ciceronian" mode was not congenial to "science." On the other hand, the closeness of character-writing to the style recommended by Bacon for the "progression" of science suggests that Croll is right when he says that "Anti-Ciceronianism" is the literary expression of science.

It seems to me that this sort of contradictory evidence cancels itself out and that we must look to something other than "science" as the cause of the decline of the character. Perhaps we can see what offended in the character by examining its later substitute, the special kind of biography favored by the Restoration. There is a close connection between the character and Restoration biography. Often the terms "character" and "life" are used interchangeably, and the genres combined. To cite the best-known examples, Halifax's *Character of Charles II* (1685) is a biography, as is Clarendon's character-laden *Life* (1670), while Halifax's *Character of a Trimmer* (1688) is a sort of autobiographical political broadside, related to the "polemic character" of the Commonwealth period but far more extended and quite different. Such is the confusion between character and biography that throughout the century many "Lives" are in effect "a bare chronicle of events in which the hero figures only as a name, and a subsequent character sketch in which his particular virtues and vices are formally enumerated." [12] Despite the confusion, writers like Halifax, Clarendon, and Burnet are beginning to evolve a new form altogether. Their formal biographies are closer than the earlier characters to Bacon's "Methods . . . more fit to win consent or belief." As such, they are further from the style recommended by Bacon for scientists than is the character. The later authors, especially the stately Clarendon, are also remote from Sprat's "Artizans, Countrymen, and Merchants."

Why did the new kind of biography replace the character? A comparison of the Overbury piece with an extract from a character embedded in Bishop Burnet's biography of "A meere Scholler," Sir Matthew Hale (1682), is instructive:

He was but of a slow speech, and sometimes so hesitating, that a stranger would have thought him of low parts, that knew not readily what to say (though ready at other times). But I never saw Cicero's doctrine de Oratore more verified in any man, that furnishing the mind with all sorts of knowledge, is the chief thing to make an excellent orator; for when there is an abundance and clearness of knowledge in the mind, it will furnish even a slow tongue to speak that which by its congruence and verity shall prevail. Such a one never wants moving matter, nor an answer to vain objectors.

The manner of our converse was as suitable to my inclination as the matter. For whereas many bred in universities, and called scholars, have not the wit, manners, or patience, to hear those that they discourse with speak to the end, but through list and impotency cannot hold, but cut off a man's speech when they hear any thing that urgeth them, before the latter part make the former intelligible, or strong (when oft the proof and use is reserved for the end), liker scolds than scholars; as if they commanded silence at the end of each sentence to him that speaketh, or else would have two talk at once. I do not remember that ever he and I did interrupt each other in any discourse. His wisdom and accustomed patience caused him still to stay for the end.[13]

In the Overbury character we have only the external traits of the scholar. With Burnet everything that happens externally must be explained as the result of some process "in the mind." "Overbury" gives us an impressionistic assortment. In Burnet we have an analysis of "parts" and what makes them work. Hale's choice phrases come from an "abundance and clearness of knowledge" in the mind. They exist as an example of an invariable law enunciated long ago by Cicero. In "Overbury" each pedantic quirk is presented only in its concrete integrity. Each detail is not, as in Burnet, a part of some causal process or an instance of some larger abstraction such as Wisdom or Patience. There is no clear distinction at all in "Overbury" between inner mental life and outer behavior. In Burnet, each external trait is the cue for a digression on how it exemplifies a larger scheme of things, usually an internal mental process. Hale's careful slowness of speech, for example, is not described concretely (as the "scholler's" speech is in the Overbury) but exists only as exemplifying the opposite of the usual law governing university scholars and as a result of another law which governs the results of "Wisdom and accustomed Patience" in the mind. Always Burnet wants us to see what makes the machine run.

I think now we can see at least one reason why the long biography replaced the short character. If, like Burnet, your main interest is in the reasons for an action, quality, or event, rather than in the action, quality, or event itself, the more causally related information you can present, the better. Concrete things are brought in only for the utilitarian function of illustrating larger abstract principles, rather than for what they represent or how delightful they are or how much we know about them or how witty we can be about them, or how they are typical of a certain sort of person commonly seen around town. A knowledge of the larger principle, in turn, will be useful itself. A good deal of information must be presented. The character or the brief sketch is too short to present processes which go on over a lifetime. Therefore they were replaced by the biography. Just as the emphasis on process determined vocabulary, figurative language, and syntax, so it altered genres as a whole.

Burnet's preface to his life of Hale is illuminating and shows how well aware the biographers were that they were doing something new. "No part of history is more instructive or delighting, than the lives of great and worthy men," begins Burnet on page three, but the instruction soon displaces the delight. Other biographies, we next discover, "do rather amuse the reader's fancy with a splendid show of greatness, than offer him what is really so useful to himself." The rest of the long preface is a consideration of the relation between arguments and utility, with the danger of "the wit and stile of the writer being more considered than the argument which they handle." Reviewing the history of the biography, Burnet tells us that, "For many ages there were no lives writ but by monks, through whose writing there runs such an incurable humour of telling incredible and inimitable passages, that little in them can be proposed as a pattern" (p. 6). What is important is the "pattern." Nothing can be useful unless it is ordered into a causal chain, and strung out in an Argument. Such a chain, of course, is the opposite of the pre-Restoration character. Earlier biographers "have fallen into another extreme, in writing lives too jejunely, swelling them up with trifling accounts of the childhood and education, and the domestic and private affairs of these persons of whom they writ, in which the world is little concerned. . . . Those transactions are only fit to be delivered to posterity, that they may carry with them some useful piece of knowledge to aftertimes" (p. 6). Over such "domestic concerns" Burnet "shall draw a veil . . . and shall avoid saying any thing of him, but what may afford the reader some profitable instruction" (pp. 10–11). Utility — "profitable instruction" — demands that everything be arranged in a "pattern" or "argument." Burnet's method is typical of the Restoration; he is right when he holds that the "humour of writing in such a manner" as the older biographers has "been quite laid down in this age" which for him is "more awakened and enlightened" (p. 7). The casual impressionism of the character, its whimsical promiscuity, was too disorderly and too personal to be useful.

The characters, in short, were too much like what passed for full-blown biography in the first part of the century. Douglas Bush says that in this period "biography, like the essay, was only detaching itself from related forms and much of it was 'impure.' " [14] These earlier biographies by Fulke Greville, Walton, Hayward, Drummond, and Fuller, for example, are all like the character in their lack of pattern, open condemnation or praise of their subject, anecdotal sketchiness, and incessant digressions. For Bush and the rest of us, true or modern biography begins with the regularized thing the Restoration wrote, with its single-minded concentration on extended causal processes in space and time. What John Harrington wrote in his preface to that ancestor of our *DNB*, Anthony A Wood's *Athenae Oxonienses*, strikes us today as self-evident: "It was thought more useful to publish, as you will now find it, in an honest plain *English* dress, without flourishes or affectation of Stile, as best becomes a History of Truth and matter of Fact." Utility determines Truth and Stile, which is "plain." "Plain" meant that everything was part of a pattern, with nothing included for its own sake:

> The Work is fitted for all Men in all Faculties, and therefore those of one Profession should not be displeased, if somewhat be inserted, which, however useless to them, may be chosen and admir'd by others. . . . Such general Collections are read by most Men with different Designs; and therefore however easie it may be for any Man to discover an Omission; it is very hard for any one Reader to pronounce one single Passage in them wholly superfluous.[15]

Fiction

Much of what we have said about character and biography also applies to fiction. In fact, many of the earlier novels purport to be little more than autobiographies in the form of letters, journals, and the like. We can now return to translations, for our period produced three interesting versions of *Don Quixote*.

> . . . y conocido á Luscinda, que después afirmó, que sola la belleza de Luscinda podía contender con aquélla. Los luengos y ruuios cabellos, no sólo le cubrieron las espaldas, mas toda en torno la escondieron debaxo de ellos, que sino eran los pies, ninguna otra cosa de su cuerpo se parecia, tales y tantos eran. En esto les siruió de peyne vnas manos, q̃ si los pies en el agua auían parecido pedaços de cristal, las manos en los cabellos semejauan pedaços de apretada nieue: todo lo qual, en más

admiración, y en más deseo de saber quién era, ponía á los tres que le mirauan. Por esto determinaron de mostrarse, y al moui-miento que hizieron de ponerse en pie, la hermosa moça alçó la cabeça, y apartándose los cabellos de delante de los ojos, con entrambas manos, miró los que el ruydo hazían: y apenas los huuo visto, quando se leuantó en pie, y sin aguarder a calçarse, ni a recoger los cabellos, asió mucha presteza vn bulto como de ropa, que junto á sí tenía, y quiso ponerse en huyda, llena de turbación, y sobre salto: mas no huuo dado seys passos, quando no pudiendo sufrir los delicados pies la aspereza de las piedras, dió consigo en el suelo.

. . . for as he after affirmed, no feature saue *Lucindas* could contend with hers. The long and golden haires did not onely couer her shoulders, but did also hide her round about, in such sort, as (her feet excepted) no other part of her body appeared, they were so neere and long. At this time her hands serued her for a Combe, which as her feete seemed pieces of crystall in the water, so did they appeare among her haires like pieces of driuen Snow. All which circumstances did possesse the three which stood gazing at her with great admiration, and desire to know what she was; and therefore resolued to show themselues; and with the noise which they made when they arose, the beauti-full mayden held up her head, and remouing her haires from before her eyes with both handes, she espyed those that had made it, and presently arising full of fear and trouble, she laid hand on a packet that was by her, which seemed to be of ap-parrell, and thought to flie away, without staying to pull on her shoes, or gather vp her haire: But scarce had she gone sixe paces when her delicate and tender feete, vnable to abide the rough encounter of the stones made her fall to the earth. (tr. Shelton, 1612)

One of the fair'st that ever Eyes beheld, except it were *Lucinda*, for that *Cardenio* would by no means allow. Instead of a Comb to disentangle her Hair, she made use of her Fingers, which by consequence were very small. That Accident made another Discovery of her Arms and Hands, surpassing in whiteness all the Ermins, or Snow that ever fell from the Sky. Which as-tonishing Beauties so ravish'd their Admiration, and encreas'd their Curiosity, that they resolv'd to accost her, and see who she was. The young Lady hearing a Noise, peep'd through her Hair, as through a Window, and seeing three Men coming toward her, only stay'd to take up a little Bundle which she had, and betook her self to her Heels with all the speed she could. But her bare tender Feet not being able to endure the rudeness of the Stones, down she fell, poor Soul. (tr. Philips, 1687)

Cardenio was not less surpriz'd than the other two, and once more declar'd, that no Face could vie with hers but *Lucinda's*. To part her deshevel'd Tresses, she onely us'd her slender Fingers, and at the same time discover'd so fine a pair of Arms and Hands, so white and lovely, that our three admiring Gazers grew more impatient to know who she was, and mov'd forward to accost her. At the noise they made, the pretty Creature started; and peeping thro' her Hair which she hastily remov'd from before her Eyes with both her Hands, she no sooner saw three Men coming towards her, but in a mighty fright she snatch'd up a little Bundle that lay by her, and fled as fast as she cou'd, without so much as staying to put on her Shooes, or do up her hair. But alas! scarce had she gone six steps, when her tender Feet not being able to endure the rough Encounter of the Stones, the poor affrighted Fair fell on the hard Ground. (tr. Motteux, 1712)[16]

I doubt that anyone in the seventeenth century consciously shared our modern preoccupation with "point of view" in fiction. Yet I think there is a significant difference in the point of view of these three translations, or at least between Shelton's and the other two. In Shelton, much more of the action is seen through the eyes of the fictional characters than in Philips and Motteux. There is little distance between characters and narrator. This comes about because Shelton concentrates more than the others on the physical details enumerated in Cervantes' text. Shelton positively delights in Cervantes' physicality. He describes precisely the extent to which the hair covers the girl, faithfully brings in Cervantes' image of the crystalline feet, and shows the exact way in which the girl parts her hair "from before her eyes with both handes." This material is either omitted altogether or only barely mentioned by the others. The difference between the concrete Shelton and the others can be seen in such details as in the last sentence, where Shelton has "the rough encounter of the stones." This is adopted by Motteux but Philips has the less sensuous "rudeness of the Stones." Shelton wants us to feel the rough encounter; Philips gives us an abstraction, "rudeness."

The later translators present the action from the point of view of the narrator of the story, rather than from that of the characters in it. There is more distance between the narrator and the characters. This is because their emphasis is not on physical description, vivid and immediate, but on the narrator's analysis of causal relations. Compare, for example, Shelton's "At this time her hands serued her for a Combe, which as her feete seemed pieces of crystall in the water, so did they appear among her haires like pieces of driuen Snow" to Philips' "Instead of a Comb to disentangle her Hair, she made use of her Fingers, which by consequence were very small." Philips has added, gratuitously, a causal relationship in the "by consequence"; this is followed by another, even more technical and impersonal, in the next clause, beginning with "That Accident made another Discovery." Motteux ignores altogether the charming business about the comb, the feet like crystal, and the snow like ermine in his haste to get to the causal relation in the "Arms and Hands" which are "so lovely, that our three admiring Gazers grew more impatient."

As we might expect, where Shelton is content to describe only the external behavior of his characters, Philips and Motteux are far more interested in "inside views." These explain, from the perspective of a detached and always reliable observer, the causes of actions in terms of clear and distinct counters like "Admiration" and "Curiosity" reacting automatically to the stimulus of "Beauties." As cultivated Restoration gentlemen, we all know, of course, what the

Beauties are which automatically excite "Admiration" and "Curiosity"; there is no need to go into specific details, as Shelton has done.

Understandably, the tone of the later translators is one of detached amusement. In Philips the girl is a "pretty Creature" and a "poor Soul" and in Motteux a "poor affrighted Fair" with "deshevel'd Tresses" instead of hair. The fine language suggests condescension, and that she is not a whole, live girl but a literary convention. Philips and Motteux (and undoubtedly Cervantes) are only half-serious about Our Heroine and "our three admiring gazers." There is a good deal of the mock-heroic in all this detached causal analysis. But Shelton seems wholly engrossed in what is going on; there is no distance at all between narrator and characters.

The difference between Shelton's and the other two translations is the difference between the earliest prose fiction, from Sidney's *Arcadia* to Nashe's *Unfortunate Traveler*, and the novels of Defoe, Richardson, or Fielding. In the earlier fiction there is a chain of static pictures, quite out of all time and space, connected by purely narrative links, with characterization generally a matter of frozen moral absolutes. In the later fiction, almost all external actions are examples of a progression of conflicting inner causes, either psychological or moral (Virtue, Benevolence, Reason, Passion, Love, Honor, and so on), all in clear chronological order. The extreme types, I suppose, of Elizabethan and later fiction are the *Arcadia* — all loosely connected narrative action, set speeches, and rich description, occurring, as the title suggests, out of space and time — and *Pamela*, in which almost nothing "happens" at all. What we do have in *Pamela* is causal development of character, mostly implicit. Therefore time is very important, and we are always made well aware of the date. Even in *Tom Jones*, the chief emphasis is not on the incidents themselves but on how they relate to the development of the main characters.[17] This tendency toward what we now know as realism has already begun in the Restoration in the preference for biographies of real people in space and time instead of ideal types as in the characters. The same thing is happening in the most popular fictional form of the period, the romance, where "verisimilitude" is replacing "ideality." [18]

That we commonly regard Defoe, Richardson, and Fielding as the first important "real" or "modern" novelists is an admission that we, too, have lost the Elizabethan taste for the "qualitatively unique." We prefer to regard all action in fiction as part of a causal series. Like Burnet, we see things as "useful" only if there is an "argument" and a "pattern" both chronological and spatial. Here is another union of Truth and Utility. In the Platonically inclined Renaissance, truth was independent of time and space, a reflection of some timeless and spaceless Ideal. With the triumph of the new nominalism, there are no more such Ideals. Events happen in a world of space-time coordinates, a doctrine which, as Burnet's preface attests, was accepted because it was useful and useful because it was accepted. Everything that is not in spatial and chronological causal sequence is whimsical, quaint, perverse, or difficult.

This is why modern innovations in fiction, such as the rearranging of time sequence and point of view in Conrad and Faulkner, or the wordplay of Joyce, were at first so curious and difficult for us. We come to fiction prepared for a reliable, omniscient, objective narrator like the one in Philips' and Motteux' translations. A deviation from this norm is a real innovation. In fact, our expectation has always opened up endless possibilities for technical experimentation. Once the utilitarian norm is established, a writer like Swift regularly obtains many of his effects by ironically undercutting one of its more simple-minded or heartless exemplars, such as Gulliver or the speaker in *A Modest Proposal*. The narrator may be ironically and subtly distinguished from the author ("Fielding" in *Tom Jones*), "sympathetic" or "unsympathetic," or "reliable" or "unreliable." [19] None of these techniques would be as effective without our post-Restoration expectation that the narrator be detached, analytical, reliable, and given to causal explanations.

Our modern innovations have gone far. But I doubt that many of them would have perplexed an Elizabethan as much as they at first did us. If not the realism and structure, then the style, so difficult for us, of *Ulysses* is fundamentally Elizabethan. How and why this mode yielded to that of our conventional novel can perhaps be seen if we compare the style of Thomas Nashe with two of the acknowledged forerunners of modern fiction, Bunyan and Defoe. Here, for example, is Nashe's Jack Wilton at Wittenberg, where he is present at "a verie solemne scholasticall entertainment of the Duke of Saxonie":

That pageant ouerpast, there rusht vpon him a miserable rablement of iunior graduats, that all cride vppon him mightily in their gibrige, lyke a companie of beggars, God saue your grace, God saue your grace, Iesus preserue your Highnesse, though it be but for an houre.

Some three halfe penyworth of Latine here also had he throwen at his face, but it was choise stuffe, I can tell you, as there is choise euen amongest ragges gathered vp from the dunghill. At the townes end met him the burgers and dunsticall incorporationers of *Wittenberg* in their distinguished liueries, their distinguished and liuery faces I mean, for they were most of them hot liuered dronkards, and had all the coate colours of sanguine, purple, crimson, copper, carnation, that were to be had, in their countenances. Filthie knaues, no cost had they bestowed on the towne for his welcome, sauing new painted their houghs and bousing houses, which commonly are fairer than their churches, and ouer their gates set the towne armes carousing a whole health to the Dukes armes, which sounded gulping after this sort, *Vanhotten, slotten, irk bloshen glotten gelderslike:* what euer the wordes were, the sense was this, Good drinke is a medicine for all diseases.

A bursten belly inkhorne orator called *Vanderhulke,* they pickt out to present him with an oration, one that had a sulpherous big swolne large face, like a Saracen, eyes like two Kentish oysters, a mouth that opened as wide euery time he spake, as one of those old knit trap doores, a beard as though it had been made of a birds neast pluckt in peeces, which consisteth of strawe, haire, and durt mixt together. He was apparelled in blacke leather new licourd, & a short gowne without anie gathering in the backe, faced before and behinde with a boistrous beare skin, and a red night-cap on his head. To this purport and effect was this broccing duble beere oration.[20]

For me the most remarkable quality of this wildly exuberant prose is that I never know what to expect next. Almost every phrase is an "unusual collocation" and therefore a personal expression. The first sentence begins formally enough with an absolute construction ("That pageant ouerpast") but it ends up in a colloquial chaos. The most obviously rhetorical devices jostle the most artless. With no warning we have emphatic or sarcastic intrusions ("but it was choise stuffe, I can tell you, as there is a choise euen amongest ragges gathered vp from the dunghill"); extravagant punning jokes ("in their distinguished liueries, their distinguished and liuery faces I mean"); quick shifts into indirect discourse; explosive alliteration ("bursten belly"); utterly unpredictable sentence structure; torrents of similes; and powerful clumps of adjectives. The boundary between nouns and adjectives, to be strictly observed in the Restoration, is blurred here. Nouns ("belly," "beere") become adjectives, as, indeed, all the "parts of speech" begin to lose their identity, often self-consciously (the pun on "liueries" and "liuery"). Does "bursten" modify "belly," "orator," or "inkhorn"? Or all three? In such densely descriptive language, so full of surprises, the exact logical relations among words do not make much difference. In "bursten belly inkhorn orator" each word has begun to lose its distinct grammatical function and lexical significance — if it ever had these in the first place. The phrase is really one Germanic compound; in effect it is a complete surprise, a sort of nonce-word, like "dunsticall." Nashe's frequent nonce words and nonce compounds are in wild contrast to the technical diction sought by the Restoration. Nonce words are subjective and for the immediate context only; technical terms ideally have the same significance in all contexts and are impersonal. Nashe, in contrast to the Restoration, is more interested in generalized, highly personal sensory impressions than in abstract logical distinctions. These impressions may come as much from the fireworks of an alliteration like "bursten belly" as from the visual image itself. Nashe wants us to see, and even to hear and smell, what is happening immediately in front of us. The surprising logic of sense perception, not that of ideas or grammar, governs sentence structure just as it governs vocabulary and syntax. Where most of us would write, "They picked out to present him with an oration Vanderhulke, an inkhorn orator with a bursting belly," Nashe puts the "bursten belly" part first, for what Vanderhulke looks like is the important thing.

Of course, these descriptive elements are never morally neutral. There is none of the Restoration's seeming objectivity at all. When Nashe tells us, with one of his irruptions of irony, that the bousing houses commonly are fairer than the churches, he is intruding and commenting on the text as surely as when he plucks us by the sleeve with his "I can tell you." In fact, there is no separation between the descriptions of physical and moral qualities. One is as absolute as the other, as Nashe's reference to the colors of the drunkard's "humors" indicates. A man is a hypocrite in the same way that he has eyes like Kentish oysters. There is no hint of moral misdeeds coming from an inner conflict between such Restoration absolutes as Reason and Passion.

Nor is there more than a hint of the Restoration's concern

for causal, and spatial and chronological, sequence. Although we can easily infer the motives of the hypocritical burghers and dunsticall incorporationers, Nashe is not interested in exploring them. He is not even interested in the way their flattery and drunkenness might be integrated into his plot; in what follows, they are forgotten while the Duke of Saxony hears Lutheran speeches, whose chief interest for Nashe is stylistic. As in the Elizabethan translations, there are no characterizations by "inside views." Nashe never concerns himself, for example, with the long-range psychological effects of Jack Wilton's incredible journey. Nor, although he is writing a travel book, does Nashe care about such causal matters as how or why his hero happens to be in this particular place at this particular time. The book is full of sentences like "Towards Venice we progrest, and took Rotterdam in our waie, that was clean out of our waie" (p. 245), where Jack meets Erasmus and More, and, a paragraph later, "So left we them to prosecute their discontented studies, and made our next journey to Wittenberg. At the very pointe of our entry into Wittenberg," and so on. Everything takes place in a practically noncausal world out of time and space. There is not a progression of events but a series of discrete narrative bits.

For all Nashe's emphasis on sensuous detail, he is not a realist, in any sense of the word. Most of the pictures are exaggerated. Needless to say, no one could have gone all those distances and seen all those people at any particular period in time. Surely Nashe could not have expected his readers to believe it really happened. *The Unfortunate Traveler* is a frankly artificial confection. Like Ben Jonson's ideal poet, Nashe is a maker, an artificer. As McKerrow says, "He, as indeed almost all the prose writers of his time, set himself deliberately to produce a kind of artistic composition, following in some measure the accepted principles of rhetoric, in which the effect would be heightened by all the well-known devices of rhetoric." [21] At the same time, though, as in the Jonsonian and classical plain style, the mind of the author intrudes at every turn. Or perhaps we should say "speaker" or "authorial voice," for Nashe himself seldom emerges in his writings.

While one hesitates to describe Nashe's style as "plain," it seems to me that it has affinities with the tradition of the classical plain style. Elsewhere Nashe indicates that he is following the *genus humile*.[22] He implies as much in our passage, for he twits Vanderhulke and all the speakers at Wittenberg for stealing quotes and stock tags out of Cicero instead of being, like himself, original. That we do not regard *The Unfortunate Traveler* as a "real" novel attests to our feeling that the classical plain style is alien to modern fiction, as it is to the norm of modern prose style in general.

Like classical plain style, Nashe's prose seeks to reveal the personality of the "author" at any particular moment. Therefore Nashe, like Bacon, required many styles; in the wideness of his range he is close to the "libertine" authors. For example, just before Jack Wilton gets to Wittenberg we have passages like the description of the effect of Surrey's Geraldine in the style C. S. Lewis called "Golden": "Her high exalted sunne beames have set the Phenix neast of my breast on fire, and I myself haue brought Arabian spiceries of sweet passions and praises to furnish out the funerall flame of my follie. . . . All the whole receptacle of my sight was vnhabited with hir rare worth" (p. 243). Then, after Wittenberg, there is the straightforward melodrama, laced with commonplaces, of the revenge and execution of Cutwolfe, though even this is broken into by the jaunty description of the executioner who "woulde cracke neckes as fast as a cooke crackes egges" (p. 327).

Now, although both Bacon and Nashe have many styles, Bacon's exist to achieve an end beyond themselves, Nashe's for their own sakes, for the delight they afford and for the

emotional attitudes they express. In fact the book itself —
its characterizations, settings, structure, and the rest — is
nothing except its styles. The completely inconsistent Jack
Wilton is not a novelistic "character" seen in relation to a
stable "society" at all. Rather he is a cluster of styles, and
there is no clear separation of Wilton's style from Nashe's.
As G. R. Hibbard puts it, in contrast to the Restoration
author's appearance of distant objectivity, Nashe

is incapable of keeping Jack, the actor and narrator, distinct
from himself, the moralist and literary critic. . . . As a realized
human being he does not exist at all. . . . The story is sheer
improvisation. . . . The hero is and does whatever Nashe's
strictly literary purpose demands he should be and do. When
his creator seeks to outdo the writers of jest books, Jack is the
accomplished practical joker; when he seeks to outdo his chroniclers, Jack is the most vivid of chroniclers; when Petrarchism
comes under fire, he becomes a gifted literary critic and clever
parodist. . . . And so one could go on. *The Unfortunate
Traveler* is held together by one thing only, the personality of
its author.[23]

Although Nashe has these affinities with the classical
genus humile, his book like "libertine" prose represents a
stage in the break-up of the separation of styles which, as
Auerbach has shown, has been so important for the representation of reality in Western literature since Homer. In
contrast to classical times, Nashe has the serious, "high"
matter — such affairs of the great as Cutwolfe's revenge —
mixed in with the "low," the ridiculous affairs of the humble, as in the treatment of Cutwolfe's executioner.

In the Judeo-Christian tradition the lives of the lowly are
not so ridiculous. The Bible treated seriously *all* subject
matter in the same "paratactic" style, often yielding sublime
effects without resort to the classical "high" style or *genus
grande* at all. There is none of this unified sublimity in
Nashe, but something like it informs *The Pilgrim's Progress*
(1678). The "paratactic" mode was congenial to a Bible-

centered Puritan like Bunyan, who provides evidence that Puritan style in general, unlike any "baroque" revival of the *genus humile*, was important in the rise of the modern English novel. Perhaps we can understand why by contrasting Jack Wilton's confrontation with Vanderhulke and Christian's with Faithful:

Now as Christian went on his way, he came to a little ascent, which was cast up on purpose that pilgrims might see before them. Up there therefore Christian went and looking forward, he saw Faithful before him upon his journey. Then said Christian aloud, "Ho-ho, so-ho; stay, and I will be your companion." At that Faithful looked behind him, to whom Christian cried again, "Stay, stay, till I come up to you." But Faithful answered, "No, I am upon my life, and the avenger of blood is behind me." At this Christian was somewhat moved, and putting to all his strength, he quickly got up with Faithful, and did also overrun him, so the last was first. Then did Christian vaingloriously smile, because he had gotten the start of his brother; but not taking good heed to his feet, he suddenly stumbled and fell, and could not rise again, until Faithful came up to help him.[24]

The contrast between Nashe and Bunyan is more profound than a mere difference of "personality." The entire conception of what the language of fiction should be doing has radically altered. Bunyan's first concern is with the pilgrim's progress, not with the specific details in themselves of each moment of the journey. Nor does Bunyan intrude conspicuously into the action. When he does come in, it is not to place a moral tag from a physical mark on his Unfortunate Traveler or his acquaintances but to illuminate the meaning of his hero's internal growth. Where Nashe's characters chiefly exist as their — and Nashe's — styles, Bunyan's are various abstract mental and moral processes, all in pretty much the same style. There are no great masses of descriptive detail in *The Pilgrim's Progress* to be relished for their own sake. Bunyan is really talking about mental or spiritual processes even when he seems to be merely "setting the scene." Like the "little ascent," everything that Christian — and the reader — sees is "cast upon purpose" by God and by Bunyan. Perhaps the only exceptions to this absence of purely "literary" machinery are the little connecting phrases with which Bunyan must, of necessity, bump along his characters: "Now as Christian went on his way"; "Then I saw in my Dream," and so on.

In such a style, in which language exists not for its own sake but to carry the burden of a larger "progress," there is little need for metaphor or any other "similitude" since, as Bunyan himself says, everything in the book, like everything in the world of the Puritan, is a metaphor already, waiting to be "unfolded" and applied in a "use":

> Put by thy curtains; look within my veil;
> Turn up my metaphors and do not fail.
> There, if thou seekest them, such things to find,
> As will be helpful to an honest mind. (p. 164)

As in the Biblical "paratactic" mode, every incident carries a heavy freight of significance. It requires no "color" from rhetorical heightening. The style therefore must be plain, in the sense that there must be no self-expressive and unexpected similitudes, strange words, and the like. The solemn, archetypal "progress" is the thing not our attitude to it. Unusual collocations of any kind — lexical, syntactic, or grammatical — would bring in too much subjectivity.

This plain style puts a heavy burden on the reader, at least on the non-Puritan reader. With only a few events brought sharply into focus, he must try to lift the veil of the mystery. What is presupposed is a common frame of reference — here, the Bible and Christian doctrine. To appreciate our passage we need not know the exact theological point and stated Biblical allusion to the last being first or even the unstated one about pride going before a fall. But we must have at least a general intuitive understanding of the Puritan outlook. Otherwise how can we make anything out of Christian's "vainglorious" overtaking of Faithful? In this Puritan style, prose does not exist as an expression of the author himself or as rhetorical heightening. Rather, it is a series of signs for mental events whose excitement and significance depend upon a context already known to the reader. Like the "nominal" style already discussed it is technical, since it depends on a special knowledge. Because nothing need be explained or qualified, it also has few complex sentences and therefore little syntactic variety — again like the nominal style.

In these respects Bunyan's style is like the other kinds of Restoration prose, including the "close, naked, natural" style recommended by Sprat. Like Puritan prose, "scientific" style sacrifices rhetorical devices because its real significance is not in itself, but in another purpose beyond itself, new discoveries leading ultimately to good "works" (that favorite word of both Puritans and Baconians). Both "science" and Puritanism are intensely empirical, for in both the most inconsequential-seeming details of life are significant, and therefore to be observed closely. Inevitably there is the same concentration, in both styles, on things rather than on words and rhetoric. The Royal Society and "science" could not possibly have influenced Bunyan. Yet the tinker of Bedfordshire writes, if not like Sprat's merchant, then certainly like the artisan and countryman that he was. Certainly his kind of allegory is remote stylistically from that of a wit and scholar like Spenser. In an Elizabethan allegory like *The Faerie Queene* everything also is related to a transcendental abstraction. But, as in Nashe, we have more a series of elaborate tableaux than Bunyan's ever-present "progress."

There is a difference, of course, between Bunyan's prose style and that of many of the Restoration writers we have considered thus far. In Lancaster's translation of Plutarch, for example, the syntax resembles elegant mathematical ratios. There is little of this formal balance in Bunyan. What then did Sprat mean by "mathematical plainness"? Did he want a Bunyan or a Dryden, a "manly" or a "polite" style? We may never be sure, but we do know that, like the other reformers of style, he wanted an easily accessible prose.

That the author of what most historians of literature regard as the first "real" novels, Daniel Defoe, was not an artisan or countryman but a merchant therefore does not seem extraordinary. In the section "Of the Trading Stile" from *The Complete English Tradesman* Defoe reveals his awareness of the connection between mercantile values and his ideal utilitarian prose:

> I might have made some apology to you for urging tradesmen to write a plain and easy stile; let me add to you, that the tradesmen need not be offended at my condemning them *as it were* to a plain and homely stile; easy, plain, and familiar language is the beauty of speech in general, and is the excellency of all writing, on whatever subject, or to whatever persons they are we write or speak. The end of speech is that men might understand one another's meaning; certainly that speech, or that way of speaking which is most easily understood, is the best way of speaking. If any man was to ask me, which would be supposed to be a perfect stile, or language, I would answer, that in which a man speaking to five hundred people, of all common and various capacities, idiots or lunaticks excepted, should be understood by them all in the same manner with one another, and in the same sense which the speaker intended to be understood, this would certainly be a most perfect stile.
>
> ALL exotic sayings, dark and ambiguous speakings, affected words, and as I said in my last, abridgment, or words cut off, as they are foolish and improper in business, so indeed are they in any other things; hard words and affectation of stile in business, is like bombast in poetry, a kind of rumbling nonsense, and nothing of the kind can be more ridiculous.[25]

There is nothing ridiculous about Defoe's first major work of fiction, *The Life and Strange Surprising Adventures of*

Robinson Crusoe. This work is about twenty years beyond our century, but it is the logical culmination of everything we have been saying about the rise of a style for modern fiction. Its author seemed to have imbibed whatever ideas of the later seventeenth century helped to create the new prose style, including, in *An Essay Upon Projects* (1697), Sprat's plan to establish an English Academy to regularize the language. Robinson Crusoe is, for all his difficulties, not an Unfortunate Traveler, but his journey is something of a Pilgrim's Progress in that he seeks, with several disastrous exceptions, one unvarying goal: not eternal bliss in the next world, but material betterment in this one. In this way he is thoroughly utilitarian. What makes Crusoe so fascinating, though, is that a certain imprudent part of him, compounded partly of sheer wanderlust and partly of a yearning to get rich quickly, makes him run away from home (which act Crusoe calls his "Original Sin") and forsake the easy, sober course to riches offered by his father.

Once Crusoe is on the island, though, he is all prudence and utility. Crusoe's very being, his *arete*, is his aptitude for the useful, and more specifically economic, arts. For Marx and many others Crusoe is *homo economicus* himself. This view must be qualified; Bonamy Dobrée is right when he says that too much has been made of *Robinson Crusoe* as the myth of acquisitive capitalism.[26] Crusoe is not interested in acquiring money *per se*, as his famous speech attests:

'O drug!' said I aloud, 'what art thou good for? Thou art not worth to me, no, not the taking off of the ground; one of those knives is worth all this heap; I have no manner of use for thee, e'en remain where thou art, and go to the bottom as a creature whose life is not worth saving.' However, upon second thoughts I took it away.[27]

The whole speech is concerned with utility, not accumulation. Money is useless in itself, but someday it might be very useful indeed. On the island, however, it is useless, as are more goods than one needs. "As it was, I had not the least advantage by it, or benefit from it; but there it lay in a drawer, and grew mouldy with the damp of the cave in the wet season; and if I had had the drawer full of diamonds, it had been the same case; and they had been of no manner of value to me, because of no use" (pp. 95–96). Crusoe is not exactly Economic Man, but he is always a utilitarian except for his "Original Sin."

The stylistic result is the impersonal, progressive kind of plainness that seems "modern" to us. Having analyzed Wilton's meeting with Vanderhulke and Christian's with Faithful, let us now look at Crusoe's first encounter with Friday:

He was a comely handsome fellow, perfectly well made; with straight strong limbs, not too large; tall and well shap'd, and, as I reckon, about twenty six years of age. He had a very good countenance, not a fierce and surly aspect; but seem'd to have something very manly in his face, and yet he had all the sweetness and softness of an European in his countenance too, especially when he smil'd. His hair was long and black, not curl'd like wool; his forehead very high and large, and a great vivacity and sparkling sharpness in his eyes. The colour of his skin was not quite black, but very tawny; and yet not of an ugly yellow nauseous tawny, as the Brasilians, and Virginians, and other natives of America are; but of a bright kind of dun olive colour, that had in it something very agreeable, tho' not very easy to describe. His face was round and plump; his nose small, not flat like the negroes, a very good mouth, thin lips, and his fine teeth well set, and white as ivory. After he had slumber'd, rather than slept, about half an hour, he wak'd again, and comes out of the cave to me; for I had been milking my goats, which I had in the enclosure just by; when he espy'd me, he came running to me, laying himself down again upon the ground, with all the possible signs of an humble thankful disposition, making many antick gestures to show it. At last he lays his head flat upon the ground, close to my foot, and sets my other foot upon his head, as he had done before; and after this, made all the signs to me of subjection, servitude, and submission imaginable, to let me know how he would serve me as long as he liv'd. I understood him in many things, and let him know I was very well pleas'd with him; in a little time I began to speak to him, and teach him to speak to me; and first, I made him know his name should be Friday, which was the day I sav'd his life; I call'd him so for the memory of the time; I likewise taught him to say Master, and then let him know, that was to be my name; I likewise taught him to say yes and no, and to know the meaning of them; I gave him some milk in an earthen pot, and let him see me drink it before him, and sop my bread in it; and I gave him a cake of bread to do the like, which he quickly comply'd with, and made signs that it was very good for him.

I kept there with him all that night; but as soon as it was day, I beckon'd to him to come with me, and let him know I would give him some cloaths, at which he seem'd very glad, for he was stark naked. (pp. 149-150)

The most obvious difference between the styles of *The Pilgrim's Progress* and *Robinson Crusoe* is the wealth of description in the latter. Critics have always praised Defoe for his ability to use details to make his thoroughly unlikely story plausible. Nashe also is detailed, yet *The Unfortunate Traveler*, though the plot is not much more fantastic than that of *Robinson Crusoe*, does not seem "realistic" at all to us. The difference lies in the *kind* of detail that each author uses. It is not enough to say that Nashe's details are "exaggerated." What makes *The Unfortunate Traveler* unreal is the same thing that makes the *Arcadia* unreal: the details are presented for their own sakes. Rather than being seen in causal relations useful to the reader or to the narrator, the details reflect the narrator's own attitudes. We could compare, for example, Nashe's "one that had a sulpherous big swolne large face" to Defoe's "The colour of his skin was not quite black, but very tawny, and yet not of an ugly yellow nauseous tawny, as the Brasilians . . . but of a bright kind of dun olive colour, that had in it something very agreeable, thou not very easy to describe." Defoe's emphasis is all, as his last phrase suggests, on the difficulty of exact, objective description, on the problem of getting the shade just right, not on the author's momentary feelings toward the subject. His careful antitheses, with their suggestion of "precision," contrast completely with Nashe's impressionistic, even tautological, massing of adjectives. Defoe's book is not about The Unfortunate Robinson Crusoe but merely Robinson Crusoe, a real, tangible, isolated modern man. The novel's title, like *Tom Jones, Roderick Random,* or *Pamela,* is simply the name of a person. But *The Unfortunate Traveler* contains a value judgment, like "A Meere Scholler." Unlike Nashe and Overbury, Defoe seems to aspire toward an objective report on a laboratory specimen.

If Crusoe is a scientist, though, he is always an "applied" scientist. Ian Watt calls him — evidently Defoe as well — "a strict utilitarian." [28] Had Crusoe gone about gathering scientific data for the sheer pleasure of it or in the spirit of pure research the book would not have been "realistic" at all, for Crusoe must always be concerned first with sheer survival and then with material comforts. Otherwise we would not recognize *Robinson Crusoe* as a novel; it would be a romantic idyll of life on a desert isle. Normally we demand for fiction to be "realistic" that there be a motive or cause for all behavior; for Defoe this means that the characters be interested in what they think is useful for themselves.

Crusoe's only important interest in Friday is utilitarian. Their relationship is immediately that of Master to slave. Crusoe looks Friday over with the impersonal acuity of a slave owner examining potential property. In fact, Friday has almost no existence apart from his being a perfect slave, as strong and docile as Defoe's idea of a Negro but capable of civilization, "with the sweetness and softness of an European." The extraordinarily detailed description of Friday's skin is not merely for its own sake, for "atmosphere." That it is not completely black is important for Crusoe, since it means that Friday combines the best qualities of negro and white. All Crusoe's interest is in Friday's usefulness for him. "Master" is the first word Crusoe teaches him, and at the end of their relationship, even after many years, Crusoe has not taught him much more, for Friday still speaks pidgin English. That the servant does not exist apart from the Master is symbolized most compellingly by Crusoe's assigning to Friday of his very name, signifying the day when their relationship began and when Friday, in effect, began to exist.

Here as throughout the novel there are none of the usual passions which control human relationships, such as loyalty to family or nation, or sex. Crusoe's companion on a desert island is no Calypso but a man; most of the affection Crusoe feels for him is that of a Master for his faithful servant. Not even the arrival of the first person Crusoe has talked to in twenty years in the midst of a harrowing skirmish with cannibals can keep our restless entrepreneur from milking his goats.

Crusoe's prudence — Economic Man's dominant trait, according to Adam Smith — is reflected in his style. There are none of Nashe's unusual collocations in it; it is the language of a man in complete control of the situation. The syntax, like the Crusoe who tells the story at his desk years after the events, is calmly balanced not sporadically and therefore obtrusively so. Often, as in the last sentence of our paragraph, there is a long succession of balanced independent clauses controlled by the "I" at the beginning of each. More often the Defoe sentence starts off with one or more loosely antithetical or at least parallel constructions, and then trails off into several details tacked on. The balance suggests judiciousness: "His face was round and plump; his nose small." The tacked-on details indicate careful observation. Here is a man coolly surveying the scene, even at the momentous occasion of Friday's arrival. Where Nashe gives us a blurred impression of the whole, Defoe's balances

make us consider and sort out each detail. Defoe calculates
its use, not its beauty or other fascination: "not flat like
the negroes, a very good mouth, thin lips, and fine teeth
well set, and white as ivory." "Very good," "fine," and
"well" in this context are adjectives of utility. Crusoe is
sizing up Friday as a slave. These are the only kind of details that interest him.

The other kinds of details are "dull." Had he begun his
journal too soon, Crusoe tells us, it

> would ha' been full of many dull things. For example, I must
> have said thus: 'Sept. the 30th. After I got to shore and had
> escap'd drowning, instead of being thankful to God for my
> deliverance, having first vomited with the great quantity of salt
> water which was gotten into my stomach, and recovering my-
> self a little, I ran about the shore, wringing my hands and beat-
> ing my head and face, exclaiming at my misery, and crying out,
> I was undone, undone, till tyr'd and faint I was forc'd to lye
> down on the ground to repose, but durst not sleep for fear of
> being devour'd. (p. 52)

These "dull" details are exactly what an Elizabethan would
have included. What Defoe does put into Crusoe's journal
gives us a good insight into his interests and methods:

> September 30, 1659. I, poor miserable Robinson Crusoe, being
> shipwreck'd, during a dreadful storm, in the offing, came on
> shore on this dismal unfortunate island, which I call'd the Island
> of Despair, all the rest of the ship's company being drown'd,
> and my self almost dead.
> All the rest of that day I spent in afflicting my self at the
> dismal circumstances I was brought to, viz. I had neither food,
> house, clothes, weapon, or place to fly to, and in despair of any
> relief, saw nothing but death before me, either that I should be
> devour'd by wild beasts, murther'd by savages, or starv'd to
> death by want of food. At the approach of night, I slept in a
> tree for fear of wild creatures, but slept soundly tho' it rain'd
> all night. (p. 53)

Even in his moment of "Despair" Crusoe is coolly sorting
out, in calm "either . . . or" constructions, each aspect of

his situation. The Despair itself is not as interesting as the straightforward observation that he "slept soundly, tho' it rain'd all night."

When Crusoe does tell us about his feelings — and he has many moments of despair and panic — it is generally only with reference to the problems of survival. There is not much stylistic heightening. As in so much literature of the Restoration and Augustan period, he is curiously detached from his own feelings, preferring to generalize about them rather than to describe them. It is as though they were happening to someone else:

> I was now landed and safe on shore, and began to look up and thank God that my life was sav'd in a case wherein there was some minutes before scarce any room to hope. I believe it is impossible to express to the life what the extasies and transports of the soul are, when it is so sav'd as I may say, out of the very grave; and I do not wonder now at that custom, viz. that when a malefactor who has the halter about his neck, is tyed up, and just going to be turn'd off, and has a reprieve brought to him; I say, I do not wonder that they bring a surgeon with it, that the surprise may not drive the animal spirits from the heart, and overwhelm him. (p. 36)

Passions are seen as examples which help prove a larger generalization, usually with reference to the struggle to prosper or survive. Therefore they are described in the same style as everything else, as, for example, when Friday prostrates himself before Crusoe. About the only times Crusoe does become rhetorical is when he generalizes about the greatest danger besetting Economic Man, the Reason-Passion conflict and its consequences:

> 'Now,' said I aloud, 'my dear father's words are come to pass: God's justice has overtaken me: I rejected the voice of Providence, which had mercifully put me in a posture or station of life wherein I might have been happy and easy. . . . I refus'd their help and assistance who would have lifted me into the world, and wou'd have made every thing easy to me, and now

I have difficulties to struggle with, too great even for nature itself to support, and no assistance, no help, no comfort, no advice.' Then I cry'd out, 'Lord, be my help, for I am in great distress.' (p. 68)

The effect of the stylistic contrast is to set off Useless Passion (Crusoe's wanderlust and greed) from Useful Prudence, dramatizing the main conflict of the book. There is a "dissociation of sensibility" here; as E. M. Novak observes, we feel that "passion appears to be grafted on to the characters, an appendage rather than an organic part of them." [29] Feelings must be kept separate from the serious business of life.

In this prose of business everything must be accounted for. This is especially true of time. Something is always happening in *Robinson Crusoe*. All periods of time are "filled in," for example, in the paragraph about the meeting with Friday: "After he had slumbered . . . . about half an hour . . . . for I had been milking my goats . . . . At last he lays his head . . . after this, made all the signs . . . . in a little time I began to speak . . . . I kept there with him all that night; but as soon as it was day, I beckon'd to him. . . ." So conscious of time is Crusoe that he names his man Friday "for the memory of the time." This Puritanical and empirical reckoning is in complete contrast to Nashe.

Similarly we are always being moved about very carefully through space. Exact relations between places and things are always spelled out: "My goats, which I had in the enclosure just by"; "his head flat upon the ground, close to my foot." As in Restoration prose, the sense of temporal and spatial progression makes the style seem "modern." Nothing is seen in its own right; everything is part of larger patterns. Even in this relatively static passage the prose is operative rather than descriptive.

The ultimate end of everything, to which all else converges, is of course what is materially useful. Insofar as any generalization can be valid about a writer so fabulously voluminous and full of contradictions, Defoe was a radical utilitarian, responsible for such extraordinary statements about "Usefulness" as "the greatest Pleasure, and justly deem'd by all good Men the truest and noblest End of Life; in which Men come nearest to the Character of our B. Saviour, who went about doing good; and even to that of our great Creator, whose goodness is ever all his Works." [30] *Robinson Crusoe*, as everyone has always said, is a book no one can put down until the end or at least until Crusoe gets off his island. I think we feel this way because we all get caught up in the various progressions of Crusoe toward the utilitarian "truest and noblest End of Life." "How will he get out of this one?" we are always asking.

But any writer can manage this sort of suspense. The significant progressions are more subtly developed. For example, Defoe always makes us aware of Crusoe's gradual progressions from absolute poverty to riches and comfort; from powerless solitude to absolute rule, first over his "family" of animals, then over Friday, various prisoners, and the physical island itself, and eventually over foreign plantations; and from unskilled naïveté to endless practical wisdom under the whip of necessity. It is wrong to regard Part I as merely a discursive string of exciting episodes interrupted by moralistic or religious reflections. Both in the microcosm of style and in the macrocosm of over-all structure the book is organized around its utilitarian progressions.

Another of the book's progressions is the growth of Crusoe's Puritanism. The simultaneous rise of Crusoe's religiosity and affluence has not gone unnoticed. Indeed, "There are probably few classrooms where *Moll Flanders* and *Robinson Crusoe* are studied which do not resound with explanations based on the rise of the middle classes, economic individualism, and the significant relationship between capitalism and the Protestant ethic." [31] Crusoe more and more sees everything in his progress as a reflection of God's plan. As the book goes on there are increasingly frequent passages, filled with Puritan intensity, like the following, when Crusoe has just discovered some "English barley" growing mysteriously on his island:

It is impossible to express the astonishment and confusion of my thoughts on this occasion. I had hitherto acted upon no religious foundation at all; indeed, I had very few notions of religion in my head, or had entertain'd any sense of any thing that had befallen me, otherwise than as a chance, or, as we lightly say, what pleases God; without so much as enquiring into the end of Providence in these things, or His order governing events in the world. But after I saw barley grow there, in a climate which I knew was not proper for corn, and especially that I knew not how it came there, it startl'd me strangely, and I began to suggest that God had miraculously caus'd this grain to grow without any help of seed sown, and that it was directed purely for my own sustenance on that wild miserable place. (pp. 58–59)

Even after Crusoe discovers that the barley has grown from some old chicken feed that he once threw down on that place it is still a "work of Providence" that the place happened to be a good spot, sheltered from the sun and free from rats. Crusoe's religion is frankly utilitarian. Like the clergymen of the Royal Society, he believes in God because he sees how useful everything is: "By the assistance of His grace, I gain'd a different knowledge from what I had before. I entertain'd different notions of things. . . . In a word, the nature and experience of things dictated to me, upon just such reflection, that all the good things of this world are no further good to us than they are for our use" (p. 95). The Puritan accounting of everything that happens is quite compatible with the entrepreneur Crusoe's accounting of all his material wealth.

In that everything that happens is a part of a progression beyond itself, the events of Crusoe's world are a sort of allegory. Like Christian, Crusoe even has obviously allegorical dreams. Defoe himself, in the beginning of the *Serious Reflections on the Life and Surprising Adventures of Robinson Crusoe* (1720) argued, though none too convincingly, that the *Life* was an allegory of his own life.[32] In this respect, then, *Robinson Crusoe* has much in common with the equally Puritan *Pilgrim's Progress*. In both these books a single man is stripped down to the state of nature — Crusoe (p. 87) actually uses this term out of Hobbes, Locke, and naturalistic philosophy — only to rise to happiness. Everything in their lives exists in relation to some larger abstraction and process, transcendental in Bunyan, transcendental and practical in Defoe.

Not without reason do we regard Bunyan and Defoe, authors of two of the most popular works of fiction of their day, as the fathers of the modern novel. Like them, we see things not in themselves but leading up to ends. The style then must progress, and it must be plain and, at least for Defoe, impersonal — in a word, modern.

Drama

If the writers of Restoration comedy were influenced by "science" they did not acknowledge their debt openly. In fact, in a number of plays — for example, Shadwell's *The Virtuoso* (1676), Aphra Behn's *The Emperor of the Moon* (1687), Settle's *The New Athenian Comedy* (1693), Wright's *The Female Vertuoso's* (1693), and Ravenscroft's *The Anatomist* (1697) — the scientist is something of a stock fool. This does not mean that the playwrights were antiscientific themselves. But the frequency with which this vein was mined, and the great popularity of a number of these plays, may well attest to a contemporary feeling that the New Philosophy was a fake, an easy target for comedy, as alchemy had been for Ben Jonson. If the plays tell us anything about the popular climate of opinion, "science" after the Restoration is more a badly misunderstood curiosity than a new metaphysic sweeping all before it.

The best of these plays is *The Virtuoso*. Sir Nicholas Gimcrack, the mad scientist, is distinguished by his florid rhetoric. His "Admirer, Flatterer, and great Confident" is Sir Formal Trifle, who is regularly mocked in the tradition of the words-things equation as "The greatest Master of Tropes and Figures: The most *Ciceronian* Coxcomb, the Noblest Orator breathing: He never speaks without Flowers of Rhetorick: In short, he is very much abounding in words, and very much defective in sense."[33] There is little difference between the styles of Sir Formal Trifle and Sir Nicholas the Virtuoso. If not for Croll and Jones, then for Shadwell, at least, Ciceronianism was not much different from the language of science:

Sir For. All the ingenious World are proud of Sir *Nicholas*, or his Physico-mechanical Excellencies.
Sir Nich. I confess I have some felicity that way; but were I as praecelling in Physico-Mechanicall Investigations, as you are in Tropicall Rhetorical Flourishes, I would yield to none.
Longv[ill]. How the Asses claw one another. (Act II, p. 30)

Rhetoric is always allied to uselessness in the Restoration, and Sir Nicholas' chief humor is his penchant for useless experiments. When he is attacked, mistakenly, by some weavers for inventing a new loom, Sir Nicholas protests: "O what will become of me! Gentlemen, Gentlemen, for Heav'ns sake do something for me; I protest and vow they wrong me, I never invented any thing of use in my life . . . . We Vertuoso's never find out anything of use" (Act V, p. 81).

Shadwell's attack is essentially humanitarian. When asked whether, on his trip to Italy to study tarantulas, he noticed the people, Sir Nicholas replies, "Oh by no means! 'Tis below a Virtuoso to trouble himself with Men and Manners.

I study Insects" (Act III, p. 49). At the end, he resolves to
do useful works but does not know how to begin. "Am I
deserted by all? Well, now 'tis time to study for use: I will
presently find the Philosophers Stone; I had like to have
gotten it last year, but that I wanted *May Dew*, being a dry
season" (Act V, p. 100). The Restoration distinguished between a "scientific" and a "utilitarian" attitude. "This foolish
Virtuoso," sneers the spruce wit Bruce, "does not consider,
that one Bricklayer is worth fourty Philosophers" (Act IV,
p. 72).

The combination, in Bruce, of hedonistic Epicureanism
— he opens the play with a tribute to *"Lucretius! . . .
great oracle or Wit and Sense"* — and hardheaded utilitarianism mark him as a typical hero of Restoration comedy. It
is the genre of utility *par excellence.* The Way of the World
or State of Nature in these plays is the way of self-interest.
Any sort of deception is acceptable as long as it works.
"Reason" is not the Virtuoso's abstract speculation but, as
in *Robinson Crusoe,* "Prudence," calculation which leads
to success. The heroes of the best of these plays — the
Dorimants, Mirabells, Valentines, Horners, and the rest —
often are made to seem as foolish as their victims. Nevertheless they triumph not because they are kindly or long-
suffering or gracious but because they are prudent. Villains
are few, though there are many fools, that is, those who are
not prudent and so do not succeed. "Success" is usually
sexual fulfillment, either in the performance of the stark
act itself or in the exclusive sexual control over another.
It is assumed that the mainspring of human conduct is the
pleasure principle. To seek pleasure (or power over others
who will provide pleasure) is natural and, in a sense, good.
To a considerable extent the villains of the Elizabethan
stage — the Edmunds and Claudiuses — become the heroes
of Restoration comedy.

Sex was not the only pleasure acknowledged by the Restoration. Intellectual pleasure, often called "wit," was a worth-while end in itself. According to some critics this was the sole purpose of the comedies. "Wit" in this sense usually means bright repartee or, as in *The Way of the World*, an extremely complicated plot. Most of this type of wit depends on another, what Fujimura has called "the notion of wit as decorum of conduct." [34] This second kind of wit is more obviously related to the utilitarian ethic. It is the cool self-control of Robinson Crusoe or of the Machiavellian rake on the rise. The successful heroes — the prototype would be Congreve's Truewit — all have it. They know how to behave in all situations and especially when to forego immediate pleasure to gain a greater later on. The fools, the Witwouds, lack this "wit." They exceed Decorum; they do not know when to stop (Sir Fopling Flutter) or how to curb their native characteristics at the right time to gain the larger ends (the country bumpkins). Laughter in Restoration comedy is chiefly egoistic and malicious, directed against these fools. Hobbes[35] as well as others had said that the source of laughter lay exactly here, in our sense of superiority to fools.

The witty characters — in the second sense of "wit" — all "have their wits about them." They undertake no action without the ultimate end in view. Nothing is done for its own sake. All actions, therefore, are seen by their actor as part of a larger scheme of things. Even though he may be driven by a great passion, the wit must always be sure of what he is doing. Therefore we always find him commenting, like Robinson Crusoe, on his own behavior. These comments, writes Norman Holland, are "a late seventeenth-century version of Donne's conceits." They "let a man be passionate but discuss his passion at the same time, as Donne's do." [36] Wanning calls this detached speech "the language of split-man observation" (p. 307). Even when he discusses his own passion, the Restoration wit is impersonal, his tone that of "the observer humorously regarding events with which he, as an actor, has the strange chance to be connected" (p. 313).

The sharpest contrast to the language of split-man observation is the language of Elizabethan comedy. Wanning's examples of comparison cannot be improved upon: the amiable raillery of Congreve's Mirabell and Shakespeare's Benedick. Benedick says:

In brief, since I do purpose to marry, I will think nothing to any purpose that the world can say against it; and therefore never flout at me for what I have said against it; for man is a giddy thing, and this is my conclusion.

Wanning sees "man is a giddy thing" as "a direct expression of the whole-man" in which "the will and the mind are to have the same purpose; for the mind must accept as the relevant direct evidence about the proper state of the emotions that which the emotions themselves offer" (p. 318). Mirabell says:

A fellow that lives in a windmill, has not a more whimsical dwelling than the heart of a man that is lodged in a woman. There is no point of the compass toward which they cannot turn, and by which they are not turned; and by one as well as another; for motion, not method, is their preoccupation. To know this, and yet continue to be in love, is to be made wise from the dictates of reason, and yet persevere to play the fool from the force of instinct.

In contrast to Benedick's "whole-man," "this," says Wanning, "is the shaping of elegant observation of one half of the split-man by his other rational half" (p. 319); it is another example of the "dissociation of sensibility." "Mirabell *never* speaks of himself as an undivided personality; he has always the same air of cool amusement at the singular antics of another fellow of the same name" (p. 316). These antics are brought in not for their own sakes, but in relation to the inexorable workings of the Method of Winning Over Women. Reason is Prudence, Wit (in sense two), and Decorum; Unreason is impulse, and the impulsive man, like Benedick, is the hero of the Elizabethan comedy but the fool in the Restoration. The man of Reason carefully reckons up the alternatives on which he must act if he is to gain his end. Always there is the contrast between The Right Way to Succeed and The Wrong Way, and this utilitarian contrast is the chief source of the measured, impersonal balance of Mirabell's prose.

Holland speaks of the "Right-way-wrong-way" figure of Restoration drama, which "does not simply compare A to B; it also compares *ways of comparing A* to B. That is, the oddity of the stated connection between A and B . . . leads us to infer other connections and we compare the *stated* connection of A to B with the inferred connections. Usually, the stated connection tends to be a 'wrong' way of relating A to B, and the inferred connections tend to be 'right' " (p. 70). In the windmill figure the stated comparison is between a man living in a windmill and a man living in a woman's heart. The figure is promptly "unfolded" in a ratio: a man living in a windmill is like a man living in a woman's heart because both are turned about helplessly. But men who live in windmills are not ordinarily lovers; in fact, one does not "live" in a windmill in the same sense that one "lives" in a woman's heart. The comparison is "only" a figure. The stated comparison is far-fetched enough to make us think of other, not merely metaphorical, ways of comparing inhabitants of windmills to lovers, and the most obvious relationship is that both are fools. As is commonly the case, the "right" way to unfold the figure is less figurative than the "wrong" way. It also has a relation to the Right Way to Succeed. Mirabell is concerned not with man as a giddy thing or with the curious nature of love but with How to Avoid Becoming a Fool "by force of instinct." The utilitarian part of the figure is less figurative because more true than the "wrong way." What is most significant here is the extent to which the nature of the figurative language is determined by the utilitarianism of the play as a whole.

Yet in the greatest of the Restoration comedies the heroes transcend the Way of the World and undo the assumptions of the State of Nature. To varying degrees, real feeling pushes aside the utilitarian necessity to dissemble. Eventually this feeling becomes too strong, and we have the ridiculous sentimental dramas of the eighteenth century. Even as early as Etherege, though, characters like Dorimant and Harriet in *The Man of Mode* stand out because, without ever questioning the prevailing criteria of success, they are able to fight through and rise above the intriguing — at which they themselves are experts. They are able to tell each other openly though ironically what their real feelings are toward each other without becoming "fools." This is hard enough for most of us in the real world; on the Restoration stage it is all but impossible. Honesty here is a real heroic triumph. It takes all of Harriet's finely controlled tact to save the day near the end of *The Man of Mode* (1676):

Dor[*imant*]. I will renounce all the joys I have in friendship and in Wine, sacrifice to you all the interest I have in other Women —
Har[*riet*]. Hold — though I wish you devout, I would not have you turn Fanatick. — Could you neglect these a while and make a journey into the Country?
Dor. To be with you, I could live there: and never send one thought to *London*.
Har. What e're you say, I know all beyond *High Park's* a desert to you, and that no gallantry can draw you farther.
Dor. That has been the utmost limit of my Love — but now my passion knows no bounds, and there's no measure to be taken of what I'll do for you from any thing I ever did before.
Har. When I hear you talk thus in *Hampshire* I shall begin to think there may be some little truth inlarg'd upon.[37]

The tact is Etherege's, too. A simple "happy ending" would be absurd here. "The play," writes Holland, "is nothing more nor less than the old sentimental story of the rake reformed, indeed redeemed, by the love of a good woman. At least that *would* be the basic form of the action were it not so variously undercut by irony" (p. 94).

The most famous and happiest balance between blunt candor and ironic guile is struck off in another proviso scene, the great one in William Congreve's *The Way of the World* (1700):

Milla[mant]. . . . . I won't be call'd Names after I'm marri'd; positively I won't be call'd names.
Mira[bell]. Names!
Milla. Ay, as Wife, Spouse, my Dear, Joy, Jewel, Love, Sweetheart, and the rest of that nauseous Cant in which Men and their Wives are so fulsomely familiar, — I shall never bear that — Good Mirabell, don't let us be familiar or fond, nor kiss before Folks, like my Lady *Fadler* and Sir *Francis*: nor go to *Hide-Park* together the first *Sunday* in a *New Chariot*, to provoke Eyes and Whispers, and then never to be seen there together again; as if we were proud of one another the first Week, and asham'd of one another ever after. Let us never Visit together, nor go to a Play together; but let us be very strange and well bred: Let us be as strange as if we had been married a great while; and as well-bred as if we were not marri'd at all.
Mira. Have you any more Conditions to offer? Hitherto your Demands are pretty reasonable.
Milla. Trifles, — as Liberty to pay and receive Visits to and from whom I please; to write and receive Letters, without Interrogatories or wry Faces on your part; to wear what I please; and choose Conversation with regard only to my own Taste; to have no Obligation upon me to converse with Wits that I don't like, because they are your Acquaintance; or to be intimate with Fools, because they may be your Relations. Come to Dinner when I please, dine in my Dressing-room when I'm out of Humour, without giving a Reason. To have my closet inviolate; to be sole Empress of my Tea-Table, which you must never presume to approach without first asking leave. And

lastly, where-ever I am, you shall always knock at the Door before you come in. These Articles subscrib'd, if I continue to endure you a little longer, I may by degrees dwindle into a Wife.

Mira. Your Bill of Fare is something advanc'd in this latter Account. Well, I have a Liberty to offer Conditions — That when you are dwindled into a Wife, I may not be beyond measure enlarged into a Husband.

Milla. You have free Leave; propose your utmost, speak and spare not.

Mira. I thank you. *Imprimis*, then, I covenant that your Acquaintance be general; that you admit no sworn Confident, or Intimate of your own Sex; no she-Friend to screen her Affairs under your Countenance, and tempt you to make trial of a mutual Secrecy. No Decoy-duck to wheedle you a *fop-scrambling* to the Play in a Mask — Then bring you home in a pretended Fright, when you think you shall be found out — And rail at me for missing the Play, and disappointing the Frolick which you had to pick me up and prove my Constancy.

Milla. Detestable *imprimis!* I go to the Play in a Mask!

Mira. *Item,* I article that you continue to like your own Face, as long as I shall: And while it passes current with me, that you endeavour not to new-Coin it. To which end, together with all Vizards for the Day, I prohibit all Masks for the Night, made of Oil-Skins and I know not what — Hog's Bones, Hare's Gall, Pig-Water, and the Marrow of a roasted Cat. In short, I forbid all Commerce with the Gentlewoman in *What-d'ye-call-it* Court. *Item,* I shut my Doors against all Bawds with Baskets, and Penny-worths of *Muslin, China, Fans, Atlases,* &c. — *Item,* when you shall be Breeding —

Milla. Ah, name it not.

Mira. Which may be presum'd, with a Blessing on our Endeavours —

Milla. Odious endeavours!

Mira. I denounce against all strait Laceing, squeezing for a Shape, 'till you mould my Boy's Head like a Sugar-loaf; and instead of a Man-child, make me Father to a Crooked-billet. Lastly, to the Dominion of the *Tea-Table* I submit. — But with *proviso*, that you exceed not in your Province; but restrain yourself to native and simple *Tea-Table* Drinks, as *Tea, Chocolate,* and *Coffee.* As likewise to Genuine and Authorized *Tea-Table* Talk — Such as mending of Fashions, spoiling Reputations, railing at absent Friends, and so forth — But that on no Account you encroach on the Men's Prerogative, and presume to drink Healths, or toast Fellows; for prevention of which I banish all *Foreign Forces*, all Auxiliaries to the *Tea-Table*, as *Orange-Brandy*, all *Aniseed*, most noble Spirit of *Clary*. — But for *Cowslip-Wine, Poppy-Water*, and all *Dormitives*, those I allow. — These *Provisos* admitted, in other things I may prove a tractable and complying Husband.

Milla. Oh, horrid *Provisos!* filthy Strong-waters! I toast Fellows! Odious Men! I hate your odious Proviso's.

Mira. Then we're agreed. Shall I kiss your Hand upon the Contract? [38]

This glorious scene is something other than the language of utility we have encountered already in Congreve and in the Restoration as a whole. It reads like Elizabethan prose; it has the joyous cumulative force, juicy specificity, and ironic bite of a Nashe, a Burton, or a Montaigne. Dale Underwood points to this resemblance when he says that Congreve, "while keeping both the abstract and intellectualized language and the complexity of awareness which distinguish Etherege's plays, returned to that comedy something of the concrete and bustling world of sensuous experience which Etherege had so extensively removed." [39] The comic strategy of the speeches lies in the contrast between the surface formality of the drawing up of the contract, with its tough-minded *Items* and *Imprimises*, and the obvious fact that both Mirabell and Millamant are, for once, forgetting the Art of Successful Dissembling and unloading whatever is on the top of their brilliant heads. Their speech is like the "Anti-Ciceronian" mode in that, instead of studied antitheses, we have a continuous "trailing effect": A consideration of names leads Millamant into a proviso against overfamiliarity in public, then into a demand for free relations with whatever part of that public she chooses; this freedom of association with others reminds her of the freedom to come to dinner whenever she chooses; freedom of the dinner-table reminds her of her authority as Empress of the Tea-Table; and, while on the subject of her authority, Mirabell must always knock on the door. Millamant wants exactly what she is doing in the language of the proviso scene — to associate freely!

Mirabell's rebuttal also resembles the "Anti-Ciceronian" progression in which a simple statement — "I covenant that your acquaintance be general" — is elaborated upon with no advance in logic. Mirabell starts predicting Millamant's behavior at the theater. Next, deception by means of a mask at this theater brings to mind deception by the mask of cosmetics, and then the gentlewoman who sells them; cosmetics and gentlewomen remind him of painted bawds, and bawds of breeding; breeding of shaping their future boy's fetal head into a sugar-loaf shape; the sugar-loaf of the Dominion of the Tea-Table; and so on.

This is the language of two people getting down to business and saying exactly what they think of each other. These two people are poised and mature, and their dialogue is controlled exquisitely by its ironic framework. Their candid but oblique and highly controlled self-revelation recalls the best tradition of the classical plain style.

The provisos themselves all have to do with questions of candor and honesty in dealings between the main characters and the rest of society. Mirabell insists that Millamant not cuckold him behind his back, while Millamant refuses to be put into situations where she must dissemble. Each demands frankness of the other. Both recognize the realities of the Way of the World. The proviso motif itself is a sort of hard-minded business contract. Its *items* and *imprimises* are often frankly or covertly sexual, and the imagery of the scene is frequently legal, political, or military. But it is a measure of their sane transcendence of this State of Nature that both of them stake out for themselves those areas, such as Millamant's Tea-Table and Mirabell's drinking of healths, which are to remain inviolate even from each other and which will preserve their individuality and integrity. They are, in short, as "natural" with each other as is possible or wise. In this way they rise above, in a more delightful and complicated way than Dorimant and Harriet, the "naturalism" of the other people in the play.

"Naturalism" has two paradoxical aspects. A "naturalist" like Montaigne, speaking from the skeptical side of Christian humanism, advocates and practices candor, honesty, moderation, and detachment. A "naturalist" like Hobbes or Machiavelli, though equally blunt, advises unrestrained and aggressive deception to succeed in the barbarous State of Nature.[40] Drama is conflict, and the conflicts inherent in the two aspects of "naturalistic" philosophy make Restoration comedy, in the hands of an Etherege, a Wycherley, or a Congreve, the exciting thing it is.

The conflict is mirrored in the two basic types of language we find in Restoration comedy. As a rule, whenever the characters are in the State of Nature deceiving one another, the language is the generalized, balanced type we have found in other genres of Restoration prose. A frequent comic strategy we find in this prose — we seldom find it in the sincerely felt passages — is the *double entendre*. In a language which wants to seem "precise" the device is inevitable. The language of the Restoration, as we have seen, is filled with catchwords like Nature, Reason, Wit, Honor, Virtue, Sense, and Idea, which are presented with an air of having only one invariable meaning but which actually can have several, one of which may be used as a comic reversal of the other. For example, in *The Country Wife* (1675) Lady Fidget is informed of Horner's supposed impotency:

Sir Jasp[er]. Hah, hah, hah, he hates Women perfectly I find.
Mrs. Dain[ty]. What pity 'tis he should!
Lady Fid[get]. Ay, he's a base rude Fellow for 't; But affectation makes not a Woman more odious to him than Virtue.

Horn[*er*]. Because your Virtue is your greatest affectation, Madam.
Lady Fid. How, you sawcy Fellow, wou'd you wrong my honour?
Horn. If I cou'd.
Lady Fid. How d'y mean, Sir?
Sir Jasp. Hah, hah, hah, no he can't wrong your Ladyship's honour, upon my honour; he poor Man — hark you in your ear — a mere *Eunuch*.
Lady Fid. O filthy French Beast, foh, foh; why do we stay? let's be gone; I can't endure the sight of him.[41]

Here the comedy turns, first, on the meaning of "Virtue." For Lady Fidget it means both "chastity" and a "good trait." In Horner's comic inversion, the "good trait" is a "bad trait" because it interferes with male success. There is no difference, after all, between "Virtue" and "affectation." "Honour" is the next word to be played with. In Lady Fidget's question it means, like "Virtue," "chastity," but also "reputation" and possibly "honesty," in the sense of "telling the truth" (which Lady Fidget is not). Therefore after Horner's puzzling (to her) "If I cou'd," Lady Fidget wonders which meaning he has in mind, and Sir Jasper tries to enlighten her with a play on words — "he can't wrong your Ladyship's honour, upon my honour" — that is funnier than he realizes. Because he does not know that Horner is lying, Sir Jasper's "honour" — in the sense of reputation — is soon to be as unreal as Lady Fidget's. All these semantic games help to establish the naturalistic and positivistic world view of the play. As Hobbes has said, "Honour" and "Virtue" are only words, mere abstract circumlocutions whose moralistic connotations serve only to hide the hard physical reality underneath.

This language is extremely artificial. Yet it has struck generations of readers as "conversational." The answer, as Wanning has pointed out, is that, "Where we go wrong is in imagining that there is anything necessarily natural about conversation" ("Some Changes," p. 309). It seems the wits of Charles' court really talked this way. Indeed Dryden, in a frequently quoted passage from the "Essay on . . . Dramatick Poetry . . . ," remarks that "by the advantage of our conversation, the discourse and raillery of our comedies excel." [42] In other words, if the Restoration writers were "conversational," it was in a very special way. As Wanning puts it, "There is obviously a sense in which Nashe and Dekker and Martin Marprelate and Middleton and Massinger are colloquial and Dryden and Cowley and Halifax and Congreve are not" (p. 307). If by "conversational" or "colloquial" we mean "spontaneous," "self-revealing," and the like, then Nashe, Dekker, the classical plain style, and Congreve's "proviso scene" are conversational. If we mean by this epithet "easy to understand," then we can apply it to the *sermo communis* of the Restoration writers, with the writers of comedies a partial exception. Neither kind of "conversational" prose excluded artifice. But the special devices the Restoration used to achieve the utilitarian goals it designated for prose are the basis of modern prose style.

Some Conclusions

In the Restoration prose became prosaic. Writers as different as Bunyan and Dryden understand prose as a vehicle for communicating intelligibly rather than revealing the mind of the author or speaker or showing off his command of literary devices. A writer like Defoe is close to this norm and is the best possible evidence that great art can emerge from utilitarian presuppositions. Once the norm is established, writers like Congreve and Swift achieve fine effects by artful deviations from it. Before the Restoration there is no settled norm at all. After the Restoration only a few mavericks like Aubrey seem unaware of what has happened to prose.

Whether the Restoration was more utilitarian than other ages is a question I leave to historians of ideas. I have no doubt, however, that it was utilitarian concerns that motivated the theorists and practitioners of the new prose. Utilitarian prose is written in all ages. To my knowledge, though, the Restoration is the first time in English history when utilitarian criteria become official doctrine for literary prose in general.

The causes for this development are difficult to isolate. I see most of them adumbrated early in the century in Bacon. Only a few of the Restoration authors however —

302

Sprat and Glanvill are notable examples — acknowledge their debt to Bacon explicitly or even seem aware of it. Whether Bacon and his followers created the new climate of opinion or are themselves responding to it is another of those horrible chicken-or-egg questions that haunt the history of ideas, and which I will not pretend to answer.

The new prose of utility is unclassical and un-Christian. I do not wish to imply that everyone in the "neoclassic" Age of Dryden lost contact with Greco-Roman civilization and turned atheist. Nor am I saying that we have not had exemplars of the classical plain style since 1660. But I am talking about the norm not variations from it. Classical prose is fundamentally an imitation of various time-honored artistic and moral ideals, while prose in the Judeo-Christian tradition is self-expression. To the Restoration reformers of style, both are generally suspect.

The decline of classical influences on prose seems to begin with the triumph of the English language over Latin at the start of the century. Imitation in the form of "Anti-Ciceronianism" is an early casualty of the deeper trends. The "neoclassicism" often attributed to Restoration prose has been overemphasized or is an aspect of utilitarianism. Other concepts used to explain the Restoration shift in sensibility such as Eliot's "dissociation of sensibility" or Weber's "Protestant Ethic" have taken quite a beating in recent years. I believe, however, that they have at least as much validity as "neoclassicism." All such terms ("science," of course, heads the list) have been helpful guides. But none is complete enough. All are aspects of the profounder concerns I have tried to describe in this book.

The Style of Tacitus

Apart from external evidence, which can never be conclusive, about the only way to verify a statement like "Tacitus influenced Bacon's style" is to compare texts from the two authors. It is a dangerous course, however.

Our first problem is that we have no "control," such as translations of identical texts. The best we can do is, first, to fall back on subjective impressionism and to select the most Baconian-seeming passage in Tacitus we can find. We can also look to external evidence to see whether, of all that Bacon might have read in Tacitus, the text chosen is the kind of passage that would have influenced him. Critics of Tacitus agree that he was at the height of his powers — and at his most characteristic — in the first six books of the *Annals*. Bacon, who quotes extensively from Tacitus, quotes more from these books than from any other of his writings. If Bacon was influenced by Tacitus, it was at least in part by these books. Almost all Bacon's quotations from Tactitus have to do with dissimulation. With its emphasis on dissimulation, Bacon must have relished the passage in the *Annals* describing the coup of Tiberius. Bacon refers to it, in fact, in the *Advancement*: "It is true that in Socrates it was supposed to be but a form of irony, *Scientiam dissimu-*

lando simulavit, for he used to dissemble his knowledge, to the end to enhance his knowledge; like the humor of Tiberius, that would reign, but would not acknowledge so much." [1] In short, if anything in Tacitus influenced Bacon, the passage I shall discuss here would have.

A second problem is that comparisons of selected passages to prove or disprove an "influence" are dangerous because every writer's manner varies and no passage can represent him completely. How can we be sure our passage is "typical" of Tacitus? About all we can do here is to trust to our general sense of style — the *Sprachgefühl* scorned by the professional linguist — which tells us that the variations from Tacitus' normal range in the passage are not fundamental.

Third, we face the obvious difficulties of comparing the styles of two different languages, one of which, to make matters worse, is ancient and much more highly inflected. Where it is possible to make statistical comparisons of specific linguistic or stylistic features in the same language, and to generalize about them with some confidence, it is almost impossible across languages. We may compare, for example, the number of conjunctions or independent verbs; but conjunctions and verbs do not necessarily have the same use or stylistic force in Latin as in English. Although we can describe with some precision the grammatical forms of Tacitus' Latin, we cannot say very much that is certain about the effect of these forms, intended or not, on Tacitus' readers. Nor — if we think of "style" as a deviation from a norm — can we know very much what the norm for historical writing was in Tacitus' day, against which we can say such-and-such a form of Tacitus' is unusual or not. Then, too, we cannot be sure that a reader of Bacon's time would respond to Tacitus in the same way that we do. For Croll, Tacitus is "somewhat grave and mysterious";[2] but how do we know that Bacon thought he was? Finally, and perhaps worst of all, there are the difficulties about the recognition of archaisms, connotations, and the like in an ancient language.

Despite all these problems we need not despair entirely. There is external evidence to help us. We have statements from Tacitus, Bacon, and their contemporaries about the two authors' stylistic intentions and effects. In addition, we may follow Stephen Ullman's suggestions.

There is no need whatever to take a defeatist view of the prospects of stylistic reconstruction. The success of the operation will ultimately depend on . . . the attitude of the critic himself, on whether his mind has been thoroughly sensitized to these problems, and whether he is fully aware of the difficulties involved and of the ways in which they can be tackled. The other condition of success is that we should have sufficient information about the linguistic background at the time the text was written. Even under the most favorable circumstances we can never hope, of course, to have a complete picture of a past state of a language and of all the expressive, suggestive, and evocatory nuances which enriched its words, its forms, and its constructions for a contemporary reader. We may, however, reach precise conclusions on a number of important points.[3]

The work of Boetticher and Draeger[4] established the now venerable tradition of considering Tacitus' style under the headings of brevity and force, variety, and poetic color. Lacking a genuine science of comparative stylistics, we shall have to settle for these categories, even though such traditional distinctions rely on what Riffaterre calls "a fragmentary metalanguage borrowed mostly from the categories of rhetoric (metaphor, hyperbole)." [5] Although the traditional categories may no longer be useful for describing modern prose, the ancients and the writers of the Renaissance consciously used them. Therefore the grouping of Boetticher and Draeger is valid, and useful for our purposes. For according to Croll, "brevity" was the *summum bonum* of the Anti-Ciceronians, and "variety" corresponds to Croll's "asymmetry."

Here, at last, is our passage:

Primum facinus novi principatus fuit Postumi Agrippae caedes,
quem ignarum inermumque quamvis firmatus animo centurio
aegre confecit. nihil de ea re Tiberius apud senatum disseruit:
patris iussa simulabat, quibus praescripsisset tribuno custodiae
adpositio, ne cunctaretur Agrippam morte adficere, quandoque
ipse supremum diem explevisset. multa sine dubio saevaque
Augustus de moribus adulescentis questus, ut exilium eius senatus
consulto sanciretur perfecerat: ceterum in nullius umquam suo-
rum necem duravit, neque mortem nepoti pro securitate privigni
inlatem credibile erat. propius vero Tiberium ac Liviam, illum
metu, hanc novercalibus odiis, suspecti et invisi iuventis caedem
festinavisse. nuntianti centurioni, ut mos militiae, factum esse
quod imperasset, neque imperasse sese et rationem facti redden-
dam apud senatum respondit. quod postquam Sallustius Crispus
particeps secretorum (is ad tribunum miserat codicillos) com-
perit, metuens ne reus subderetur, iuxta periculoso ficta seu
vera promeret, monuit Liviam ne arcana domus, ne concilia
amicorum, ministeria militum vulgarentur, neve Tiberius vim
principatus resolveret cuncta ad senatum vocando: eam condicionem esse imperandi, ut non aliter ratio constet quam si uni
reddatur.
    At Romae ruere in servitium consules, patres, eques. quanto
quis inlustrior, tanto magis falsi ac festinantes, vultuque composito, ne laeti excessu principis neu tristiores primordio, lacrimas
gaudium, questus adulationem miscebant. Sex. Pompeius et Sex.
Appuleius consules primi in verba Tiberii Caesaris iuravere,
apudque eos Seius Strabo et C. Turranius, ille praetoriarum
cohortium praefectus, hic annonae; mox senatus milesque et
populus. Nam Tiberius cuncta per consules incipiebat, tamquam
vetere re publica et ambiguus imperandi: ne edictum quidem,
quo patres in curiam vocabat, nisi tribuniciae potestatis prae-
scriptione posuit sub Augusto acceptae. verba edicti fuere pauca
et sensu permodesto: de honoribus parentis consulturum, neque
abscedere a corpore, idque unum ex publicis muneribus usurpare.
sed defuncto Augusto signum praetoriis cohortibus ut imperator
dederat; excubiae, arma, cetera aulae; miles in forum, miles in
curiam comitabatur. litteras ad exercitus tamquam adepto
principatu misit, nusquam cunctabundus nisi cum in senatu
loqueretur. causa praecipua ex formidine, ne Germanicus, in
cuius manu tot legiones, immensa sociorum auxilia, mirus apud

populum favor, habere imperium quam exspectare mallet. dabat et famae, ut vocatus electusque potius a re publica videretur quam per uxorium ambitum et senili adoptione inrepsisse. postea cognitum est ad introspiciendas etiam procerum voluntates inductam dubitationem: nam verba vultus in crimen deterquens recondebat.[6]

The first crime of the new reign was the murder of Postumus Agrippa. Though he was surprised and unarmed, a centurion of the firmest resolution despatched him with difficulty. Tiberius gave no explanation of the matter to the Senate; he pretended that there were directions from his father ordering the tribune in charge of the prisoner not to delay the slaughter of Agrippa, whenever he should himself have breathed his last. Beyond a doubt, Augustus had often complained of the young man's character, and had thus succeeded in obtaining the sanction of a decree of the Senate for his banishment. But he never was hardhearted enough to destroy any of his kinsfolk, nor was it credible that death was to be the sentence of the grandson in order that his stepson might feel secure. It was more probable that Tiberius and Livia, the one from fear, the other from a stepmother's enmity, hurried on the destruction of a youth whom they suspected and hated. When the centurion reported, according to military custom, that he had executed the command, Tiberius replied that he had not given the command, and that the act must be justified to the Senate.

As soon as Sallustius Crispus who shared the secret (he had, in fact, sent the written order to the tribune) knew this, fearing that the charge would be shifted on himself, and that his peril would be the same whether he uttered fiction or truth, he advised Livia not to divulge the secrets of her house or the counsels of friends, or any services performed by the soldiers, nor to let Tiberius weaken the strength of imperial power by referring everything to the Senate, for "the condition," he said, "of holding empire is that an account cannot be balanced unless it be rendered to one person."

Meanwhile at Rome people plunged into slavery — consuls, senators, knights. The higher a man's rank, the more eager his hypocrisy, and his looks the more carefully studied, so as neither to betray joy at the decease of one emperor nor sorrow at the rise of another, while he mingled delight and lamentations with his flattery. Sextus Pompeius and Sextus Apuleius, the consuls, were the first to swear allegiance to Tiberius Caesar, and in their presence the oath was taken by Seius Strabo and Caius Turranius, respectively the commander of the praetorian cohorts and the superintendent of the corn supplies. Then the Senate, the soldiers and the people did the same. For Tiberius would inaugurate everything with the consuls, as though the ancient constitution remained, and he hesitated about being emperor. Even the proclamation by which he summoned the senators to their chamber, he issued merely with the title of Tribune, which he had received under Augustus. The wording of the proclamation was brief, and in a very modest tone. "He would," it said, "provide for the honours due to his father, and not leave the lifeless body, and this was the only public duty he now claimed."

As soon, however, as Augustus was dead, he had given the watchword to the praetorian cohorts, as commander-in-chief. He had the guard under arms, with all the other adjuncts of a court; soldiers attended him to the forum; soldiers went with him to the Senate House. He sent letters to the different armies, as though supreme power was now his, and showed hesitation only when he spoke in the Senate. His chief motive was fear that Germanicus, who had at his disposal so many legions, such vast auxiliary forces of the allies, and such wonderful popularity, might prefer the possession to the expectation of empire. He looked also at public opinion, wishing to have the credit of having been called and elected by the State rather than of having crept into power through the intrigues of a wife and a dotard's adoption. It was subsequently understood that he assumed a wavering attitude, to test likewise the temper of the nobles. For he would twist a word or a look into a crime and treasure it up in his memory.[7]

Tacitus achieves "brevity," first of all, by omission. Background information is lacking. There is no introduction. Tacitus assumes we are intimately connected with even such minor figures as Sallustius Crispus. He avoids repetition, for example, "*nihil de ea re Tiberius . . . disseruit*," where the pregnant "*ea re*" does duty for "*caedes*" or a synonym, since we already know what has happened; or "*mox senatus milesque et populus*," with "*iuravere*" or a synonym for it omitted and the English forced to supply the clumsy "did the same," weakening the dramatic effect. Tacitus prunes auxiliaries and main verbs: *"exubiae arma, cetera aulae"* (no *"erant"*); *"vultuque composito, ne laeti"* (no *"viderentur"* or *"essent"*) *"excessu principis"*; and so on. Idioms are shortened. *"Duravit"* serves for the usual *"duravit mentem."* Asyndeton contributes to the effect of speed or onrushing: *"consules, patres, eques"*; *"verba vultus"*; *"lacrimas gaudium, questus adulationem."* Terse, simple, often archaic verbs replace longer ones, such as *"ponere"* for *"proponere."* Tacitus also achieves concise power in the force of his word order by the violent contrast of *"servitium"* (slavery) next to *"consules, patres, eques."* There is power, too, in Tacitus' device of forming adjectives from nouns, somewhat in the manner of *Time* magazine, as in *"novercalibus"* (step-motherly). Tacitus uses genitives with great force and suggestiveness. *"Primum facinus novi principatus"* insinuates that many more crimes are to follow. The same use is made, as is possible in English, of the imperfect tense: *"patris iussa simulabat,"* *"questus adulationem miscebant,"* *"nam verba vultus in crimen detorquens recondebat."* In this way Tacitus suggests the oppressive, corrupt atmosphere of the Roman court. Participles (*"detorquens"*) have the same effect, which would be lost in the relative clause for which they are a concise substitute. Violence is suggested in the harsh, extremly elliptical ablative absolutes — *"iuxta periculosa"* (for *"cum iuxta periculosum esset"*) *"ficta seu ver promeret."*

We have seen how Tacitus obtains forceful brevity by various devices of omission. He also obtains it by the figures of thought, as opposed to the Gorgian figures of sound (the distinction of Croll and Williamson). Zeugma abounds in Tacitus, here in *"habere imperium quam exspectare mallet,"* with the sinister overtones suggested by the "point" of the zeugma. Anaphora suggests the scurrying of the soldiers — "*miles in forum, miles in curiam comita-batur.*" Metaphors are often violent — "*ruere,*" "*detor-quens,*" "*ne vim principatus resolveret.*" "*Festinavisse*" ans "*festinantes*" add to the general turbulence. There are a host of words which suggest the underhanded qualities of Tiberius' court, like "*arcana domo,*" "*inrepsisse,*" and "*re-condebat.*" These figures, metaphors, and suggestive words create the Tacitean atmosphere of noisy tumult amid, and concealing, silent conniving. Anaphora, zeugma, oxymo-ron, and chiasmus are often antithetical. This antithesis is effective at dramatic moments: "*quanto quis inlustrior, tanto magis falso ac festinantes . . . lacrimas gaudium, ques-tus adulationem*"; "*excubiae arma, cetera aulae*" (the transla-tor is forced to render the antithesis as: "He had the guard under arms, with all the other adjuncts of a court," losing all brevity and therefore dramatic force); and "*illum metu, hanc novercalibus odiis.*"

Under variety, Tacitus uses many devices which seem to serve no purpose other than asymmetry. Short sentences clash with long ones ("*At Romae . . . eques. quanto . . . miscebant.*") and long members ("*sed defuncto . . . dede-rat*") with short ("*excubiae . . . aulae*"). Passages of in-nuendo alternate with plain narration. Asymmetry in Taci-tus' context is the syntactical embodiment of the tumultuous world of Tiberius' court, which is always described in a disjointed way, by such devices as throwing singulars and plurals together ("*consules, patres, eques*") or different parts of speech ("*falsi ac festinantes*"). Ramsay has described Tacitus' "truncated periods": "Several subordinate ideas are introduced under one principal verb, but they are expressed by single words, usually Ablatives or Participles, loosely connected (if at all), instead of by complete subordinate sentences." [8] A fair sample of the asymmetrical period is the last sentence of the first paragraph, "*Quod post-quam . . . uni reddatur.*" The main verb is "*monuit,*" but it is overwhelmed by a swarm of subordinate ideas, mostly in the form of those constructions which can float freely apart from the rest of the sentence: appositives (*"particeps secretorum"*); parenthetical expressions (*"is ad tribunum miserat codicillos"*); ablative absolutes (*"iuxta periculoso"*); and participial phrases (*"metuens . . . promeret"*). Symmetry is constantly being established (*"ne arcana . . . ne consilia . . . ministeria . . ."*) only to be shattered in the next clause, and even in the clause itself by the omission of *"ne"* before *"ministeria."* Following the mind of the speaker reflected in the thought of Sallustius Crispus, the "trailing effect" is marked. The sentence is saved from anarchy only by Crispus' pointed *sententia*. But this, too, is asymmetrical, since it represents a shift into indirect discourse and metaphor.

Boetticher and Draeger's third quality, poetic color, is a bit nebulous and often difficult to separate from the other two. Some of the devices already noted under the head of brevity, especially the figures of thought, elevate the style also. Other devices serve only elevation, gravity, or dignity. These are largely borrowed from poetry, such as the use of an abstract word in a concrete sense, like *"auxilia"* in *"immensa sociorum auxilia"* or *"mors"* in *"Agrippa morte"* and *"mortem nepoti,"* or the echoing of phrases from the poets.[9] Alliteration and assonance subtly reinforce dramatic effects. Tacitus uses *s*'s to insinuate the evil, hidden quality of tyranny: *"sensu permodestu," "inrepsisse," "praescripsisset," "suspecti et invisi iuvenis caedem festinavisse," "falsi et festinantes."* Choking oppression is also suggested in the quick, tight sequences of nouns or adjectives of which Tacitus is fond: *"tanto magis falsi ac festinantes."* Transitive verbs are unusually frequent, contributing to the rapid movement; Tacitus, as we have seen, omits the undramatic forms of *esse* whenever he can. Finally, with his dislike of repetition Tacitus has an extraordinary number of heightening circumlocutions for things he must mention again and again, especially death, as here: *"caedes," "mors," "confecit," "excessu,"* and the magniloquent *"supremem explevisset."*

The end result is high drama. For example, the high point of our passage — the rushing *"in servitium"* of the consuls, senators, and knights — is made quite vivid by the metaphor *"ruere";* the violent juxtaposition of *"servitium"* with *"consules, patres, eques,"* the asyndeton suggesting their rushing, pell-mell, into slavery; a snarling alliteration and assonance (*"falsi ac festinantes"*) and the sudden introduction into the narrative, at this climactic point, of the description of the aristocrats' behavior, sharply pointed by elaborate antithetical constructions. The feeling of rush and haste is maintained by the terse *"mox senatus milesque et populus," "excubiae arma, ceterea aulae," "miles in forum, miles in curiam comitabatur."* In dramatic contrast to this feeling is Tacitus' careful introduction of the names of some of the suppliants. The solemn effect of a passing pageant of minor figures marching to their doom under the power of a great emperor is typical. It is characteristic of Tacitus to establish a scene in this way, by a few swift strokes in which feeling is generalized, rather than by concrete details of description. He is a master of "atmosphere" — Racine's "plus grand peintre de l'antiquité" (in the preface to *Brittanicus*). Impending doom and dramatic irony are also latent in the ominous way Tacitus opens and closes paragraphs and scenes: *"Primum facinus novi principatus"; "eam condicionem esse imperandi, ut non aliter ratio constet quam si uni reddatur"; "At Romae ruere in servitium consules, patres, eques";* and *"nam berba vultus in crimen detorquens recondebat."* Even Tacitus' "digressions" are often dramatic. The incident about Sallustius Crispus breaks up the melodrama. But his advice is dramatically ironic, for Tiberius' failure to have everyone's account rendered to himself is very nearly his downfall, as in the Sejanus episode, while Tiberius' heeding of Crispus' advice is apparent in the next scene. Tacitus has established the atmosphere of all of Tiberius' reign at the very beginning.

Tacitus also handles characterization like a dramatist. Except for the few formal portraits, it is implied rather than stated directly. Events, past and present, suggest things without Tacitus' telling us what they are. Tiberius' speech is *"sensu permodesto,"* "in a very modest tone," that is, Tiberius is dissimulating, in contrast to the great and popular Germanicus. Specific situations are repeated, so that, without comment on Tacitus' part, characterization is achieved. For example, Tiberius is seen making two lying speeches (the allegedly trumped-up order from Augustus ordering Agrippa's death, and the unctuous promise to perform the rites sincerely). More than anything else, it is his methods of characterization which cast doubt on the objectivity of Tacitus as a historian. His portrait of Tiberius is patently biased, that of Germanicus idealized. Tacitus' facts are accurate, but not the significance he gives to them. A fact satisfactory to Tacitus' bias receives more attention than one which is not, though both will be mentioned. For example, more attention is given to the behavior of the sycophants than to Tiberius' modest refusal to be emperor. Facts which contradict his emotional bias Tacitus characteristically shrugs off with an imputation of hypocrisy or an inappropriate comment: "He looked also at public opinion, wishing to have the credit of having been called and elected by the State rather than of having crept into power through the intrigues of a wife and a dotard's adoption. It was subsequently understood that he assumed a wavering attitude, to test likewise the temper of the nobles." Tacitus' imputation of motives is often gratuitous: "It was more probable that Tiberius and Livia, the one from fear, the other from a stepmother's enmity. . . ." Whenever the facts remotely suggest it, Tacitus falls back on the stock motifs — often very effective — of the schools of declamation: the Wicked Tyrant, the Enforced Suicide, the Unjust Condemnation, the Pathetic Death, and so on. The repetitions embody his pessimism, which sees evil endlessly repeating itself in history.

Tacitus is clearly interested in more than events, although he calls his work the *Annals*. Like his predecessors, his response to history is an ethical one. Where the prime concern of the modern historian is in the truth or falsity of an event, Tacitus is concerned with its moral significance, and its emotional value. No fact or event is morally or emotionally neutral. Tacitus himself is involved in it. Nothing "just" happens, or happens because of circumstances or fortune (Tacitus' two or three allusions to Fate do not change this overwhelming impression).[10] His conviction that Tiberius is a bad man colors Tacitus' entire characterization. Not only is Tacitus concerned with immorality in particular persons but in the world at large, which he sees in abject decline, save for a few heroes like Germanicus, Agricola, and Noble Savages in Germany; these have retained the old virtue of the Republic which he yearns for but knows to be a hopeless anachronism. *Everyone* at Rome rushes into slavery, "*consules, patres, eques . . . mox senatus milesque et populus.*" After reading Tacitus, we do not remember too clearly anything that has happened, for the events are smothered in emotional, moral, and psychological ambiguities. But we do remember personalities, and we have a picture of the times as a whole. Put another way, Tacitus' idea of history determines his style. For if no event is neutral, then it takes on the overtones and ambiguity of poetry, oratory, and drama.

Tacitus' practice follows from his theory.

My purpose is not to relate at length every motion, but only such as were conspicuous for excellence or notorious for infamy. This I regard as history's highest function, to let no worthy action be uncommemorated, and to hold out the reprobation of posterity as a terror to evil words and deeds.[11]

I have to present in succession the merciless biddings of a tyrant, incessant prosecutions, faithless friendships, the ruin of innocence, the same causes issuing in the same results, and I am everywhere confronted by a wearisome monotony in my subject matter. . . . But of many who endured punishment or disgrace under Tiberius, the descendants yet survive; or even though the families themselves may be now extinct, you will find those who, from a resemblance of character, imagine that the evil deeds of others are a reproach to themselves. Again, even honour and virtue make enemies, condemning, as they do, their opposites by too close a contrast.[12]

With this moral passion Tacitus hoped to reconcile an ideal of objectivity.

Hence my purpose is to relate a few facts about Augustus — more particularly his last acts, then the reign of Tiberius, and all which follows, without either bitterness or partiality, from any motives to which I am far removed.[13]

I would not deny that my elevation was begun by Vespasian, augmented by Titus, and still further advanced by Domitian; but those who profess inviolable truthfulness must speak of all without hatred.[14]

The tension between objectivity and moral fervor generates the complexities of Tacitus' style — "ostensible equity of suspended judgement, but implying the worst" (Syme, I, p. 347).

The closest Bacon comes to the Tacitean conception of history is in his discussion of Lives.

And although many men more mortal in their affection than in their bodies, do esteem desire of name and memory but as a vanity and ventosity,
> Animi nil magnae laudis egentes;
[souls that have no care for praise;] which opinion cometh from that root, *non prius laudes contempsimus, quam laudanda facere desivimus;* [men hardly despise praise till they have ceased to

deserve it;] yet that will not alter Salomon's judgement. *Memoria justi cum laudibus, at empiorum nomen putrescat;* [the memory of the just is blessed; but the name of the wicked shall rot;] the one flourisheth, the other either consumeth to present oblivion, or turneth to an ill odour. And therefore in that style or addition, which is and hath been long well received and brought in use, *felicis memoriae, bonae memoriae,* [of happy, of pious, of good memory,] we do acknowledge that which Cicero saith, borrowing it from Demosthenes, that *bona fama propria possessio defunctorum;* [good fame is all that a dead man can possess;] which possession I cannot but note that in our times it lieth much waste, and that therein there is a deficience. (*Advancement, Works,* VI, pp. 194–195)

At first this recalls Tacitus. But in fact Bacon advocates Lives not for their potential moral benefit for posterity, but rather to clear up reputations, to set the record straight. The subject of the passage is *fama*, not ethics.

Notes

Introduction

1. The best analysis of these problems is at the beginning of the first and fourth chapters of Andrews Wanning's unpublished thesis "Some Changes in the Prose Style of the Seventeenth Century" (Cambridge University, 1936). See also Sol Saporta, "The Application of Linguistics to the Study of Poetic Language," in *Style in Language*, ed. T. Sebeok (Cambridge, Mass., 1960), pp. 82–93.

2. Two good recent bibliographies of the new stylistics are Paul Doherty, "Stylistics — A Bibliographical Survey," *CEA Critic* (May, 1966), pp. 1, 3–4, reprinted in *Teaching Freshman Composition*, eds. G. Tate and E. P. J. Corbett (New York, 1967), pp. 329–334; and R. W. Bailey and D. M. Burton, *English Stylistics: A Bibliography* (Cambridge, Mass., 1967).

3. *Style, Rhetoric, and Rhythm: Essays by Morris W. Croll*, eds. J. Max Patrick, Robert O. Evans, John M. Wallace, and R. J. Shoeck (Princeton, 1966), p. 195.

4. R. F. Jones' writings on our topic are collected in the *Festschrift* in his honor, *The Seventeenth Century* (Palo Alto, 1961).

5. Marshall McLuhan, *The Gutenberg Galaxy* (Toronto, 1962), pp. 228 ff.

6. "On Defining Style," in N. E. Enkvist, J. Spencer, and M. Gregory, *Linguistics and Style* (London, 1964), pp. 1–56.

Chapter One

1. "Juste Lipse et le mouvement anti-cicéronien," *Revue du seizième siècle*, II (1914), pp. 200–242; " 'Attic Prose' in the Seventeenth

Century," *Studies in Philology,* XVIII (1921), pp. 79–128; "Attic Prose: Lipsius, Montaigne, Bacon," *Schelling Anniversary Papers* (New York, 1923), pp. 117–150; "Muret and the History of 'Attic' Prose," *PMLA,* XXXIX (1924), pp. 254–309; "The Baroque Style in Prose," in *Studies in English Philology,* eds. K. Malone and M. B. Ruud (Minneapolis, 1929), pp. 427–456. See also Croll's introduction to Lyly's *Euphues* (London, 1916), pp. xv–lxiv. All of Croll's significant writings have been gathered in *Style, Rhetoric, and Rhythm: Essays by Morris W. Croll,* eds. J. Max Patrick, Robert O. Evans, John M. Wallace, and R. J. Schoeck (Princeton, 1966). This edition has invaluable bibliographical materials on the scholarship on Anti-Ciceronianism since Croll. All future citations from Croll are taken from the Princeton edition, hereafter referred to as *Style.*

2. The survival of the Gorgian-Isocratic style, not based on logic, is, according to Croll, apparent in Book Three of the *Rhetoric.* The presence of both the essay and the oratorical styles here "exactly represents the state of unstable equilibrium which had necessarily followed Plato's attack on oratory" (*Style,* p. 56).

3. There is some question as to whether the three "characters" of style originate with Theophrastus, Cicero, or the author of the *Rhetorica Ad Herennium.* For a discussion of this question, as well as an excellent survey of the *genera dicendi,* see the articles of G. Hendrickson, "The Peripatetic Mean of Style and the Three Stylistic Characters," *American Journal of Philology,* XXV (1904), pp. 125–146; and "The Origin and Meaning of the Ancient Characters of Style," *AJP,* XXVI (1905), pp. 249–260.

4. Croll's position here (in 1929) represents something of a shift from his earlier (1914) view:

En somme, l'époque du mouvement anti-cicéronien fut celle qui précéda Descartes, l'époque de la philosophie de Bacon, période qui semble à des certains moments avoir comblé le gouffre qui nous sépare du moyen âge et paraît à d'autre bien plus lointaine, bien plus médiévale, que l'âge si simple de premières années de la Renaissance. (*Style,* p. 27)

In 1914 Croll associates Attic prose with Baconian science; in 1929 he associates it with Cartesianism as well.

5. Richard Foster Jones and others, *The Seventeenth Century* (Palo Alto, 1951), pp. 75–76. In this *Festschrift* are conveniently reprinted, with minor corrections, Jones' articles on science and English prose style: "Science and English Prose Style in the Third Quarter of the Seventeenth Century," *PMLA,* XLV (1930), pp.

977–1009; "The Attack on Pulpit Eloquence in the Restoration: An Episode in the Development of the Neo-Classical Standard for Prose," *Journal of English and Germanic Philology*, XXX (1931), pp. 188–217; "Science and Language in England of the Mid-Seventeenth Century," *JEGP*, XXXI (1932), pp. 315–331.

6. In his last article on our topic, Jones dealt with the difficult question of the survival of rhetoric in the Royal Society ("The Rhetoric of Science," in *Restoration and Eighteenth-Century Literature* [Chicago, 1963], pp. 1–35). He limits it to the Cartesian and atomistic wings of the Society. It is a consequence of their need to make their "mechanical" conceptions clear. Because of its figures, Jones claims it has "much in common" (p. 15) with Croll's "Anti-Ciceronianism." Sir Kenelm Digby and Walter Charleton are Jones' principal examples. Sprat and the later Glanvill, on the other hand, are in the Baconian wing, which evolved the dominant stylistic doctrine of the Society. The Baconians reject rhetoric because of their utilitarianism.

It seems to me that Jones is right to see "utilitarianism" (rather than "science," as he had earlier held) as the distinctive feature of the Baconians' stylistic theory. Nevertheless, his opposition of plain Baconian versus rhetorical Cartesian and atomist is open to some major objections. The Baconians can also become rhetorical on utilitarian grounds, as in Sprat's *History of the Royal-Society*, or get caught up in jargon, as in the writings of Hooke. And a Cartesian-mechanical-atomistic thinker like Hobbes could write severely indeed. Actually the distinctions are not as sharp as Jones maintains; most of the fellows held a healthy respect for both Descartes and Bacon.

The utilitarians of the Society do not condemn figurative language altogether but only a certain *kind* of figure. Most, though certainly not all, of the figures used by Digby and Charleton would meet with Sprat's approval, for they are obviously merely explanatory or a clear concession to rhetorical necessity. Jones quotes the following passage as an example (pp. 12–13): "Notwithstanding the perspicuity of these Arguments, we shall not superorogate, to heighten the lustre of so desirable a Truth, by the vernish of a convenient and pregnant Simile, or two. If we attractively observe a *Chameleon* catching Gnats and other small Flyes in the Aer, for his food. . . . Why should we not conceive, that this Electricity or Attraction may hold a very neer Analogy to that attraction of Gnats, by the exerted and nimbly retracted tongue of a Chameleon . . ." (Charleton,

Epicuro-Gassendo-Charletoniana [1654], pp. 343-346). No Elizabethan or "Anti-Ciceronian" was ever so self-conscious about a figure. Charleton here is as utilitarian as Sprat. For his utilitarian theory of prose style, see his *Brief Discourse Concerning the Different Wits of Men* (London, 1669), pp. 19-20.

For an appreciation of the "rhetoric of science" in general in the seventeenth century the indispensable sources are the writings of Marjorie Nicolson.

7. Morris Croll and R. S. Crane, review of R. F. Jones' "Science and English Prose Style," *Philological Quarterly*, X (1931), p. 185.

8. *The Seventeenth Century*, p. 109. Cf. J. Spingarn's introduction to his edition of *Critical Essays of the Seventeenth Century* (Oxford, 1908), I, pp. xxvi-xlviii.

9. R. F. Jones, "The Moral Sense of Simplicity," in *Studies in Honor of Frederick W. Shipley*, Washington University Studies, New Series, Language and Literature, XIV (1941); *The Triumph of the English Language* (Palo Alto, 1953).

10. In the scholarship on the controversy since Jones and Croll the Jonesians are in the majority. In a review of Jones' article on the effect of science on pulpit oratory, Moody E. Prior (*Philological Quarterly*, XI [1932], pp. 179-180) questioned Jones' understanding of seventeenth-century science. Prior held that Jones limited science to Baconianism at the expense of Cartesianism, which was equally significant. Cartesianism admitted rhetoric, as is apparent in the evolution of Glanvill's prose — rhetorical under the influence of Descartes, plain under the sway of the Baconian Royal Society. The findings of Fraser Mitchell, in his *English Pulpit Oratory from Andrewes to Tillotson* (London, 1931), in general support Croll over Jones with regard to the sermon. F. P. Wilson ("English Letters and the Royal Society," *Mathematical Gazette*, XIX [1935], pp. 343-354), like Carson Duncan long before in *The New Science and English Literature in the Classical Period* (Menasha, 1913), summarizes places in English literature where science is mentioned, and seems to accept Jones' thesis. Another Jonesian, Clark Emery, suggests in "John Wilkins' 'Universal Language'," *Isis*, XXXVIII (1948), pp. 174-185, that Wilkins' scheme for a language based on a "Real Character" influenced Sprat's ideal of a close, naked, natural way of speaking," and thereby influenced English prose. This idea is developed at length in George Williamson's *The Senecan Amble* (Chicago, 1951), pp. 278 ff., and in a valuable unpublished Harvard dissertation by Benjamin deMott, "A Study of Constructed Lan-

guages in England With Special Reference to their Relations with Science and Attitudes Toward Literary Style, 1605-1686" (1953). Joan Bennett, in "An Aspect of the Evolution of Seventeenth-Century Prose" (*Review of English Studies*, XVII [1941], p. 281) offers us a survey of changes in prose imagery and metaphor when "English prose transformed itself" — "the sixty odd years between . . . *The Advancement of Learning* and . . . the self-confident reply of the Royal Society." Mrs. Bennett's insistence on such a transformation and her note that "his learned articles tend to confirm and complete the picture I have tried to sketch" put her in Jones's camp. Replying to Mrs. Bennett, Hugh Mac-Donald in "Another Aspect of Seventeenth-Century Prose," *Review of English Studies*, XIX (1943), pp. 33-43, concedes the tidying influence of the Royal Society as evidenced in the evolution of Glanvill and Cowley described by Jones. But MacDonald argues for the existence of a universal plain style from the days of King Alfred. He cites pleas for the kind of style favored by the Royal Society by such earlier men as (the Ciceronian!) Ascham, Hall, and Jonson. He suggests another influence, political pamphleteering and journalism, in particular that of Roger L'Estrange. Deloney. Middleton, Howell, and Walton were also plain, though untouched by science. Like MacDonald, Andrews Wanning modifies Jones though Wanning is not a Crollian. In his brilliant unpublished Cambridge University thesis, "Some Changes in the Prose Style of the Seventeenth Century" (1936), Wanning accepts Jones' division of seventeenth-century prose into sharply opposed pre- and post-Restoration styles.

This survey suggests that Jones's thesis that Baconian science itself worked a profound transformation on English prose has been generally accepted, albeit with considerable modification, including some amendments from Jones himself. The Crollians are outnumbered, although Croll's description of Anti-Ciceronianism has never run into any serious trouble. In almost all the general literary and cultural histories of the period Jones' point of view seems to be regarded as the sound, orthodox position. For example, F. P. Wilson says of Bacon that

"his prose style — or rather styles, for he had several — cannot easily be squared with the tenets of his followers, whether we think of the aphoristic style of the *Essays*, where the *brevitas* of Tacitus and Lipsius is carried as far as it can go in the English language, or think of the eloquence of many a passage in the

Advancement, where he is preaching the gospel of science. . . .
But in the third quarter of the century the plain style triumphed."
(*Seventeenth Century Prose* [Berkeley, 1961], p. 5)

Wilson, like J. R. Sutherland, criticizes Jones for attributing the
triumph of the plain style solely to so limited a movement as
the Royal Society, but both go along with Jones's contention that
"there are good reasons for claiming that after 1660 English prose
made a fresh start" and that "as we move further away from the
sixteenth-century and early seventeenth-century imitators of
Seneca, it becomes more and more difficult to isolate any influence
that he still may have exerted" (Sutherland, *On English Prose*,
[Toronto, 1957], p. 67).

Exception to Jonesian orthodoxy has been taken by a formidable Crollian, George Williamson. In his awesomely docu-
mented *Senecan Amble*, he holds that, "As it was the Anti-Ciceronian style that Bacon advanced, so it is the Anti-Ciceronian
style from which the Royal Society programme derived" (p. 276).
Williamson is supported by Jackson Cope and H. W. Jones in
their edition of Sprat's *History of the Royal-Society* (St. Louis,
1958). But even the editors of the Princeton edition of Croll agree
with R. F. Jones that Restoration prose is anti-Senecan (pp. 5,
48–49).

Chapter Two

1. *Style, Rhetoric, and Rhythm: Essays by Morris W. Croll*, eds.
   J. Max Patrick, Robert O. Evans, John M. Wallace, and R.
   Shoeck (Princeton, 1966), p. 195.
2. *Works*, eds. J. Spedding, R. Ellis, and D. Heath (Boston, 1861),
   XII, pp. 84–86. All quotations from Bacon are from this edition,
   hereafter referred to as *Works*. The bracketed English translations of Bacon's Latin phrases are the editors', not mine. Bacon
   wrote a Latin revision of the *Advancement of Learning*, the
   De Augmentis Scientiarum. Wherever there are significant differences, I have quoted from the Spedding edition's translation
   of the *De Augmentis*.
3. William Hazlitt, "Lectures on the Age of Elizabeth," *The
   Collected Works*, ed. P. Howe (London, 1931), V, pp. 326–345.
4. Sir Ronald Syme, *Tacitus* (Oxford, 1958), I, p. 347.
5. *Essays*, ed. E. A. Abbott (London, 1899), and W. A. Wright
   (London, 1862).

6. Sister Mary Faith Schuster, "Philosophy of Life and Prose Style in Thomas More's *Richard III* and Francis Bacon's *Henry VII*," *PMLA*, LXX (1955), p. 483.

7. John Speed, *The History of Great Britaine . . . to our most gracious Soueraigne King James* (London, 1614), p. 741.

8. For a survey of early English historiography see G. P. Krapp's still valuable *The Rise of English Literary Prose* (New York, 1915), ch. VII, IX; Leonard Dean, *Tudor Theories of History Writing* (Ann Arbor, 1947); F. S. Fussner, *The Historical Revolution: English Historical Writing and Thought*, 1580–1640 (New York, 1962); and Herschel Baker, *The Race of Time* (Toronto, 1966).

9. Although it would be impossible here to prove the resemblance conclusively, one might compare Carlyle's treatment of an accession with passages from Bacon and Tacitus, quoted in the Appendix:

— Tuesday 31st May 1740, between one and two o'clock in the afternoon, Friedrich Wilhelm died; age fifty-two, coming August 15th next. Same day Friedrich his Son was proclaimed at Berlin; quilted heralds, with sound of trumpet and the like, doing what is customary on such occasions. (*The History of Frederick the Great*, in *Works*, ed. H. D. Trail [New York, 1900], XIV, p. 274)

Here the brevity is truly Tacitean rather than Baconian in that it works to emphasize the dramatic immediacy of the occasion — the efficient Prussian haste with which the young Friedrich is installed. Time is dramatic, so Carlyle gives us the exact time and place, in the manner of a modern radio broadcast. The abruptness is also Tacitean, as is the innuendo of "doing what is customary on such occasions" — that is, mere pomp and ceremony do not matter. Like Tacitus, Carlyle drives straight to the emotional core of an event not by elaborate descriptions of concrete externals but by a suggestion of movement or general atmosphere (cf., in the Appendix, Tacitus' *mox senatus milesque et populus*.) They are both masters of crowd scenes. Also Tacitean is the harsh, almost colloquial slackness of "Friedrich Wilhelm died; age fifty-two, coming August 15th next."

Following this scene, we have the death of the older Friedrich, thoroughly Tacitean in its extended pathos and hero-worship (cf. the death of Germanicus) and the actual accession, which reads like a translation of the passage in the appendix beginning *At Romae ruere in servitium:*

In Berlin, from Tuesday 31st May 1740, day of the late King's death, till the Thursday following, the post was stopped and the gates closed; no estafette can be despatched, though Dickens and all the other Ambassadors are busy writing. On the Thursday, Regiments, Officers principal Officials having sworn, and the new King being fairly in the saddle, estafettes and postboys shoot forth at the top of their speed; and Rumour, towards every point of the compass, apprises mankind what immense news there is. (p. 278)

Here there is Tacitean abruptness, innuendo, and the like again, as well as asyndeton ("Regiments, Officers, principal Officials" — cf. Tacitus' *consules, patres, eques,* where asyndeton serves an identical dramatic purpose); personification ("Rumour"); a violent shift into the historical present; and a taste for the strange ("estafette") and the colloquial ("in the saddle"). There is even Tacitus' fractured symmetry ("stopped . . . closed . . . despatched . . . busy writing"). Behind everything, of course, as so often in Tacitus, is Carlyle's moral fervor against the pigmies who oppose the Hero.

The style of Carlyle, then, is not far from Tacitus'. But it is hard to imagine two styles more unlike than Carlyle's and Bacon's.

Though upset by Tacitus' animus against Christianity, Carlyle thought him "the wisest, most penetrating man of his generation" (*Works,* XXVI, p. 398).

10. Essay "Of Great Place," *Works,* XII, p. 112.
11. Vincent Luciani, "Bacon and Guicciardini," *PMLA,* LXII (1947), p. 109.
12. *Aphorisms on the Composition of the Primary History, Works,* VIII, p. 359.
13. A. A. Hill, "Towards A Literary Analysis," *University of Virginia Studies,* IV (1951), p. 151.
14. E.g., Leonard Dean, "Sir Francis Bacon's Theory of Civil History Writing," *ELH,* VIII (1941), pp. 161-183; F. J. C. Hearnshaw, *TLS,* April 8, 1926; G. P. Krapp, *loc. cit.;* Vincent Luciani, *op. cit.;* Thomas Wheeler, "Sir Francis Bacon's Conception of the Historian's Task," *Renaissance Papers* (1955), pp. 40-46; and Wheeler's "The Purpose of Bacon's History of Henry the Seventh," *Studies in Philology,* LIII (1957), pp. 1-13.
15. Bacon's lumping together of history and science is apparent in titles like the *History of Dense and Rare,* the *History of Winds,* and the *History of Life and Death.* This use of "History" has roots deep in antiquity back to the age of Thucydides and the Ionian scientists; cf. Werner Jaeger, *Paideia,* tr. G. Highet

(New York, 1960), I, pp. 388 ff. See also Bacon's *Aphorisms on the Composition of the Primary History* (*Works*, VIII, pp. 357–381), where the directions for the writing of natural history are identical with those for civil history. History is truer than "idle" imagination (poetry) and "litigious" reason (philosophy).

16. For the relation of the essays to the *Advancement* see R. S. Crane, "The Relation of Bacon's *Essays* to his Program for the Advancement of Learning," *Schelling Anniversary Papers* (New York, 1923), pp. 87–105, and W. G. Crane, *Wit and Rhetoric in the Renaissance* (New York, 1937), pp. 137–148. For the relation of the *History* to the *Advancement* see the articles listed in note 13. There is also Bacon's own testimony in the *Advancement* (*Works*, VI, p. 192–193):

> And if it shall be seen that the greatness of this work may make it less exactly performed, there is an excellent period of a much smaller compass of time, as to the story of England; that is to say, from the Uniting of the Roses to the Uniting of the Kingdoms; a portion of time, wherein to my understanding, there hath been the rarest variety that in like number of successions of any hereditary monarchy hath been known. For it beginneth with the mixed adoption of a crown by arms and title; an entry of battle, an establishment by marriage; and therefore times answerable, like waters after a tempest, full of working and swelling, though without extremity of storm; but well passed through by the wisdom of the pilot, being one of the most sufficient kings of all that number.

17. *Advancement*, *Works*, VI, p. 359. There is an extensive literature on the relation of Bacon to Machiavelli; for example, N. Orsini, *Bacone e Machiavelli* (Genoa, 1936), which lists all the parallels in an appendix; Vincent Luciani, "Bacon and Machiavelli," *Italica*, XXIV (1947), pp. 26–40: Thomas Wheeler, "Bacon's Henry VII as a Machiavellian Prince," *Renaissance Papers* (1957), pp. 111–116; the introduction to Abbott's edition of the *Essays*; and the works on Bacon's theory of history mentioned in note 13.

18. *The Letters and Life of Francis Bacon Including All His Occasional Works*, ed. J. Spedding (London, 1861–1874), V, p. 189.

19. For example, "Of Death," *Works*, XII, p. 87, from the *Annals* of Tacitus, VI, 50 and the *History*, I, 41; "Of Simulation and Dissimulation," p. 95, from the *Annals*, V, 1, and II, 76; "Of Seditions and Troubles," pp. 123–124, from the *History*, I, 7, and II, 39, and the *Annals*, III, 4; "Of Vain-Glory," p. 262, from the *History*, II, 80; "A Fragment of an Essay on Fame," p. 284, from the *History*, II, 80, *Annals*, I, 5. See also "Of Great Place,"

"Of Friendship," "Of Riches," "Of Prophecies," and the rest of "Of Seditions and Troubles" for other Tacitean allusions.

20. Croll, *Style*, p. 193; Bacon, *Letters and Life*, II, p. 25. The letter to Greville is reprinted and discussed by V. F. Snow in "Francis Bacon's Advice to Fulke Greville on Research Techniques," *Huntington Library Quarterly*, XXIII (1959–1960), pp. 369–378. The letter was sent in Essex' name.

21. Letter to the Earl of Rutland, *Letters and Life*, II, p. 12.

22. *Advancement*, *Works*, VI, p. 120. Croll claims that the Anti-Ciceronians praised Cicero as a master of rhetoric only. "The Anti-Ciceronian critics, even the boldest of them, always keep an Augustan and Ciceronian orthodoxy in reserve; and even Montaigne will admit that if an abstract literary excellence, independent of the practical and moral uses of the works in which it is displayed, be the basis of one's judgment, the Augustan age and the ages that resemble it are on a higher plane than any others" (*Style*, p. 193). But in the preceding quotation Bacon praises Cicero for his "practical and moral uses" as well as his "literary excellence." See also in the *Advancement*, pp. 352 and 360, where the praise for Cicero's "wise and weighty" discourses is even stronger. This kind of pro-Ciceronian statement would seem to disqualify Bacon as an Anti-Ciceronian, at least as defined by Croll.

23. Croll, *Style*, p. 192; Bacon, *Temporis Partus Masculus*, *Works*, VII, p. 20.

24. See Jacob Zeitlin, "The Development of Bacon's Essays, With Special Reference to the Question of Montaigne's Influence on Them," *Journal of English and Germanic Philology*, XXVII (1928), pp. 496–519, and R. S. Crane, "The Relation of Bacon's Essays." Cf. Douglas Bush, *English Literature in the Earlier Seventeenth Century*, 2nd ed. (New York, 1962), pp. 169–197: "The essays are, morally, something of a jumble." For an analysis of Bacon's moral dilemma and its legacy see Loren Eisely, *Francis Bacon and the Modern Dilemma* (Lincoln, 1962).

25. Pierre Villey sees the influence of Montaigne on these essays in "Montaigne a-t-il eu quelque influence sur Francis Bacon?" *Revue de la Renaissance*, XII (1911), pp. 121–158; XIII (1912), pp. 21–46, 61–82. Reprinted as *Montaigne et Bacon* (Paris, 1913).

26. *De Augmentis*, *Works*, II, p. 127. Croll maintains here (*Style*, p. 190) that Bacon is speaking of his own style, and also of abuses of Attic prose that had grown up between the time of the *Advancement* (in which the quotation does not appear) and the *De*

Augmentis some twenty-odd years later. It seems to me unlikely that anyone, and especially the confident Bacon, would condemn his own style so strongly.

27. *Advancement, Works,* VI, pp. 118-120. The full passage reads:

Martin Luther . . . was enforced to awake all antiquity, and to call former times to his succors to make a party against the present time; so that the ancient authors, both in divinity and in humanity which had long time slept in libraries, began gradually to be read and revolved. This by consequence did draw on a necessity of a more exquisite travail in the languages original wherein these authors did write, for the better understanding of those authors and the better advantage of pressing and applying their words. And thereof grew again a delight in their manner of style and phrase, and an admiration of that kind of writing; which was much furthered and precipitated by the enmity and opposition that the propounders of those (primitive but seeming new) opinions had against the schoolmen; who were generally of the contrary part, and whose writings were altogether in a differing style and form; taking liberty to coin and frame new terms of art to express their own sense and to avoid circuit of speech, without regard to the pureness, pleasantness, and (as I may call it) lawfulness of the phrase or word. And again, because the great labour then was with the people . . . for the winning and persuading of them, there grew of necessity in chief price and request eloquence and variety of discourse, as the fittest and forciblest access into the capacity of the vulgar sort. So that these four causes concurring, the admiration of ancient authors, the hate of the schoolmen, the exact study of languages, and the efficacy of preaching, did bring in an affectionate study of eloquence and copie of speech, which then began to flourish. This grew speedily to an excess; for men began to hunt more after words than matter; and more after the choiceness of the phrase, and the round and clean composition of the sentence and the sweet falling of the clauses, and the varying and illustration of their works with tropes and figures, than after the weight of matter, worth of subject, soundness of argument, life of invention, or depth of judgment.

28. Karl Wallace, *Francis Bacon on Communication and Rhetoric* (Chapel Hill, 1943), and Maurice B. MacNamee, *Literary Decorum in Francis Bacon,* St. Louis University Studies, Series A, Humanities, I, no. 3 (1950). See also W. S. Howell, *Logic and Rhetoric in England, 1500-1700* (Princeton, 1956), pp. 364-375, and G. Williamson, *The Senecan Amble* (Chicago, 1951), ch. VI.

29. Croll, *Style,* p. 89; MacNamee, *Literary Decorum.*

30. Wallace comes to the same conclusion (*Communication and Rhetoric,* pp. 152-153):

Principally because of Bacon's hints for the writing of natural history, those scholars interested in the development of prose style suggest that the Lord Chancellor favors what Professor Croll calls an Attic, "essay" or "philosophical" style of expression, rather than a Ciceronian, "oratorical" manner of composition. . . . It must be observed, however, that Bacon, so far as one can deduce his theory of style, by no means commits himself in precept or in practice to a single "character" of language expression. . . . He clearly sees that the natural and witty aspects of the *genus humile* when applied generally can become as distasteful, affected, and vain as the Ciceronian ornamentation against which Erasmus Muret, and Montaigne were in rebellion. He . . . cannot be neatly fitted into the style of the *genus humile*. The later Essays are far from being concise, pointed, and antithetical; copious in illustrations, they are discursive rather than compact. And although the early Essays are often brief, studiously balanced, and aphoristic, it is doubtful that Bacon thus wrote because he had become a disciple of Attic prose; rather, he thought of himself as a scientist in morals, collecting observations on conduct and affairs for the observation and criticism of others; he was handing on the lamp and used such a style not because he was rebelling against Ciceronian elegance, but because he thought the manner appropriate to the subject matter.

31. Robert P. Tristram Coffin and A. M. Witherspoon, eds., *Seventeenth Century Prose and Poetry* (New York, 1929), p. 37.

32. *Novum Organum*, Book I, *Works*, VIII, Aphorism lxxxi, p. 113. Cf. Aphorisms xcviii, xcix, cix.

33. Robert Hannah, *Francis Bacon: The Political Orator* (New York, 1923), p. 15. Hannah brings in much evidence to show Bacon's saturation in the Bible.

34. *Advancement, Works*, VI, p. 352. Bacon insisted that the Bible was "for use, and not to ostentation" (p. 97). Here is one of the many points where he sounds like a Puritan. Bush (*English Literature*, p. 284) summarizes "the general affinities between Baconian science and rational Puritanism" as follows: "impatience of traditional authority and useless learning; the critical and empirical instinct; the ideal of action rather than contemplation; belief in utility, progress, and reform, in the study of God's creation and in 'works' as a religious and humanitarian duty and pleasure; and — what is not really inconsistent with that — the disposition to segregate the religious and the secular, the divine and the 'natural.' "

35. *Advancement*, p. 354; Ecclesiastes 9:14–15. Bacon continues:

Here the corruption of states is set forth, that esteem not virtue or merit longer than they have use of it." The Bible has a different moral: "Then said I, Wisdom is better than strength:

nevertheless the poor man's wisdom is despised, and his words are not heard. The words of wise men are heard in quiet more than the cry of him that ruleth among fools. Wisdom is better than weapons of war: but one sinner destroyeth much good." Bacon's interpretation of this passage illustrates his use of the Bible and of literature in general. The moral in the Bible is not straightforward political wisdom, but a melancholy reflection on the psychology of fools in general, and its consequences for the wise. Bacon regards "Solomon" as he regards Machiavelli: they are valuable because they examine "business" in a "discourse upon examples."

36. Thirdly, whereas I could have digested these rules into a certain method or order which, I know, would have been more admired, as that which would have made every particular rule, through his coherence and relation unto other rules, seem more cunning and more deep; yet I have avoided so to do, because this delivery of knowledge in distinct and disjoined aphorisms doth leave the wit of man more free to turn and toss, and to make use of that which is so delivered to more several purposes and applications. For we see all the ancient wisdom and science was wont to be delivered in that form; as may be seen by the parables of Solomon, and by the aphorisms of Hippocrates, and the moral verses of Theognis and Phocylides, but chiefly the precedent of the civil law, which hath taken the same course with their rules, did confirm me in my opinion. (*Maxims of the Law*, Preface, *Works*, XIV, pp. 182–183)

37. *Advancement*, pp. 289, 291–292. Aphorisms, which insinuate, are associated with the Probative or Initiative method; Methods (Bacon is invariably confusing in his terminology), which teach, are Magistral.

38. See MacNamee, *Literary Decorum*, pp. 35–40, and R. S. Crane's "The Relation of Bacon's *Essays*," which relates the shift to Bacon's feeling that moral subjects are best treated in Methods. For Bacon morality, in any sense of the word, was a "science popular": "It is true that in sciences popular, as moralities, laws, and the like, yea and divinity (because it pleaseth God to apply himself to the capacity of the simplest), that form may have use . . . but the subtilty of nature and operations . . . will not be enchained in those bonds; for Arguments consist of Propositions of Words; and Words are but the current tokens or marks of Popular Notions of things" (*Advancement*, p. 266).

39. "Acts of free associative thinking cannot be expressed completely in words; the whole process is inherently illogical, intuitive, and punctuated by irrelevancies. As soon as we attempt to express our thoughts, even to ourselves, we re-arrange them and drastically

prune away redundant and incoherent features. For the purposes of our articulated speech or writing this process is carried out still more ruthlessly, and we strive to cast our thoughts into a form that is not only comprehensible to ourselves, but to our hearers; the results of unrestricted thinking are refined and ordered in accordance with logical canons." (H. Head, *Aphasia and Kindred Disorders of Speech* [Cambridge, England, 1904], I, p. 52)

40. Bacon's word "traditio" reflects a usage which is now obsolete. In Bacon's rhetorical theory it refers usually to its root meaning of "handing over," "the expressing or transferring our knowledge to others," or "Delivery" (*Advancement*, p. 282). There are two principal kinds of Traditio, the Magistral and the Probative or Initiative. The former is associated with "Methods," the latter with Aphorisms. For Bacon, aphorisms are the Traditio Lampadis, the Handing-on-of-the-Lamp style. "*Proinde eam inter Deside-ratam numerabimus, eamque Traditionem Lampadis, sive Metho-dum ad Filios, apellabimus*" (*De Augmentis, Works*, II, p. 429). Spedding translates *Methodum ad Filios* as "Method of Delivery to Posterity" (*De Augmentis, Works*, IX, p. 124) and appends the following note (II, pp. 429–430): "I understand by *filios* in this passage not so much those who are qualified to be disciples, as those who will carry on the work. The *traditio lampadis* refers to the Greek torch-races, in which there were relays of runners, and each as he was spent handed the torch to a fresh man. The *methodus ad filios* is the method which, having in view the continual progression of knowledge, hands over its unfinished work to another generation, to be taken up and carried forward."

41. There is a considerable literature on the Renaissance habit, which was taught in the schools, of collecting commonplaces. For its relation to Bacon see the remarks on Bacon in E. N. S. Thompson, *The Seventeenth Century Essay* (Iowa City, 1926) and in W. G. Crane, *Wit and Rhetoric in the Renaissance* (New York, 1937). In his monumental *Les sources et l'évolution des Essais de Montaigne* (Paris, 1908), Pierre Villey shows how Montaigne collected them.

42. Zeitlin, "The Development of Bacon's Essays"; R. S. Crane, "The Relation of Bacon's *Essays*," pp. 98–105.

43. Lucius Annaeus Seneca, *Epistulae Morales*, xxiv, 6, tr. R. M. Gummere, Loeb Library (London, 1924), I, pp. 172–175. Cf. Bacon, *Letters and Life*, VI, p. 183; "And this I shall do, my Lords, *in verbis masculis*, no flourishing or painted words, but such words as are fit to go before deeds."

44. William Summers ed., *Select Letters of Seneca* (London, 1910), Introduction, *passim*.

45. Cf. the essay, "Of Seeming Wise," *Works*, XII, p. 165: "Some are never without a difference, and commonly by amusing men with a subtilty, blanch the matter; of whom A. Gellius saith, *Hominem delirum, qui verborum minutiis rerum frangit pondera:* [a trifler, that with verbal points and niceties breaks up the mass of matter]." Gellius is referring to Seneca, but Bacon, as usual, misquotes. The note on this passage in S. H. Reynolds' edition of the *Essays* (Oxford, 1906), pp. 182–183, is illuminating:

> We learn from a passage in the *Advancement of Learning* that Bacon was aware that it was about Seneca that these words or something like them had been used. "As was said of Seneca, 'Verborum minutiis rerum frangit pondera.'" Now the comments of Aulus Gellius on the style and matter of Seneca are found in the *Noctes Atticae*, xii, chap. 2. He is termed '*nugator homo verborum Seneca piget: inepti et insubidi et insulsi hominis joca non praeteritio*, etc.' But the words in Bacon's text do not occur. The nearest approach to them is in the better balanced and more considered censure of Quintilian: "Si non omnia sua amasset; si rerum pondera minutissimus sententiis non fregisset, consensu potius eruditorum quam puerorum amore comprobaretur" De Instit. Orat. X. cap. I, sec. 130. It would seem that Bacon had read both the preceding passages and, by confusing their authorship and adding something of his own, had evolved the sentence which he ascribes to Aulus Gellius. *He thus shows us, all the more clearly, what his opinion of Seneca must have been*" (Italics mine).

46. Thompson, *The Seventeenth Century Essay*; W. G. Crane, *Wit and Rhetoric in the Renaissance*, pp. 138–148.

47. Cf. epistles xix, xl, xl, xlvi, lix, lxxxv, c, cxiv.

48. For the rhetorical history of the plain style in antiquity, and its relation to the epistle, see the articles of Hendrickson already cited and Wesley Trimpi, *Ben Jonson's Poems: A Study of the Plain Style* (Palo Alto, 1962), ch. I. See also Chapter Four, pp. 133–141.

49. *The Senecan Amble*, pp. 183–185. More than anyone else, Williamson seems to be aware of the affinities of Senecan style with the Gorgian *genus grande*.

50. *Temporis Partus Masculus*, *Works*, VII, p. 20. The translation here is by Basil Montagu from his edition of Bacon's *Works* (London, 1837), III, p. 546. The Latin is as follows: "Nam levius malum est, quod philologorum parens extisti, ac tuo ductu et auspiciis plurimi, ingenii fama et cognitionis rerum populari et

molli jucunditate capti et contenti severiorem veri pervestigatio-
nem corruperunt. Inter quos fuere Marcus Cicero et Annaeus
Seneca et Plutarchus Charoneus."

51. *The Great Instauration*: "The Plan of the Work," *Works*, VIII,
p. 49. Cf. Basil Willey, *The Seventeenth Century Background*
(New York, 1934), p. 44: " 'Man should not dispute and assert,
but whisper results to his neighbor.' The words are Keats's, but
they well express the aspiration which was in Bacon."

There is a modern translation of the *Questiones* by John Clarke,
with notes by Sir Archibald Geikie, in *Physical Science in the
Time of Nero* (London, 1910).

52. For a discussion of Lipsius' "hopping" Senecanism, for which
there is no parallel in Bacon, see *The Senecan Amble*, ch. V, and
Basil Anderton, *Sketches From a Library Window* (New York,
1923), pp. 29–30. In the letter to Greville (Letters and Life, II,
p. 22), Bacon attacks Lipsius as a writer of epitomes which "will
no more make a man a good Civilian, Common Lawyer, Logician,
Naturalist, Politician, nor Soldier, than the seeing of the names
of London, Bristol, York, Lincoln, and some few other places of
note, in a Mercator's general map will make a stranger understand the cosmography of England."

53. Bernard Andreas (d. 1521?), *Historia Regis Henrici Septem*, reprinted in James Gairdner, *Memorials of King Henry VII* (London, 1858), pp. 1–75. In addition to Speed, Polydore Vergil, Hall,
and Andreas, Bacon was indebted to Stowe, the Cotton manuscript collections, Fabyan, and various other documents, such as
the Rolls of Parliament. See Bush, *English Literature*, p. 227.

54. James Gairdner says:

Another curious error that has crept into all our histories is also
traceable, not indeed to the words of Bernard André, but to a
singular misreading of them by one of Bacon's contemporaries.
Bacon himself tells us that though accompanied in his entry by
troops of noblemen, Henry rode in a close chariot, "as one that,
having been some time an enemy to the whole State and a proscribed person, chose rather to keep state and strike a reverence
into the people than to fawn upon them." What Bacon, however,
relates as a fact is only a conjecture in the pages of his contemporary Speed, who shows us clearly on what it was grounded.
Henry, according to Speed, eschewed popular acclamations, "for
that, as Andreas saith, he entered *covertly*, meaning *belike*, in a
horse-litter or close chariot." The close chariot, then, is a mere
inference from the words of Andreas (Bernard André) as read by
Speed. But the MS. of Bernard André does not say that Henry
entered the city covertly, but joyfully (*laetenter*, not, as Speed
quotes the word, *latenter*), and the whole aspect of the matter is

thus completely changed. Henry had no fear of a good reception by the citizens, and he was not so impolitic as to cool their ardor by reserve on his part. He was received by the Lord Mayor and city companies at Shoreditch, and met, as Polydore Vergil and Hall assure us, with a very warm and enthusiastic welcome, every one pressing forward "gladly to touch and kiss that victorious hand!" (*Henry the Seventh* [London, 1926], pp. 33-34)

Bacon's rejection of Hall and Vergil (whom he at other times follows, as Spedding shows in his edition) in favor of Speed is characteristic. Wherever there are several possibilities, Bacon chooses the one most in accord with Machiavellian theories.

55. Polydore Vergil, *Anglica Historia* (1534), ed. and tr. Denys Hay, Camden Series (London, 1950), LXXIV, pp. 3-5.

56. Edward Hall, *The Vnion of the Two Noble and Illustre Famelies of Lancastre and Yorke* (1542; reprinted London, 1809), pp. 422-423.

57. *Aphorisms on the Composition of the Primary History, Works,* VIII, p. 360.

58. Marjorie Walters, "The Literary Background of Francis Bacon's Essay 'Of Death,'" *Modern Language Review,* XXXV (1940), p. 6.

59. Jeremy Taylor, *The Rule and Exercises of Holy Dying,* ch. III, sec. 7, no. 4, in *The Whole Works,* eds. R. Heber and C. P. Eden (London, 1854), III, p. 339. Montaigne, in his treatment of the passage (*Essais,* [Paris, 1595], I, xix), keeps Seneca's intimacy and wealth of detail, but unlike Taylor, rejects Seneca's rhetorical elevation:

Je crois, à la verité, que ce sont ces mines et appareils effroyables dequoy nous l'entournons, qui nous font plus de peur qu'elle; une toute nouvelle forme de vivre; les cris des mères, des femmes, et des enfants; la visitation de personnes estonnées et transies; l'assistance d'un nombre de valets pasles et esplorez; une chambre sans jour; des cierges allumez; nostre chevet assigé de medecins et de pescheurs; somme, tout horreur et tout effroy autour de nous; nous voyla desja ensepvelis et enterrez. Les enfants ont peur de leurs amis mesmes, quand ils les voyent masquez: aussi avons nous. Il faut oster le masque aussi bien les choses que des personnes: oste qu'il sera, nous le trouverons au dessous que cette mesme mort qu'un valet ou simple chambrière passèrent dernierement sans peur.

Chapter Three

1. Extensive biographical and bibliographical materials on Glanvill are in Jackson Cope, *Joseph Glanvill, Anglican Apologist* (St.

Louis, 1956); Ferris Greenslet, *Joseph Glanvill* (New York, 1900); and the *DNB*.

2. R. F. Jones and others, *The Seventeenth Century* (Palo Alto, 1951), p. 91.

3. Morris Croll, review of R. F. Jones' "Science and English Prose Style," *Philological Quarterly*, X (1931), p. 185.

4. G. Williamson, *The Senecan Amble* (Chicago, 1951), p. 281.

5. Evelyn notes for April 4, 1679, that Pritchard, Bishop of Gloucester, "preach'd in a manner very like bishop Andrews, full of divisions, and scholastical." Even in 1683 (July 15) Evelyn could hear "A stranger, an old man, [who] preach'd on 6 Jerem. 8 . . . much after Bp. Andrews's method, full of logical divisions, in short and broken periods, and Latine sentences, now quite out of fashion in the pulpit, which is grown into a far more profitable way, of plaine and practical discourses." The entry illustrates how a member of the Royal Society reacted *against* "Senecan" style, replacing it with the plain style on utilitarian grounds of "profit." (Quoted in Fraser Mitchell, *English Pulpit Oratory From Andrewes to Tillotson* [London, 1931], p. 308; for a summary of the endurance of the older sermon styles after the Restoration see Mitchell, pp. 308 ff.)

6. "Joseph Glanvill, Anglican Apologist: Old Ideas and New Style in the Restoration," *PMLA* (1954), p. 250.

7. Joseph Glanvill, *The Vanity of Dogmatizing* (London, 1661), pp. 136–142.

8. *Style, Rhetoric, and Rhythm: Essays by Morris W. Croll*, eds. J. Max Patrick, Robert O. Evans, John M. Wallace, and R. J. Shoeck (Princeton, 1966), p. 12.

9. "Address to the Royal Society" in *Scepsis Scientifica* (London, 1665), sig. c₃.

10. "Against Confidence in Philosophy" in *Essays on Several Important Subjects in Philosophy and Religion* (London, 1676), p. 25. The pages of each essay in this collection are numbered separately.

11. "Modern Improvements of Useful Knowledge" (formerly, in a different version, *Plus Ultra*) in the *Essays*, pp. 34–35.

12. *The Seventeenth Century*, p. 89; cf. Thomas Birch, *History of the Royal Society* (London, 1756), p. 500.

13. Thomas Sprat, *The History of the Royal-Society of London* (London, 1667), p. 40.

14. See also p. 141, "For like School-boys, we give over as far as our

Masters can teach us"; and p. 226, "Opinions are the *Rattles* of immature intellects."

15. "Address to the Royal Society," *Scepsis Scientifica*, sig. a₂.
16. "Modern Improvements of Useful Knowledge," *Essays*, pp. 54–55.
17. Cf. Moody Prior's introduction to his reprint of the *Plus Ultra* (New York, 1931), pp. viii–ix.
18. *The Vanity of Dogmatizing*, p. 227. The expression was popularized by Whitehead and Carl Becker.
19. R. K. Merton, "Science, Technology, and Society in Seventeenth-Century England," *Osiris*, IV (1938), pp. 360–632; Christopher Hill, *The Century of Revolution* (London, 1961). See also "Puritanism, Pietism, and Science" and "Science and Economy of 17th Century England" in Merton's *Social Theory and Social Structure* (New York, 1965), pp. 574–627. R. F. Jones' recent (1961) revision of *Ancients and Moderns* (St. Louis) and Richard Westfall's *Science and Religion in Seventeenth Century England* (New Haven, 1958) are excellent introductions to this large topic. The most recent survey is Margery Purver, *The Royal Society: Concept and Creation* (Cambridge, Mass., 1967). For correctives to the school of Merton and Hill, see L. S. Feuer, *The Scientific Intellectuals: The Psychological and Sociological Origins of Modern Science* (New York, 1963). Feuer argues, not very convincingly, for a "hedonist-libertine ethic" as the major influence on the early scientists. See also M. M. Knappen, *Tudor Puritanism* (Chicago, 1939); P. H. Kochner, *Science and Religion in Elizabethan England* (San Marino, 1953); M. Curtis, *Oxford and Cambridge in Transition* (Oxford, 1959); and H. F. Kearney, "Puritanism, Capitalism, and the Scientific Revolution," *Past and Present*, XXVIII (1964), pp. 81–101. For guidance on these matters I am indebted to a brief but illuminating conversation with Mrs. Barbara Shapiro of Pitzer College.
20. Margaret Wiley, *The Subtle Knot* (Cambridge, Mass., 1952), pp. 220–221.
21. In Thomas White's *SCIRI, Sive Sceptices & Scepticorum a Jure Disputationis Exclusio* (London, 1665), sig. a.
22. Joseph Glanvill, *Scir$\frac{e}{i}$ Tuum Nihil Est* (London, 1665), sig. a.
23. All of Glanvill's works on witchcraft are collected in *Sadducismus Triumphatus* (London, 1681), the chief source of his posthumous fame.

24. Quoted in Henry George Lyons, *The Royal Society 1660–1940* (Cambridge, England, 1944), p. 10. Later in his career Boyle became more interested in "pure" science and less interested in the Invisible College. See Kearney, "The Scientific Revolution," pp. 97–98.

25. Quoted in Lyons, *The Royal Society*, p. 32. Wren's florid manner indicates that he is consciously appealing to the "wits." If so, he is following Bacon's and Sprat's utilitarian allowance of rhetoric for the "use" of knowledge.

26. For discussion of the Stubbe-Glanvill controversy, with its lengthy bibliography, see, in addition to the works on the early Society cited above, Appendix B to J. Cope and H. W. Jones' edition of Sprat's *History of the Royal-Society of London* (St. Louis, 1958); and Herschel Baker, *The Wars of Truth* (Cambridge, Mass., 1952), pp. 362–366.

27. Joseph Glanvill, *A Praefatory Answer to Henry Stubbe* (London, 1671), p. 44. The brackets are Glanvill's. Glanvill was correct as to Stubbe's duplicity; see Westfall, *Science and Religion*, p. 23.

28. Thomas Sprat, *The Life and Writings of Mr. Abraham Cowley*, in J. Spingarn, ed., *Critical Essays of the Seventeenth Century*, (Oxford, 1908) II, p. 138.

29. Cf., for example, Sprat's assertion that in the recent plague "the greatest losers endured with such undaunted firmness of mind . . . the best *Moral* Philosophy, too, may be learn'd from the shops of the *Mechanicks*" (p. 121).

30. From the "Advertisement to the Reader" prefixed to the *History*.

31. *Life and Writings of Cowley*, Spingarn, II, pp. 128–129.

32. Joseph Glanvill, *An Essay Concerning Preaching* (London, 1678), p. 18. See also Glanvill's *A Seasonable Defense of Preaching, and the Plain Way of It* (London, 1678), for a similar theory. Twelve of Glanvill's sermons are available in the *Discourses, Sermons, and Remains* (London, 1671).

33. For a discussion of Glanvill's sermon style and reputation as a preacher, see Jackson Cope's *Joseph Glanvill, Anglican Apologist*, pp. 159–166.

Chapter Four

1. Joseph Glanvill, "Anti-Fanatick Theologie and Free Philosophy" in *Essays on Several Important Subjects in Philosophy and Religion* (London, 1676), p. 43.

2. *Style, Rhetoric, and Rhythm: Essays by Morris W. Croll,* eds. J. Max Patrick, Robert O. Evans, John M. Wallace, and R. J. Shoeck (Princeton, 1966), p. 89.

3. G. Williamson, *The Senecan Amble* (Chicago, 1951), pp. 286–287.

4. J. Cope and H. W. Jones, Introduction to Thomas Sprat's *The History of the Royal-Society of London* (St. Louis, 1958), pp. xxix–xxx.

5. R. F. Jones, in *The Seventeenth Century* (Palo Alto, 1951), p. 106. Cf. A. C. Howell, "*Res et Verba:* Words and Things," *ELH,* XIII (1946), pp. 131–142. Howell agrees that in the seventeenth century "the term *res,* meaning *subject-matter,* seems to become confused with *res,* meaning *things,* and the tendency to assume that *things* should be expressible in *words,* or conversely, words should represent *things,* not metaphysical and abstract concepts, may be discerned" (p. 131).

6. Wesley Trimpi, *Ben Jonson's Poems: A Study of the Plain Style* (Palo Alto, 1962), p. 90.

7. *Phaedrus,* c. 275, in *The Dialogues of Plato,* tr. Benjamin Jowett (New York, 1907), I, pp. 580–581.

8. *Phaedrus,* c. 278, p. 583. Aristotle follows Plato in making rhetoric" the opposite of "dialectic" at the very outset of the *Rhetoric;* but Aristotle tries to reconcile them. According to Ammonius, Theophrastus, influenced by Aristotelian canons of appropriateness, again defines the difference between the philosophical and rhetorical styles in terms of the words-things relation. Rhetoric has reference to persuading the *hearers,* the plain style to the *thinking* of the *speakers,* and to mental things:

Language is divided into two types, according to the philosopher Theophrastus, the one having reference to the hearers, the other to the matter concerning which the speaker aims to convince his audience. To the division with reference to the hearers belong poetry and rhetoric. Therefore its function is to choose the more stately words, and not those which are common and vulgar, and to interweave them with each other harmoniously to the end that by means of them, such as vividness, sweetness and other qualities of style, together with expansion and contraction, all employed at the suitable moment, the listener should be charmed and, with respect to intellectual persuasion, overmastered. The division looking to the matter will be the especial concern of the philosopher, refuting the false and setting forth the true. (Ammonius, *Aristotelis De Interpretatione,* ed. Wallies [Berlin, 1897], p. 65; tr. G. Hendrickson, "The Origin and Meaning of the Ancient Characters of Style," *American Journal of Philology,* XXVI [1905], p. 255)

According to Greek theory, then, the plain style has reference to "things" or "matter" in the soul of the speaker. Oratory has no connection with "things" in this sense, being concerned with the arts of persuasion. As such, classical *oratory* is nearer in intention than the classical *plain* style to the plain style advocated by Glanvill and his allies. The Royal Society's plain style also has reference to the reader or listener rather than to the mind of the author or speaker.

9. Cicero, *Orator*, 51, tr. H. M. Hubbell, Loeb Library (Cambridge, Mass., 1952), p. 345.

10. *Orator*, 63–64, p. 353. But, Cicero hastens to add, "all speaking is oratory." Like Aristotle before him, Cicero is trying to reconcile the division, "*absurdum et inutile et reprehendum*" (*De Oratore*, III, 61) between oratory and the plain style (cf. *De Oratore* III, 69–73, *Brutus*, 23).

11. *De Oratore*, III, 149, tr. H. Rackham, Loeb Library (Cambridge, Mass., 1948), p. 119; 149, p. 121.

12. *Rhetorica Ad Herennium*, tr. H. Caplan, Loeb Library (Cambridge, Mass., 1954), pp. 265 ff. For a discussion of the ultimate origin of the "characters" of style, see the articles of Hendrickson on the subject (ch. 1, n. 3).

13. M. Grant and G. Fiske, "Cicero's Orator and Horace's Ars Poetica," *Harvard Studies in Classical Philology*, XXXV (1924), pp. 1–74.

14. The crucial Horatian texts are in the *Ars Poetica* and the *Sermones*. For example, Horace praises his model, the satirist Lucilius, in a passage quoted endlessly by Renaissance "Anti-Ciceronian" theorists on the plain style: "He in olden days would trust his secrets to his books, as if to faithful friends, never turning elsewhere for recourse, whether things went well with him or ill. So it comes that the old poet's whole life is open to view, as if painted on a votive tablet" (*Sermones*, II, i, 30–34, in *Satires, Epistles and Ars Poetica*, tr. H. R. Fairclough, Loeb Library [Cambridge, Mass., 1947], p. 129). Another passage reveals the ultimate indebtedness of the equation of words to things in Horace (as in Cicero before and Seneca after) to the *Socraticae chartae*:

Of good writing the source and font is wisdom. Your matter the Socratic pages can set forth and when matter is in hand words will not be loath to follow. . . . I would advise one who has learned the imitative art to look to life and manners for his model, and draw from thence living words. At times a play marked by attractive passages and characters fitly sketched, though lacking in charm, though without force and art, gives the people more delight and holds them better than verses void of thought, and sonorous trifles. (*Ars Poetica*, 309–322, p. 477)

Horace simply assumes that the soul is a *speculum* of "genuine life" (*vera vita*): "In truth it is preferable to cast aside toys and to learn wisdom; to leave to lads the sport that fits their age, and to search out words that will fit the music of the Latin lyre, but to master the rhythms and measures of a genuine life. Therefore I talk thus to myself and silently recall these precepts" (*Epistles*, II, ii, 141–144, p. 437). The "rhythms and measures of a genuine life" imply the conversational norms which Socrates, Cicero, and the author of the *Ad Herennium* had assigned to the plain style, in which words approximate things. For Horace, this norm determines the character of epistles and satires: "Hence it is not enough to make your hearer grin with laughter — though even in that there is some merit. You need terseness, that the thought may run on, and not become entangled in verbiage, that weighs upon wearied ears. You also need a style now grave, often gay, in keeping with the role, now of orator or poet, at times of the wit, who holds his strength in check and husbands it with wisdom. Jesting oft cuts hard knots more forcefully and effectively than gravity" (*Sermones*, I, x, 7–15, pp. 116–117). Grant and Fiske conclude that "so far as Horatian poetry consists of *sermones* (and *epistulae*) it clearly falls under the canon of the plain style, for the sermo *par excellence* is the *genre* in which the plain style realizes its peculiar virtues" ("Cicero's Orator," p. 40). These "peculiar virtues" depend on the equivalence of words to things, that is, to the character of the author. In contrast to the *contentio* of the epic and tragic poets the sermo "aims at relaxing emotional tension — at least the *sermo apta ad docendum et delectandum*, such as a Platonic dialogue or a Horatian satire — by an exhibition of character, whether in the orator himself, in the personages he depicts, especially in his *narratio*, or in the characters produced by the poets on the comic stage" (*ibid.*, p. 34).

15. Juvenal, *Satires*, I, 85–86, tr. G. G. Ramsay, Loeb Library (Cambridge, Mass., 1940), p. 9.
16. Persius, *Satires*, I, 1, tr. G. G. Ramsay, Loeb Library (Cambridge, Mass., 1940), p. 316. Persius insists on revealing his own character as well:

Nay, indeed, it is no aim of mine that my page should swell with dark pretentious trifles, fit only to give solidity to smoke. To yourself alone, Cornutus, do I speak; I now shake out my heart to you at the bidding of the Muse; it is a joy to me to show you, beloved friend, how large a portion of my soul is yours. Strike it and note carefully what part of it rings true, what is but paint and plaster of the tongue. It is for this that I would ask for a hundred throats: that I may with clear voice proclaim how deeply I have planted you in the recesses of my heart, and that my words may render up all the love that lies deep and unutterable in my inmost soul. (*Satires,* V, 19–29, p. 371)

Similar reflections on the four related genres of the plain style recur throughout antiquity. Thalia, muse of the epigram, cautions Martial to reject the lofty style: "Let those themes be written by men grave overmuch, and overmuch austere, whom at midnight their lamp marks at their wretched toil. But do you dip your little Roman books in sprightly wit; let Life recognize and read of her own manners" (*Epigrams,* VIII, iii, 15–17, tr. W. Ker, Loeb Library [Cambridge, Mass., 1947], II, p. 7). The words of Martial's book equal his own soul: "Why do you require a title? Let two or three verses be read; all will cry that you, a book, are mine" (XII, iii, 17–18, p. 321). Pliny echoes Horace's emphasis on the conversational variety of the epistle as a mirror of the wayward moods of the soul: "In these poems I joke, play, love, sorrow, complain, grow angry, describe something now in a concise, now in a higher style" (*Epistulae,* IV, 14, tr. W. Melmoth and W. Hutchinson, Loeb Library [Cambridge, Mass., 1931], p. 317). Demetrius, like everyone else, assigns letters to the plain style and relates them, with qualifications, to the philosophical style of the Platonic dialogue, to conversation, and to the equation of words to things (the contours of the processes of thought): "The letter, like the dialogue, should abound in glimpses of character. It may be said that everyone reveals his own soul in his letters. In every form of a composition it is possible to discern the writer's character, but in none so clearly as the epistolary. . . . A letter is designed to be the heart's good wishes in brief" (*On Style,* 227, tr. W. R. Roberts, Loeb Library [Cambridge, Mass., 1953], p. 441). Roberts questions the traditional authorship of Demetrius.

17. Quintilian, *Institutio Oratoria,* VIII, Preface, 17, tr. H. E. Butler, Loeb Library (Cambridge, Mass., 1933), III, p. 187.

18. Cicero long since laid down this rule in the clearest of language, that the worst fault in speaking is to adopt a style inconsistent with the idiom of ordinary speech and contrary to the common

feeling of mankind. But nowadays our rhetoricians regard Cicero as lacking both polish and learning; we are far superior, for we look upon everything that is dictated by nature as beneath our notice, and seek not for the true ornaments of speech, but for meretricious finery, as though there were any real virtue in words save in their power to represent facts. And if we have to spend all our life in the laborious effort to discover words which will at once be brilliant, appropriate, and lucid, and to arrange them with exact precision, we lose all the fruit of our studies. And yet we see the majority of our modern speakers wasting their time over the discovery of single words and over the elaborate weighing and measurement of such words when discovered. (VIII, Preface, 25, p. 191)

19. VIII, Preface, 30–35, pp. 193–195. This natural style (for Quintilian, the basis of eloquence in general) must not be completely conversational:

> There are still some critics who deny that any form of eloquence is purely natural, except that which closely resembles the ordinary speech of everyday life, which we use to our friends, our wives, our children, and our slaves, a language, that is to say, which contents itself with expressing the purpose of the mind without seeking to discover anything in the way of elaborate and far-fetched phraseology. . . . There is some truth in this contention, and we shall therefore be careful not to depart from the more exact usage of ordinary speech to the extent that is done by certain authors. On the other hand, that is no reason for calumniating the man who . . . succeeds in improving upon the bare necessaries of style. For the common language of every day seems to me to be of a different character from the style of an eloquent. (XII, x, 40–43, Loeb Library, IV, pp. 471–473)

Quintilian's model for this artistic plainness is, as always, Cicero, whom Quintilian considers superior to any Silver Latin writer, including Seneca. Quintilian does "not know what can be added to the charms" of Cicero's style, "except perhaps reflections to suit the taste of our own times" (XII, x, 46, pp. 475–477). Ciceronian eloquence, however, is only elevated conversation. "Those subtle teachers . . . have laid it down that the paradigm is best suited for actual speech and the enthymeme for writing. My own view is that there is absolutely no difference between writing well and speaking well" (XII, x, 51, p. 479).

20. For similar statements, cf. *Epistulae* cxiv, 1–3; xl, 1; c, 2.

21. *Epistulae*, Loeb Library, Vol. III, c, 4–5, pp. 151–153. F. I. Marchant has shown how Seneca's theory follows from his philosophy, with its roots in the Socratic and Ciceronian ideals. There is

a close connection between Seneca's style and his philosophy. The perfectly wise man, the man who follows nature absolutely, is so seldom seen as to be practically a myth (ep. 42). Following nature is an approximation varying in degree and in kind with the individual. If, then, excellence in writing depends on conformity to nature, it follows that a man's style is determined by his character. And this is what Seneca teaches. He adopts as an expression of his own view the Greek proverb, modernized by Buffon, that a man's speech corresponds to his life, that the style is the man. Language . . . is the dress of the mind and the qualities of the one are like the qualities of the other. . . . It is the character of the mind that determines the character of the style, good or bad. ("Seneca and his Theory of Style," *American Journal of Philology*, XXVI [1905], p. 47)

22. Erasmus, *Ciceronianus* (1528), tr. Izora Scott in *Controversies Over the Imitation of Cicero* (New York, 1910), p. 123.

23. Ralph Lever, *The Art of Reason* (London, 1573), pp. 11–12.

24. Sir Philip Sidney, *Works*, ed. A. Feuillerat (London, 1926), III, p. 132.

25. Montaigne, "A Consideration Upon Cicero," *Essayes*, tr. Florio, (New York, 1933), Book I, ch. xxxix, p. 201.

26. *The Overburian Characters*, Percy Reprints (Oxford, 1936), p. 19.

27. J. Vives, *Opera Omnia*, ed. G. Mejansius (Valencia, 1782), II, p. 227. Quoted and translated in Trimpi, *Ben Jonson's Poems*, p. 44.

28. Roger Asham, *The Schoolmaster*, "Of Imitation" (1570), in *The Whole Works*, ed. J. Giles (London, 1865), III, pp. 264–265.

29. Marc-Antoine Muret, *Opera Omnia*, ed. C. H. Frotsher (Leipzig, 1834), I, p. 339. Quoted and translated in Trimpi, p. 44.

30. Ben Jonson, *Discoveries*, in *Ben Jonson*, eds. C. H. Herford and P. Simpson (Oxford, 1947), VIII, p. 628.

31. Vives, *Opera Omnia*, VI, pp. 297–298. Tr. Trimpi, pp. 61–62.

32. Justus Lipsius, *Institvtio Epistolica*, in *Epistolarvm Selectarvm* (Antwerp, 1605), VII, p. 9. Quoted and translated in Trimpi, pp. 62–63. Cf. Horace, *Sermones*, II, i, 33.

33. Lipsius, *Institvtio*, IX, pp. 11–12. Quoted and translated in Trimpi, p. 64.

34. *Discoveries*, p. 625. There are at least five other similar statements in the *Discoveries*: "*There* cannot be one colour of the mind; another of the wit. If the mind be staid, grave, and compos'd, the wit is so; that vitiated, the other is blowne, and deflowr'd" (p. 592); "What is so furious, and *Bethl'em*-like, as a vaine sound of chosen and excellent words, without any subject of *sentence*, or *science* mix'd?" (p. 574); "In all speech, words and sense, are as

the body, and the soule. The sense is as the life and soule of Language, without which all words are dead" (p. 621); "The conceits of the mind are Pictures of things, and the tongue is the Interpreter of those Pictures. . . . Neither can his mind be thought to be in tune, whose words doe jarre" (p. 628); "What figure of a Body was *Lysippus* ever able to forme with his Graver, or *Apelles* to paint with his Pencill, as the Comedy to life expresseth so many, and various affections of the minde?" (p. 640).

35. Jonas Barish, *Ben Jonson and the Language of Prose Comedy* (Cambridge, Mass., 1960), p. 87.

36. Quintilian, X, i, 129–130; Bacon, *Advancement, Works,* VI, p. 292.

37. Roger Ascham, *The Schoolmaster,* "Of Imitation," in *The Whole Works,* III, p. 211. A letter of Ascham to Sturm in 1550 is evidence that he regarded "Anti-Ciceronians" as the prime debasers of style: "I do not know what all the Oxford men are about, but some months ago, at Court, I fell in with a man from that University who, by his preference of Lucian, Plutarch, Herodian, Seneca, Aulus Gellius, and Apuleius seemed to bring both of those tongues down to their latest and most debased Age" (*Works,* I, pp. lxii and 190; quoted in *The Senecan Amble,* p. 61).

38. Ascham is not the only old-fashioned humanist to think this way. For example, quoting the same Ciceronian passage used by Jonson, Sir Thomas Elyot reminded his contemporaries that

they be much abused that suppose eloquence to be only in wordes or coleurs of Rhetorike, for, as Tulli saith, what is so furiouse or mad a thinge as a vaine soune of wordes of the best sort and most ornate, contayning neither connynge or sentence? Undoubtedly very eloquence is in euery tonge where any mater or acte done or to be done is expressed in wordes clene, propise, ornate, and comely. (*The Gouvernour* [London, 1531], I, pp. 116–117)

39. Montaigne, "Of the Institution and Education of Children," in *Essayes,* tr. Florio (New York, 1933), Book I, ch. xxv, p. 110.

40. Erich Auerbach, *Mimesis,* tr. W. Trask (Princeton, 1953), p. 272, on the *Confessions,* pp. 58–63. For more on Augustine and the *sermo humilis* in relation to Christian style see Auerbach's *Literary Language and Its Public,* tr. R. Manheim (London, 1965), ch. I.

41. Robert Burton, *The Anatomy of Melancholy,* Everyman's Library (London, 1932), I, p. 29.

42. Richard Whitlock, Preface to *Zootomia* (1654), in *Two Seventeenth-Century Prefaces,* ed. A. K. Croston (London, 1949),

p. 16. See G. Williamson, "Richard Whitlock, Learning's Apologist" in Williamson's *Seventeenth-Century Contexts* (London, 1960).

43. Long before the rise of libertine prose in the age of Whitlock and Browne the Renaissance had recognized that a mode whose intention is self-revelation need not be artless. Letter-writing, for example, the prime self-revelatory genre of the classical plain style, was bound by an elaborate system of tropes, schemes, and even the standard Ciceronian oratorical divisions, all of which the Renaissance had long since codified in handbooks on letter-writing. Significantly, of the many examples of letters reproduced in the leading manuals of Angel Day, William Fullwood, and Abraham Fleming, Cicero's epistles far outnumber everyone else's, and Seneca's appear hardly at all. Evidently Cicero was regarded as more "natural" and "plain" than Seneca. All of the manuals define the epistle in the traditional way (often with the debt to the tradition explicitly indicated) as "a declaration (by writing) of the mindes of such as be absent, one of them to another, even as though they were present" (William Fullwood, *The Enimie of Idlenesse* [1582; reprinted, Potsdam, 1907], p. 47). All the theorists require a conversational norm: "By letter we may absence make/ even presence self to be/ And talke with him, as face to face/ together we did see" (Fullwood, p. 41). But spontaneity and self-revelation do not exclude artifice: "And although pregnant wit ensuing by nature was the foremost cause that first bred the inuention of Letters, and that euery one naturally can speake, or in some sort or other let downe their meaning: yet Arte preuayling in the cause, and by cunning skill marshalling euery thing his due order, place, and proportion, how much more the same is then beautified, adorned, and as it were into a new shape transmuted by such kind of knowledge" (Angel Day, *The English Secretoire* [London, 1595], p. 1). Even in the *genus humile* assigned by Day to the familiar letter there is "a certaine kind of elegancie, pleasant and neat conueyance" (p. 10). Despite what Day says, however, the kind of "Arte" employed by libertine self-revelation is apt to be eccentric and complicated rather than "pleasant and neat," as in the classical plain style.

44. Sir Thomas Browne, *Religio Medici* (1642), "To the Reader," Everyman's Library (New York, 1951), p. xxii. Alexander Ross's attack on the *Religio* anticipates Restoration theory. According to Ross in the *Medicus Medicatus* (London, 1645) Browne "tells us, that many things in it are not to be called unto the *rigid test of*

reason being delivered Rhetorically" (sigs. A₃–A₄). Therefore Browne cannot be taken seriously. Ross objects especially to Browne's metaphors, which "cast a mist upon the thing defined; every Metaphor being more obscure than proper Words" (pp. 20–21).

45. For a survey of the various meanings of *mimesis* in antiquity see Richard McKeon, "The Concept of *Mimesis*," *Modern Philology*, XXXIV (1936), pp. 1–35.

46. In *Controversies Over the Imitation of Cicero*, p. 84.

47. Sir Henry Savile, note appended to his translation of Tacitus' *Life of Agricola* (London, 1591).

48. Sir William Cornwallis, "Of Vanity," in *Essays* (1601), ed. Don Cameron Allen (Baltimore, 1946), p. 175:

> Of wordes first, for it is one of the first things we do. They are but the Lackies of reason, of which to send more then will performe the business is superfluous. Me thinkes, an *esse videatur* at the close of a period is as nice as a Tumbler ending his tricks with a caper, and *Tullie's Venit, imo in Senatum Venit*, moves me no more against *Catiline* than the first *Venit*. Mee thinkes this same retorick, the child of words, is but a pickled Herring to bring on drinke; for his diuisions and repetitions are for nothing but to bring his memory acquainted with his tongue and to make three words of one. How shall a man hope to come to an ende of their workes, when hee cannot with two breathes saile through a Period, and is sometimes grauelled in a Parenthesis? I wonder how *Cicero* got the people of *Rome* tyed so fast to his tongue, for were his matter no better then his stile, hee should not persuade me to looke upon him? I make as great difference between *Tacitus'* and *Senecae's* stile and his as Musitians betweene *Trenchmore* and *Lachrymae*. Mee thinkes the braine should ligge at the hearing a *Tullian* sound, and sit in counsaille when it heares the other.

49. Douglas Bush, *English Literature in the Earlier Seventeenth Century*, 2nd ed. (New York, 1962), p. 192.

50. R. F. Jones, "The Moral Sense of Simplicity," in *Studies in Honor of Frederick W. Shipley*, Washington University Studies, New Series, Language and Literature, XIV (1941), p. 2.

51. In *The New England Mind: The Seventeenth Century* (New York, 1939) Perry Miller shows how "the Puritan aesthetic led Puritans to the conclusion that because a sermon was plain it was also 'profitable'" (p. 333). William Haller, in *The Rise of Puritanism* (New York, 1947), demonstrates that Puritan imagery was "drawn from nature and the common life of the field, the home, the shop and the roadside" for purely utilitarian reasons. Like the scientists, the early Puritans objected to "meta-

physical wit, learned allusions, tags of Greek and Latin, snatches from the heathen poets and philosophers, and all figures of speech depending upon recondite knowledge" because "many members of the audience were sure to miss the point," not, I would add, because of Anti-Ciceronian imitation (p. 141). Cf. Harold Fisch, "The Puritans and the Reform of Prose-Style," *ELH*, XIX (1952), 229–248:

> In the Restoration period, it is thus impossible to distinguish clearly a Puritan and a scientific element in the development of plain prose. All now seems to be striving in the same direction. . . . An important feature of the Restoration is that particular techniques of language, such as that adopted by the Puritans for their special doctrinal purposes (the austere style), or that adopted by the scientists for their special needs (the plain style of the report), or by the moral philosophers for the purpose of psychological realism (the Senecan style), are now losing their distinctive characteristics and are being merged together as a standard for all men of good taste. (pp. 247–248)

52. Baxter is quoting a statement of Glanvill's on Baxter's own style:

> There is a smartness accompanying your pen that forces what you write into the heart by a sweet kind of irresistible violence; which is so proper to your serious way, that I never met it equal'd in any other writings. And therefore I cannot read them without an elevation, and emotions which I seldom feel in other perusals. And when you are ingag'd in doctrinal and controversial matters, I no less apprehend in them your particular excellencies. I find a strength, depth, concinnity and coherence in your notions, which are not commonly elsewhere met withall. . . . And methinkes there is a force in your way of writing, which overpowers opposition (*A Second True Defence of the Meer Non-Conformist*, [London, 1681], p. 180).

53. For a study of "Enthusiastic" prose, see Jackson Cope, "Seventeenth-Century Quaker Style," *PMLA*, LXXXI (1956), p. 725–754.

Chapter Five

1. Ben Jonson, *Discoveries*, in *Ben Jonson*, eds. C. H. Herford and P. Simpson (Oxford, 1947), VIII, pp. 590–591.
2. Sir Francis Bacon, *The Advancement of Learning*, in *Works*, eds. J. Spedding, R. Ellis, and D. Heath (Boston, 1861), VI, pp. 119–120.
3. *Style, Rhetoric, and Rhythm: Essays by Morris W. Croll*, eds. J.

Max Patrick, Robert O. Evans, John M. Wallace, and R. J. Schoeck (Princeton, 1966), p. 95.

4. Basil Willey, *The Seventeenth Century Background* (New York, 1934), p. 35.

5. L. C. Knights, "Bacon and the Seventeenth-Century Dissociation of Sensibility," in *Explorations* (New York, 1943), p. 115.

6. See H. Fisch and H. W. Jones, "Bacon's Influence on Sprat's *History of the Royal-Society*," *Modern Language Quarterly*, XII (1951), pp. 399–406.

7. Thomas Sprat, *The History of the Royal-Society of London* (London, 1667), p. 111.

8. P. 332. In his *Observations on M. de Sorbiere's Voyage to England* (London, 1665), Sprat lumps together Seneca with Cicero as "Rhetoricians," any one of whom will serve as well as the other. Replying to Sorbiere's attack on Clarendon's lack of oratorical training, Sprat asks, "Whence did he fetch this Idea of Eloquence? Let him produce his notes out of *Aristotle, Tully, Quintilian, Seneca*, or any of the *Rhetoricians* of Antiquity; And then let him tell me, whether they do not all with one *voyce* consent that an *Orator* must of necessity be acquainted with all sorts of useful knowledge?" (pp. 201–202).

9. Thomas Sprat, *Life and Writings of Mr. Abraham Cowley*, in *Critical Essays of the Seventeenth Century*, ed. J. Spingarn (Oxford, 1908), II, p. 129.

10. John Webster, *Academiarum Examen* (London, 1654), p. 18.

11. Forty years after Webster, William Wotton in *Reflections Upon Ancient and Modern Learning* stands up for antiquity's faith in language against the modern passion for "matter":

> The Humour of the Age which we live in is exceedingly altered. Men apprehend or suspect a Trick in every Thing that is said to move the Passions of the Auditory in Courts of Judicature or in the *Parliament-House*. They think themselves affronted when such Methods are used in Speaking. . . . And therefore, when Men have spoken to the Point, in as few words as the Matter will bear, it is expected they should hold their Tongues. Even in the Pulpit, the Pomp of Rhetorick is not always commended; and very few meet with Applause who do not confine themselves to speak with the severity of a Philosopher as well as with the Splendour of an Orator — two things not always consistent. (*Critical Essays of the Seventeenth Century*, III, p. 213)

"Ancients and moderns" is not simply humanists against scientists; Swift, for example, in the *Battle of the Books*, puts Rymer and Bentley among the moderns.

349

12. Seth Ward, *Vindiciae Academiarum* (Oxford, 1654), p. 19.

13. John Wilkins, *An Essay Towards a Real Character* (London, 1668), "To the Reader," p. 1.

14. Robert Boyle, *Some Considerations Touching the Style of the Holy Scriptures* (London, 1663), p. 101. Boyle's *Some Considerations Touching the Usefulnesse of Experimental Naturall Philosophy* (London, 1663) is one of the outstanding utilitarian tracts of the century.

15. Francis Glisson, *A Treatise of the Rickets* (London, 1651), Preface. Quoted in R. F. Jones, *The Seventeenth Century*, p. 80.

16. Robert Plot, *A Natural History of Oxfordshire* (London, 1676), p. 2. Quoted in R. F. Jones, *The Seventeenth Century*, p. 83.

17. Joshua Childrey, *Britania Baconica* (London, 1661), sigs. B₈–B₄.

18. Fraser Mitchell, *English Pulpit Oratory From Andrewes to Tillotson* (London, 1931), pp. 401–402.

19. Robert Boyle, *The Sceptical Chymist* (London, 1661), Preface, p. 9.

20. John Wilkins, *Ecclesiastes* (London, 1704), sig. A. Originally published in 1646.

21. In contrast to classical theory and, one would think, common sense, Wilkins holds that "rhetorical flourishes" *detract* from "Majesty": "It will not become the Majesty of a Divine Ambassage, to be garnished out with flaunting affected Eloquence." For his theory of style Wilkins does indeed cite Seneca's theory, but then immediately condemns Senecan practice: " 'Tis a sign of low thoughts and designe, when a Man's chief study is about the polishing of his phrase and words" (*Ecclesiastes*, pp. 251–252).

22. Symon Patrick, *A Friendly Debate Between a Conformist and a Non-Conformist* (London, 1669), pp. 144–145).

23. Symon Patrick, *A Discourse of Profiting by Sermons* (London, 1683), pp. 5–6. Almost all Patrick's many writings are on religious affairs. But in *A Brief Account of the Sect of Latitude-Men, Together With Some Reflections upon the New Philosophy* (London, 1662; Augustan Reprints, Los Angeles, 1963), Patrick praises the New Philosophy, not for itself but for its uses: first, for everyday practical benefit (much of the tract is taken up with an anecdote about a broken clock that can be repaired, not by jargon-ridden scholastics, but by an "ingenious Gentleman that had used to take in pieces his own Watch and set it together again" [p. 87]); and second, for potential benefits for Anglican apologetics ("True Philosophy can never hurt sound

Divinity"). Less empirical doctrines will serve the cause just as well, though. A "Cambridge Platonist," Patrick also thinks Platonism might be useful "no less against the open violence of *Atheisme*, than the secret treachery of *Enthusiasm* and *Superstition*" (p. 24). Florid and impassioned, with an occasional Brownesque turn, the style as well as the argument of the *Brief Account* reflects the necessities of rhetorical persuasion, not "science."

24. John Eachard, *The Grounds and Occasions of the Contempt of the Clergy* (1670), in *Dr. Eachard's Works* (London, 1705), pp. 22–23. As the quotation suggests, Eachard seems to have thought of the New Philosophy as a mere passing fad. In *Some Observations on an Answer to the Enquiry* (*Dr. Eachard's Works*, pp. 119–125) Eachard ridicules the young wits who pretend to be scientists by using the new jargon, which is just as useless as the old.

   Eachard's most notable imitator is John Phillips, in *Speculum Crape-Gownorum* (London, 1682).

25. At the opening of Oxford's Sheldonian theatre Evelyn and a presumably discomfited John Wallis (the great mathematician) heard South's oration, "the first part of which consisted of satyrical invectives against *Cromwell*, fanaticks, the Royal Society, and new philosophy; the next, of encomiasticks, in praise of the archbishop, the theatre, the vice-chancellor, the architect, and the painter; the last, of execrations against fanaticks, conventicles, comprehension, and new philosophy, damning them *ad inferos, ad gehennam*" (letter of Wallis dated July 17, 1669, in Robert Boyle, *Works*, V, p. 514; cf. Evelyn's diary, July 9, 1669; quoted in R. F. Jones, *Ancients and Moderns* [St. Louis, 1961], p. 225). South's view of learning was precisely opposite that held by the Royal Society. For a mighty invective against knowledge for its leading only to restlessness, hard work, and antagonism, see the sermon called "Increase of Knowledge Attended With Sorrow." One sentence, "How are Galileo and Copernicus persecuted, and Descartes worried by almost every pen!" is the only evidence for any acquaintance of South's, in his published works, with the New Philosophy. The speech at the Sheldonian theatre shows that South was all on the side of the persecutors.

26. Robert South, *Sermons* (Oxford, 1842), I, p. 449.

27. Robert South, *Works* (London, 1823), III, p. 33. Quoted in Mitchell, *English Pulpit Oratory*, p. 316.

28. Sir Isaac Barrow, "Against Foolish Talking and Jesting," *The-*

ological Works (Oxford, 1830), I, pp. 407–408. I am indebted to Mitchell's discussion of Barrow, in *English Pulpit Oratory*, pp. 321–329.

29. Edward Stillingfleet, "A Sermon Preached at a Publick Ordination," *Works* (London, 1710), I, pp. 366–367.

30. Gilbert Burnet, *A History of My Own Time* (London, 1818), III, p. 149. Dryden's famous remark to Congreve that "if he had any talent for *English* Prose, it was owing to his having often read the Writings of the great Archbishop Tillotson" (William Congreve, *Works* [London, 1923], IV, p. 184), while not true — Dryden had already developed his prose style before Tillotson had fairly begun preaching — illustrates how fashionable Tillotson had become. See Louis Locke, *Tillotson* (Copenhagen, 1954), p. 114.

31. Gilbert Burnet, *A Sermon Preached at the Funeral of . . . John* [Tillotson] . . . *Lord Archbishop of Canterbury* (London, 1694), pp. 13–14.

32. John Tillotson, "The efficacy, usefulness, and reasonableness of divine faith," *Works* (London, 1748), IX, pp. 255–56.

33. Samuel Parker, *A Discourse of Ecclesiastical Politie* (London, 1670), p. 76. Parker, a member of the Royal Society, did not do things by halves. His utilitarianism ran so deep that, "When asked, 'What was the best body of divinity?' Parker is said to have answered, 'That which would help a man to keep a coach and six horses was certainly the best' (*Somers Tracts*, ii, 507); and the facts of his life show that the character for flexibility of conscience and self-seeking which he obtained among contemporaries was not undeserved" (*DNB*).

34. James Arderne, *Directions Concerning the Matter and Stile of Sermons* (London, 1671), pp. 50 ff.; Edward Fowler, *The Principles and Practices of Certain Moderate Divines, Abusively called Latitudinarians* (London, 1671), p. 112; Gilbert Burnet, *A Discourse of the Pastoral Care* (London, 1692), p. 225.

35. William Perkins, *The Art of Prophecying* (London, 1607), pp. 132–136. Originally published in 1592.

36. Richard Baxter, *Gildas Silvianus; The Reformed Pastor* (London, 1656), p. 123.

37. John Geree, *The Character of an Old English Puritan or Non-Conformist* (London, 1659), p. 2.

38. Richard Parr, *The Life of the Most Reverend Father in God, James Ussher* (London, 1686), pp. 48–49. Quoted in Mitchell, *English Pulpit Oratory*, p. 229.

39. Meric Casaubon, *A Letter . . . to Peter du Moulin . . . Concerning Natural Experimental Philosophie* (London, 1669). Because it raises some vital questions which the age did not care to answer, Casaubon's little-known *Letter* is of considerable importance for seventeenth-century intellectual history. For a discussion, see Jones, *Ancients and Moderns* (1961), pp. 241–244.

40. Another philosopher who wrote in the old "Senecan" mode while accepting the new theory of the plain style was Nathaniel Fairfax, one of the last — and strangest — of the "libertines." Fairfax is well aware of the Royal Society's stylistic ideals, but his enthusiasm for its utilitarian aspects leads him to write in a most unscientific style, for example:

> Even the slighted and off-cast in the mouths of Handy-crafts-men and Earth-tillers shall be better drawn and more patly brought in. And inasmuch as that *Fellowship* of *Worthies* in *London,* who are now embodied under the name of *Royal,* have given us already so many new things, and are daily starting more, neither named nor known by those before us; and for the enriching of the *English* tongue, as well as fulfilling of *Englands* store, have thought fit their discoveries should almost wholly come abroad in our own Speech, as they are happily made in our own Land. . . . For inasmuch as almost the whole of those words, that we speak in things or knowledges of things that are not body, are taken from things that are body . . . so all the words about body and hangers on to body that we have to do with, are either such as flow from or mainly well fall in with those that are utter'd by Workmen, for such things as are done by hand-deed. (*A Treatise of the Bulk and Selvedge of the World* [1674] in *Two-Seventeenth-Century Prefaces,* ed. A. K. Croston [London, 1949], pp. 39–40)

41. Meric Casaubon, *A Treatise Concerning Enthusiasme* (London, 1655), p. 140.

42. Thomas Hobbes, *Leviathan* (1651), Everyman's Library (New York, 1950), p. 16. But cf. *The Answer of Mr. Hobbes to Sir William Davenant's Preface Before Gondibert,* in Spingarn, *Critical Essays,* III, p. 60: [Fancy] consisteth not so much in motion as in copious Imagery discreetly ordered & perfectly registered in the memory."

43. Robert Ferguson, *The Interest of Reason in Religion* (London, 1675), pp. 279–280. Ferguson's work has not received the attention it deserves.

44. John Dryden, Preface to *Annus Mirabilis* (1667), in *The Political Works,* ed. A. Noyes (Cambridge, Mass., 1909), p. 25. For Dry-

den's connection with the Royal Society, as well as his general intellectual background, the standard work is still Louis Bredvold, *The Intellectual Milieu of John Dryden* (Ann Arbor, 1934).

45. Andrews Wanning, "Some Changes in the Prose Style of the Seventeenth Century" (unpublished dissertation, Cambridge University, 1936), p. 186. In this chapter and the next I am heavily indebted to Wanning's thesis. It is the finest study I have ever read of the general history of style in the seventeenth century. On pp. 40-49, Wanning has an especially cogent piece on what are, for all practical purposes, the two main ideas of "plain" style.

46. In the "Life of Plutarch" Dryden describes Seneca's style harshly: "We may call it a shattered eloquence, not vigorous, not united, not embodied, but broken into fragments; every part by itself pompous, but the whole confused and unharmonious. His Latin . . . has nothing in it for the purity and elegance of Augustus and his times" (*Works*, eds. Sir Walter Scott and George Saintsbury [Edinburgh, 1882–1893], XVII, p. 75).

47. John Locke, *An Essay Concerning Human Understanding*, Everyman's Library (New York, 1961), III, iii, 1, p. 15.

48. For a discussion of Descartes' theory of language and its relation to modern linguistics see Noam Chomsky, *Cartesian Linguistics* (New York, 1966).

49. J. Middleton Murry, *The Problem of Style* (Oxford, 1960), p. 5.

50. Samuel Parker, *A Free and Impartial Censure of the Platonick Philosophie* (Oxford, 1666), p. 63.

51. S. T. Coleridge, Lecture XIV, "On Style," from *Literary Remains* in *Miscellaneous Criticism*, ed. T. M. Raysor (Cambridge, Mass., 1936), p. 218. This lecture is filled with brilliant observations on seventeenth-century prose style.

52. Aristotle, *Rhetoric*, tr. J. H. Freese, Loeb Library (Cambridge, Mass., 1926), 1410b, pp. 167–168.

53. E. A. Burtt, *The Metaphysical Foundations of Modern Science* (New York, 1924); A. N. Whitehead, *Science and the Modern World* (New York, 1925); Basil Willey, *The Seventeenth Century Background* (New York, 1934); Theodore Spencer, *Shakespeare and the Nature of Man* (New York, 1951). For a discussion of seventeenth-century nominalism in its historical setting and in relation to literature see Bredvold, *The Intellectual Milieu of John Dryden*, ch. II. For a general view of this burgeoning field, see S. Toulmin, D. Bush, *et al.*, *Seventeenth-Century Science and the Arts* (Princeton, 1961).

54. Thomas Baker, *Reflections Upon Learning, Wherein is shewn*

the *Insuffiency Thereof, in severall Particulars. In order to evince the Usefulness and Necessity of Revelation* (London, 1700), p. 45. The extraordinary title speaks for itself.

Chapter Six

1. Andrews Wanning, "Some Changes in the Prose Style of the Seventeenth Century," unpublished dissertation (Cambridge University, 1936).
2. Plutarch, "Of Envy and Hatred," in *Morals*, tr. Philemon Holland (London, 1603), p. 234; tr. P. Lancaster (London, 1684), I, pp. 425-426.
3. See Rulon Wells, "Nominal and Verbal Styles," in *Style in Language*, ed. T. Sebeok (Cambridge, Mass., 1960), pp. 213-220.
4. I owe these distinctions to John Wilson, *Language and the Pursuit of Truth* (Cambridge, England, 1956), pp. 23 ff.
5. Montaigne, *Essais* (Paris, 1595), II, x, p. 266; tr. John Florio (London, 1603), p. 239; tr. Charles Cotton (London, 1686), II, pp. 140-141.
6. Gustav Stern, "Meaning and Change of Meaning," *Goteborgs Hogskolas Ausskrift*, XXXVIII (1932), p. 308.
7. Angus MacIntosh, "Patterns and Ranges," *Language*, XXXVII (1961), p. 333.
8. For a modern bibliography of the famous distinction of Saussure, see Stephen Ullman, *Language and Style* (Oxford, 1964), p. 25.
9. Benjamin Boyce, *The Theophrastan Character in England to 1642* (Cambridge, Mass., 1947), p. 176.
10. *The Overburian Characters*, Percy Reprints (Oxford, 1936), p. 33.
11. Sir Francis Bacon, *The Advancement of Learning* in *Works*, eds. J. Spedding, R. Ellis, and D. Heath (Boston, 1861), VI, p. 291.
12. Donald A. Stauffer, *English Biography Before 1700* (Cambridge, Mass., 1930), p. 271.
13. Gilbert Burnet, *Notes on the Life and Death of Sir Matthew Hale* (Dublin, 1815), pp. 122-123. First published in 1682.
14. Douglas Bush, *English Literature in the Earlier Seventeenth Century*, 2nd ed. (New York, 1962), p. 230.
15. J. Harrington, "To the Reader" of Anthony A Wood's *Athenae Oxoniensis* (London, 1691).
16. Miguel de Cervantes, *El Ingenioso Hidalgo Don Quixote de la Mancha* (Madrid, 1605), I, xxviii, pp. 149-150; tr. Thomas Shelton (London, 1612), pp. 283-284; tr. J. Philips (London, 1687), p. 136; tr. P. Motteux (London, 1712), pp. 329-330.

17. I am indebted in this discussion of the general theory of the early novel to Ian Watt, *The Rise of the Novel* (Berkeley, 1957), especially chapters I and III.

18. On this subject see A. J. Tieje, "The Theory of Characterization in Prose Fiction Prior to 1740," *University of Minnesota Studies in Language and Literature*, V (1916), pp. 1–131.

19. The best discussion of these matters is Wayne Booth's *The Rhetoric of Fiction* (Chicago, 1961).

20. Thomas Nashe, *The Unfortunate Traveler*, in *Works*, ed. R. B. McKerrow (London, 1904–1910), II, pp. 247–248. Originally published in 1594.

21. Nashe, *Works*, V, p. 111.

22. See W. Staton, "The Characters of Style in Elizabethan Prose," *Journal of English and Germanic Philology*, LVII (1958), pp. 197–207, especially pp. 204–207 for Nashe's references to the plain style.

23. G. R. Hibbard, *Thomas Nashe* (London, 1962), p. 178.

24. John Bunyan, *The Pilgrim's Progress*, eds. J. B. Wharey and R. Sharrock (Oxford, 1960), p. 66. Originally published in 1678.

25. Daniel Defoe, "Of the Trading Stile," Letter III of *The Complete English Tradesman* (London, 1725). Quoted in *Daniel Defoe*, ed. J. T. Boulton, (New York, 1965), p. 227. This book is a selection of Defoe's nonfictional writing, with an excellent introduction by the editor on the relation of Defoe's style to the Baconian tradition.

26. On this topic see M. E. Novak, *Economics and the Fiction of Daniel Defoe* (Berkeley, 1962), and the same author's *Defoe and the Nature of Man* (Oxford, 1963). Dobrée's remarks are on p. 418 of his *English Literature in the Early Eighteenth Century* (London, 1959).

27. Daniel Defoe, *The Life and Strange Adventures of Robinson Crusoe*, Everyman's Library (New York, 1945), pp. 43–44. Originally published in 1719.

28. *The Rise of the Novel*, p. 69.

29. Novak, *Defoe and the Nature of Man*, p. 133.

30. Daniel Defoe, *The Case of the Protestant Dissenters in Carolina* (London, 1706), p. 5.

31. Novak, *Economics and the Fiction of Daniel Defoe*, p. viii.

32. On *Robinson Crusoe* as allegory see E. B. Benjamin, "Symbolic Elements in *Robinson Crusoe*," *Philological Quarterly*, XXX (1951), pp. 206–211 and R. W. Ayers, "*Robinson Crusoe*: 'Allusive Allegorick History,'" *PMLA*, LXXXII (1967), pp. 399–407.

On Defoe and the tradition of the spiritual autobiography, see G. A. Starr, *Defoe and Spiritual Autobiography* (Princeton, 1965).

33. Thomas Shadwell, *The Virtuoso* (London, 1676), Act I, p. 4. For Shadwell's sources in the transactions of the Royal Society see Claude Lloyd, "Shadwell and the Virtuosi," *PMLA*, XLIV (1930), pp. 472-494.

34. T. Fujimura, *The Restoration Comedy of Wit* (Princeton, 1952), p. 36.

35. Thomas Hobbes, *Leviathan*, Everyman's Library (New York, 1950), pp. 45-46.

36. Norman Holland, *The First Modern Comedies* (Cambridge, Mass., 1959), p. 36.

37. George Etherege, *The Man of Mode*, in *Dramatic Works*, ed. G. Brett-Smith (Boston, 1927), Act V, Scene ii; II, pp. 278-279. Originally published in 1676.

38. William Congreve, *The Way of the World*, in *Works*, ed. M. Summers (London, 1923), Act IV, Scene i; III, pp. 56-57. Originally published in 1700.

39. Dale Underwood, *Etherege and the Seventeenth-Century Comedy of Manners* (New Haven, 1957), p. 161.

40. On "naturalism" and the influence of Hobbes on the Restoration playwrights see Fujimura, *The Restoration Comedy of Wit*, pp. 43 ff.

41. William Wycherley, *The Country Wife*, in *Works*, ed. M. Summers (London, 1924), Act I, Scene i; II, p. 13. Originally published in 1675.

42. John Dryden, "Essay on the Dramatick Poetry of the Last Age," in *Essays*, ed. W. P. Ker (Oxford, 1900), I, p. 175.

Appendix

1. On Bacon, Tacitus, and dissimulation, see E. B. Benjamin, "Bacon and Tacitus," *Classical Philology*, LX (1965), pp. 102-110.

2. *Style, Rhetoric, and Rhythm: Essays by Morris W. Croll*, eds. J. Max Patrick, Robert O. Evans, John M. Wallace, and R. Shoeck (Princeton, 1966), p. 194.

3. Stephen Ullman, *Language and Style* (Oxford, 1964), p. 172.

4. W. Boetticher, *Lexicon Taciteum* (Berlin, 1830) and A. A. Draeger, *Syntax und Stil des Tacitus* (Leipzig, 1868). Among the works on Tacitus, I have benefited most from B. Walker, *The Annals of Tacitus* (Manchester, 1952); Ronald Syme, *Tacitus*

(Oxford, 1958); Gaston Boissier, *Tacitus and Other Roman Studies*, tr. W. G. Hutcheson (London, 1906); and the introduction and notes to H. Furneaux' edition of the *Annals* (Oxford, 1965).

5. Michael Riffaterre, "Criteria for Style Analysis," *Word*, XV (1959), p. 165.

6. *Annals*, ed. Furneaux, I, 6–7, pp. 187–190.

7. Tacitus, *The Complete Works*, tr. A. J. Church and W. J. Brodribb, Modern Library (New York, 1942), pp. 6–7.

8. G. G. Ramsay, *The Annals of Tacitus* (New York, 1904), p. lxi.

9. For example, *"dabat et famae"* from Horace's *"das aliquid famae"* (*Sat.* II, ii, 94).

10. See Walker, ch. XII, for a discussion of Tacitus' fatalism.

11. *Annals*, III, 65; Church and Brodribb, p. 137.

12. *Annals*, IV, 33; Church and Brodribb, p. 63.

13. *Annals*, I, 1; Church and Brodribb, p. 3.

14. *History*, I, 1; Church and Brodribb, p. 419.

Bibliography

The following is a list of works discussed in this book in which the utilitarian plain style of the seventeenth century is defended or at least described. Where only a few pages of a long text are in any way relevant, I have cited page numbers. I do not claim to have read all the manifestos and other statements about the new plain style that were published, but I do think all the important ones are here.

Most of the entries on this list can be found in a similar bibliography, Appendix C of Andrews Wanning's unpublished thesis, "Some Changes in the Prose Style of the Seventeenth Century" (Cambridge University, 1936).

Arderne, James. *Directions Concerning the Matter and Stile of Sermons.* London, 1671.

Bacon, Sir Francis. *The Advancement of Learning* (1605), in *Works*, eds. J. Spedding, R. Ellis, and D. Heath. Boston, 1861. Vol. VI, pp. 85–412.

———. *Aphorisms on the Composition of the Primary History*, n.d., in *Works*. Vol. VIII, pp. 357–371.

———. *De Augmentis Scientiarum* (1632), in *Works*. Vol. II, tr. in Vol. VIII.

Baker, Thomas. *Reflections Upon Learning, Wherein is shown the Insufficiency Thereof, in severall Particulars. In order to evince the Usefulness and Necessity of Revelation.* London, 1700.

Barrow, Sir Isaac (d. 1677). "Against Foolish Talking and Jesting," in *Theological Works*. Oxford, 1830. Vol. I, pp. 383–418.

Baxter, Richard. *Gildas Silvianus; The Reformed Pastor.* London, 1656.

———. *A Second True Defence of the Meer Non-Conformist.* London, 1681. P. 180.

Boyle, Robert. *Some Considerations Touching the Style of the Holy Scriptures.* London, 1663.

Burnet, Gilbert. *A Discourse of the Pastoral Care.* London, 1692. Pp. 108–109; 215–234.

———. *A Sermon Preached at the Funeral of . . . John* [Tillotson] *. . . Lord Archbishop of Canterbury.* London, 1694.

———. *Notes on The Life and Death of Sir Matthew Hale* (1682?). Dublin, 1815.

Casaubon, Meric. *A Treatise Concerning Enthusiasme.* London, 1655.

Charleton, Walter. *A Brief Discourse Concerning the Different Wits of Men.* London, 1669.

Childrey, Joshua. *Britania Baconica.* London, 1661. Sig. B₃–B₄.

Defoe, Daniel. "Of Academies" from *An Essay Upon Projects* (1697) in *Daniel Defoe,* ed. J. T. Boulton. New York, 1965. Pp. 27–31.

Dryden, John. Preface to the *Annus Mirabilis* (1667) in *The Poetical Works,* ed. A. Noyes. Cambridge, Mass., 1909. Pp. 23–28.

Evelyn, John. *Diary,* ed. E. S. de Beer. Oxford, 1955. Entry for July 15, 1683.

Eachard, John. *The Grounds and Occasions of the Contempt of the Clergy* (1670) in *Dr. Eachard's Works.* London, 1705.

Fairfax, Nathaniel. "To the Reader" of *A Treatise of the Bulk and Selvedge of the World* (1674) in *Two Seventeenth-Century Prefaces,* ed. A. K. Croston. London, 1949.

Ferguson, Robert. *The Interest of Reason in Religion.* London, 1675.

Fowler, Edward. *The Principles and Practices of Certain Moderate Divines, Abusively Called Latitudinarians.* London, 1671.

Geree, John. *The Character of an Old English Puritan or Non-Conformist.* London, 1659.

Glanvill, Joseph. *The Vanity of Dogmatizing.* London, 1661.

———. "Address to the Royal Society" in *Scepsis Scientifica.* London, 1665.

———. *Plus Ultra.* London, 1668. Reprinted as "Modern Improvements of Useful Knowledge" in *Essays on Several Important Subjects in Philosophy and Religion.* London, 1676.

———. "Anti-Fanatick Theologie and Free Philosophy" in *Essays.* London, 1676.

———. *An Essay Concerning Preaching.* London, 1678.

———. *A Seasonable Defense of Preaching, and the Plain Way of It.* London, 1678.

Glisson, Francis. Preface to *A Treatise of the Rickets.* London, 1651.

Harrington, John. "To the Reader" of Anthony A Wood's *Athenae Oxoniensis.* London, 1691.

Hobbes, Thomas. *The Answer of Mr. Hobbes to Sir William Davenant's Preface Before Gondibert* (1650) in *Critical Essays of the Seventeenth Century*, ed. J. Spingarn. London, 1909. Vol. II, pp. 59–67.

———. *Leviathan* (1651). New York, Everyman's Library, 1961. Book I, ch. 4–8.

Locke, John. *An Essay Concerning Human Understanding* (1690). New York, Everyman's Library, 1961. Book III.

Parker, Samuel. *A Discourse of Ecclesiastical Politie*. London, 1670. Pp. 74 ff.

———. *A Free and Impartial Censure of the Platonick Philosophie*. Oxford, 1666. Pp. 63–80.

Patrick, Symon. *A Discourse of Profiting by Sermons*. London, 1683.

———. *A Friendly Debate Between a Conformist and a Non-Conformist*. London, 1669.

Perkins, William. *The Art of Prophecying* (1592). London, 1607.

Phillips, John. *Speculum Crape-Gownorum*. London, 1682.

Plot, Robert. *A Natural History of Oxfordshire*. London, 1676. P. 2.

Ross, Alexander. *Medicus Medicatus*. London, 1645.

Sergeant, John. *The Method to Science*. London, 1696.

South, Robert. "The Fatal Imposture and Force of Words" (1668) in *Sermons*. Oxford, 1842. Vol. I, pp. 439–461.

Sprat, Thomas. *The History of the Royal-Society*. London, 1667.

Stillingfleet, Edward (d. 1699). "A Sermon Preached at a Publick Ordination," in *Works*. London, 1710. Vol. I, pp. 366–367.

Tillotson, John (d. 1694). "The Necessity of Repentance and Faith" in *Works*. London, 1748. Vol. VII, p. 223.

Ward, Seth. *Vindiciae Academiarum*. Oxford, 1654.

Webster, John. *Academiarum Examen*. London, 1654.

Wilkins, John. *An Essay Towards a Real Character*. London, 1668.

———. *Ecclesiastes* (1646). London, 1704.

Wotton, William. *Reflections Upon Ancient and Modern Learning* (1694) in *Critical Essays of the Seventeenth Century*, ed. J. Spingarn. London, 1909. Vol. III, pp. 210–215.

The following works are not discussed in my text, but are also relevant to the utilitarian plain style.

Cudworth, Ralph (d. 1688). *A treatise concerning eternal and immutable morality*. London, 1731. Pp. 144–145.

Dryden, John. Preface to the *Religio Laici* (1682) in *The Poetical Works*, ed. A. Noyes. Cambridge, Mass., 1909. Pp. 157–162.

A Free and Impartial Inquiry into the Causes of that very great Esteem and Honour that the Non-conforming Preachers are generally in with their Followers. By a Lover of the Church of England, and Unfeigned Piety. London, 1673.

Gother, John. *Good Advice to the Pulpits.* London, 1687.

Locke, John. *Of the Conduct of the Understanding.* London, 1706. Sections xxiv, xxix, xxxi, xxxii.

Malebranche, Father. *His treatise concerning the search after truth,* tr. T. Taylor. London, 1700. Pp. 90–99.

More, Henry. *Enthusiasmus Triumphatus.* London, 1656.

Pemble, William (d. 1623). "Vindiciae Gratiae: a plea for grace," in *Works.* Oxford, 1659. Pp. 1–141.

Petty-Southwell Correspondence, 1676–1687, ed. M. Lansdowne. London, 1927. Pp. 150–151, 324.

Sherlock, William. *A Discourse Concerning the Knowledge of Jesus Christ.* London, 1674. Pp. 1, 55, 69–70, 81–82, 194, 254.

Index